# Thinking an

## The Mind

Edited by

**Carolyn N. Hedley**
**Patricia Antonacci**
**Mitchell Rabinowitz**
*Fordham University*

**LEA** LAWRENCE ERLBAUM ASSOCIATES, PUBLISHERS
1995 Hillsdale, New Jersey                               Hove, UK

Lawrence Erlbaum Associates, Inc., Publishers
365 Broadway
Hillsdale, New Jersey 07642

Cover design by Jan Melchior

**Library of Congress Cataloging-in-Publication Data**

Thinking and literacy : the mind at work / edited by Carolyn N.
    Hedley, Patricia Antonacci, Mitchell Rabinowitz.
        p.      cm.
    Includes bibliographical references and index.
    ISBN 0-8058-1547-3. — ISBN 0-8058-1548-1 (pbk.)
    1. Cognitive learning.   2. Literacy.   I. Hedley, Carolyn N.
II. Antonacci, Patricia.   III. Rabinowitz, Mitchell.
LB1062.T45   1995
370.15′2—dc20                                            94-29571
                                                            CIP

Printed in the United States of America
10  9  8  7  6  5  4  3  2  1

*To our students and our teachers
who have entered the community
of learners through collaboration,
co-constructing the knowledge that
shapes our dispositions for thinking.*

# Contents

# Preface

The rapidly increasing knowledge of how the mind works and the changing structures for educating youth are the impetus for this work. Each of the authors has worked to bring fresh perspectives of how to reach the learner, by humanizing models for learning while acknowledging increasing technological change that is bound to be part of our educational future. Concern and respect for the learner combined with the overwhelming technology for accessing knowledge has become focal. Current research for studying the mind tells us that what the mind processes and the kinds of information the mind receives from the environment is, in fact, forming and reforming the processes and neural maps of the mind in a continuing construction process. Even as it receives information from its own neural processing and from the kinds and amount of stimulation from its environment, the mind is restructuring itself. It is imperative that educators look at what and how the mind works, simply because we can be more effective in teaching and learning. We now know we can make a positive difference in cognitive development by what we do with this new information.

The book begins with Part I on the theoretical constructs of cognitive processing that describe the processes of literacy learning, developed in Part II. Contexts for learning and strategies for fostering learning become Parts III and IV of the work. In chapter 1, the Hedleys develop the themes of the book in their discussion of thinking, literacy, and the mind. Definitions of these terms and discussion of what research is telling us about their development and functions is culminated by applications for education. This chapter sets the theme for the rest of the book. Searle, in chapter 2 on consciousness, defines *consciousness* somewhat differently from the Hedleys as "those subjective states of sentience or awareness that begin when one wakes in the morning from a dreamless sleep and continue throughout the day until one goes to sleep at night . . ." (pp. 21–22). Bransford (chapter 3) characterizes the problem-solving process, defining problem solving as a constructive process of mind rather than a fixed body of information changing only when informed by epistemological development. Smith (chapter 4) takes one aspect of the creative process, the *roadmap theory*, and examines the paradoxical nature of creativity and the variance of its functions. He demystifies creativity only to lead us to new questions, in effect remystifying creativity once again. At the level of actual reading, Marzano (chapter 5) begins his work with applications of mediated instruction leading to a highly theoretical discussion of cognitive processing during reading: His model includes the general task processor, the information screener, the propositional network processor, the word processor, and the macrostructure generator. At first glance, one wonders if Marzano is turning to a behavioristic model, but he assures us that "[t]he lofty goals regarding enhanced thinking and reasoning . . . will be reached only through a concentrated effort to better understand the situated thinking and reasoning within the various content domains" (p. 97). The first part of the book on cognitive theory ends with Comstock's (chapter 7) discussion of television and its effect on academic achievement. Is there an association between the two? Comstock develops the traits that are associated with television viewing: cognitive abilities, vocabulary, interests, impulse control, perceptual and spatial responses, imaginativeness, and creativity. In some ways his views based on research are pessimistic regarding the relationship between viewing television and scholastic achievement.

Part II begins with a refreshing chapter by Baron, who finds language explainable; she brings new meaning to the concepts of language as social, functional, and variable in its acquisition. In any case, language acquisition is coherent; "language orienteers of all ilk use remarkably similar approaches in working to break the language code" (p. 131). Rabinowitz and Steinfeld (chapter 8) develop a model and computer program for teaching vocabulary, the SIVL Tutor, demonstrating how one learns a second language. Bologna (chapter 9) provides us with a comprehensive view of the competencies that the young child brings to reading. Her synthesis of the literature indicates that an integration of processes—perceptual, cognitive, and language, combined with social competence and affective development—are essential concerns for learning success. Developmentally appropriate practice (DAP) becomes operationalized in her discussion. In chapter 10, Ehri is consistently concerned with word reading processes while learning to read. She advocates a more systematic approach to phonics instruction during the first year of reading instruction. Although she endorses whole language practices, she advocates that teachers have a better working knowledge of the many aspects of reading acquisition, including letter-sound knowledge. The rest of her chapter is devoted to how these word-reading processes work for children and how teachers can better teach them using informal assessment to determine what children need to know and do to read effectively.

Contexts for thinking and literacy in Part III is introduced by London. In chapter 11 on the case for multiculturalism as a means for transforming education, London tells us that we have a moral imperative to promote multiculturalism, including its universal values. Reevaluating curriculum in the light of the moral imperatives within the concept of multicultural curriculum will cause conflict, but anything less than such commitment betrays the vision of our history. This lofty beginning is followed by Carver's discussion (chapter 12) of how to use cognitive apprenticeships on a large scale. Her work alone is worth the price of the book, as one of the most useful explications of how to do cognition as apprenticeship. Educators often use the term without explanation of how cognitive apprenticeships work; Carver has resolved our anxieties. Johnson-Holubec, Johnson, and Johnson (chapter 13) give us a masterful explanation of cooperative learning in reading and language arts; ultimately these authors promote cooperative learning as the most natural way to learn reading and language by building base groups that give academic and social support. Finally, in chapter 14, Bernhardt and Antonacci describe two blueprints for learning and thinking in classrooms, pointing out that criteria for analysis of classrooms and the artifacts of learning in such environments can be defined. The discussion of how thinking environments or the lack of them can affect the learner is fascinating.

Strategies for thinking and learning, Part IV, follows easily from the contexts for learning portion of the book because many of these contexts include strategies as part of that context. Following the blueprint described in the previous chapter, Antonacci and Colasacco (chapter 15) create a program (TACLE) that fulfills all of the demands in the search for a thinking environment. Through provision of apprenticeships to teachers and students alike in the Yonkers schools, situated and problem-based learning meet the requirements of thoughtful work, processes made visible, and participatory assessment. In a similar vein, Ciardello (chapter 16) uses case-based instruction to motivate high school students. This type of instruction is situational and narrative, involving active participation and decision-making. Finally, Vacca and Newton conclude with a chapter (17) on response to literature, first by defining *response*, then by discussing response theory and moving its premises to a response-based curriculum. Vacca and Newton summarize their chapter and our work:

> Instruction from a response-based perspective must, therefore, focus on eliciting and nurturing readers' first interactions with text. It must also focus on sharing both the process and the result of those first interactions with peers. Classroom discussion, writing tasks and metacognitive activities can play a central role in facilitating meaning construction before, during, and after reading events. (p. 300)

—*Carolyn N. Hedley*
—*Patricia Antonacci*
—*Mitchell Rabinowitz*

# Part I

# THEORETICAL VIEWS OF COGNITIVE PROCESSING AND LITERACY

# Chapter 1

# Thinking and Literacy: The Mind at Work in the Classroom

Carolyn N. Hedley
W. Eugene Hedley
*Fordham University*

The title of this chapter was taken from The 1993 Reading Institute, held at Fordham University: *Literacy and Thinking: The Mind at Work in the Classroom.* The broad, ambitious title was chosen to insure a wide exchange of ideas for the development of models of literacy and thinking in deciding new agendas for learning. Three key concepts in the title are *thinking, literacy,* and *mind.* Each of these concepts is undergoing change and development as a result of recent research and publications: namely, Edelman (1992), writing on the relation of brain and mind; new translations and commentaries on Vygotsky's psychological approach to thinking (Kozulin, 1990; Vygotsky, cited in Rieber & Carton, 1987); and new work on the origins of speech and literacy (Lewin, 1993). Educators may want to reflect on these developments and determine how recent conceptualizations of literacy, thinking, and the mind inform educational practice.

In the first section, the concept of the mind/brain relationship is discussed, drawing on the work of cognitive psychologists and neurophysiologists with special attention to the work of Nobel laureate, Gerald Edelman. In the next section, we consider the concept of thinking as a complex phenomenon using the analyses of the Russian psychologist, Lev Vygotsky, including recent applications of his research. The third section develops literacy from a historical and anthropological perspective; a distinction is drawn between the development of human speech and the development of a written language. The last section develops notions of what teachers do while teaching literacy, thinking, and knowledge of content, based on the discussion in the preceding sections.

## THE MIND

In this section, we discuss the relationship between the human brain and consciousness. Current research in neurobiology is producing a "picture" of the brain as an enormously complex and dynamic organ. The potential for neuronal structuring may be of genetic origin, but the way neurons organize themselves to carry out the various functions of consciousness is dependent upon how groups of neurons respond to stimuli from both within and outside the organism. Human consciousness emerges as a dynamic, constantly changing, and unique phenomenon of each individual. The most fascinating aspect of this emerging picture of the mind is the role of language in the development of human consciousness. Before we discuss the role of language, we must remind ourselves that the human mind or consciousness is not a *thing* or entity, but a function—the word *mind* refers to the results of processes of interaction between the brain and the whole organism, including the brain and the environment.

The concept of mind has had a long history as a subject of philosophical speculation and inquiry. Until this century, the development of a theory of mind was focused upon what kind of substance might account for all the manifestations of what one might call *mind*. At the beginning of this century, science led the way in a shift of attention from the concept of mind as substance to that of function. Ernst Cassirer in his book, *Substance and Function* (1923), traced the history of this scientific change. John Dewey (1916) suggested that when certain nouns proved to be a source of philosophic concern or confusion, such problems might be resolved by simply changing the noun form of the confusing term to its gerund or verb form. As a means of not treating *mind* as object, the philosopher considers its function as expressed in the gerund form *minding*. This process of creating verb forms removes the temptation to consider mind as a substance that is fixed and focuses on mind as functions and processes that change. "What is a mind?" is a confusing question, but "Mind the children!" or "Mind your manners!" are clear enough commands. They are orders to focus your attention, to fully attend, or to direct your intentional processes to moving events. This switch to the function of minding does not lead to simplicity when dealing with the concept of minding. The nature of the function of minding in "Mind the children!" will depend upon the individual children in the group involved, upon the complex nature and current physical and psychological state of the individual doing the minding, and upon the entire situation and context in which the minding is being done. An analysis of functions turns out to be anything but simple, and introduces additional complexities and processes.

Attempting to view the concept of mind as function has revealed greater complexity and produced new attempts at philosophic resolution. At one end of the spectrum are those who attempt to reduce the concept of mind to the physical operation of the brain. A convincing model that emerges from this endeavor is that of the computer model of the human mind. The inadequacy of this model has been pointed out by Roger Penrose (1989) and Gerald Edelman (1992). At the other end of the spectrum are those who reduce mind to a set of behaviors. But behaviorists encounter great difficulties when they try to objectify the internalized functions of mind that have no behavioral manifestation. Both of these views fail to take into account the mediating function of mind or consciousness. It is the function of mind or rather, mind *is* the function by which human consciousness operates on all that is external to it; human consciousness, in turn, is shaped by the results of this operation. Phenomenologists such as Edmund Husserl and American pragmatists, particularly Peirce and James, advocated the study of the transactional function of human consciousness early in this century. During the same period, the Soviet psychologist Lev Vygotsky performed a large number of clinical studies based on this transactional function. He took exception to the rather static "developmental" studies of Piaget for the very reason that they failed to take into account the transactional aspect of human consciousness. Today, Nobel prizewinner Gerald Edelman is the leading contributor in the effort to fully understand how the human brain functions upon an external *reality*, how perceived reality functions to alter consciousness, and how the brain functions to allow an external reality to operate on itself. Edelman's recent work, *Bright Air, Brilliant Fire* (1992), serves as our guide to the brief discussion of human consciousness that follows.

We will not belabor the distinction between the concepts of the *mind* and *human consciousness*. For our purposes, *mind* will refer to a highly directed human consciousness, a mind that is purposefully or intentionally focused on a problem to be solved or a situation to be resolved. The concept of *mind* is of limited value when trying to understand the relationships between the physiology of a human brain and the functions of human consciousness. A person may be said to have a good mind, to be mindless, or to have a poor mind. What is meant is that some persons are able to attend purposefully for a significant period of time and to be successful in dealing with situations and problems. The mindless show little ability to sustain their attention for more than a brief period, with little success at problem solving. A person of poor mind may be able to focus his or her attention, but with poor results at problem solving. These distinctions fail to take us beyond a common behavioral understanding. The concept of *human consciousness* possesses a far richer range of meaning, allowing us to make a closer connection to the neurophysiology of the brain and to identify and categorize the numerous functions involved in human consciousness. In other words, the term *mind* seems to lend itself to behavioral manifestations of human consciousness. *Human consciousness* is used in the following discussion as a broad concept involving these functions, but implying other functions that may not be manifest; *mind* refers to a more limited set of behaviors and functions of consciousness.

The first point to be made concerns the incredible complexity of the brain—that biological organ essential to consciousness:

> Indeed, the circuits of the brain look like no others we have seen before. The neurons have treelike arbors that overlap and ramify in myriad ways. Their signaling

is not like that in a computer or a telephone exchange; it is more like the vast aggregate of interactive events in a jungle. And yet despite this, brains give rise to maps and circuits that automatically adapt their boundaries to changing signals. Brains contain multiple maps interacting without any supervisors, yet bring unity and cohesiveness to perceptual scenes. And they let their possessors (pigeons, for example) categorize as similar a large if not endless set of diverse objects, such as pictures of different fish, after seeing only a few such pictures. (Edelman, 1992, p. 69)

Not only are neurons clustered to perform functions of consciousness, but these clusters in turn form maps that allow for the integration of a wide range of functions. At the level of higher consciousness, we find in the human brain the neuronal capability to generate maps of maps.

A few points to further illustrate the complexity of the brain should be noted. First, the cerebral cortex, which composes the part of the brain associated with higher brain functions, is made up of some 10 billion nerve cells or neurons. Each neuron is connected to other neurons at points called *synapses*. There are about one million billion synapses in the cortex, or about 1 billion connections in half a single cubic centimeter of brain (about the size of a peanut). Extending this concept, our neurons are often arranged into maplike connections. These maps can react to multisource stimulations that are received from two-dimensional sources and are able to produce reactions appropriate to a three- or four- (time) dimensional world. These maps can also connect with each other. Millions of fibers within the brain serve to connect these maps forming maps of maps. Finally, as Edelman (1992) stated:

A piece of brain tissue is an intricate network that responds to electrical and chemical signals in three-dimensional space and in time. It sends out dynamic patterns and receives and responds to such patterns. These patterns affect each other and, through other nerve connections, the action of other organs of the body. . . . The brain is a master controller and its rhythmic patterns alter how you breathe, pump blood, digest your food, and move. (p. 22)

The brain with its neurons is a genetically acquired organ. However, what particular neurons will group, what and how groups of neurons form maps, and how maps of maps are developed are determined jointly by the unique, genetically determined brain and the interaction of the whole organism with its environment and with its brain and the brain with the whole organism. Basically, the brain is a correlator. "It correlates temporal inputs during its own development, and it correlates the properties of signals and scenes in its adult functioning to give rise to consciousness" (Edelman, 1992, p. 149).

A second point concerns the rise of consciousness itself. Keep in mind that the capacity for consciousness must preexist in a biological sense. It is the interaction of the brain with the entire organism and its environment out of which consciousness arises. The brain must develop its capacity of perception through a process of interaction with an environment. It must develop the mapping needed to allow for the formation of concepts. What is needed is, of course, determined by this same interaction between the brain and its environment. The creation of the elaborate feedback *loops* are essential for memory.

Edelman (1992) made a distinction between *primary* consciousness and *higher-order* consciousness. This distinction is of particular relevance to educators. *Primary consciousness,* defined as the awareness that integrates biological needs with the categorization process of external stimuli, is present in varying degrees in many members of the animal kingdom. This integration or *scenario* is retained in memory. Primary consciousness is "limited to the remembered present. It is necessary for the emergence of higher-order consciousness, and it continues to operate in animals capable of higher-order consciousness" (p. 149).

The role of language is key to the development of higher-order consciousness. Edelman's summary puts it clearly:

> Higher-order consciousness arises with the evolutionary onset of semantic capabilities, and it flowers with the accession of language and symbolic reference. Linguistic capabilities require a new kind of memory for the production and audition of the coarticulated sounds that were made possible by the evolution of a supralaryngeal space. The speech areas mediating categorization and memory for language interact with already evolved conceptual areas of the brain. Their proper function in a speech community connect phonology to semantics, using interactions with the conceptual areas of the brain to guide learning. This gives rise to a syntax when these same conceptual centers categorize the ordering events occurring during speech acts. As a syntax begins to be built and a sufficiently large lexicon is learned, the conceptual centers of the brain treat the symbols and their references and the imagery they evoke as an "independent" world to be further categorized. A conceptual explosion and ontological revolution—a world, not just an environment—are made possible by the interaction between conceptual and language centers. (pp. 149–150)

This brief summary cannot begin to do justice to the complexity of the view of mind or consciousness presented by Edelman. To connect the function of consciousness to both its neurobiological and evolutionary sources is to reject a reductionist simplicity and to accept as fundamental the complexity and uniqueness of individual consciousness. Such an approach provides a rich insight into the role of language and learning. Not only can the *mystical* aspect of consciousness be accounted for in terms of the brain's complexity and how the complexity becomes structured, but the distinction between the *world* of primary consciousness and the *world* of higher order consciousness begins to make *evolutionary sense.* The world of higher order consciousness is seen as a socially based symbolic world—and a world that is at the same time uniquely individual.

## THINKING

Reflections on the essential relation of thought to language are the focus of this section. Edelman's work focused upon the neurophysiology of the brain and its relation to consciousness and on the relation between higher consciousness and language. In contrast, the work of the psychologist Lev Vygotsky concentrated on the development of language and its mediating role on thinking. Vygotsky used the study of language development as the key to understanding thought and cognitive functioning.

Vygotsky's contributions to the understanding of the process of thinking may be considered contemporary even though his work and research took place some 60 years ago. His ideas and writings became available to the Western world relatively recently, in particular with the publication in 1962 of the English translation of his *Thought and Language*. Since that time, Vygotsky's stature as both psychologist and theorist has steadily grown. Any serious discussion of the relation of thinking and language must include the consideration of his major contributions to this field.

From his own psychological research, Vygotsky concluded that initially thought and speech develop from different origins. This position is consistent with the neurophysiological studies of Edelman. However, once both are established in the individual, their development proceeds under reciprocal influence. They become mutually interdependent and from this point forward an advancement in one area stimulates advancement in the other. Furthermore, any failure to advance in either speech or thinking retards or precludes advancement in the other. The two functions of thought and speech form a unity out of their interdependent relationship; from this process, speech becomes intellectual and thought becomes verbal. "The cases of pathological dissolution and involution of functions . . . also indicate that the *relation* between thought and speech is not an unchangeable one" (Vygotsky, 1988, p. 68). Vygotsky summarized his findings as follows:

1. Thought and speech have different genetic roots.
2. The two functions develop along different lines and independently of each other.
3. There is no clear-cut and constant correlation between them in phylogenesis.
4. Anthropoids display an intellect somewhat like man's *in certain respects* (the embryonic use of tools) and a language somewhat like man's *in totally different respects* (the phonetic aspect of their speech, its release function, the beginnings of a social function).
5. The close correspondence between thought and speech characteristic of man is absent in anthropoids.

6. In the phylogeny of thought and speech, a prelinguistic phase in the development of thought and a preintellectual phase in the development of speech are clearly discernible. (pp. 79–80)

From and during the interaction of thought and speech, concepts develop. Vygotsky identified two types of concept formation: the *scientific* and the *spontaneous*. Scientific concepts are generated out of factual knowledge. They are the product of the self's interaction with a socially preexisting reality comprised of structured and interrelated bodies of knowledge. The most structured knowledge in this social reality is presented by means of formal schooling; during the educational process scientific concepts are usually acquired. Spontaneous concepts are generated out of the individual's reflections on his or her own experiences.

Concepts arising in these two modes are not to be conceived of as being independent of each other, in spite of their differing origins. In fact, the two types of concepts maintain a mediating relationship from the outset. Vygotsky termed this relationship a *dialogue*. The dialogue is responsible for the continuing development of our concepts. Scientific concepts give structure and order to our spontaneous concepts and spontaneous concepts bring reality and individuality, or a sense of personal ownership to our scientifically acquired concepts. The mediating relationship or dialogue between scientific and spontaneous concepts constitutes what Vygotsky termed the *zone of proximal development* (ZPD). An examination of this zone reveals that the socially based scientific concepts precede the development of concepts based upon individual reflection. The emergence of thought in the individual is socially acquired, and the structure inherent in social thought or concepts is a prerequisite for the development of internal or individual concepts. This forms a basis for Vygotsky's educational directive that instruction precedes development.

In his research with children, Vygotsky inquired into the role of inner speech. How does language development in children account for both the internal and external uses of language? Vygotsky's research showed that the earliest speech in a child is social. It is only later that speech begins to divide into a form of speech designed for oneself and into a distinct form of speech for others. This later form is focused upon the task of communication. At this later stage of speech development we witness outward interpsychological relations becoming converted into inner psychological mental functions. Also, we witness the earlier development of overt dialogue being converted into a form of internal dialogue. In short, Vygotsky's studies of children point to the initial social origin of both thought and language. The very recent neurobiological studies of Edelman would seem to support this conclusion.

A final point Vygotsky made in connection with the development of thought and language concerns *meaning* in connection with word meaning. Vygotsky held that a distinction must be made between the *sense* of a word and its *meaning*.

In short, the sense of a word is the class or category of objects, acts, or experiences to which it refers. A child may have a sense of the word, cat, for instance, but the meaning of the term is continuously being expanded and refined. The meaning of a word is derived from the entire context in which it is used—including, but not limited to, the sense of the word. Thus, the young child will acquire the sense of a large number of words, but will be only beginning the process of developing the meaning of words. The meaning of words is acquired through a continuous process of interaction between the individual and the environment, between scientific and spontaneous concepts, and between instruction and development. The sense of a word may be readily acquired, but the meaning of a word continually develops both internally within the individual and externally as social reality. It is interesting to note that Edelman's work also revealed the primacy of categorization over communication in human consciousness and in the development of symbolic functioning.

## LITERACY

The impact of literacy on thought and cognitive development is the emphasis in this section. An anthropological and historical view of language evolution and development will be our first focus. The work of Robert Lewin (1993) is the basis for this section. However, the impact of literacy on thought and thinking is best described in the historical setting of ancient Greece. The implications for classroom practice are most profound.

*Homo erectus* appeared on the scene some 1.7 million years ago. For 1 million years prior to this and for 1.5 million years after, the evolution of the brain and the physiology required for speech followed an essentially biological pattern. As Roger Lewin (1993) wrote in *The Origin of Modern Humans*:

> Between 2.5 million and 250,000 years ago, the pace of technological change (and, by inference, language-induced cultural change) closely parallels increase in brain size and therefore looks like biological evolution. After that, and particularly in the more recent Upper Paleolithic times, brain size remains the same while technological change gathers apace—a sure sign of the modern human mind (equipped with modern human language?) at work. In other words, real cultural evolution had kicked in. (p. 165)

Modern human language did not just appear on the evolutionary scene. It required, first of all, the evolution of a brain anatomy that would allow the treatment of sounds as symbols and permit their storage in memory. The development of language required the physical development of a voice box that could produce a wide range of sounds. A bit of this evolutionary process remains in evidence. A human infant has a very limited set of sounds available—not unlike those of adult primates. The larynx of primates, including humans, is located high in the neck. However, only in humans does the larynx move lower in the neck with advancing maturity. The changing voice phenomenon in the teenager signals the acquisition of the full range of human sound production. This increased range of sound is due to the increased size of the laryngeal space made possible by the descent of the larynx. Human beings pay a price for this. Primates and human infants are able to swallow and breathe at the same time due to the location of their larynx. Adult humans cannot. An attempt to do so results in a tendency to choke.

The need for language and its use is of ancient origin. Earliest forms of man had to make do with the recognition of visual categories or patterns and to learn appropriate responses to them (e.g., the mate, the enemy, some prey). Dealing with the "buzzing blooming confusion" in this manner restricted early hominids to a day-by-day existence. As speech and language evolved, these visual categories could be captured in speech, facilitating through verbal means a recall of visual patterns for later use. Speech was responsible for making possible the common sharing of visual patterns, especially in relation to the rearing of the young. The further development of speech led to the development of the facility to create categories of categories. This, in time, led to the assembly of categories into myths—a visual and verbal world. It is within this world, or culture, that language as a tool for communication evolves. However, a primary function of language was and continues to be that of categorization rather than simply communication. In fact, it is the use of language to categorize the infinite multiplicity of sensory data into manageable units and to label these units for subsequent recall and use that makes communication possible.

There remains one further, dramatic step in the development of modern languages: the evolution of literacy. As ancient Greeks would recount this occurrence:

> Cadmus had brought Greece "gifts of the mind": vowels and consonants yoked together in tiny signs, "etched model of a silence that speaks"—the alphabet. With the alphabet, the Greeks would teach themselves to experience the gods in the silence of the mind, and no longer in the full and normal presence, as Cadmus himself had the day of this marriage. (Calasso, 1993, pp. 390–391)

Ancient Greece, especially Athenian culture, converted itself from a purely oral society to a literate one in a matter of a few centuries. It is important to note the effects of this transition in order to fully appreciate the impact of literacy upon contemporary Western civilization. For ancient Greece, the advent of literacy brought about a transition from *mythos* to *logos* as the dominant mode of thought and of problem solving. Poetry, prior to the advent of literacy, was inseparable from music, rhythm, dance, and dramatic performances. If a lengthy speech is to become the common property of a culture and be remembered generation to generation it must be accompanied and reinforced by these mnemonic devices; otherwise, it must be written down. Poetic forms of ordinary speech gave way to prose. Logical and linear forms of explanation and expression emerged. In short, history, science, and philosophy were born.

Even more important was the impact upon human thought processes. The linear and logical aspect of written language added new patterns for thinking. These rational new patterns and their corresponding written forms provide an effective prod to memory, allowing greater permanence to both individual and collective decisions. For example, Pericles admonished judges to make no judgment that was not based upon *written* laws. A government of laws and not of men has as its prerequisite a literate citizenry. In addition to the linear and logical impact upon human thought, written language facilitates the capacity to extrapolate in both a forward and backward direction. Thus, the individual acquires the ability to construct an extended, coherent, and permanent past and to project a more manageable future. Interpolation is greatly facilitated by the possession of a written language. It is possible to take a bit of the past (history) and to extrapolate to a future. However, it is equally important to be able by means of interpolation to determine possible steps necessary to carry one from this past toward the projected future. And most important, literacy makes memory (personal and collective) both permanent and objective.

The effects of literacy upon thinking are striking. It not only makes historical thinking possible, but it makes history possible. It provides the basis for analytical thinking and more effective methods for problem solving. Literacy also provides for the orderly expansion or growth of a language. Beyond all the effects listed, literacy provides the most effective means for arriving at consensus among large populations regarding linguistic categories and meanings, providing a more stable basis for communication. The world of Western civilization was dramatically changed and subsequently shaped by Cadmus' gift of an alphabet to the Greeks. The development of the written word allowed the gods to remove themselves from the everyday affairs of man, for they had provided a means for man to control his own destiny. Now that man had a history, he could begin to create a future.

Before turning to an examination of the implications for education, it will be helpful to restate some of the key notions that emerge from the three areas of inquiry that lie outside of the usual purview of those concerned with language and education. First, the brain is a dynamic, ever-changing organ. Its neuronal maps develop and change in response to both internal and external stimuli. The product of the brain at any given moment in time is a unique, individual consciousness. Second, language and the development of a brain capable of symbolic functioning is essential to the emergence of a higher consciousness. The visual and verbal functions of the brain are developed independently and in different brain locations. These functions are interrelated by means of neural mapping and by maps of maps. Third, conceptual language must precede the development of higher consciousness. Concept formation or the formation of categories takes precedence over the communication function of language. The sense of a word will be acquired prior to its meaning, which is a developmental process that is developed by use in communicating. In this sense, instruction must precede development. Fourth, written language is a significantly different process than spoken language. It has a fundamental impact upon our thinking and upon how we see the world. It is only with a written language that analytic and logical skills can arise. With the advent of literacy, man transcended his past and acquired a history and, by logical extrapolation, a future. Finally, it must be recognized that literacy is the cornerstone of Western civilization. The history of Western civilization begins with the Greek alphabet in about the eighth century B.C. From this point forward, Western civilization had a history and its future was shaped by those forms of thoughts that are the hallmark of literacy.

## IMPLICATIONS FOR EDUCATION

In our discussion of the mind, thinking, and literacy, and the implications of this discussion for education, it becomes important to sort out the ideas that have currency for educational practice. What kind of a curriculum fosters the development of physiological dynamics of the brain? It can be demonstrated that newly processed information and incremental information are processed in different neural patterns, patterns formed by the thinking process itself during the process of thinking in response to external and internal stimuli. The product of the brain at any given moment in time is a unique, individual consciousness (Edelman, 1992). It can be extrapolated that learning will be an individual process, whether intended or not.

Language and the development of the symbolic functions of the brain are essential to the emergence of higher consciousness, that is, higher level thinking. The imaging process, visual functions, and verbal functions are situated in different brain locations. Their development, however, depends not only on external stimuli but on the interaction and mapping that evolves among them. Mental processes developed in response to sensory input aid the learner to move from a direct life experience, including all of its symbolic forms, to the use of imagery, visual thinking, and verbal thinking. All of these forms of thought and perhaps others must be fostered in the educational setting. Conceptual language (basic verbal concepts) precede the brain's development of higher level thinking (Vygotsky, as translated by Rieber & Carton, 1987). Moreover, instruction precedes development of cognitive processes and higher level thought. The zone of proximal development is stimulated and directed by what one learns through instruction, modeling, and scaffolding.

Finally, written language is a significantly different process from spoken language. Only with written discourse can logic and analysis of events arise. History, poetry, and the rational development of disciplined study cannot occur without the written word. A civilization may have a past within the oral tradition, but a society has a history (a common memory) only with its graphic, permanent forms of presentation. Likewise, poetry as a separate art form cannot exist in an illiterate society, but it develops and grows in a manifestly different way with its written expression. Thus literacy becomes the cornerstone of educational practice from literature and science to computerized electronic modes. None of these disciplines exist with any rational development or systematization apart from a written language. Thus, educators must seek forms that not only utilize written language, but create new forms of language to accommodate new knowledge.

## Educational Concerns

Questions arise from these premises: How can we facilitate the development of a relationship between sensory and visual stimuli and/or the experience of human living and linguistic categories, or the concepts that one develops before higher level consciousness occurs? How can we aid in the transition of the child's consciousness or his or her basic concepts to higher consciousness? How can we insure that instruction occurs which precedes or augments new levels of conceptual cognitive development? If literacy has been deemed essential for a civilization to progress, how can we develop the notion of literacy as an across-the-curriculum priority? We ask these questions in a unified group, because the practices that qualify as answers to one question are part of the answers to the rest. If these questions are treated separately or in a linear or hierarchical manner, the whole is lost, and the concepts we are trying to convey are violated.

## Practices for Thinking and Literacy

One academic who looked at educational practice in terms of the concerns mentioned earlier is David Perkins (1992) in his book *Smart Schools*. The smart school is energetic, informed, and thoughtful. Perkins discussed practices that promote just such schools. He feels that we must be clear, having firm objectives about what we teach; that we must offer an authentic, challenging curriculum; that we must give accurate, informative feedback, including authentic assessment; that instruction should promote reflection; and that we should use many forms of instruction, including didactic teaching, coaching, the Socratic method, cooperative and problem-based situated learning.

To promote thinking, he recommended understanding learning processes such as explaining and generalizing, using examples and analogies. The development of mental images and visual thought, problem-solving techniques, levels of understanding, attention to subject matter in terms of problem solving, methods of justification and explanation, and the formation of good questions and generative topics are forcefully presented in the book. Does the curriculum promote the language of thinking: reasons, evidence, hypothesis, strategies, graphic organizers, a culture of thinking? Does it encourage intellectual passion, such as curiosity, truth, persistence? These functions for instructing were upheld by Perkins. Mental images are developed and used to integrate the themes of the curriculum. In his discussion of distributed intelligence, he advocated thinking on paper and cooperative, collegial teaching with graphic organizers, along with the management functions that promote learning and help with task dimensions and procedures. In the section on cognitive economy, he concluded that we must increase the complexity of cognitive tasks, that they must be related to life, that this approach to curriculum development should be cost-effective and feasible, employing authentic assessment while fulfilling many of the demands of conventional instruction.

In short, Perkins defined in detail the kind of classrooms we advocate, a fine overview of processes that govern good education. What we would like to develop in the remainder of this chapter are examples of thinking, literate behaviors created by complex, relevant learning tasks, with specific techniques for teaching. Examples of literacy behaviors in the development of minding, thinking, and languaging (emphasizing its written forms of reading and writing) will demonstrate applications of educational use.

We may have well-organized, interesting, informative texts, as an example, for science. We are familiar with the strategies of the whole-language classroom and theme learning for scientific concepts, but educators are careless with the development and quality of interaction that occurs during cooperative group learning. We must attend to greater structure for higher level thought that engages the learner in a greater respect and understanding of the power and necessity of the written word for developing a greater use of more complex and more abstract thinking.

Problem-situated learning regarding a scientific concept in the collaborative groups involves discussion. What may not be stressed is the graphic presentation of the logic that should dominate such interaction. The dynamics of discussion should include diagrams, minutes, and the reading of notes to augment logic and developmental task-oriented discussion. Without literate presentations such as books, a written agenda, and the blackboard for ideas, the progression of investigation and the production of highly developed insights are less likely to occur.

A recent issue of *The Reading Teacher* devotes the entire publication to "New Definitions of Reading in the Content Areas" and focuses on the necessity of bringing higher level thought and literacy activities to the content of the disciplines. It is gratifying to note that information for the concepts we endorse is reaching the classroom right along with the theory and research that support such practice.

In this issue, Harste (in R. J. Monson & M. P. Monson, 1994) stated:

> It's very important that a teacher plan to plan in advance by looking at those topics that might be of importance and interest to students. You come to curriculum

possibilities by systematically rotating topics under investigation through the disciplines, through the sign systems, and also, in some ways through the kinds of personal and social knowledge that the group you are working with has already shared. Teachers can't do for kids what they haven't done for themselves, so they should begin asking some questions. What would a historian want us to learn about this particular topic? A biologist? What generalizations would a philosopher want us to walk away with? An artist? (pp. 519–520)

What follows this introduction is a series of articles, the first of which advocates the use of graphic organizers, such as the Venn diagram for demonstrating likenesses and differences between the Greeks and Romans, an H-Map comparing and contrasting hot and cold air, a jot chart for categorizing information, and a card sort for definitions of Biomes. From these organizers, students move to visual examples of the concepts presented, including maps and realia, then go on to writing from the sketchy information of the advance (graphic) organizer. Knowledge of vocabulary, savvy for working in jigsaw-collaborative groups, and the multiple perspectives suggested previously by Harste (Hadaway & Young, 1994) are learned during this progression.

A second article (Lewis, Wray, & Rospigliosi, 1994) developed notions of scaffolding using such techniques as the prior knowledge revision frame. Heading the page is the topic (Rabbits) and the half completed sentences: *Before I began this topic, I thought that . . .* followed halfway down the lined page by *I learned that . . .* and ending with *Finally I learned that. . . .* The learner has a scaffold for many of the science and other activities that he needs to explore his own prior knowledge and acquired information from reading. Moving on through the journal, Casteel and Isom (1994) wrote of the reciprocal processes in science and literacy, demonstrating the principle of literacy as being essential to scientific learning with the integration of literacy processes (reading, writing, speaking, listening, thinking, and imaging) as being the means by which literate behaviors and scientific behaviors are processed. See Fig. 1.1.

Fallon and Allen (1994) developed the notion that kindergarten writing (including diagrammatic art and illustrations) can be used across the curriculum in social studies, math, science, and literature as a means of developing emergent literacy and a bank of content knowledge. The principles of curriculum design include:

1. Children contributed to curriculum development.
2. Children wrote daily on topics of their own choosing as well as in response to teacher-directed topics related to content area learning.
3. Children read and listened to a wide variety of poetry, informational and fictional literature every day.
4. Children had someone who listened—really listened—to what they said and wrote. (p. 551)

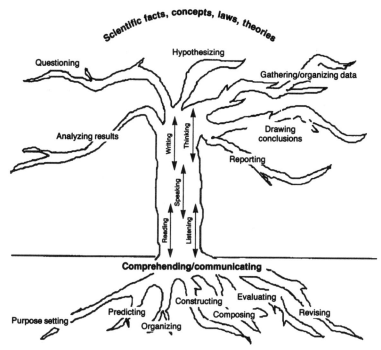

FIG. 1.1. Illustration of the supportive nature of literacy processes to science understanding. From Casteel and Isom, 1994. © Copyright 1994 by International Reading Association. Reprinted with permission.

How do these examples of children's working demonstrate, or provide examples, models and scaffolding for the educator?

Harste (in R. J. Monson & M. P. Monson, 1994) clearly addressed concepts of individual learning and the necessity of integrating conceptual development to knowledge possessed by the group one is teaching; he stressed that knowledge of symbolic systems and themes across curriculum areas is essential for the development of generalizable knowledge of the learner. He suggested epistemic knowledge be claimed through the eyes of the biologist, the physicist, the archaeologist, and the philosopher.

The examples of moving from visual and verbal experience to the graphic organizer, to group discussion, and to collection of artifacts (Hadaway & Young, 1994) is a demonstration of the concept of moving from visual thinking to higher level thought (graphic organizers) to writing and group discussion. Clearly, higher level thinking becomes a collective concern; group production of literate forms is requisite. In each of these examples, students move through conceptual levels via literacy events, whether using scaffolding to explore prior and acquired knowledge about rabbits in the Lewis et al. (1994) article or the literacy processes engaged in *across the kindergarten curriculum* developed by Fallon and Allen (1994).

Even more gratifying, processes for developing thinking about thinking are being forwarded in Casteel and Isom's work, including questioning, hypothesizing, gathering/organizing data, analyzing results, drawing conclusions, and reporting. Literacy events are organized around purpose setting, predicting, organizing, constructing, composing, evaluating, and revising as parallel processes developed as part of scientific literacy (Fallon & Allen, 1994).

Teachers are clearly beginning to see the relationship between literacy behaviors and content-area learning. "Biology is not plants and animals. It is language about plants and animals. . . . Astronomy is not planets and stars. It is a way of talking about planets and stars" (Postman, as cited in Casteel & Isom, 1994, p. 540). Developing principles from practice, Fallon and Allen (1994) not only demonstrated how children are encouraged to develop their own thinking around areas of conceptualization across the kindergarten curriculum, but also showed how visual, verbal, lifelike experiences are used to move children into conceptually sophisticated and somewhat abstract mental processing of rationalized social and scientific concepts.

The examples from *The Reading Teacher*, written by teachers, demonstrate that teachers have "got it" in terms of what classrooms are going to be like. What they may not realize as they go for the gold of deeper, more involved learning and thinking, is the role that literacy plays in civilized society. The information gleaned from the videocassette player (or glommed onto from the information highway), while a valid, vital learning experience, had better include the literacy activities of reading, writing, listening, speaking, thinking, and visualizing. Literacy has been undersold as a civilizing activity in our time; if we are doing anything in this chapter it is making the case for literacy.

## REFERENCES

Calasso, R. (1993). *The marriage of Cadmus and Harmony*. New York: Knopf.

Cassirer, E. (1923). *Substance and function*. Chicago: The Open Court.

Casteel, C. P., & Isom, B. A. (1994). Reciprocal processes in science and literacy. *The Reading Teacher, 47*(7), 538–545.

Dewey, J. (1916). *Democracy and education*. New York: Macmillan.

Edelman, G. M. (1992). *Bright air, brilliant fire*. New York: Basic Books.

Ellis, J. M. (1993). *Language, thought, and logic*. Evanston, IL: Northwestern University Press.

Fallon, I., & Allen, J. (1994). Where the deer and the cantaloupe play. *The Reading Teacher, 47*(7), 546–551.

Hadaway, N. L., & Young, T. A. (1994). Content literacy and language learning: Instructional decisions. *The Reading Teacher, 47*(7), 522–527.

Kozulin, A. (1990). *Vygotsky's psychology*. Cambridge, MA: Harvard University Press.

Lewin, R. (1993). *The origin of modern humans*. New York: Scientific American Library.

Lewis, M., Wray, D., & Rospigliosi, P. (1994). . . . And I want it in your own words. *The Reading Teacher, 47*(7), 528–537.

Monson, R. J., & Monson, M. P. (1994). Literacy as inquiry: An interview with Jerome C. Harste. *The Reading Teacher, 47*(7), 519–520.

Penrose, R. (1989). *The emperor's new mind.* New York: Oxford University Press.
Perkins, D. (1992). *Smart schools.* New York: Free Press.
Posner, M. I., & Raichle, M. E. (1994). *Images of mind.* New York: Freeman.
Rieber, R. W., & Carton, A. S. (Eds.). (1987). *The collected works of L. S. Vygotsky.* New York: Plenum.
Rose, S. (1992). *The making of memory.* New York: Doubleday.
Vygotsky, L. (1988). *Thought and language.* Cambridge, MA: MIT Press.

# Chapter 2

# The Problem of Consciousness

John R. Searle
*University of California, Berkeley*

The most important scientific discovery of the present era will come when someone—or some group—discovers the answer to the following question: How exactly do neurobiological processes in the brain cause consciousness? This is the most important question facing us in the biological sciences, yet it is frequently evaded, and frequently misunderstood when not evaded. In order to clear the way for an understanding of this problem, I am going to begin to answer four questions: 1. What is consciousness? 2. What is the relation of consciousness to the brain? 3. What are some of the features that an empirical theory of consciousness should try to explain? 4. What are some common mistakes to avoid?

## WHAT IS CONSCIOUSNESS?

Like most words, *consciousness* does not admit of a definition in terms of genus and differentia or necessary and sufficient conditions. Nonetheless, it is important to say exactly what we are talking about because the phenomenon of consciousness that we are interested in needs to be distinguished from certain other phenomena such as attention, knowledge, and self-consciousness. By *consciousness* I simply mean those subjective states of sentience or awareness that begin when one awakes in the morning from a dreamless sleep and continue throughout the day until one goes to sleep at night or falls into a coma, or dies, or otherwise becomes, as one would say, *unconscious*.

Above all, consciousness is a biological phenomenon. We should think of consciousness as part of our ordinary biological history, along with digestion, growth, mitosis, and meiosis. However, though consciousness is a biological phenomenon, it has some important features that other biological phenomena do not have. The most important of these is what I call its *subjectivity*. There is a sense in which each person's consciousness is private to that person, a sense in which he is related to his pains, tickles, itches, thoughts, and feelings in a way that is quite unlike the way that others are related to those pains, tickles, itches, thoughts, and feelings. This phenomenon can be described in various ways. It is sometimes described as that feature of consciousness by way of which there is something that it's like or something that it feels like to be in a certain conscious state. If somebody asks me what it feels like to give a lecture in front of a large audience, I can answer that question. But if somebody asks what it feels like to be a shingle or a stone, there is no answer to that question because shingles and stones are not conscious. The point is also put by saying that conscious states have a certain qualitative character; the states in question are sometimes described as *qualia*.

In spite of its etymology, consciousness should not be confused with knowledge; it should not be confused with attention; and it should not be confused with self-consciousness. I consider each of these confusions in turn.

Many states of consciousness have little or nothing to do with knowledge. Conscious states of undirected anxiety or nervousness, for example, have no essential connection with knowledge.

Consciousness should not be confused with attention. Within one's field of consciousness there are certain elements that are at the focus of one's attention and certain others that are at the periphery of consciousness. It is important to emphasize this distinction because *to be conscious of* is sometimes used to mean *to pay attention to*. But the sense of consciousness that we are discussing here allows for the possibility that there are many things on the periphery of one's consciousness—for example, a slight headache I now feel, or the feeling of the shirt collar against my neck—which are not at the center of one's attention. I will have more to say later about the distinction between the center and the periphery of consciousness.

Finally, consciousness should not be confused with self-consciousness. There are indeed certain types of animals, such as humans, that are capable of extremely complicated forms of self-referential consciousness which would normally be described as self-consciousness. For example, I think conscious feelings of shame require that the agent be conscious of himself or herself. But seeing an object or hearing a sound, for example, does not require self-consciousness. And it is not generally the case that all conscious states are also self-conscious.

## WHAT ARE THE RELATIONS BETWEEN
## CONSCIOUSNESS AND THE BRAIN?

This question is the famous *mind–body problem*. Although it has a long and sordid history in both philosophy and science, I think, in broad outline at least, it has a rather simple solution. Here it is: Conscious states are caused by lower level neurobiological processes in the brain and are themselves higher level features of the brain. The key notions here are those of *cause* and *feature*. As far as we know anything about how the world works, variable rates of neuron firings in different neuronal architectures cause all the enormous variety of our conscious life. All the stimuli we receive from the external world are converted by the nervous system into one medium, namely, variable rates of neuron firings at synapses. And equally remarkable, these variable rates of neuron firings cause all of the color and variety of our conscious life. The smell of the flower, the sound of the symphony, the thoughts of theorems in Euclidian geometry—all are caused by lower level biological processes in the brain; and as far as we know, the crucial functional elements are neurons and synapses.

Of course, like any causal hypothesis, this one is tentative. It might turn out that we have overestimated the importance of the neuron and the synapse. Perhaps the functional unit is a column or a whole array of neurons, but the crucial point I am trying to make now is that we are looking for causal relationships. The first step in the solution of the mind–body problem is: Brain processes *cause* conscious processes.

This leaves us with the question: What is the ontology, what is the form of existence, of these conscious processes? More pointedly, does the claim that there is a causal relation between brain and consciousness commit us to a dualism of *physical* things and *mental* things? The answer is a definite no. Brain processes cause consciousness but the consciousness they cause is not some extra substance or entity. It is just a higher level feature of the whole system. The two crucial relationships between consciousness and the brain, then, can be summarized as follows: Lower level neuronal processes in the brain cause consciousness and consciousness is simply a higher level feature of the system that is made up of the lower level neuronal elements.

There are many examples in nature in which a higher level feature of a system is caused by lower level elements of that system, even though the feature is a feature of the system made up of those elements. Think of the liquidity of water, or the transparency of glass, or the solidity of a table, for example. Of course, like all analogies, these analogies are imperfect and inadequate in various ways. But the important thing that I am trying to get across is this: There is no metaphysical obstacle, no logical obstacle, to claiming that the relationship between brain and consciousness is one of causation and at the same time claiming that consciousness is just a feature of the brain. Lower level elements of a system can cause higher level features of that system, even though those features are features of a system made up of the lower level elements. Notice, for example, that just as one cannot reach into a glass of water and pick out a molecule and say, "This one is wet," so one cannot point to a single synapse or neuron in the brain and say, "This one is thinking about my grandmother." As far as we know anything about it, thoughts about grandmothers occur at a much higher level than that of the single neuron or synapse, just as liquidity occurs at a much higher level than that of single molecules.

Of all the theses that I am advancing in this chapter, this one arouses the most opposition. I am puzzled as to why there should be so much opposition, so I want to clarify a bit further what the issues are: First, I want to argue that we simply know as a matter of fact that brain processes cause conscious states. We don't know the details about how it works and it may well be a long time before we understand the details involved. Furthermore, it seems to me that an understanding of how exactly brain processes cause conscious states may require a revolution in neurobiology. Given our present explanatory apparatus, it is not at all obvious how, within that apparatus, we can account for the causal character of the relation between neuron firings and conscious states. But, at present, from the fact that we do not know *how* it occurs, it does not follow that we do not know *that* it occurs. Many people who object to my solution (or dissolution) of the mind–body problem object on the grounds that we have no idea how neurobiological processes could cause conscious phenomena. But that does not seem to me a conceptual or logical problem. That is an empirical/theoretical issue for the biological sciences. The problem is to figure out exactly how the system works to produce consciousness, and since we know that in fact it does produce consciousness, we have good reason to suppose that there are specific neurobiological mechanisms by way of which it works.

There are certain philosophical moods we sometimes get into when it seems absolutely astounding that consciousness could be produced by electrobiochemical processes, and it seems almost impossible that we would ever be able to explain it in neurobiological terms. Whenever we get in such moods, however, it is important to remind ourselves that similar mysteries have occurred before in science. A century ago, it seemed extremely mysterious, puzzling, and to some people metaphysically impossible that life should be accounted for in terms of mechanical, biological, chemical processes. But now we know that we can give such an account, and the problem of how life arises from biochemistry has been solved to the point that we find it difficult to recover, difficult to understand why it seemed such an impossibility at one time. Earlier still, electromagnetism seemed mysterious. On a Newtonian conception of the universe, there seemed to be no place for the phenomenon of electromagnetism. But with the development of the theory of electromagnetism, the metaphysical worry dissolved. I believe that we are having a similar problem about consciousness now. But once we recognize the fact that conscious states are caused by neurobiological processes, we automatically convert the issue into one for theoretical-scientific investigation. We have removed it from the realm of philosophical or metaphysical impossibility.

## SOME FEATURES OF CONSCIOUSNESS

The next step in our discussion is to list some (not all) of the essential features of consciousness that an empirical theory of the brain should be able to explain.

### Subjectivity

As I mentioned earlier, this is the most important feature. A theory of consciousness needs to explain how a set of neurobiological processes can cause a system to be in a subjective state of sentience or awareness. This phenomenon is unlike anything else in biology, and in a sense, it is one of the most amazing features of nature. We resist accepting subjectivity as a ground floor, irreducible phenomenon of nature because, since the 17th century, we have come to believe that science must be objective. But this involves a pun on the notion of objectivity. We are confusing the *epistemic* objectivity of scientific investigation with the *ontological* objectivity of the typical subject matter in science in disciplines such as physics and chemistry. Because science aims at objectivity in the epistemic sense that we seek truths that are not dependent on the particular point of view of this or that investigator, it has been tempting to conclude that the reality investigated by science must be objective in the sense of existing independently of the experiences in the human individual. But this last feature, ontological objectivity, is not an essential trait of science. If science is supposed to give an account of how the world works and if subjective states of consciousness are part of the world, then we should seek an (epistemically) objective account of an (ontologically) subjective reality, the reality of subjective states of consciousness. What I am arguing here is that we can have an epistemically objective science of a domain that is ontologically subjective.

### Unity

It is important to recognize that in nonpathological forms of consciousness we never just have, for example, a pain in the elbow, a feeling of warmth, or an experience of seeing something red, but we have them all occurring simultaneously as part of one unified conscious experience. Kant called this feature "the transcendental unity of apperception." Recently, in neurobiology it has been called "the binding problem." There are at least two aspects to this unity that require special mention. First, at any given instant, all of our experiences are unified into a single conscious field. Second, the organization of our consciousness extends over more than simple instants. So, for example, if I begin speaking a sentence, I have to maintain in some sense at least an iconic memory of the beginning of the sentence so that I know what I am saying by the time I get to the end of the sentence.

## Intentionality

*Intentionality* is the name that philosophers and psychologists give to that feature of many of our mental states by which they are directed at, or about states of affairs in the world. If I have a belief or a desire or a fear, there must always be some content to my belief, desire, or fear. It must be about something even if the something it is about does not exist or is a hallucination. Even in cases when I am radically mistaken, there must be some mental content which purports to make reference to the world. Not all conscious states have intentionality in this sense. For example, there are states of anxiety or depression in which one is not anxious or depressed about anything in particular but is just in a bad mood. That is not an intentional state. But if one is depressed about a forthcoming event, that is an intentional state because it is directed at something beyond itself.

There is a conceptual connection between consciousness and intentionality in the following respect. Although many, indeed most, of our intentional states at any given point are unconscious, nonetheless, in order for an unconscious intentional state to be genuinely an intentional state it must be accessible in principle to consciousness. It must be the sort of thing that could be conscious even if it, in fact, is blocked by repression, brain lesion, or sheer forgetfulness.

## The Distinction Between the Center and the Periphery of Consciousness

At any given moment of nonpathological consciousness I have what might be called a *field of consciousness*. Within that field I normally pay attention to some things and not to others. So, for example, right now I am paying attention to the problem of describing consciousness but giving very little attention to the feeling of the shirt on my back or the tightness of my shoes. It is sometimes said that I am unconscious of these. But that is a mistake. The proof that they are a part of my conscious field is that I can at any moment shift my attention to them. But in order for me to shift my attention to them, there must be something there to which I was previously not paying attention but to which I am now paying attention.

## The Gestalt Structure of Conscious Experience

Within the field of consciousness our experiences are characteristically structured in a way that goes beyond the structure of the actual stimulus. This was one of the most profound discoveries of the Gestalt psychologists. It is most obvious in the case of vision, but the phenomenon is quite general and extends beyond vision. For example, the sketchy lines drawn in Fig. 2.1 do not physically resemble a human face. If we actually saw someone on the street that looked like that, we

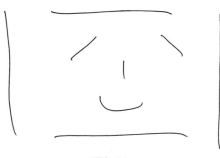

FIG. 2.1.

would be inclined to call an ambulance. The disposition of the brain to structure degenerate stimuli into certain structured forms is so powerful that we will naturally tend to see this as a human face. Furthermore, not only do we have our conscious experiences in certain structures, but we also tend to have them as figures against backgrounds. Again, this is most obvious in the case of vision. Thus, when I look at the figure I see it against the background of the page. I see the page against the background of the table. I see the table against the background of the floor, and I see the floor against the background of the room, until we eventually reach the horizon of my visual consciousness.

## The Aspect of Familiarity

It is a characteristic feature of nonpathological states of consciousness that they come to us with what I call the *aspect of familiarity*. In order for me to see the objects in front of me as, for example, houses, chairs, people, or tables, I have to have a prior possession of the categories of houses, chairs, people, and tables. But that means that I will assimilate my experiences into a set of categories that are more or less familiar to me. When I am in an extremely strange environment, in a jungle village, for example, and the houses, people, and foliage look very exotic to me, I still perceive that as a house, that as a person, that as clothing, that as a tree, or a bush. The aspect of familiarity is thus a scalar phenomenon. There can be greater or lesser degrees of familiarity. But it is important to see that nonpathological forms of consciousness come to us under the aspect of familiarity. Again, one way to consider this is to look at the pathological cases. In Capgras' syndrome, the patients are unable to acknowledge familiar people in their environment as the people they actually are. They think the spouse is not really their spouse but is an impostor, etc. This is a case of a breakdown in one aspect of familiarity. In nonpathological cases it is extremely difficult to break with the aspect of familiarity. Surrealist painters try to do it. But even in the surrealist painting, the three-headed woman is still a woman, and the drooping watch is still a watch.

## Mood

Part of every normal conscious experience is the mood that pervades the experience. It need not be a mood that has a particular name to it, like depression or elation, but there is always what one might call a flavor or tone to any normal set of conscious states. So, for example, at present I am not especially depressed, I am not especially ecstatic, nor indeed am I what one would call simply "blah." Nonetheless, there is a certain mood to my present experiences. Mood is probably more easily explainable in biochemical terms than several of the features I have mentioned. We may be able to control, for example, pathological forms of depression by mood-altering drugs.

## Boundary Conditions

All of my nonpathological states of consciousness come to me with a certain sense of what one might call their *situatedness*. Though I am not thinking about it, and though it is not part of the field of my consciousness, I nonetheless know what year it is, what place I am in, what time of day it is, the season of the year, and usually even what month it is. All of these are the boundary conditions or the situatedness of nonpathological conscious states. Again, one can become aware of the pervasiveness of this phenomenon when it is absent. So, for example, as one gets older there is a certain feeling of vertigo that comes over one when one loses a sense of what time of year it is or what month it is. The point I am making now is that conscious states are situated and they are experienced as situated even though the details of the situation need not be part of the content of the conscious states.

## SOME COMMON MISTAKES ABOUT CONSCIOUSNESS

I would like to think that everything I have said so far is just a form of common sense. However, I have to report, from the battlefronts as it were, that the approach I am advocating to the study of consciousness is by no means universally accepted in cognitive science or even neurobiology. Indeed, until quite recently many workers in cognitive science and neurobiology regarded the study of consciousness as somehow out of bounds for their disciplines. They thought that it was beyond the reach of science to explain why warm things feel warm to us or why red things look red to us. I think, on the contrary, that it is precisely the task of neurobiology to explain these and other questions about consciousness. Why would anyone think otherwise? Well, there are complex historical reasons, going back at least to the 17th century, why people thought that consciousness was not part of the material world. A kind of residual dualism prevented people from treating consciousness as a biological phenomenon like any other. However, I am not going to attempt to trace this history. Instead I am going to point out some common mistakes that occur when people refuse to address consciousness on its own terms.

The characteristic mistake in the study of consciousness is to ignore its essential subjectivity and to try to treat it as if it were an objective third-person phenomenon. Instead of recognizing that consciousness is essentially a subjective, qualitative phenomenon, many people mistakenly suppose that its essence is that of a control mechanism or a certain kind of set of dispositions to behavior or a computer program. The two most common mistakes about consciousness are to suppose that it can be analyzed behavioristically or computationally. The Turing test disposes us to make precisely these two mistakes, the mistake of behaviorism and the mistake of computationalism. It leads us to suppose that for a system to be conscious, it is both necessary and sufficient that it has the right computer program or set of programs with the right inputs and outputs. I think you have only to state this position clearly to enable you to see that it must be mistaken. A traditional objection to behaviorism was that behaviorism could not be right because a system could behave as if it were conscious without actually being conscious. There is no logical connection, no necessary connection between inner, subjective, qualitative mental states and external, publicly observable behavior. Of course, in actual fact, conscious states characteristically cause behavior. But the behavior that they cause has to be distinguished from the states themselves. The same mistake is repeated by computational accounts of consciousness. Just as behavior by itself is not sufficient for consciousness, so computational models of consciousness are not sufficient by themselves for consciousness. The computational model of consciousness stands to consciousness in the same way the computational model of anything stands to the domain being modeled. Nobody supposes that the computational model of rainstorms in London will leave us all wet. But they make the mistake of supposing that the computational model of consciousness is somehow conscious. It is the same mistake in both cases.

There is a simple demonstration that the computational model of consciousness is not sufficient for consciousness. I have given it many times before so I will not dwell on it here. Its point is simply this: *Computation is defined syntactically.* It is defined in terms of the manipulation of symbols. But the syntax by itself can never be sufficient for the sorts of content that characteristically go with conscious thoughts. Just having zeros and ones by themselves is insufficient to guarantee mental content, conscious or unconscious. This argument is sometimes called "the Chinese room argument" because I originally illustrated the point with the example of the person who goes through the computational steps for answering questions in Chinese but does not thereby acquire any understanding of Chinese.[1] The point of the parable is clear but it is usually neglected. *Syntax by itself is not sufficient for semantic content.* In all of the attacks on the Chinese room argument, I have never seen anyone come out baldly and say they think that syntax is sufficient for semantic content.

---

[1]Searle, J. R. (1980). Minds, brains, and programs. *Behavioral and Brain Sciences, 3*, 417–457.

However, I now have to say that I was conceding too much in my earlier statements of this argument. I was conceding that the computational theory of the mind was at least false. But it now seems to me that it does not reach the level of falsity because it does not have a clear sense. Here is why.

The natural sciences describe features of reality that are intrinsic to the world as it exists independently of any observers. Thus, gravitational attraction, photosynthesis, and electromagnetism are all subjects of the natural sciences because they describe intrinsic features of reality. But such features such as being a bathtub, being a nice day for a picnic, being a $5 bill, or being a chair, are not subjects of the natural sciences because they are not intrinsic features of reality. All the phenomena I named—bathtubs, and so on—are physical objects and as physical objects have features that are intrinsic to reality. But the feature of being a bathtub or a $5 bill exists only relative to observers and users.

Absolutely essential, then, to understanding the nature of the natural sciences is the distinction between those features of reality that are intrinsic and those that are observer-relative. Gravitational attraction is intrinsic. Being a $5 bill is observer-relative. Now, the really deep objection to computational theories of the mind can be stated quite clearly. Computation does not name an intrinsic feature of reality but is observer-relative and this is because computation is defined in terms of symbol manipulation, but the notion of a *symbol* is not a notion of physics or chemistry. Something is a symbol only if it is used, treated, or regarded as a symbol. The Chinese room argument showed that semantics is not intrinsic to syntax. But what this argument shows is that syntax is not intrinsic to physics. There are no purely physical properties that zeros and ones or symbols in general have to determine that they are symbols. Something is a symbol only relative to some observer, user, or agent who assigns a symbolic interpretation to it. So the question, "Is consciousness a computer program?" lacks a clear sense. If it asks, "Can you assign a computational interpretation to those brain processes that are characteristic of consciousness?" the answer is that you can assign a computational interpretation to anything. But if the question asks, "Is consciousness intrinsically computational?" the answer is that nothing is intrinsically computational. Computation exists only relative to some agent or observer who imposes a computational interpretation on some phenomenon. This is an obvious point. I should have seen it 10 years ago, but I did not.

## ACKNOWLEDGMENTS

This article was originally published in *Experimental and Theoretical Studies of Consciousness*. Wiley, Chichester (Ciba Foundation Symposium 174). The theses advanced in this chapter are presented in more detail and with more supporting argument in *The Rediscovery of the Mind* by J. R. Searle, 1992, Cambridge, MA: MIT Press.

# Chapter 3

# Creative Cognition:
# Demystifying Creativity

Steven M. Smith
*Texas A&M University*

Although creative activities are obviously a function of mental processes, creativity has not been typically studied within the contemporary science of cognitive psychology. Part of the reason for this lack of attention to creative thinking is that there has not been a clearly defined paradigm for studying creativity using a cognitive-processing approach. In a recent book (Finke, Ward, & Smith, 1992), however, my colleagues and I established and articulated a creative-cognition paradigm, calling for the study of creativity from the point of view of the mental processes that give rise to creative behavior. Although our original efforts in this area focused on our own laboratory research, there is now a growing number of researchers exploring the cognitive processes and mental structures that underlie creativity (e.g., Smith, Ward, & Finke, in press).

The predominant approach to creativity in psychological research has been psychometric in nature, focusing on creative people and their personality traits. Those individuals who have made the greatest creative contributions in their fields of endeavor have been studied, often in depth, in order to discover what personality factors creative geniuses may have in common. This personality approach may be useful for distinguishing creative people from uncreative ones, but it is not particularly useful in terms of telling us how to think creatively if we do not already do so.

The creative-cognition view states that there are patterns of cognition that set the stage for creative discoveries, patterns that can be found in people in all domains of creative endeavor. This approach focuses not on creative products or people, but on creative thinking itself. In doing so, we change from the question of who is creative to that of how people think creatively.

Before proceeding further, it will be useful to define what I mean by the term *creativity*, an elusive concept that resists a clear definition. The main problem is that there are few, if any, characteristics that are absolutely necessary for a product to be considered creative. Therefore, I have taken what is known as a "family resemblance" approach, defining creativity as a set of shared properties, none of which are necessary or sufficient for something to be considered creative, but all of which are common in creative products. These shared properties include novelty, imaginativeness, practicality, emergence (new qualities that can emerge when old elements are combined), ambiguity, meaningfulness, incongruity, and divergence (being different from the ordinary). Defined in this way, creativity can be understood without pigeonholing it in any absolute way. It is important to avoid oversimplifying the sometimes paradoxical concept of creativity.

## THE PARADOXES OF CREATIVITY

The subject of creativity is riddled with paradoxes. Resolving and clarifying these paradoxes are important for our understanding of creativity. For example, one paradox is that our society needs and treasures creativity, yet at the same time pressures, censors, and shuns those who do not conform to social norms. Conformity does not bring about innovation or novelty, qualities of creative ideas and products. Given the degree of conformity we see in the world, it is not surprising that so few people are considered to be creative. Why, then, in spite of pressure to conform, does our society continue to produce and revere creative people?

It also seems paradoxical that imagination and practicality are the two primary qualities of creative products. These are usually viewed as opposites, rather than as qualities that go together. Imagination so often seems impractical, and practicality seems so unimaginative. How can imaginative ideas be realistic?

Creative thinking may involve special mental processes, such as insight or divergent thinking. Paradoxically, creativity is also thought to be part of our regular "armamentarium" of cognitive abilities, playing an important role in such everyday activities as speaking and dreaming. Does creative thinking involve special skills, or normal everyday ones?

Another paradox is that creativity involves the use of old or expert knowledge, yet it also requires that we do things in new ways. Should we use our prior knowledge in creative thinking, or should we reject it? How are we to distinguish between wisdoms when we are told on the one hand not to fall into a rut in our thinking, yet are also warned to have the sense not to repeat the mistakes of history?

Finally, it seems paradoxical that creative people have been described as having personality traits that are mutually exclusive or contradictory, such as reflectivity and spontaneity, or childlike playfulness and mature wisdom. How is it possible to be both reflective and spontaneous? The answer may be simply that creative people are reflective at certain times and spontaneous at other times. This apparently simple answer, however, leads to some challenging questions: Is it meaningful to characterize a person as having opposite traits? Are there noncreative people who are also both reflective and spontaneous, but not in a creative way? And most importantly, when are the appropriate times to be reflective and spontaneous if creativity is the desired outcome?

This last question is probably the most useful one, and should be framed in terms of creative processes. An adequate understanding of the process should enable us to address questions such as the stages of creativity in which reflectivity is most needed, and those in which spontaneity is more appropriate. At what point in the process are knowledge and wisdom most important, and when is childlike imagination needed? The approach I have taken is aimed at understanding the processes that underlie creative thinking.

The same cognitive structures and processes involved in noncreative cognition can be used to explain creative thinking. This approach may help to "demystify" creativity, because the mysterious ways in which ideas appear to be created may seem less baffling when expressed in terms that are used to explain everyday thinking. That creative thinking, in one form or another, is not an everyday activity, however, is not a valid assumption. Furthermore, that noncreative cognition is perfectly well understood is equally untenable. The process of demystifying creativity by casting it in terms of cognitive processes and mental structures may help to lift the mystery from some phenomena, but it is unlikely to remove all of the mystery and excitement involved in creative thinking.

Creative cognition involves many complex mental activities, such as formulating and reconceptualizing problems, generating divergent ideas, transcending mental blocks, visualizing, exploring ideas, discovering interesting combinations of ideas, using and adapting one's expert knowledge, discovering insight, and refining ideas. Examples of basic cognitive processes that underlie these activities include encoding, storage and retrieval of information, attention, mental imaging, conceptualization, analogical reasoning and rule-based thinking, and metacognition. Cognitive structures involved in creative thinking include concepts, images, language structures, mental models, schemata, distributed networks, and prototypes. Only a few of these basic underlying cognitive processes and structures will be discussed in the present chapter, but all of them are involved in both creative and noncreative thinking. The goal of creative cognition is not necessarily to describe a certain path to successful creativity, but rather to understand basic cognitive structures and processes well enough to know how to set the stage for creative ideas, discoveries, and products.

## THE ROADMAP THEORY OF CREATIVE THINKING

The "roadmap" theory of creative thinking combines a number of conventional theoretical mechanisms into an integrated system that is intended to explain a broad array of phenomena, and resembles other theories in important ways (e.g.,

Newell, Shaw, & Simon, 1962). Although the theory by no means addresses all of the important issues in creative cognition, it nonetheless provides a context for understanding many important aspects of creative thinking. The roadmap theory, as considered here, will incorporate ideas about planful thinking, the logical "tree" structures that planful thinking can produce, a "generative search" process, metacognitive monitoring, fixation, incubation, and insight.

The basic idea of the roadmap theory is to conceive of consciousness as moving from one place to the next, beginning with an initial problem state, and ending with a goal or solution state. The road along which one moves is determined by the plans used to guide thinking. Fixation corresponds to dead-end branchings of the road, and incubation allows escape from dead ends. Several examples, some historical, some from laboratory research, and some from everyday life, will be considered in the context of the roadmap theory.

## Plans

A *plan* refers to an abstract cognitive structure that represents a general approach to a situation, and includes rules for manipulating information, making decisions, and guiding behavior. Plans can be general (e.g., how to get through college) or specific (e.g., how to tie your shoes). When a plan is selected for dealing with a situation, the plan's rules are applied until the goals of the plan are successfully attained, whereupon the plan is abandoned. The knowledge state with which one begins is the initial representation of the problem. Given an initial representation of the problem and a plan for dealing with the situation, one can create a roadmap of the possible steps that one might potentially take in carrying out the plan.

The roadmap can be plotted as a hierarchical tree structure, such as the one shown in Fig. 3.1. Thinking in such a structure begins at the top and works its way down, searching for information that will lead, knowledge state by knowledge state, to the anticipated goal of the plan that is guiding one's thinking. The top of the tree structure (labeled *Begin Search* in Fig. 3.1) constitutes the initial representation of a question or problem on which one is working. At each branch in the tree one may choose the next step in one's thinking from the various possibilities offered by the plan. Choosing the next step allows one to descend through the tree structure in search of a target or goal state.

## Generative Search

We may commonly think of a search as having a single well-defined goal or target. For example, a math problem such as $845 \times 2509 = ?$ appears to have a very obvious set of rules that guide the problem solver step by step to the single correct solution, using a clearly circumscribed series of rules. The question "How many *y*s are there in the word *psychology*?" involves a similar direct search path, as well as a clear-cut answer. Not all questions are addressed and answered in

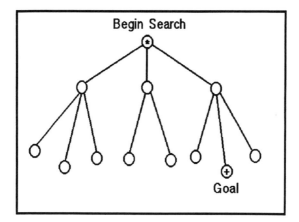

FIG. 3.1. Circles indicate choice points in a hierarchy of possible knowledge states. Movement from one knowledge state to another is done according to the rules of the plan guiding the search. The generative search typically begins at the top of the map and works its way down, step-by-step, in search of a goal.

such a clear-cut fashion. For example, "What should you serve for dinner when you have important guests?" has many possible considerations, and many possible answers, some better than others.

The exploration of one's knowledge in search of ideas and information that may lead to a solution is an open-ended process that I refer to as a *generative search*. At each choice point one can generate many possible *next steps* to pursue. Any step may appear to be a promising lead or a useless dead end. As you generate and gather information, you arrive at potential goals, targets, and solutions to the original problem. Important to this theory is the fact that the targets and solutions and goals being sought are not explicitly stored facts that reside passively in memory, with the goal of the problem solver being merely to find answers that are already there. Goal states are achieved by being constructed, step-by-step, using not only preexisting knowledge, but also new ideas that emerge during a generative search from combinations of existing knowledge. This generative, constructive approach to how knowledge is used thus explains how the same cognitive system can carry out both narrowly defined convergent tasks, such as math problems, and broad, ill-defined problems, including those that require creative solutions.

## Monitoring

Metacognitive *monitoring*, like introspection, refers to the act of attending to one's own thoughts. In the roadmap theory presented here, self-monitoring is an important element for determining the directions taken by the generative search. At each branching, or choice point, the thought process may proceed either in ways that fulfill the goals and constraints of one's current guiding plan, or in directions that are inappropriate for reaching an optimal solution. As thinking continues from one knowledge state to the next, the appropriateness of one's choices can be gauged in terms of the number of subgoals and constraints that are satisfied along the way. The more subgoals and constraints that become satisfied when thinking takes a particular direction, the closer one feels to the final goal, and the more likely one is to persist in that direction. This part of the thought process refers to *verification*, or verifying that one's mental work has been appropriate.

Monitoring one's thinking is very useful for keeping problem solving on track, particularly for tasks that are highly familiar. A potential drawback of the verification process, however, is that partial verification of one's thinking may guide one blindly down a path that cannot lead to a solution. Such events refer to *dead-end branchings*, and will be discussed at length to describe their important role in creative cognition.

### Fixation: Dead-End Branchings

Fixation in problem solving refers to getting stuck in one's work on a problem. More generally, the term has been used to refer to any of a number of ways that remembering, solving problems, or creative thinking can be at least momentarily blocked (e.g., Smith & Blankenship, 1991). The simplest type of cognitive block is *interference* in memory, also known as *response competition*. When two different memories become learned, the two corresponding responses can be thought of as competing with each other when an attempt is made to retrieve one of the memories. One memory (to be called the *blocker*) can intrude upon consciousness, blocking a similar memory (the *target* of the search) from being retrieved. When the blocker is stronger than the target, it wins the competition, causing a *memory block*.

In terms of the roadmap theory, interference occurs when the direction of one's thinking leads to retrieval of a blocker, rather than to the planned target of one's search (Fig. 3.2). A turn in one's cognitive roadmap toward a blocked pathway is a *dead end*, a point from which one cannot discover a correct target without abandoning the blocked path. The ease with which one can abandon a dead end depends on how strong a blocker is, and how far one has taken a blocked path; it is not always easy to tell at which point one has taken a wrong turn on one's mental highway.

A number of factors can contribute to the cognitive fixation that can occur when one has taken a dead-end path. Two classes of factors that will be considered here are *typical thinking* and *recent experience*. Typical thinking is the result of long-term experience, caused by repeated use of parts of the mental roadmap in habitual ways. The major problems with typical thinking when new, creative ideas are sought are that thinking can proceed automatically, based on unfounded,

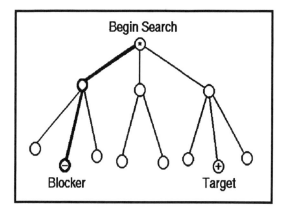

Begin Search

Blocker

Target

FIG. 3.2. Heavier lines indicate stronger or likelier paths caused by recency or frequency of use. A search may be diverted down a dead end if a blocker is typical or has been recently encountered.

implicit assumptions, and that old paths are unlikely to lead to new ideas. Recent experiences can make inappropriate ideas at least temporarily stronger. Although recent encounters with blockers may be less of a problem than typical thinking in many situations that require creative thinking, recency nonetheless provides a means of manipulating and studying mental blocking in experimental settings.

One type of typical thinking that leads to dead-end paths is called *functional fixity* (e.g., Maier, 1931). This term refers to a difficulty in seeing an object as being useful for reasons other than the ways the object is typically used. Maier's now classic "two-string" problem could be solved only by seeing that a pair of pliers could be used as a weight for a pendulum, rather than for their more typical purpose.

One of my favorite examples of a real-life problem involving functional fixity happened to a former professor of mine who started up her car one morning only to discover that her radiator cap was missing. A negligent mechanic had failed to replace the cap the previous day when her car had been repaired. She sensibly decided to drive back to the garage to retrieve the missing radiator cap, and to offer a few choice words to the errant mechanic. Even more sensibly, she decided to get something for a temporary replacement to keep the radiator from disgorging its contents while she drove to the garage. What was she to use as a temporary replacement for a radiator cap?

I have posed this problem to thousands of students, and their answers almost always show a clear pattern of functional fixity. The first answers likely to be offered are to use other objects used to cap things in automobiles, such as the gas cap or oil cap. The functional fixity shown here is very specific, focusing on other very similar objects. These initial ideas must be discarded on the basis that even if one of those caps did fit, another cap would still be needed to replace the replacement. Students then move on to other materials in the home that are typically used to close off things, such as saran wrap, aluminum foil, or a rag. Again, typical, functionally fixated thinking fails in this case because none of these typical materials could withstand the radiator heat and pressure, even for a brief time.

The professor's solution was inspired, and surpassed or escaped functional fixity; she grabbed a large potato from the vegetable bin and jammed it into the opening of the radiator—one size fits all! Her solution was creative and elegant (and inexpensive). The "potato plug" worked, an idea that required novel thinking, unconstrained by the mental dead ends offered by typical thinking, allowing her to drive safely to the garage.

The thinking involved in this situation can be illustrated by the mental roadmap in Fig. 3.3. The likeliest first steps involve either alternative automobile parts or common household materials used for wrapping. Typical thinking thus begins with the very first step, taking dead-end turns on the mental path. Although vegetables typically function in capacities other than auto parts, the potato had qualities (e.g., size, composition, availability) that made it an ideal temporary radiator cap. Sometimes, even brief mental excursions can lead to surprising ideas.

Typical thinking can involve a number of different types of trap for the problem solver, some of them due to inappropriate implicit assumptions. One such trap is illustrated by the following popular riddle:

> It was a dark and stormy night when a man and his son drove around Dead Man Curve. The car suddenly lost traction and skidded into a great oak tree, killing the man instantly, and throwing the boy from the car. An ambulance arrived quickly and sped the boy to the emergency room for surgery. Moments after the boy was wheeled into the operating room, the surgeon emerged, hands trembling, and said, "I cannot operate on this boy. He is my son!" How is this possible?

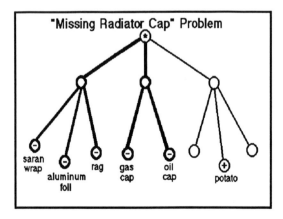

FIG. 3.3.  Two entire branches of this roadmap represent typical directions of thinking that lead down dead ends in the radiator-cap problem.

When I pose this problem to my students, the first solutions they try are that the boy was the dead father's adopted son and the surgeon's biological son (or vice versa), the man is the boy's grandfather, the man is a minister (a type of father), or that the mother lied to her husband all those long years ago about who the real father was. These incorrect attempts are diagrammed in Fig. 3.4, which shows the dead-end branchings that solvers usually take. Importantly, all of the inappropriate paths bear the implicit assumption that surgeons are men. In this case, an unwarranted sex-role stereotype prevents people from seeing the obvious solution; the surgeon is his mother.

How obvious should the solution be if not for sex-role stereotypes? See for yourself as you try this slightly altered version of the surgeon problem:

> It was a dark and stormy night when a woman and her son drove around Dead Man Curve. The car suddenly lost traction and skidded into a great oak tree, killing the woman instantly, and throwing the boy from the car. An ambulance arrived quickly and sped the boy to the emergency room for surgery. Moments after the boy was wheeled into the operating room, the surgeon emerged, hands trembling, and said, "I cannot operate on this boy. He is my son!" How is this possible?

The surgeon is obviously the boy's father, a man. No one even considers this to be a riddle, because it doesn't require altering an unconscious stereotype to solve it.

Recent experience can also strengthen paths that lead to blockers. An important consequence of this is that recent experience can be experimentally manipulated and researched, whereas the typicality of a particular train of thought varies greatly among people. Different people have different stereotypes, and they also differ in terms of other implicit assumptions that they may make. These differences make typical thinking difficult to study, because the experimenter cannot

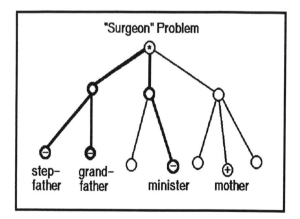

FIG. 3.4. A prejudicial sex-role stereotype, that surgeons are men, prevents thinking from taking the appropriate path to the otherwise obvious solution in the surgeon problem; the surgeon is the boy's mother.

control that variable. Recent experience, however, can be controlled, and therefore has proven a valuable tool for research on fixation and related mental blocks.

The first researcher to capitalize upon the hypothesis that recent experience can block solutions to problems was Luchins (e.g., Luchins & Luchins, 1970). His now famous water jar problem demonstrated the importance of mental set, what he referred to as *mechanization* of thought. The task in which water jar problems are given involves the subject solving a long series of similar problems that require mathematical solutions. When subjects discover that a single, moderately complex algorithm (B − A − 2C) can be repeatedly used to solve every problem, they typically speed up work, solving each one very quickly. At one point in the sequence, a problem is inserted that cannot be solved with the recently discovered algorithm, but can be solved by an extremely simple algorithm (A + B). Subjects typically get stuck when they get to the special problem, failing to see the obvious solution because of their recent problem-solving experience. The mental set found in solving a series of Luchins' water jar problems can be explained as the result of a temporary strengthening of a blocker's (B − A − 2C) path.

I have also conducted numerous experimental studies on the subject of fixation in which blocks are introduced in the laboratory by exposing subjects beforehand to blockers. My studies have used a broad variety of cognitive tasks and materials, a few of which I will presently describe. These studies all show that recent experiences can cause fixation in memory, problem solving, and creative thinking.

One set of experiments to be described used Remote Associates Test (RAT) problems (Smith & Blankenship, 1991), which are commonly used to test creative thinking. For RAT problems one must find a single word (the solution) that is strongly related to each of three test words that are given. For example, for the RAT problem "CAR-SHOE-TOP" the solution is "box," because it makes a two-word phrase or a compound word with each of the three test words: "box-CAR," "SHOE-box," and "box-TOP." Other examples of RAT problems are shown in Table 3.1.

TABLE 3.1
Sample RAT Problems, Solutions, and Blockers

| RAT Problems | | | Solution | Blocker |
|---|---|---|---|---|
| ARM | COAL | STOP | pit | rest |
| BALL | STORM | WHITE | snow | cloud |
| SHIP | PARKING | SUIT | space | jump |
| DECK | SCOTCH | RECORDER | tape | flight |
| APPLE | HOUSE | FAMILY | tree | green |
| CAT | SLEEP | BOARD | walk | black |

*Note:* Every solution word makes a two-word phrase or compound word with each of the three problem words. Every blocker makes a phrase with two of the three problem words.

The reason that RAT problems are considered to test an important aspect of creative thinking is that they require the problem solver to engage in a type of atypical thinking referred to as *remote association* (e.g., Mednick, 1962). For remote association one must think not of common associates of the test words, but of unusual ones, because there is one unusual associate in common for all three test words. For example, common associates of the RAT word "ARM" might be "leg" or "hand"; common associates of "COAL" are "mine" and "black"; and common associates for "STOP" are "sign" and "bus." A remote associate of all three test words, ARM, COAL, and STOP, is "pit," which makes the combinations "ARM-pit," "COAL-pit," and "pit-STOP."

Blocker words were found that were not quite correct answers; each blocker makes a two-word phrase or compound word with only two of the three test words. For example, the blocker word "horn" fits with two of the RAT words from the "CAR-SHOE-TOP" example ("CAR-horn" and "SHOE-horn"), but does not fit with the third RAT word (TOP). In our experiments on fixation effects, we introduced the blocker words in a task that was ostensibly unrelated to the later tasks in the experiment (i.e., the RAT problems). For example, the blockers were sometimes used as stimuli in what was called a test of short-term memory (e.g., Smith & Schumacher, 1992).

We have repeatedly found that recent viewing of blocker words impedes performance on RAT problems (Smith & Blankenship, 1991; Smith & Schumacher, 1992). Furthermore, even when subjects who have seen blockers are able to solve the RAT problems, they take considerably more time in doing so, as compared to control-group subjects who see unrelated words rather than blockers in their incidental "short-term memory" task. Figure 3.5 depicts this fixation or blocking in a RAT problem. The mental path to "horn" is momentarily strengthened, relative to the path that leads to the correct answer, "box."

Although the RAT tests remote association, it is not intended as a test that requires subjects to be highly imaginative. An open-ended activity, referred to as a *creative generation* task, examines more creative, imaginative thinking (e.g., Smith, Ward, & Schumacher, 1993). In this task, subjects are asked to create as many new objects as they can for a given category. For example, Smith et al. asked subjects to sketch and label as many new ideas as they could for toys, or to create new animals for an imaginary inhabited planet similar to Earth. Although not all the college students in the experiments were creative, a large number of them came up with fascinating and creative ideas in a brief experimental session.

Recent experiences with novel toys or imaginary animals were experimentally introduced by Smith et al. (1993) in the form of examples. Some subjects saw three examples of imaginary animals, each of which happened to have four legs, antennae, and a tail, or three examples of imaginary toys, each of which used a ball, electronics, and required a high degree of physical activity. Certainly, not all imaginary creatures and toys must have these features. Smith et al. found that

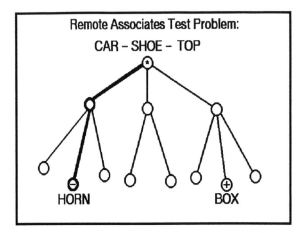

FIG. 3.5.   Recent experience with the blocker word "horn" draws thinking down an inappropriate path in the "CAR-SHOE-TOP" Remote Associates Test problem. The appropriateness of both the phrases "CAR-horn" and "SHOE-horn" make the dead end even more compelling. The correct target, "box," is weaker if it has not been recently seen.

viewing the examples fixated subjects, constraining their creative thinking in this generation task. Those who saw examples were far more likely to include the example features in their sketches than subjects who had seen no examples. The conformity shown by subjects who had seen examples appeared to be involuntary, and was every bit as strong an effect even when subjects were explicitly instructed to generate ideas that were as different as possible from the examples.

An even more realistic creative-generation task was used by Jansson and Smith (1991), who had engineering designers generate novel designs for specified creative-design problems. For example, designers in one experiment were asked to "design a measuring cup that blind people can use," or, in another, to "design an inexpensive, spillproof coffee cup that does not use a straw or a mouthpiece." Half of the designers were shown examples, and half were not. The examples often contained obvious design flaws. For example, the example shown for the spillproof coffee cup had a mouthpiece, which was specifically forbidden, because hot coffee drunk through a mouthpiece without taking in air would scald one's mouth. Nonetheless, more than 50% of the students who saw an example created designs of cups with mouthpieces, even though they were expressly ruled out in the instructions. Only 11% of the control subjects committed the same error in their designs.

This constraining of creative thinking, termed *design fixation* by Jansson and Smith, again can be explained by the roadmap theory. In Fig. 3.6 the mental path leading to ideas for spillproof cups with mouthpieces is shown to be temporarily strengthened by the recent experience with the fixating example. Control subjects are not similarly constrained, generating many more designs of spillproof cups without mouthpieces.

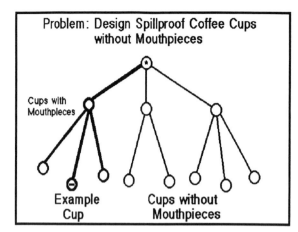

FIG. 3.6. Design fixation results from temporary strengthening of mental paths that lead to designs with mouthpieces.

## RESOLVING MENTAL BLOCKS

So far, I have focused on fixation and blocking, situations that prevent discovery of solutions along one's mental highway. I now turn to the issue of resolving impasses, escaping from dead-end branchings of the road along which one is thinking.

The notion of *incubation effects* has been popular since Wallas (1926) proposed it as a stage of problem solving. The idea of incubation is that after initial attempts at creative problem solving lead to impasses, it may be beneficial to put the problem aside rather than continuing to work at it. If work is interrupted, then an insightful idea may pop into one's head when one returns later to the problem, or even while one is engaged in an unrelated activity. Anecdotally, people often discover this pattern of incubation in their own everyday lives. Furthermore, famous historical examples abound in which sudden insights burst into scientists' minds unexpectedly, while they were engaged in unrelated activities (e.g., Archimedes' discovery of the displacement principle while at the baths; Kekulé's discovery of the benzene ring as he dozed in a chair).

Unfortunately, several factors have contributed to the notion that sudden-insight experiences after incubation periods are caused by mysterious, unconscious forces that labor invisibly at difficult problems while the conscious mind, which was too stupid to solve the problem in the first place, relaxes on vacation. One contributing factor is that famous, insightful scientists may not be good cognitive psychologists, and therefore attribute their incubated insights to the wrong causes. A second factor is that the name that has been assigned to the phenomenon, *incubation*, is a metaphor that suggests something that develops invisibly, and then hatches suddenly, without much warning. Just because the phenomenon has the name *incubation*, however, does not mean that invisible-idea development occurs in the unconscious mind. Finally, a factor that has contributed to this mysterious view of incubation is the surprising dearth of laboratory evidence of the phenomenon; without empirical evidence, inappropriate assumptions are not easily rejected.

The theory of incubation and insight that I endorse does not assume unconscious processes, and is supported by ample empirical evidence (e.g., Smith, 1994; Smith & Blankenship, 1989, 1991; Smith et al., in press). This theory states that incubation and subsequent insight experiences begin with cognitive impasses, as illustrated in the roadmap theory in this chapter. An impasse occurs when one's mental set yields too strong a tendency to take a dead-end branching of a cognitive path. Because the mental set that leads to a dead end can be caused by recent experience or typical thinking, then the way to avoid the dead end is to approach the problem with a different mental set, one that is less likely to lead into the same trap. Incubation, then, has its beneficial effect by: (a) making one's initial mental set less recent, and (b) taking one into different contexts that are associated with different mental sets.

Evidence that leaving one's typical setting enhances incubation and insight comes from historical examples. Archimedes and Kekulé had their insights while away from their work. Poincaré's famous mathematical insight occurred while he was stepping onto a bus, and Nobel laureate Kary Mullis got the idea of polymerase chain reaction while on a midnight drive. Ample evidence that making blocker experiences less recent facilitates incubation comes from laboratory studies that show how performance recovers after blockers are shown if retests are delayed (Smith & Blankenship, 1989, 1991; Smith & Schumacher, 1992; Smith & Vela, 1991).

This view of incubation and insight that involves altered mental sets is thus demystified to some degree. The idea that one's mental set changes over time or in new contexts fits not only with personal experience, but with historical examples as well. The theory is consistent with laboratory evidence on incubation effects, as well as studies that show the suddenness of insight experiences (e.g., Metcalfe, 1986; Metcalfe & Weibe, 1987). The logic of the theory does not depend upon the idea of mysterious, invisible, unconscious processes, of which we have neither empirical nor experiential evidence. Thus, an important aspect of creativity is neither glorified nor denied, but explained in clear and verifiable terms.

## SUMMARY

In the present chapter I have outlined and illustrated an approach for demystifying creativity that involves careful examination and research on the mental processes that are involved in creative thinking. The roadmap theory provides a context for understanding a broad range of phenomena, from everyday thinking and remembering to the creative phenomena of fixation, incubation, and insight. As such, the theory can help to resolve some of the paradoxes of creativity noted at the beginning of this chapter.

For example, whether fixation, incubation, and insight involve special processes can be addressed. These phenomena have been explained herein as special results of thinking within a very understandable cognitive system. The creative-cognition approach has now led to specific experimental findings of these phenomena under conditions predicted by the theory (e.g., Smith & Blankenship, 1991; Smith et al., 1993; Smith & Vela, 1991).

Another paradox, that creative thinking must both use and reject old knowledge, is also understandable from the creative-cognition point of view. At least some expert knowledge must be present if one is to carry out a successful generative search. One must monitor, however, for times when the knowledge used to guide a search is inappropriate, and reformulate problems when such impasses are reached. Should our classrooms emphasize knowledge or creativity? Clearly, they must do both. True creativity is not possible without knowledge, yet without knowing how to use one's knowledge creatively, one can solve only old types of problems.

An important implication of the position taken up in this chapter is that creative thinking is understandable and describable in terms of cognition, and therefore can be learned. In the past, researchers have focused on testing and identifying which individuals are creative. The creative-cognition approach implies that nearly anyone with an appropriate knowledge base can generate creative ideas if they learn to use that knowledge in creative ways.

The present chapter by no means covers the range of ideas being researched in creative cognition (see Finke et al., 1992; Smith et al., in press). A brief list of other topics in creative cognition includes:

1. Conceptualization and conceptual combination, including emergent properties, and reconceptualization
2. Analogical reasoning, a conceptual way of generalizing old knowledge to new situations
3. Visualization, both of abstract relations and concrete forms
4. Computational models (usually computer simulations) of creative cognition.

As can be seen from this list, the roadmap theory only scratches the surface of research in creative cognition.

## REMYSTIFYING CREATIVE THINKING

Understanding aspects of creative thinking demystifies the phenomenon in certain respects, but it also leads to new questions. How do people know when to persist on a mental road, and when to abandon the path? If blocks occur beyond our awareness, how can we learn to detect them? Once we have successfully abandoned a dead end, how do we find a more appropriate path? A creative-cognition approach helps us understand old questions about creativity, but in the process, provides new mysteries to be explored. In a sense, the business of demystifying creativity has the additional effect of remystifying it, guiding our future exploration of creative thinking.

## REFERENCES

Finke, R. A., Ward, T. B., & Smith, S. M. (1992). *Creative cognition: Theory, research, and applications.* Cambridge, MA: MIT Press.

Jansson, D. G., & Smith, S. M. (1991). Design fixation. *Design Studies, 12*(1), 3–11.

Luchins, A. S., & Luchins, E. H. (1970). *Wertheimer's seminars revisited: Problem solving and thinking* (Vol. 3). Albany: Faculty–Student Association, State University of New York.

Maier, N. R. F. (1931). Reasoning in humans. II. The solution of a problem and its appearance in consciousness. *Journal of Comparative Psychology, 12*, 181–194.

Mednick, S. A. (1962). The associative basis of the creative process. *Psychological Review, 69,* 220–232.

Metcalfe, J. (1986). Premonitions of insight predict impending error. *Journal of Experimental Psychology: Learning, Memory, and Cognition, 12*, 623–634.

Metcalfe, J., & Wiebe, D. (1987). Intuition in insight and noninsight problem solving. *Memory and Cognition, 15*, 238–246.

Newell, A., Shaw, J. C., & Simon, H. A. (1962). The process of creative thinking. In H. E. Gruber, G. Terrell, & M. Wertheimer (Eds.), *Contemporary approaches to creative thinking.* New York: Atherton Press.

Smith, S. M. (1994). Getting into and out of mental ruts: A theory of fixation, incubation, and insight. In R. Sternberg & J. Davidson (Eds.), *The nature of insight.* Cambridge: MIT Press.

Smith, S. M., & Blankenship, S. E. (1989). Incubation effects. *Bulletin of the Psychonomic Society, 27*, 311–314.

Smith, S. M., & Blankenship, S. E. (1991). Incubation and the persistence of fixation in problem solving. *American Journal of Psychology, 104*, 61–87.

Smith, S. M., & Schumacher, J. S. (April, 1992). *A test of transfer-appropriate fixation in problem solving.* Paper presented at the meeting of the Midwestern Psychological Association, Chicago, IL.

Smith, S. M., & Vela, E. (1991). Incubated reminiscence effects. *Memory & Cognition, 19*(2), 168–176.

Smith, S. M., Ward, T. B., & Finke, R. A. (in press). *The creative-cognition approach.* Cambridge: MIT Press.

Smith, S. M., Ward, T. B., & Schumacher, J. S. (1993). Constraining effects of examples in a creative generation task. *Memory & Cognition, 21*, 837–845.

Wallas, G. (1926). *The art of thought.* New York: Harcourt, Brace, & World.

# Chapter 4

# Creating Contexts for Community-Based Problem Solving: The Jasper Challenge Series

Brigid Barron, Nancy Vye, Linda Zech, Dan Schwartz,
John Bransford, Susan Goldman, James Pellegrino,
John Morris, Steve Garrison, Ronald Kantor[1]
*Vanderbilt University*

At the present time there are calls from within and outside the educational community to reconceptualize learning goals for students, as well as the roles teachers play in this learning (NCTM, 1989). No longer are the basics defined as reading, writing, and arithmetic, but as the ability to think critically, reason, reflect, engage in argumentation, and develop the capacity for independent learning. These new goals constitute what has been termed the "thinking curriculum" (Resnick & Klopfer, 1989) and are being espoused not only by educators but also by members of the business community who recognize the need for workers who can be independent learners and decision makers (Senge, 1990).[1]

These learning goals call for dramatic changes in our current educational environments. For the past several years, the Cognition and Technology Group at Vanderbilt (CTGV), a group of researchers at Vanderbilt's Learning Technology Center, has been experimenting with technologies that can help facilitate the process of moving toward thinking curricula. This chapter continues a discussion we began earlier in which we traced the evolution of our thinking about the role cognitive psychology might play in implementing such approaches to instruction. Our discussion in that chapter focused on three different models of the role of

---

[1]As is evident from the contents of this chapter the Learning Technology Center is a multidisciplinary and highly collaborative environment. We point out the many advantages of this organization in this chapter. One of the consequences of such an organization is that many have ownership over a particular project. This multiownership is reflected in the large number of authors listed on this paper.

cognitive psychology in research: (a) the curricular elaboration model, in which one changes some aspect of the curriculum but leaves all other aspects of educational practice intact; (b) the classroom restructuring model, in which one attempts to change the overall nature of the teaching and learning process that occurs in classrooms; and (c) the learning communities model, in which the goal is to create a dynamic system that breaks the isolation of classrooms and provides a basis for continual adaptation to changing conditions.

The focus of this chapter is on further analyses of the characteristics of effective learning communities and ways to help develop them. Our discussion is organized into four parts. First, we use our own organization, the Learning Technology Center, as an example of a functioning, learning community and contrast it with the structure and functioning of typical classrooms. We then describe central features of our early attempts at establishing classroom-based learning communities. Second, we discuss our newest SMART (Special Multimedia Arenas for Refining Thinking) programs, titled *The Jasper Challenge Series*, that utilize technology to help teachers and students break the boundaries of their classrooms and create functioning learning communities. Third, we discuss studies of the "value added" by SMART for student and teacher achievement and motivation. We conclude with a discussion of what we have learned thus far and a summary of ideas for further research.


## THE IMPORTANCE OF LEARNING COMMUNITIES
## AND AN EXAMPLE

A number of theorists argued that there have been two major phases of the cognitive revolution. DeCorte, Greer, and Verschaffel (in press) noted that the focus of the first phase was primarily on analyses of individual thinkers and problem solvers. There was a deemphasis on affect, context, culture, and history (Gardner, 1985). DeCorte et al. noted that a second phase of the cognitive revolution has arisen as a reaction to these limitations. The second phase includes attempts to relocate cognitive functioning within its social, cultural, and historical contexts (e.g., Brown, Collins, & Duguid, 1989; Suchman, 1987; Yackel, Cobb, Wood, Wheatley, & Merkel, 1990).

In many ways, social context is to individuals as water is to fish: The effects are so pervasive that it is easy to overlook them. For example, it is easy to overlook the fact that the social conditions necessary for the deployment of most psychological experiments are very special; they are based on a set of conditions in which participants temporarily become "subjects" who allow experimenters to rule (Bransford, 1981). In such contexts, what is said or read is interpreted in a particular manner, perhaps limited to the ecology of the experimental setting. Thus, in an experimental context it is natural to have "subjects" decide that utterances such as "paper" or "Bill has a red car" are examples of English words and sentences, respectively. However, try walking up to someone (preferably a stranger) and simply say "paper" or "Bill has a red car." In this type of setting the listeners' expectations are very different than they are in an experimental context. They become agitated because, despite knowing what you said, they have no idea what you mean or intend (e.g., Bransford, 1981; Bransford & Nitsch, 1978).

The role played by students in typical classrooms is often analogous to the role played by "subjects" in experiments. Students learn to adopt the role of passive receivers of wisdom that is dispensed from teachers, textbooks, and other media (Brown, 1992). The role of the teacher is to deliver information and manage learning. In Dewey's words, education is seen as nothing but preparation for living. He argued that this was the wrong model: "I believe that education, therefore, is a process of living and not a preparation for future living" (Dewey, 1897, p. 78). The idea of making education a process of living is a very interesting one to pursue. We believe that one way to make education come alive is to enrich its connections with the larger social ecology.

## The Learning Technology Center as an Example of a Learning Community

We have found it useful to reflect on the kinds of social environments within which we work as professionals. Our immediate environment, the Learning Technology Center (LTC), supports almost continual learning. It is a very different environment from those found in most classrooms in schools. Some important dimensions of difference follow.

*Projects vs. Lessons.* The activities of the LTC are organized around projects rather than around lessons presented by teachers. Our projects almost always require the discovery of new knowledge. There is no "right answer" that someone is withholding from us and no single authority to whom we turn to tell us what is correct. In the process of pursuing goals relevant to our projects, we engage in "just in time" knowledge acquisition. The knowledge may come from reading, from our own experimentation, or from visits by outside experts. Usually it comes from a combination of these sources. Our knowledge-acquisition activities are almost always means to important ends rather than ends in themselves. And they frequently generate new foci for investigations.

*Collaboration and Distributed Expertise.* The LTC is a multidisciplinary group made up of cognitive psychologists, developmental psychologists, special education researchers, content specialists in areas such as literacy, mathematics, science, and public policy, and experts in computer and video design. Instead of assuming that everyone needs to know and learn the same thing (an assumption commonly found in classrooms), we assume that no single individual is an expert in every area and explicitly acknowledge the importance of *distributed expertise* (e.g., Brown, Ash, Rutherford, Nakagawa, Gordon, & Campione, 1993). In the LTC, different individuals take the role of teacher or learner depending on the relationship between their expertise and the part of the project being worked on at any moment. Thus, instead of a fixed hierarchy of roles, our center is organized around a principle of heterarchy (basically, a flexible hierarchy), where different individuals occupy leadership roles depending on momentary needs. Because any single project usually requires different leaders at different points in time, our projects almost always have multiple authors. We frequently reflect this by publishing as a group, namely the Cognition and Technology Group at Vanderbilt (CTGV).

Especially valued in our LTC is the role played by *intelligent novices*—individuals who are committed to learning with understanding yet do not have the expertise required to understand the particular domain (e.g., some aspect of math or science) being addressed in a project (e.g., see Brown, Bransford, Ferrara, & Campione, 1983; Bruer, 1993). Intelligent novices help keep the experts attuned to the kinds of issues faced by learners who are attempting to develop competence in new domains. In addition, respect for the role of intelligent novices encourages a continual exploration of information outside one's specific areas of expertise. This has helped each of us develop a respect for the expertise, values, and traditions that others bring to our group.

*Intrinsic and Extrinsic Motivation.* Work at the LTC is based on a combination of intrinsic and extrinsic motivation. Most everyone is interested in what they are doing and hence is intrinsically motivated. Nevertheless, there are always aspects of a project that are taxing and tedious. Furthermore, there are many things that compete for one's time. Therefore, extrinsic deadlines play an important role in determining what gets accomplished within particular time frames.

The presence of important deadlines, and activities designed to meet them, contributes to an emotional climate that is far from steady state and boring. In many classrooms, the only deadlines are tests that often involve a great deal of guessing about what to study. Our deadlines in the LTC tend to be much more self-defined than in most classroom contexts. We define the goals we are attempting to accomplish, so preparation for meeting these deadlines is much less of a guessing game.

*Connectedness to a Broad Community of Audiences.* Our work would seem much less meaningful if we were our only audience. Much of the excitement, and most of the opportunities for new learning, come from interactions with diverse audiences that furnish us with new points of view. For example, we interact with fellow academicians, politicians, principals, teachers, students, parents, and business leaders. Each of these groups has very different perspectives, and each provides important points of view.

Our connections to broader communities also supply us with numerous models of ways to do things. For example, we often have opportunities to compare our responses to various grant solicitations to those of other academicians. And we have learned from observing how nonacademic groups (e.g., members of the business community) plan and communicate various ideas. No one ever forces us to copy their approaches. We have the freedom to choose whether to appropriate ideas from other groups that might help us better achieve our goals.

*Frequent Opportunities for Formative Self-Assessment.* Implicit in each of the points discussed earlier is the fact that we have frequent opportunities for formative self-assessment. By comparing our current thinking with others, and by subjecting our in-progress products to the scrutiny of others through reviews and presentations, we are able to continually find weaknesses and improve. This is very different from typical classrooms where the test at the end of the unit or year is usually summative and there are few real opportunities to revise.

*The Use of Tools to Improve Efficiency.* We could not do our work without the availability of tools that support productivity. Computer software for word processing coupled with computer networks for collaboration are elements that we absolutely need. Also necessary is software for planning, data analysis, and archiving. The tools that we employ are used continuously. We do not simply learn a set, use it for a while, and then learn about a new set. This may be contrasted to classrooms where powerful tools are often missing. Even when they are present, they are often presented for a set of isolated lessons and never used again.

*Support for Technology.* It is important to note that there is a great deal of support for the technological tools we use. A number of individuals in our LTC are experts in technology and hence can help others who may need to learn something new or may be experiencing problems. Without this support, most of us would never attempt to use the tools that we find so valuable. In contrast, typical classrooms rarely have the technology for powerful tools, let alone the technical support needed to keep things going and growing.

## The Evolution of Our Attempts to Build Learning Communities

Our reflections on the differences between typical classrooms and our own learning community have influenced the way we think about ways to transform classrooms to meet new learning goals. We do not assume that classrooms should be identical to our Learning Technology Center. Nevertheless, it appears to us that there is much to be gained by students and teachers from changing the structure of how teachers teach and how students learn.

Discussion in CTGV (1994) documents some of the ways in which we have gradually changed our approach to helping schools develop learning communities. For example, we started by emphasizing only problem- and project-based activities, moved to the idea of breaking the isolation of classrooms by creating a "challenge series" that was organized around these activities, and, most recently, have increased opportunities for formative assessment by teachers and students, as well as opportunities to try new sets of tools. Important elements of learning communities have emerged from our work.

*Project-Based Activity.*   In much of our work on learning communities (CTGV, 1994) we have begun with problem-based curricula followed by a student-generated projects (CTGV, 1992). This is a departure from the activities of our center, which focuses almost exclusively on projects. We encourage schools to begin with problem-based curricula that provide models for inquiry and allow students to develop a common ground for discussion. Our assumption is that appropriate models increase the quality of the projects that students subsequently pursue.

In most of our studies, students' work has been organized around a set of videodisc-based problems called *The Adventures of Jasper Woodbury*, developed by the CTGV at Vanderbilt (1990, 1991, 1993b). The Jasper series was designed to help students learn to think and reason about problems that require extended effort to solve. Each video in the series consists of a narrative that ends with a challenge to resolve some dilemma faced by the main characters in the story. The information relevant to resolving the dilemma is embedded in the narrative. Students formulate the subproblems involved in solving the problem and search the video for the important information.

*The Adventures of Jasper Woodbury* represents an approach to instruction we have been testing called *anchored instruction* (CTGV, 1990). The basic idea behind this approach is to create anchors or macrocontexts that situate learning in the context of real-world problems. Anchors have the following features that make them ideal for helping to build learning communities within classrooms:

1. They are quite complex and this complexity affords opportunities for students to be engaged in the problem-solving process for extended periods of time. Video-based stories make this complexity manageable.
2. They provide an excellent context for collaborative learning because individuals invariably notice different aspects of problems; hence this collaborative noticing pays off.
3. Anchors have multiple solutions. This feature affords opportunities for students to engage in lively dialogue about their chosen solutions. Because there is not a single right answer, students can begin to engage in the evaluation of ideas and take intellectual responsibility for their choices as they defend them to their peers.

4. As noted earlier, anchors provide models of approaches to problems that increase the quality of student-generated projects.
5. Engaging anchors can be shown to other members of the community (business leaders, principals, superintendents, politicians), who can try to solve them and, ideally, receive help from "experts" who are students from the schools (see CTGV, 1994).

The CTGV has conducted a number of studies to investigate issues of learning and transfer resulting from problem-solving experiences with the Jasper series. Because of space limitations it is not possible to provide a review of the research that has been completed. For the interested reader, reviews are available in a number of places (e.g., CTGV, 1992a, 1992b, 1993a, 1993b, in press).

An example of one of the Jasper episodes is called *The Big Splash*, in which a young man named Chris is trying to develop a business plan around the idea of selling tickets to a dunking booth at his school's fun fair. In order to get a loan from the principal that would fund his plan, Chris needs to convince her that he has thought through all the components of the plan, including an estimate of total revenue, an itemized list of expenses, and a plan for how he will work out the logistics of implementation. The challenge for students is to sort through the pros and cons of various methods of filling the pool, use some survey data provided in the video to select the ticket price that would generate the most money, and then use the sample data to estimate how much would be made on the day of the fair.

In addition to working on *The Big Splash*, students work on related analogous problems designed to deepen their understanding of some of the mathematical concepts. Analogous problems engage students in a form of what-if thinking by starting with the original problem and altering some aspect of it. For example, in the adventure Chris estimated the best ticket price at $1.00. What if he had charged $1.50? Would his plan have worked?

***Collaboration and Distributed Expertise.*** Our work with problem- and project-based curricula has almost always involved an emphasis on having students work in small groups to generate and solve problems and communicate their ideas about solutions. Most students prefer working in groups on Jasper and subsequent projects rather than working on them in isolation. In addition, when students work collaboratively to solve problems, they usually cover more of the possibilities in the problem space than when they work alone (e.g., Barron, 1991; McNeese, 1992).

***Intrinsic Plus Extrinsic Motivation.*** The teachers with whom we have worked have been volunteers who are intrinsically interested in improving their teaching practices. In addition, the Jasper problems are designed to be intrinsically interesting for students to watch and, especially, to solve.

We have tried to increase the levels of excitement in classrooms even further by introducing external challenges for which students and teachers must prepare. Sometimes the challenges have involved the presentation of original plans to members of the community who ask relevant (and tough) questions and allow students to carry out the plans that pass muster. At other times the challenges have involved the opportunity to participate in live satellite-based challenges (CTGV, 1994). In each case we have tried to create for the classroom teacher some of the advantages available to sports coaches and drama, theater, and band leaders; namely, the excitement of preparing for a real deadline in order to test one's mettle and do one's best.

*Connectedness to a Broad Community of Audiences.*   The challenges noted earlier are designed to connect students to other classrooms as well as to other members of the community. In the process, students interact with real audiences and see a rich set of models of how things can be done.

*Frequent Opportunities for Formative Assessment.*   In our earliest work on learning communities, our challenges were summative rather than formative. Gradually we have increased our efforts to help make thinking visible in the classrooms so that ideas can be evaluated and revised. Three ways discussed in CTGV (1994) to help make thinking visible are as follows:

1. Most work is conducted collaboratively in small groups who are encouraged to discuss issues.

2. There is a focus on explanation-oriented student presentations, and students have repeated opportunities to give them.

3. We developed a simple device that make it possible for students to anonymously answer a question and for the teacher to immediately share the responses of all students with the class. For example, the teacher can show a frequency distribution that makes the range of responses quite clear to students. The responses to these questions can then be used to generate class discussion that reveals students' thinking in more depth. The questions might focus on how groups are functioning, how well students understand their work on the problem, and students' feelings about presentations. Our assumption is that when thinking is "made visible" then the information needed for formative assessment is available for the teacher and students to use.

Since writing the CTGV (1994) paper, we have significantly increased opportunities for formative assessment by introducing our SMART Challenge videos in conjunction with work on Jasper. SMART challenges are discussed in more detail later.

*The Use of Tools to Improve Efficiency.*   We have gradually increased the kinds of tools made available to teachers and students. Pedagogical tools include the use of videodisc players for the problem-based curricula, optional uses of computer tools such as electronic calculators and spreadsheets, and use of assessment tools like the ones discussed. In our SMART challenges, we include the introduction of just-in-time conceptual tools (e.g., the idea of making timelines, graphs, and other types of representations) that teachers and students can use.

***Support for Technology.*** We noted earlier that all of us in the LTC require and expect support for the technology we use to do our work. Teachers need and deserve similar levels of support. In our research programs we are able to provide that support to them. However, as we seek ways to institutionalize change, we are committed to helping school systems find the kinds of support that teachers need.

## THE SMART EXPERIMENT

Our goal in this section is to discuss our most recent attempt to create learning communities. We refer to it as our SMART (Special Multimedia Arenas for Refining Thinking) experiment. This experiment attempted to assess the "value added" of the components of learning communities discussed previously.

The SMART project used a new set of four video programs (called *The Jasper Challenge Series*) in addition to the Jasper problem *The Big Splash* and its analogs. The goal of the Challenge programs was to create opportunities for students and teachers to obtain feedback about their solutions, provide encouragement to revise, showcase examples of well-articulated reasoning, and offer ways to think about some of the more difficult concepts embedded in the problem. Our hope was that programs that focused on student reasoning would convey models of mathematical reasoning and levels of expectations, as well as provide teachers with ideas about how to communicate and understand difficult concepts. In addition, we hoped that the content of the programs would stimulate discussion and provide additional opportunities for making thinking visible. Table 4.1 summarizes the design principles used to develop the Challenge programs.

### The Challenge Programs

Four Challenge programs were created. Each focused on a different part of the problem-solving process in *The Big Splash*. The first program was a general introduction; the second program focused on expenses; the third focused on revenue; and the fourth focused on a set of analogous problems that had to do with sampling.

Table 4.2 summarizes the content of the four programs that complemented *The Big Splash* episode. These programs are described in greater detail later, using the second *Jasper Challenge* show to instantiate the general descriptions.

TABLE 4.1
Design Principles of the *Jasper Challenge* Programs

1. Engaging programs with an authentic purpose
2. Built-in opportunities for revision and chances to improve
3. Use of authentic audiences (the learning community) to energize learning
4. Showcase student explanations to communicate standards
5. Stimulate discussion through sharing ideas across classrooms
6. Communicate values of self-assessment and reflection
7. Introduce new conceptual tools to teachers and students that support sensemaking

### Program Content and Organization

Each SMART program is composed of four major segments called *Smart Lab, Roving Reporter, Toolbox,* and *The Challenge.* The programs are hosted by a character named Steve, a young man with an exuberant, zany personality, who welcomes the students to each show, interacts with another character in *Toolbox,* interviews students as the *Roving Reporter,* and delivers *The Challenge* at the end of each show. *Smart Lab* and *Roving Reporter* relied on data from students in classrooms that were participating in *The Jasper Challenge Series* learning community implementation (described later). First, we describe each of the four segments of the shows comprising *The Jasper Challenge Series.*

*Smart Lab.* The focus and purpose of *Smart Lab* is to provide feedback to students about decisions they have made in the course of their work on *The Big Splash.* This was accomplished by having students respond in writing to a series of questions about their work. The responses of all students participating in the learning community (approximately 100 students) were then summarized and represented graphically or in a table that was shown as part of the show. The host of *Smart Lab* is a young woman named Denise. She explains the graph or table to students and frequently provides some commentary about the range of responses or poses some question to students that is designed to encourage them to think about the reasonableness of various alternatives.

For example, in the second show, Denise uses a computer to graphically display students' responses, reproduced in Fig. 4.1. This graph illustrates the percentage of students who selected various options for filling the pool that would be used with the dunking machine. Denise describes the axes and then reports the percentage of students selecting each plan. She comments that some students were quite creative and chose to combine methods for filling the pool, such as using the school hose plus the water truck from the pool store. Denise next shows a graph that relates the *most commonly* calculated total expenses for each plan chosen. She explains that there were so many estimates, even for the same plan, that she just graphed the expense that was most frequently calculated for each. After summarizing the data, Denise warns that these total expenses are not nec-

TABLE 4.2
Content of the *Jasper Challenge* Programs

| Show | Smart Lab | Roving Reporter | Toolbox | The Challenge |
|---|---|---|---|---|
| 1 | Student attitudes towards complex problem solving | Introduction to students, teachers, and principals in learning community | Discussion of use of bar graphs to display data | Watch *The Big Splash*<br>Begin work on expenses<br>Generate itemized list |
| 2 | Method of pool filling<br>Total expenses | Student explanations of:<br>Pool-filling method<br>Itemized expenses<br>Timelines | Timelines to compare plans<br>Computer animation illustrating relation of rate of water flow to time to fill pool | Revise plan for pool filling<br>Revise itemized expenses<br>Draw a timeline for your plan<br>Estimate total revenue |
| 3 | Revised pool-filling method<br>Revised total expenses<br>Best ticket price choices<br>Estimations of total revenue | Student explanations of:<br>Best ticket price<br>Total revenue<br>Pie charts<br>Revised plans | Part/whole representation illustrating extrapolation from sample to whole population<br>Computer animation illustrating cumulative frequency to determine best ticket price | Revise estimate of revenue<br>Evaluate huckster plans<br>Take several samples of size 60. Think about whether if Chris took another sample of 60 his estimate would be the same |
| 4 | Flaws in huckster plans<br>Reliability of samples<br>Monte Carlo data for sample size 60 | Student explanations of:<br>Critiques of hucksters<br>Why 60 is a good sample size | Estimates of total revenue graphed based on 100 samples of size 15, 60, and 90<br>Use of above graphs to discuss reliability of sample estimates in relation to size | Prepare for *The Big Challenge*<br>Evaluate each plan and identify flaws<br>Choose the "best" plan |

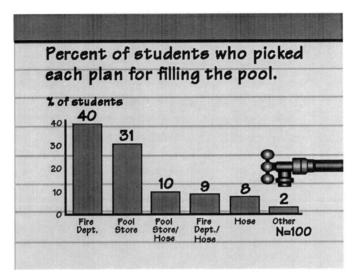

FIG. 4.1.   Smart Lab graph summarizing students' pool-filling plans.

essarily correct and she questions whether there should be so many expense estimates for the same plan. She suggests that it might be time to double-check and see if there might be expenses that were missed, extra expenses that didn't need to be there, or calculation errors.

*Roving Reporter.*   In *Roving Reporter*, video clips are shown of Steve interviewing various students in the learning community about the problem solving they have been doing. Teachers nominated students whom they thought were doing an exemplary job. The purpose of this segment was to showcase student reasoning and provide an opportunity for members of the learning community to react to various ideas. For example, in the second show, *Roving Reporter* featured 10 different interviews of students describing the plan they had generated for filling the pool and their expenses. One student provided the following rationale for his group's decision to use the fire department:

> Because we thought that the school hose would take too long and the pool, the pool store would probably cost and we didn't want to waste the money and we thought about the fire department having to go out on a call but it pumps 1,000 gallons a minute, an um, and there are 2,500 gallons in the pool so its going to take 2 minutes, 2½ minutes. I don't think they'll be called in that 2½ minutes and its not going to take that long to pump it out, plus they get it for free.

This particular rationale sets a nice context for asking students if they can begin to quantify the amount of risk associated with relying on the fire truck to bring the water. One of the analogous problems for *The Big Splash* reminds students of the data on number of calls and false alarms per week that was provided in the adventure. Through what-if thinking using additional data in the analogous problems, students can begin to think about differentially "risky" situations.

Other students featured in the second show rejected using the fire department, feeling that the plan entailed too much risk. Another group outlined in detail their plan for using the school hose plus the pool store, thereby minimizing both risk and cost, as well as ensuring that the pool could be filled by the fair's starting time.

*Toolbox.* *Toolbox* is hosted by a character named Dave, whose specialty is generating visual representations to aid problem solving. Steve visits Dave in each show and engages Dave in conversation about the problem solving in *The Big Splash.* Dave provides ideas for visual representations that can be conceived of as "tools" for thinking, problem solving, and communicating. We chose visual representations for a number of reasons, including their usefulness for revealing patterns and communicating mathematical ideas in a nonprocedural way. *Toolbox* was not designed to give away solutions but rather to provide scaffolding for students' conceptual understanding of the mathematics and problem solving. Many of the tools also suggested ways for students to revise their solutions.

In the second show, *Toolbox* begins with Steve asking Dave if he has any pictures or diagrams that would help determine the best plan. Dave suggests a timeline. In the course of completing the timeline they realize that they need to determine how long it will take to fill the pool using various pool-filling methods. Dave uses his computer to illustrate dynamically "fill time" as a function of the rate of water flow. A still of this representation is shown in Fig. 4.2. As the computer shows the number of gallons filled up in 30-second increments, Steve makes a table to record the results. The segment ends with Steve wondering about alternative ways to fill the pool and suggests to the audience that they think about it.

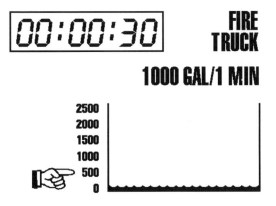

FIG. 4.2.  Still of pool-filling graphic from *Toolbox.*

*The Challenge.* Each show ended by giving the students a new problem-solving challenge to focus on. These challenges were delivered by Steve and included a challenge to revise their work based on feedback they had just received. A second part of the challenge was to begin work on a new part of the problem. In the second show, students were to reconsider their plan for filling the pool, revise estimates of total expenses and begin working on estimates of the total revenue they could expect on the day of the fair. Steve suggested they draw a diagram to help explain their estimates of total revenue.

### *A Revised Culminating Event:* The Big Challenge

While developing and presenting an original business plan was quite moti-vating to students in several of our initial studies on learning communities (CTGV, 1994), it was not possible to "scale up" this type of performance when working with a large number of classrooms. We decided to create a live, interactive event that was broadcast on our local PBS-TV station. Interactivity was achieved by giving each participating class a cellular phone, which students used to call in their critiques of a set of flawed business plans. In addition, each class was called by the host of the show and was asked to explain the class' analysis of a particular plan. Students had prepared their responses in advance to all but one of the business plans. The novel plan provided students with the challenge of "thinking on their feet" during the live broadcast: After the plan was shown on the air, students had 10 minutes to call the TV station with an analysis of the flaw(s) in the plan. The students' answers were then summarized and the data were dis-played on the show for all the students to see. For example, one plan involved a proposal for a can-crushing machine that would accept cans and give the depositor a few cents in exchange. The owner of the machine could then collect additional money when the cans were turned in for recycling. An estimate was given for how much money could be made with this business. The major flaw in this plan was in revenue estimation: The number of cans deposited during a 1-hour period on a Saturday morning were counted and generalized to 24 hours a day, 7 days a week, thereby providing an inflated revenue estimate.

### A "Value-Added" Study of the *Jasper Challenge Series*

To look at the added benefit of *The Jasper Challenge* programs for student learning and attitudes, a set of inner-city classrooms participated in a 6-week study. All classes followed the same curriculum (*The Big Splash* and related analogous problems) and all participated in *The Big Challenge*. However, ap-proximately half of the classes received *The Jasper Challenge* programs and the other classes did not. Classes were matched within school on their previous year's mathematics achievement scores and then randomly assigned to one of two types of implementations (*Jasper-only* or *Jasper plus Jasper Challenge* programs).

## Student Characteristics

The students and teachers who participated in this study were recruited from among the fifth-grade teachers and classrooms within two schools, yielding 9 classrooms and 208 students. Instruction took the place of the regularly scheduled mathematics class. Of the 9 classrooms, 2 were Chapter I mathematics classes. (The Chapter I program serves economically disadvantaged students who are experiencing academic difficulty.)

## Sequence of Instruction

In preparation for *The Big Challenge*, students spent approximately 10 class sessions solving *The Big Splash*, 6 sessions on analogous problems, and 2 sessions evaluating business plans. All classes spent the same amount of time on each part of the problem as well as on the analogous-problem activities. Students in the *Jasper-only* classrooms also received the challenges that were shown in the programs but they were in written form and delivered by project personnel.

## Professional Development Sessions

All teachers attended three 2-hour professional development sessions. The first professional development session provided an overview of *The Big Splash*, learning goals for students, and focused on solving the expenses challenge. The second session focused on revenue, and the third focused on the analogous problems. During these sessions, ideas for using visual representations to facilitate students' conceptual understanding and problem solving were discussed. These were the same representations that were featured in *Toolbox*. This was done to insure that *all* teachers had access to the same conceptual tools, even *Jasper-only* teachers.

## Findings

In the discussion that follows we report our findings in three areas: student learning, student attitudes, and reactions to *The Big Challenge*.

### Student Learning

To look at the effects on students' knowledge of business planning and sampling concepts, an instrument focusing on those concepts was developed. It was administered to students at the start of the study and following *The Big Challenge*. The assessment items focused around a business-planning scenario that was structurally identical to *The Big Splash*, although the cover story and the numbers were different. The scenario involved a student named Allison, who wanted to have a booth at her school's fun fair. She decided on a game in which students fish for plastic ducks swimming in a pool. If they caught a duck, they received a prize. Several different question formats were used, including open-ended items, items that required manipulation of survey data, multiple-choice items, and justification of multiple-choice responses. A set of sample items is provided in Table 4.3. In the next section, we talk about four different measures of student learning derived from this assessment instrument.

*Composite Measure of All Concepts.* The business-planning assessment included a set of 16 multiple-choice questions that covered topics such as selecting an appropriate sample size, using an appropriate sampling method to obtain a representative sample, vocabulary, planning, and recognition of a distribution that would result from taking 100 samples of size 15 versus 100 samples of size 80.

As illustrated in Fig. 4.3, all students gained relative to their pretest performance. However, the *Jasper-plus* students who had received the four *Jasper Challenge* programs gained significantly more. Interestingly, univariate analyses of each of the 16 individual items revealed significant effects of time for each item but no interactions. Given the advantage of the *Jasper-plus* group on the composite score, the absence of an interaction between the factors of group and time on the individual items suggests that the advantage for the *Jasper-plus* group was a general one, rather than specific to one content area.

*Justification of Answers.* For a subset of the multiple-choice items described, students provided written justifications for their answers. Figure 4.4 shows the proportion of students who had selected the correct answer and were able to

TABLE 4.3
Sample Items From Business Planning Assessment

---

*Extrapolation*
II. From the 80 students she surveyed, Allison determined the best ticket price and how much money she would make by charging this ticket price. She should multiply this amount by ___ in order to figure out total revenue. Explain your choice.

(a) 8     (b) 6     (c) 4     (d) 5

*Survey Method*
III. What do you think would be the best way for Allison to give out her survey? Explain your answer.

(a) give it to all her friends     (b) give it to every third person in her home room
(c) give it to every fourth person on her school bus     (d) give it to every fifth person at the school assembly

*Sample Size*
IV. Allison decided to give a survey to a sample of students at her school to find out how many people might be willing to buy a ticket to her Fishing for Prizes game. There are 400 people who go to her school. How many people would you tell her to get to complete her survey?

(a) 10     (b) 80     (c) 200     (d) 300

---

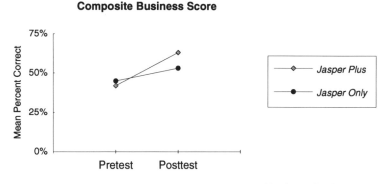

FIG. 4.3.  Student performance on an assessment of business planning.

provide a correct justification for their choices. On the first two items represented in Fig. 4.4 we found that students who had received the programs were significantly more likely to correctly justify their selected answers. On these items the percentage of students in the *Jasper-plus* group who justified their answers correctly was twice as large as the percentage of students in the *Jasper-only* group. These items had to do with recognizing distributions generated from different sample sizes and with extrapolating from the sample to the population. On the remaining items, there was a tendency for students in the *Jasper-plus* group to more frequently provide correct justifications for their correct answers. The group differences were not significant, however.

***Generation of Elements of a Good Business Plan.***    In an open-ended planning question, students were asked to generate as many ideas as they could to help Allison develop a good business plan. Responses were scored for the presence of a number of different elements, such as suggesting that she estimate income,

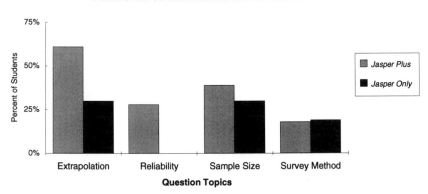

FIG. 4.4.  Student performance on items requiring justification.

determine expenses, evaluate time, and use a survey. Our analyses suggest that more students indicated the need to think about expenses and income at posttest than at pretest, regardless of group. However, the likelihood of suggesting that Allison use a survey was significantly greater in the *Jasper-plus* group than in the *Jasper-only* group at posttest, shown in Fig. 4.5. Note, however, that the frequencies with which students made suggestions in any of these categories were relatively low, no more than 30–35% in any category. The low percentage of students who made these suggestions indicates that this was a difficult item for students. The difficulty may have been due to the item form, which required high level planning and that students compose an elaborate written response.

*Using Survey Data to Estimate Revenue.* Students were given a set of survey data that Allison had hypothetically collected. The data consisted of the number of students who were willing to pay each of three prices for a ticket to her booth. In *The Big Splash*, the protagonist, Chris, collects similar survey data. To determine the best ticket price students needed to use the notion of cumulative frequency to figure out how many students would buy tickets at each price. In order to estimate total revenue on the day of the fair they needed to extrapolate these survey results to the whole population. On the assessment instrument students were asked to do three things with the "Allison" data. First, they were asked to use it to determine the best ticket price. Second, they were asked to estimate total revenue for the school based on a given ticket price. Third, they were asked to determine the number of people who would buy tickets if she charged a particular price. A composite score was created that summarized students' performance on these three problems. As Fig. 4.6 shows, both groups of students improved from pre- to posttest and there was no difference at posttest between the groups. Students in both instructional groups learned how to work with survey data that was similar to the data presented in *The Big Splash*.

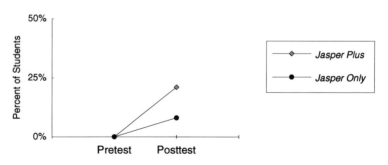

**Would Use a Survey to Make a Business Plan**

FIG. 4.5.  Students' generation of elements of a good business plan.

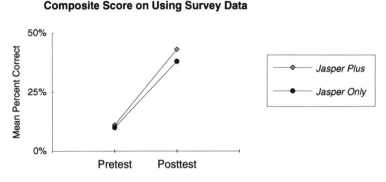

FIG. 4.6.  Students' use of survey data to estimate revenue.

In summary, both groups of students improved in their ability to answer questions about a business-planning scenario that relied on concepts taught in the context of *The Big Splash*. However, students who participated in the ongoing learning community via *The Jasper Challenge* programs did significantly better on some measures of student learning, including the overall composite score and the justification of responses to some items.

### Student Attitudes

In addition to examining the effect of *The Jasper Challenge* programs on student learning, we were interested in whether these programs might impact student attitudes. We adapted an instrument we had previously developed to measure attitudes related to solving episodes in *The Adventures of Jasper Woodbury* (CTGV, 1993a, 1993b, in press; Pellegrino et al., 1991). In the present context, we focus on the results of four scales: interest in business planning, confidence in business planning, anxiety about complex mathematical problem solving, and belief in the value of knowing what other students are thinking.

The results of our analyses indicated that the students in the learning community (*Jasper-plus* students), as compared to the students in the *Jasper-only* group, showed significantly greater positive changes in attitudes on two scales: interest and confidence in business planning. Both groups reported decreases in anxiety about complex mathematical problem solving and increases in the perception that knowing the thinking of other students is helpful.

### Student Reactions to The Big Challenge

Following their participation in *The Big Challenge*, we asked students to fill out a 17-item questionnaire in which they used a Likert scale, ranging from 1 to 6, to rate how much they agreed with a particular statement. These questions included topics such as how much they enjoyed the show, how prepared they felt, how confident they felt, how much they enjoyed listening to other students explain their answers, and how they liked the characters in the show. Significant differences between the students who had received the *Jasper Challenge* programs were found on 7 items. These items and their means are listed in Table 4.4. There were no differences on the remainder of the items. Both groups of students enjoyed the characters and style of the show and enjoyed hearing other students explain their answers. The finding that students in the *Jasper-plus* implementation felt more prepared suggests that there may well be value-added by the *Jasper Challenge Series* in terms of students' self-confidence with respect to performances that reach into the wider community or that deal with a larger mathematical arena. This is an important goal if we want students to enter the broader community as productive and willing mathematical thinkers.

## Lessons Learned and Future Directions

In this project we attempted to implement in classrooms some features of our own organization (the LTC) that support continued learning. We now reflect on each of these with respect to our impressions of how they functioned in the implementation. We also provide a brief report of our current research efforts.

### Problem- and Project-Based Curriculum

The problem-based activities in which students engaged were quite motivating. As we anticipated from prior experience, students enjoyed working on the Jasper adventures and became invested in finding good resolutions to the dilemmas that were presented. The problems were successful in eliciting multiple perspectives and students engaged in debate about their solutions.

### Collaboration and Distributed Expertise

Generally, students did a good job of collaborating to solve the Jasper problems and analogs. Nevertheless, we noticed that students did not automatically know how to work together for mutual understanding when there were disagreements

TABLE 4.4
Student Reactions to *The Big Challenge*

| Items | Means | |
|---|---|---|
| | *Jasper-only* | *Jasper-plus* |
| I felt prepared for *The Big Challenge*. | 4.43 | 5.17 |
| I thought the Challenge questions were easy. | 4.19 | 4.73 |
| I would like to participate in another program like this one. | 4.78 | 5.40 |
| I liked hearing other students explain their thinking on TV. | 4.71 | 5.11 |
| It would have been more exciting to have all the questions be about plans we had never seen before. | 3.46 | 4.44 |

about how to approach a part of a problem. Learning to communicate still remains an issue and we are beginning to work on how to help teachers facilitate collaboration within their classrooms.

### Intrinsic and Extrinsic Motivation

All students had *The Big Challenge* to look forward to. However, we believe that the opportunity to see and discuss the four intervening video programs (*The Jasper Challenge Programs*) increased the excitement and motivation in our experimental classrooms. Students reported looking forward to the programs and liking them very much.

### Connectedness to a Broad Community of Audiences

It is our impression that being connected with students in other classrooms increased students' attention to the programs and enthusiasm for revising their work. We obtained anecdotal evidence that the participation of students in the *Roving Reporter* segments led to a focus on preparing good explanations. Students were all eager to be interviewed, and they reported that they enjoyed seeing other students being interviewed about their work. In addition, students consistently mentioned being aware of other students working on the problem. This awareness was most evident in their responses to *Smart Lab* and *Roving Reporter*, where their peers' thinking was made visible. There was also some indication that teachers were aware of this broader community, because they mentioned it frequently in their classes and encouraged students to think about this broader community as they worked.

In the future we hope to add the use of E-mail to the SMART project in order to provide a more direct means of communication among students in different classrooms about their problem solving. We are interested in how this type of interactivity might further support and motivate self-assessment and reflection. As we describe later, we have already provided this resource for teachers and have found it to be quite valuable.

### Frequent Opportunities for Formative Assessment

New ideas for problem solving and opportunities for formative assessment were provided in *Smart Lab, Toolbox*, and *Roving Reporter*. We observed that students spontaneously appropriated the visual representations featured in *Toolbox* and reported learning these from Steve and Dave. Thus, these outside influences were used as intellectual resources within the classroom community. However, the degree to which the programs were used as opportunities for formative assessment varied as a function of teacher. Our classroom observations indicated that there were marked individual differences in how teachers understood the purpose of the programs and how they utilized them in their classrooms. Some teachers simply showed them to students one time without much discussion. Other teachers were quite systematic in trying to mediate the different program segments for students, spent time insuring that their students comprehended what they were seeing, and used the programs to stimulate discussion.

### The Use of Tools and Support for Technology

Teachers quickly became comfortable with the videodisc technology. In addition, many noted that the conceptual tools provided in the Jasper programs were useful for them as well as their students. Teachers also expressed a desire for additional tools; especially ones that would allow them to more easily communicate with one another. We mention these in our discussion of next steps.

### Next Steps

In our current work we are trying to increase the power of the Learning Community model by capitalizing on opportunities to work more closely with teachers. To do this we are collaborating closely with a group of teachers, some of whom worked with us last year, to generate and test ways to use the programs to facilitate formative assessment, enrich classroom dialogue, and increase student reflection. The model we have been following involves extensive and continuing professional development. We meet with teachers before and after each of the *Jasper Challenge* programs are used in their classrooms. The meeting before is used to brainstorm about ways to use the programs, and the meeting afterward is spent sharing teachers' experiences in trying these ideas out. We are also spending time in the classrooms on a daily basis to better understand how the ideas are translated into practice and to learn about teachers' perceptions of what transpires in the classrooms. Another aspect of the continuing support for the teachers involves use of the Internet for communications. Teachers have been provided with computers, modems and Vanderbilt University accounts that allow them to use electronic mail to talk with each other, with us, and to access the many resources available over the Internet.

### SUMMARY

In this chapter we described a project for middle-school students that adapted organizational principles we have found to be powerful in our own learning organization. These ideas led to the development of a series of video programs called the *Jasper Challenge Series*, which linked classrooms to each other and to the larger community. We described a "value-added" study designed to investigate the potential benefits of the *Jasper Challenge* programs. The study we conducted yielded data that are promising for our initial attempts to develop classroom-based learning communities. Especially interesting is the finding that students in the *Jasper-plus* program group were better able to justify their answers. Whether this was the result of a greater focus on justification in the classrooms we cannot be sure; but it will be a topic of attention in future research.

Our informal observations indicated that there was a great deal of variability in how teachers use the programs. In our current research we are working with teachers on ideas of how to use these programs to further foster the development of learning communities within and across classrooms. Ideally, this will produce even better learning for the students and teachers, as well as for us.

For a number of reasons, we believe that the development of learning communities may be necessary for successful educational reform. One reason is that the challenge of changing one's teaching practices is much too great to be affected by one or two "teacher development" workshops. It seems impossible to accomplish this type of change without frequent opportunities for ongoing feedback, discussions, and support. A second reason for the importance of learning communities derives from the fact that most students who work in problem- and project-based curricula are going to generate questions that frequently outdistance the expertise of any single individual. The opportunities and values of true learning communities make it possible to work in a climate of distributed expertise. A third reason why learning communities are so important is the effects they can have on the research community. The chance to participate in learning communities composed of students, teachers, parents, and business leaders provides opportunities for researchers to broaden their experiences and better understand the kinds of issues that are crucial to teachers and students in the schools.

## ACKNOWLEDGMENT

The preparation of this chapter and the research reported herein were supported by a grant from the National Science Foundation (NSF MDR-9252908). The ideas expressed do not necessarily reflect the views of the National Science Foundation.

## REFERENCES

Barron, B. J. S. (1991). *Collaborative problem solving: Is team performance greater than what is expected from the most competent member?* Unpublished doctoral dissertation, Vanderbilt University, Nashville, TN.

Bransford, J. D. (1981). Social-cultural prerequisites for cognitive research. In J. H. Harvey (Ed.), *Cognition, social behavior, and the environment* (pp. 557–569). Hillsdale, NJ: Lawrence Erlbaum Associates.

Bransford, J. D., & Nitsch, K. E. (1978). Coming to understand things we could not previously understand. In J. F. Kavanaugh & W. Strange (Eds.), *Speech and language in the laboratory, school, and clinic* (pp. 267–307). Cambridge, MA: MIT Press. Reprinted in H. Singer & R. Ruddell (Eds.), *Theoretical models and processes of reading.* Newark, DE: International Reading Association.

Brown, A. L. (1992). Design experiments: Theoretical and methodological challenges in creating complex interventions in classroom settings. *The Journal of the Learning Sciences, 2*(2), 141–178.

Brown, A. L., Ash, D., Rutherford, M., Nakagawa, K., Gordon, A., & Campione, J. C. (1993). Distributed expertise in the classroom. In G. Salomon (Ed.), *Distributed cognitions: Psychological and educational considerations* (pp. 188–228). New York: Cambridge University Press.

Brown, A. L., Bransford, J. D., Ferrara, R. A., & Campione, J. C. (1983). Learning, remembering, and understanding. In J. H. Flavell & E. M. Markman (Eds.), *Handbook of child psychology: Vol. 3. Cognitive development* (4th ed., pp. 78–166). New York: Wiley.

Brown, J. S., Collins, A., & Duguid, P. (1989). Situated cognition and the culture of learning. *Educational Researcher, 18,* 32–41.

Bruer, J. T. (1993). *Schools for thought.* Cambridge, MA: MIT Press.

Cognition and Technology Group at Vanderbilt. (1992). The Jasper series as an example of anchored instruction: Theory, program description, and assessment data. *Educational Psychologist, 27,* 291–315.

Cognition and Technology Group at Vanderbilt. (1993a, March). Anchored instruction and situated cognition revisited. *Educational Technology, 33,* 52–70.

Cognition and Technology Group at Vanderbilt. (1993b). The Jasper series: Theoretical foundations and data on problem solving and transfer. In L. A. Penner, G. M. Batsche, H. M. Knoff, & D. L. Nelson (Eds.), *The challenge in mathematics and science education: Psychology's response* (pp. 113–152). Washington, DC: American Psychological Association.

Cognition and Technology Group at Vanderbilt. (1994). From visual word problems to learning communities: Changing conceptions of cognitive research. In K. McGilly (Ed.), *Classroom lessons: Integrating cognitive theory and classroom practice* (pp. 157–200). Cambridge, MA: MIT Press/Bradford Books.

Cognition and Technology Group at Vanderbilt. (in press). The Jasper series: A design experiment in complex, mathematical problem-solving. In J. Hawkins & A. Collins (Eds.), *Design experiments: Integrating technologies into schools.* New York: Cambridge University Press.

DeCorte, E., Greer, B., & Verschaffel, L. (in press). Center for instructional psychology and technology. In D. Berliner & R. Calfee (Eds.), *Handbook of Educational Psychology.* New York: Macmillan.

Dewey, J. (1897). My pedagogic creed. *The School Journal, 543,* 77–80.

Gardner, H. (1985). *The mind's new science: A history of the cognitive revolution.* New York: Basic Books.

Hickey, D. T., Pellegrino, J. W., Goldman, S. R., Vye, N. J., Moore, A. L., & Cognition and Technology Group at Vanderbilt (1993). *Interests, attitudes, and anchored instruction: The impact of one interactive learning environment.* Paper presented at the American Educational Research Association annual meeting, Atlanta, GA.

Lampert, M. (1986). Knowing, doing, and teaching multiplication. *Cognition and Instruction, 3,* 305–342.

Lampert, M. (1990). When the problem is not the question and the solution is not the answer: Mathematical knowing and teaching. *American Educational Research Journal, 27,* 29–63.

McNeese, M. D. (1992). *Analogical transfer in situated cooperative learning.* Unpublished doctoral dissertation, Vanderbilt University, Nashville, TN.

National Council of Teachers of Mathematics. (1989). *Curriculum and evaluation standards for school mathematics.* Reston, VA: Author.

Pellegrino, J. W., Hickey, D., Heath, A., Rewey, K., Vye, N. J., & Cognition and Technology Group at Vanderbilt (1991). *Assessing the outcomes of an innovative instructional program: The 1990–1991 implementation of the "Adventures of Jasper Woodbury."* (Tech. Rep. No. 91-1). Nashville, TN: Vanderbilt University, Learning Technology Center.

Resnick, L. B., & Klopfer, L. E. (Eds.). (1989). *Toward the thinking curriculum: Current cognitive research.* Alexandria, VA: Association for Supervision and Curriculum Development.

Senge, P. M. (1990). *The fifth discipline: The art and practice of the learning organization.* New York: Doubleday.

Suchman, L. (1987). *Plans and situation action: The problem of human–machine communication.* Cambridge: Cambridge University Press.

Yackel, E., Cobb, P., Wood, T., Wheatley, G., & Merkel, G. (1990). The importance of social interaction in children's construction of mathematical knowledge. In T. J. Conney (Ed.), *Teaching and learning mathematics in the 1990s.* 1990 Yearbook of the National Council of Teachers of Mathematics (pp. 12–21). Reston, VA: National Council of Teachers of Mathematics.

# Chapter 5

# Enhancing Thinking and Reasoning in the English Language Arts

Robert J. Marzano
*Mid-Continent Regional Educational Laboratory*

In the last decade, there has been a great deal of discussion about the need for enhancing the thinking and reasoning of American students. For example, the National Science Board Commission on Precollege Education in Mathematics, Science and Technology (1983), the College Entrance Examination Board (1983), the National Education Association (Futrell, 1987) and the American Federation of Teachers (1985), have all strongly advocated the direct teaching of thinking and reasoning as a necessary component of school reform.

The initial reaction to these calls was to develop a wide variety of programs and practices to enhance generic-thinking skills. To illustrate, in 1991, the Association for Supervision and Curriculum Development published an anthology of programs and practices to enhance thinking and reasoning (Costa, 1991). These volumes described scores of practices and programs for enhancing specific thinking and reasoning skills. In recent years, however, there has been a strong trend to a more situated view of thinking and reasoning (Glaser, 1984, 1985; Resnick, 1987). That is, rather than viewing thinking and reasoning as a set of generic metacognitive and cognitive skills that can be applied to any domain, current research and theory point to the domain-specific nature of thinking and reasoning. In other words, thinking and reasoning processes in mathematics have characteristics that differentiate them from thinking and reasoning processes in science that differentiate them from thinking and reasoning processes in geography, and so on. In effect, each domain has metacognitive and cognitive processes that uniquely define thinking and reasoning within that domain. Consequently, to answer the question: How does one enhance thinking and reasoning in the English language arts?—one must answer the prior question: What are the metacognitive and cognitive processes indigenous to the English language arts? Although one could make a case that there are many, reading, writing, listening, and speaking seem to be almost unanimously included in English language arts curricula (Farrell, 1991). Enhancing thinking and reasoning in the English language arts, then, is a matter of enhancing the metacognitive and cognitive components of reading, writing, speaking, and listening. Given the limitation of space, I focus on reading in this chapter. Ideally, the model provided for reading can be easily extrapolated to writing, speaking, listening, or any other metacognitive/cognitive process considered central to the English language arts. (For a more detailed discussion of this model as it applies to other processes, see Marzano & Paynter, 1994.) Before discussing reading, we first consider a generalized pedagogy which, I assert, is the basis for enhancing thinking and reasoning for any metacognitive/cognitive process. The basic term for this pedagogy is *mediated instruction.*

## MEDIATED INSTRUCTION

The pedagogy of mediated instruction draws heavily from the work of Israeli psychologist Reuven Feuerstein (Feuerstein, 1980; Feuerstein, Rand, Hoffman, & Miller, 1980). Working with learning-disabled students, Feuerstein found that learning can be greatly enhanced if a skilled adult (a teacher) focuses on enhancing specific skills while students are engaged in some task in which the skills are being used. Feuerstein referred to this as *mediated learning.* At its core, mediated learning relies on the informed judgment of the teacher to identify those elements on which to provide students with guidance and support. As the learner is involved in a complex process, the "mediator" is continually monitoring the learner's weaknesses and strengths—identifying where students need help and where they do not. From this perspective, mediated learning is quite compatible with Russian psychologist Lev Vygotsky's concept of *zone of proximal development* (Vygotsky, 1962).

In simple terms, Vygotsky explained that skill development can be thought of as occurring in a zone, which he referred to as the zone of proximal development. Within this zone, learners can execute some skills independently, yet others they cannot. However, within the zone, those skills that cannot be executed independently can be performed with "a little help" from a skilled teacher. Of course, the key component to such an approach is the teacher's ability to identify those skills that can be enhanced with external support. As Hansen and Graves (1992) noted, "Thus it is up to the adult to find out what the child needs and/or wants. This information is what is most learnable" (p. 814).

The ultimate goal, then, of mediated instruction is to enhance the emerging metacognitive and cognitive components of a complex mental process. In this chapter, we consider the metacognitive and cognitive components of the complex process of reading. However, as a brief aside, it is useful to describe the meaning of the terms *metacognition* and *cognition* as they are used in this chapter, since they are used so frequently in so many different ways.

All complex processes have cognitive and metacognitive components. The cognitive components have been labeled the "blue-collar" elements of a complex process (Sternberg, 1984, 1988). They commonly deal with the acquisition and use of information within a specific situation. Many researchers in cognitive science assert that cognitive components are organized as complex "if . . . then" structures referred to as *production systems* (Anderson, 1982, 1983). In brief, production systems contain knowledge of the conditions under which certain mental skills and abilities should be activated and the actual steps involved in the skills and abilities themselves.

Most mental processes that might seem quite simple on the surface contain multilayered production systems. For example, Anderson describes the process involved in simple additions as involving over 60 productions (Anderson, 1983). In spite of their complexity, cognitive components are commonly executed with little or no conscious thought once they have been learned to the level of automaticity (LaBerge & Samuels, 1976). In fact, unless learned to a level of automaticity, cognitive components might overtax the capacity of short-term memory, since much of one's short-term memory is necessary for the execution of metacognitive components.

The metacognitive components of a complex process perform the "white-collar" work of complex processes (Sternberg, 1984, 1988). They are used to plan, monitor, and evaluate the performance and interaction of the cognitive component. Where cognitive components are performed with little or no conscious thought, metacognitive components by definition are performed in a conscious and hopefully thoughtful manner. As a number of theorists note, the use of metacognitive components is the key ingredient in being a self-regulated learner within any domain (Flavell, 1977, 1981; Paris & Lindauer, 1982; Paris, Lipson, & Wixson, 1983).

A common assumption is that thinking and reasoning refer only to the metacognitive elements of a complex process. This assumption contains only some elements of truth. When a cognitive component is functioning effectively, there is little need for metacognitive attention to it. However, when a cognitive component is functioning ineffectively or must be altered to enhance its capacity, then it requires a great deal of metacognitive attention to make the necessary alterations. This has been dramatically illustrated in what is referred to as *repair theory* in mathematics. For example, once learners have acquired the mental steps (algorithm) for performing subtraction, they will execute those steps with little conscious effort and, consequently, need little metacognitive attention. However, when learners find that their algorithms do not work well for more complex subtraction problems, they must devote a great deal of metacognitive attention to repairing and adapting their inadequate algorithms (Lehn, 1983).

In effect, then, enhancing thinking and reasoning for a complex process, such as reading, is a matter of rendering its metacognitive components more conscious and self-regulatory, and ensuring that its cognitive components are executed efficiently and are properly adapted to situational changes. All this should be done in the context of mediated instruction, which is the focused interaction of a skilled teacher with a learner while the learner is involved in a complex process, with the intent of enhancing the learner's competence in the metacognitive and cognitive components of that process. Quite obviously, the key to the success of mediated instruction is a thorough understanding on the part of teachers of the complex process they are attempting to mediate. In other words, for teachers to enhance thinking and reasoning within the reading process (or writing process, or listening process, or speaking process), they must have a thorough under- standing of the reading process (or writing process, or listening process, or speaking process). Additionally, they must be able to recognize indicators of difficulties with specific components of the reading process and have a ready stock of tactics and strategies to alleviate identified difficulties. In the section that follows, we consider the reading process in depth along with indicators of difficulties in specific metacognitive and cognitive components of that process, as well as techniques for enhancing performance in those components.


## UNDERSTANDING AND MEDIATING
## THE READING PROCESS

One of the basic conclusions of a long history of research is that reading is a very complex process. In fact, in the early 1900s psychologist Edmund Huey (1915/1974) noted that:

> ... to completely analyze what we do when we read would almost be the acme of a psychologist's achievement for it would be to describe very many of the most intricate workings of the human mind as well as to unravel the largest story of the most remarkable specific performance that civilization has learned in all its history. (p. 6)

In spite of its complexity, great advances have been made in our understanding of reading. In fact, in recent years some cognitive scientists—those who simulate human thought using computers—have been able to construct programs that for all practical purposes can read (see Just & Carpenter, 1987). These programs have literally thousands of component parts or production systems. Fortunately, for the purpose of mediated instruction, we can use a much simpler model. In this chapter I use a *parallel processing* model adapted from the field of cognitive science.

Parallel processing refers to the simultaneous execution of a number of separate, but interactive components (Rumelhart, 1989; Simon & Kaplan, 1989). Figure 5.1 depicts the interaction of the following components:

1. The general task processor
2. The information screener
3. The propositional network processor
4. The word processor
5. The macrostructure generator

The different sizes of the processing components in Fig. 5.1 are meant to represent the fact that "taller" processors pass on information to or influence those processors with smaller representations. Perhaps a more accurate representation of the interrelationship among the five processors is presented in Fig. 5.2. This

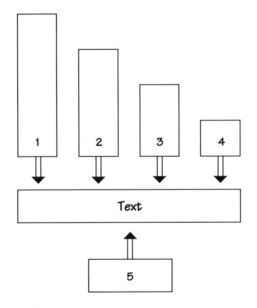

1. The general task processor
2. The information screener
3. The propositional network processor
4. The word processor
5. The macrostructure generator

FIG. 5.1. Processing components of reading. From *New Approaches to Literacy: Helping Students Develop Reading and Writing Skills* (p. 28) by R. J. Marzano and D. E. Paynter, 1994, Washington, DC: American Psychological Association. Copyright 1994 by American Psychological Association. Reprinted by permission.

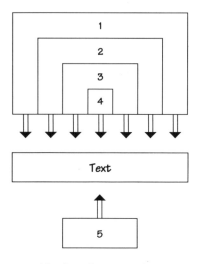

FIG. 5.2. Alternate model of reading processing components. From *New Approaches to Literacy: Helping Students Develop Reading and Writing Skills* (p. 29) by R. J. Marzano and D. E. Paynter, 1994, Washington, DC: American Psychological Association. Copyright 1994 by American Psychological Association. Reprinted by permission.

figure illustrates that the word processor operates in the context of the propositional network processor, which operates in the context of the information screener, and so on. One level passes on information to the levels below it. Additionally, the lower levels can pass on information to the higher levels. However, in general, the flow of information is from the top down.

The issue of the flow of information is an important one. At one time it was assumed that within the reading process, information flowed from the bottommost elements to the topmost components. This was called a *bottom-up* model. Perhaps the prototypic bottom-up model of reading was that presented by Phillip Gough (1972). The following is a description of Gough's account of what happens during one second of reading:

1. The reader recognizes the bars, slits, edges, curves, angles, and breaks in a letter.
2. The reader identifies the specific letter signified by the recognized bars, slits, edges, and so on.
3. The reader continues this process for all the letters in the specific word on which he or she is focusing.
4. The reader organizes the identified letters into a pattern.
5. The reader searches his or her lexical memory in an attempt to match the identified pattern with a known word.

6. When a match is made, the recognized word is placed in a semantic memory buffer. (pp. 337–338)

For Gough, reading was conceptualized as a process of adding up the meaning of the pieces. As words are understood, the meanings of phrases and sentences are gradually constructed. As more and more sentences are understood, the meaning of paragraphs are gradually constructed, and so on. Reading instruction, then, from this perspective, involves mastering the building-block skills involved in the process. First, you master one skill, then you master another. Of course, the skills that should be mastered first are those that relate directly to the first steps of the reading process—recognizing letters and letter/sound relationships. Commonly, the list of skills to be mastered with a bottom-up approach to reading instruction include the following:

- Recognizing letters
- Recognizing letter/sound relationships
- Using phonics rules
- Breaking words into syllables
- Figuring out words from context
- Figuring out words using word parts
- Recognizing sentence patterns
- Asking and answering literal questions
- Asking and answering inferential questions

This view of reading instruction dominated public instruction until the late 1960s when Kenneth Goodman (1967) presented a paper at the annual meeting of the American Educational Research Association that drastically changed the perception of educators as to the nature of the reading process and, consequently, the nature of reading instruction. Instead of a precise process of using skills in a bottom-up fashion, Goodman characterized reading as much more of an imprecise, meaning-driven activity:

> More simply stated, reading is a psycholinguistic guessing game. It involves an interaction between thought and language. Effective reading does not result from precise perception and identification of all elements, but from skill in selecting the fewest, most productive cues necessary to produce guesses which are right the first time. The ability to anticipate that which has not been seen, of course, is vital in reading, just as the ability to anticipate what has not yet been heard is vital in listening. (p. 2)

Based on this theory of reading as driven by meaning, Goodman hypothesized a reading process very different from that described by Gough. It can be summarized in the following way:

1. The reader scans along a line of print from left to right and down the page, line by line.
2. He fixes at a point to permit eye focus. Some print is central in focus, some is peripheral, allowing the reader to consider single words or short phrases.
3. Guided by his knowledge of language, his purpose for reading, the type of text being read, and his understanding of the topic, he picks up semantic and graphic cues.
4. At this point, he makes a guess or a tentative choice as to the meaning of the word or phrase.
5. He uses the representation of the text that he has already created to determine the reasonableness of his choice.
6. If the choice is acceptable, expectations are formed about the nature and meaning of the text that have not as yet been processed.
7. The cycle continues.

A comparison of this process with the one described by Gough discloses at least one major difference. Whereas the process described by Gough is a bottom-up one in which understanding is driven by recognizing the smallest parts first, the reading process, as described by Goodman, is driven from the top down. The readers' purpose for reading determines what they look for in the text, which determines where they look, and so on.

It is the meaning-driven, top-down nature of reading that is the basis of mediated instruction. Very simply, it makes little sense to reinforce any metacognitive or cognitive component of the reading process in isolation, because each component requires information from higher level components. However, it does make sense to attend to specific components while students are engaged in the overall process of reading. This wholistic aspect of mediated instruction cannot be overemphasized. Working on any component part of reading (or any other complex process) in isolation is, by definition, an artificial endeavor, because it will not reflect the complexity of a given component's use as it interacts with superordinate and subordinate components.

What, then, are the metacognitive and cognitive components of reading, and how do they interact?

**The General Task Processor**

The job of the general task processor is to monitor the extent to which the learner is getting closer to or further away from some goal. Such monitoring is highly metacognitive in nature. According to cybernetic theory, all complex processes, such as reading, are fundamentally goal-seeking activities (Glasser, 1981; Powers, 1973). What this implies, of course, is that effective reading involves the identification of a specific goal or purpose for reading. There are at least three major goals or purposes for reading that are monitored by the general task processor.

One general purpose for reading is to simply enjoy an experience vicariously. This is particularly true when you read fiction. In their review of the seminal work of Louise Rosenblatt in reader response, Anderson and Rubino (1991) classified such a purpose as "aesthetic" in nature—focused on the enhancement of the reader's self-experiences. When you read Ernest Hemingway's *The Old Man and the Sea*, for example, you vicariously experience what it is like to be an elderly fisherman battling a great fish. This enhances your experiential base.

A second major purpose for reading is to gather information for a specific task. For example, if you are engaged in the task of researching the controversy behind the assassination of President John Kennedy, you would surely read selected books and articles on the topic. Again, to use Rosenblatt's classification, such a purpose is more *efferent* in nature (Anderson & Rubino, 1991)—focused on the assimilation or accommodation of new information.

A third general purpose for reading is to affirm what you think you know. This too is classified as efferent. Readers operating from this purpose seek to verify their knowledge base. For example, while working on the research task about the Kennedy assassination, you might check the facts you think you know in an effort to be precise. You would again read over certain books and articles, but your purpose would be to verify what you know rather than gather new information.

In summary, there are three general purposes for reading: to experience events and situations vicariously, to gather new information, and to validate what you know.

***Mediating the General Task Processor.***    Mediating the general task processor is a matter of enhancing the reader's metacognitive control of this high-level information-processing component. Problems within the general task processor occur when readers have established no clear purpose for reading or when they have not kept an established purpose in mind. Evidence that readers have not set a clear purpose for reading or have lost sight of that purpose, is that they have trouble attending to what they are trying to read. Not surprisingly, when we lose sight of why we are engaged in an activity, we quickly lose interest in the activity.

The first step in mediating the general task processor is to bring the student's purpose for reading to a conscious level. For example, a teacher might ask the student, "What are you trying to accomplish by reading this book or this passage?" If the student has no clear purpose for reading ("I don't know, I'm just reading it."), the teacher might then help the student establish one by asking questions such as the following:

- Are you reading this to enjoy it—to experience something new?

- Are you reading this to find some specific information?
- Are you reading this to check to see if you are accurate about something you think you know?

With a goal for reading established or made salient, the reader can monitor progress toward the goal. This is done through a series of self-regulatory questions. For example, if your purpose is to experience situations vicariously, then it is useful to continually relate the information in the text to your personal life by asking self-regulatory questions such as the following:

- Have I ever done anything like this?
- Have I ever felt the same way as the characters I am reading about?
- Have I ever thought in the manner in which the characters are thinking?
- How are my experiences similar and different from those depicted in the text?
- Does this story help me understand something currently going on in my own life?

When your purpose for reading is to gather new information, it is commonly done for a specific task. Self-regulatory questions for this purpose include the following:

- Is this information useful to me?
- Does this information meet some specific need related to my project?

Finally, readers whose purpose is to verify what they know about a topic will commonly scan a text very quickly, looking for specific pieces of information. As they do so, they continually ask themselves, "Does this agree with or disagree with what I know about the topic?"

As teachers work with students during mediated instruction they move from cuing self-regulatory questions like those above to helping students ask and answer such questions without prompting.

**The General Information Screener**

While reading, the learner is constantly making decisions about the information contained in the text. In effect, the reader is screening information as he reads to determine whether it is reasonable—whether it should be accepted without further review or whether it should be rejected. If information is judged to be reasonable, it is integrated into the learner's existing knowledge base. But, if the information is judged to be unreasonable, then it is processed in a very different way. Such screening is again highly metacognitive.

To illustrate how the general information screener works, imagine that you are reading a book about the war in Vietnam—a topic you have been interested in for quite some time. As you read the book, you might encounter certain facts that "don't seem right"—they might even contradict what you think you know about Vietnam. In such cases, you would look to see if evidence has been provided ("Where's the proof for this?"). If evidence was not provided, you would refrain from accepting the information as true ("I don't believe this, even if the book says so."). If evidence was provided, you would make a determination as to the sufficiency of that evidence. Again, if you concluded that the evidence was not adequate, you would refrain from integrating the new information into your knowledge base. However, if you determined that the evidence was sufficient, then the information would be considered a legitimate addition to what you already know about the topic ("I guess I was wrong. It must have happened the way the book says."). In simple terms, the information screener determines the reasonableness of information given the current knowledge base of the reader.

*Mediating the Information Screener.*    Evidence that readers are experiencing difficulties with the general information screener is that they cannot describe whether the information being read seems reasonable. For example, if a teacher asks students to comment on the reasonableness of what they are reading, and the students cannot answer or do not understand what is being asked, it is probably an indication that they are having difficulty at the information-screening level.

Where effective processing at the general task-processor level involves asking and answering a variety of self-regulatory questions, effective processing at the information-screening level involves the use of more well-defined strategies. Many strategies have been developed to aid in the analysis of the reasonableness of information. De Bono (1985), for example, has designed scores of highly specific procedures to this end. Beyer (1988) has developed a number of more general procedures. A generic strategy follows, which includes the major components of a variety of the tactics others have devised:

1. Ask yourself, "Does this information make sense to me based on what I know about the topic?" If yes, then keep on reading.
2. If no, ask yourself, "Does the author provide evidence for the information that does not seem reasonable to me?"
3. If no, then refrain from accepting the information as valid.
4. If yes, then try to determine how sound the evidence is.
5. If the evidence provided is sound, then accept it as new information about the topic.
6. If the evidence provided is not sound, then do not accept the new information until better evidence is provided.

This process is presented in flow chart form in Fig. 5.3. Of course, to use this strategy, a student must understand some basic principles regarding sound evi-

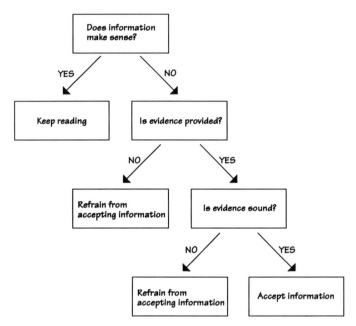

FIG. 5.3. Information screening strategy. From *Tactics for Thinking: Teacher's Manual* (p. 76) by R. J. Marzano and D. E. Arredondo, 1986, Alexandria, VA: Association for Supervision and Curriculum Development. Copyright 1986 by Mid-Continent Regional Educational Laboratory. Adapted by permission.

dence. Fortunately, research and theory by theorists such as Toulmin and his colleagues (Toulmin, 1958; Toulmin, Rieke, & Janik, 1981) have identified common errors that render evidence unsound. In Table 5.1 these are grouped into three basic categories:

1. Errors based on faulty logic.
2. Errors based on attack.
3. Errors based on weak reference.

When mediating the reading process to enhance the information screener, a teacher might initially guide a student through the strategy depicted in Fig. 5.3 by asking questions like the following: "Does this information make sense to you based on what you know about the topic?" "If not, does the writer provide evidence . . . ?" and so on. Ultimately, the mediator's goal is to help students internalize the strategy so that they might use it at will. According to current research and theory, the internalization of a complex strategy like that depicted in Fig. 5.3 requires that it progress through a number of phases (Anderson, 1990; Fitts & Posner, 1967). The first of these phases involves the construction of a model representing the steps involved in the strategy. A teacher presenting the

TABLE 5.1
Common Informal Fallacies

*Category I: Errors based on faulty logic*

Errors that fall into this category use a type of reasoning that is flawed in some way or is simply not rigorous. Such errors include:

   a. *Contradiction:* The writer or speaker presents information that is in direct opposition to other information within the same argument.
   b. *Accident:* The writer or speaker fails to recognize that an argument is based on an exception to a rule.
   c. *False cause:* The writer or speaker confuses a temporal order of events with causality, or someone oversimplifies a complex causal network.
   d. *Begging the question (circularity):* The writer or speaker makes a claim and then argues for it by advancing grounds whose meaning is simply equivalent to that of the original claim.
   e. *Evading the issue:* The writer or speaker sidesteps an issue by changing the topic.
   f. *Arguing from ignorance:* The writer or speaker argues that a claim is justified simply because its opposite cannot be proved.
   g. *Composition and division:* The writer or speaker asserts about a whole something that is true of its parts. Division involves asserting about all of the parts something that is true about the whole.

*Category II: Errors based on attack*

Informal fallacies in this category all use the strategy of attacking a person or position.

   h. *Poisoning the well:* The writer or speaker is committed to his position to such a degree that he explains away absolutely everything others offer in opposition to his position.
   i. *Arguing against the person:* The writer or speaker rejects a claim on the basis of derogatory facts (real or alleged) about the person making the claim.
   j. *Appealing to force:* The writer or speaker uses threats to establish the validity of a claim.

*Category III: Errors based on weak references*

Informal fallacies that fall into this category appeal to something other than reason to make their point; however, they are not based on attack.

   k. *Appealing to authority:* The writer or speaker evokes authority as the last word on an issue.
   l. *Appealing to the people:* The writer or speaker attempts to justify a claim on the basis of popularity.
   m. *Appealing to emotion:* The writer or speaker uses an emotion-laden or "sob" story as proof for a claim.

steps depicted would, in effect, be providing students with the necessary information to accomplish phase one of the process of internalizing an information-screening strategy. During the second phase of the process, the learners adapt the strategy to their own needs and styles. This means that learners will quite naturally change the steps presented in Fig. 5.3 and augment the list of fallacies presented in Table 5.1. Finally, in the third phase, the learners are provided with enough practice to perform the strategy with relative ease. In short, helping students internalize a specific strategy through mediated instruction requires emphasizing the strategy over an extended period of time so that students might adapt and practice the strategy.

## The Propositional Network Processor

The next processing component of reading is at the propositional network processor. Although basically cognitive in nature, it might be at the core of reading comprehension. A number of psychologists assert that propositions are the basic units of thought (Kintsch, 1974, 1979; Kintsch & van Dijk, 1978; van Dijk, 1977; van Dijk & Kintsch, 1983). In simple terms, "a proposition is the smallest unit of information that can stand as a separate assertion; that is, the smallest unit about which it makes sense to make the judgment of true or false" (Anderson, 1990, p. 123). Psychologists Herbert and Eve Clark have noted that there is a finite set of types of propositions (Clark & Clark, 1977). The following sentences represent the major types of propositions:

1. Todd walks.
2. Todd is handsome.
3. Todd eats fruit.
4. Todd is in London.
5. Todd gave a toy to Christine.
6. Todd walks slowly.
7. Todd hit Christine with a pillow.
8. Sorrow overcame Todd.

Each of these sentences can be affirmed or denied, yet none of their component parts can. That is, you could determine if it is true that "Todd walks" or "Todd is handsome," but you could not confirm or deny "Todd," "walks," or "handsome" in isolation. A proposition, then, might be described as the basic unit of thought.

More complex thoughts are constructed by combining propositions into propositional networks. For example, Fig. 5.4 represents the propositional network underlying the statement: "Bill went to the store, where he met his sister. They brought their father a coat." As you read, you organize the information into networks like that in Fig. 5.4. The more text you read, the more networks you create.

Central to the process of constructing propositional networks is making inferences. Although there has been much written about the great variety of inferences in reading (see Graesser & Bower, 1990), two types appear to be basic to the comprehension and understanding of a text: (a) default inferences, and (b) reasoned inferences. Default inferences are those you commonly make about persons, places, things, events, and abstractions. For example, when you read

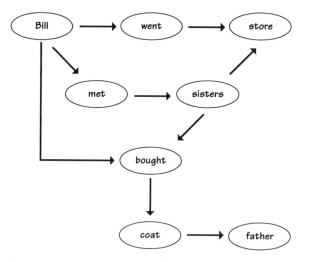

FIG. 5.4. Propositional network. From "Towards a Theory-Based Review of Research on Vocabulary" by R. J. Marzano (1993, p. 31). Copyright 1993 by Ginn. Reprinted by permission.

the sentence "Bill has a dog," you immediately add information such as: "the dog has four legs," "the dog likes to eat bones," "the dog likes to be petted," and so on. In other words, you have information about dogs stored in long-term memory that you automatically call on. In the absence of information to the contrary, you infer that the general information you have is true about the dog, even though it is not explicitly mentioned in the text.

Reasoned inferences are another way that we add information that is not explicit in a text. Such inferences are not part of our general knowledge. Rather, they are conclusions that can be logically drawn from premises implicit or explicit in the text. For example, when you read that "experimental psychologists believe that you have to test generalizations to see if they are true," and then read about a psychologist who is presented with a new theory by a colleague, you will quite naturally conclude that the psychologist will probably suggest that the theory should be tested. This inference did not come from your general knowledge base about psychologists, but was induced from the earlier information you read about experimental psychologists.

Default inferences and reasoned inferences, then, help the reader construct propositional networks for the information in a text because they put "implied meat" on the "explicit bones" of a text. Yet, default and reasoned inferences are simply the data used to create propositional networks. The process of constructing propositional networks is primarily one of constructing mental models.

Some psychologists assert that the construction of mental models is at the heart of all understanding (Johnson-Laird, 1983, 1985). That is, to understand a situation or experience, we must make a mental model of it. In simple terms, there are two basic formats for constructing mental models: (a) images of epi-sodes, objects, persons, places, and things; and (b) images of tokens. Images of episodes, objects, persons, places, and things are used when we are reading information that is fairly concrete in nature. In such cases, we form images of the concrete information contained in the text. For example, when you read a description of a beautiful mountain scene, you picture the scene in your mind in a very concrete way. When you read about Abraham Lincoln and specific events that happened to him, you generate mental pictures of Lincoln and those events. Images of tokens are commonly used when we read abstract information. In such cases, we construct an image of tokens for the information we are reading. Johnson-Laird describes tokens as arbitrary symbols that represent the key fea-tures of the information in the text. For example, when you comprehend the statement "Five of the beachcombers were athletes," you form a mental image of a set of beachcombers, some of whom have the added distinction that they are athletes. The beachcombers might be depicted as people, as stick figures, as small circles, or as any number of arbitrary representations (Johnson-Laird, 1983).

These concrete and abstract imagery models are fundamentally episodic in nature (Kosslyn, 1980; Paivio, 1971; Tulving, 1972). They form the basis for constructing propositional networks like Fig. 5.4, which are semantic in nature. In other words, based on the images the readers have constructed, they form semantic propositional networks.

In summary, the propositional network processor is responsible for making default and reasoned inferences. The information generated from these inferences, along with the explicit information in the text, is then used to create episodic mental models represented as concrete and abstract images. These are then trans-lated into propositionally based semantic networks.

*Mediating the Propositional Network Processor.*   Evidence that students are having difficulty at the level of the propositional network processor is fairly straightforward—the students have trouble describing the interrelationships among the ideas within the last few sentences they have read. For example, students who have just read a paragraph describing how Christmas trees are harvested and brought to market, but can describe only the Christmas tree their family had last year, are probably not processing information well at the network processor level.

There are a number of strategies that can be employed to enhance students' performance in creating propositional networks. First, students can be aided in making default inference. A teacher can facilitate the generation of useful default inferences by helping students identify key concepts that are not explicitly de-scribed in the text.

To illustrate, assume that students are reading a passage in which the concept of "equilibrium" is central. However, the passage does not provide much explicit information about equilibrium. At first the teacher might simply help students identify that information which must be inferred for the text to make sense. Upon examination of the text, the teacher might conclude that the following characteristics must be inferred:

1. When two elements reach equilibrium, they have usually undergone a change of state.
2. There is a specific process involved in reaching a state of equilibrium (the element greater than the other element on some dimension is lessened in that dimension, or the element lesser than the other element becomes greater in that dimension).

Armed with this awareness, the teacher would then ask the students questions that might help them identify the important characteristics of equilibrium that are not explicit in the text. For example, the teacher might ask the following questions:

- What are some basic changes that occur when something reaches a state of equilibrium?
- What is the basic process involved in reaching a state of equilibrium?
- How does this implied information about equilibrium help you understand about what you have just read?

Ultimately, though, the students must be able to independently identify key default inferences if thinking and reasoning are to be enhanced within the reading process. This would involve enhancing the students' ability to ask and answer self-monitoring questions such as:

- What are the key ideas and terms that are being used in this text?
- What is not stated about these key concepts and terms that I should keep in mind as I read?

The second type of inference that is important to the propositional network processor is the *reasoned* inference. Although there are many types of reasoned inferences, the ones that are most frequently used by readers deal with premises that *quantify* attributes. For example, when you read that "most sharks are harmless to humans unless provoked" and then later read that a young girl is swimming in an area frequented by sharks, you can reason that the girl will probably not be harmed. In effect, statements that quantify the likelihood or certainty of events are the premises from which reasoned inferences are made. Commonly, such statements include quantifiers such as *all, some, many, more, no, few, seldom,* and *never* (Copi, 1972; Klenk, 1983).

To help a student make reasoned inferences, a teacher might first identify quantitative statements and then help the student think through reasoned inferences. For example, after identifying the quantitative statement about sharks and the subsequent statement about the young girl swimming, the teacher might help stimulate reasoned inference with questions like the following:

- What have you read that will help you draw conclusions about the young girl swimming?
- What are the specific implications of the information?

Eventually, the questions cued by the teacher would be replaced with adequate cuing and practice by self-monitoring questions like the following:

- What have I read that can tell me how probable or absolute a potential event is?

We saw in the previous section that inferences are ultimately translated into mental representations or mental models. A teacher might first provide students with an awareness of this aspect of propositional network processing by helping students create mental representations of information in a text. If the text being read contains information that is fairly concrete, then the teacher might simply ask the students to describe what they see, smell, taste, touch, or hear. For example, as the students are reading a story, the teacher would occasionally stop them and ask questions such as:

- What mental pictures did the last few lines you read stimulate in your mind?
- Was there anything to smell, taste, touch, or hear?

If the text being read contains information that is more abstract, then the images the students create must necessarily contain tokens or symbols. Symbolizing abstract content can be challenging. In fact, a reader must be quite creative in many instances to construct an image for abstract content. Psychologist John Hayes demonstrates using the following equation:

$$F = \frac{(M^1, M^2)\ G}{r}.$$

The equation states that Force ($F$) is equal to the product of the masses of two objects ($M^1$ and $M^2$) times a constant $G$ divided by the square of the distance between them ($r$). To symbolize this, Hayes (1981) recommends the image of two large globes in space with the learner in the middle trying to hold them apart:

If either of the globes were very heavy, we would expect that it would be harder to hold them apart, than if both were light. Since force increases as either of the masses ($M$'s) increases, the masses must be in the numerator. As we push the globes further apart, the force of attraction between them will decrease as the force of attraction between two magnets decreases as we pull them apart. Since force decreases as distance increases, $r$ must be in the denominator. (p. 126)

Guiding students through the creation of episodic images like those above provides students with an important awareness about the functioning of the propositional network processor. At a self-regulatory level, however, students must eventually form the habit of asking themselves questions like the following:

How can I represent this information?
Are there symbols I have to imagine?

In summary, the propositional network processor can be mediated by helping students to (a) make default and reasoned inferences, and (b) create mental images of concrete and abstract information. Eventually, students must develop the habit of asking specific self-regulatory questions.

**The Word Processor**

Perhaps the processing component of reading that has been studied the most is the word processor. Before describing the role of the word processor, it is important to recognize that the words within a proposition are representations of abstractions. That is, when you read, you do not store propositional networks with words in them as depicted in Fig. 5.4. Rather, the components of the propositional networks you store are *concepts*. For example, when you represent the proposition "Fish swim" in your mind, the words *fish* and *swim* are not actually stored as components of the proposition. You use words only when you want to express the content of a proposition to yourself or to someone else. Psychologists Turner and Greene (1977) explained, "The actual word or words which are chosen to represent the concept are word tokens for the abstract concept. It is important to understand that the abstract concept can and may be represented by a number of words in a given language" (p. 3). In short, the job of the word processor is to recognize words that are symbols for concepts. Understanding the job of the word processor, then, will be facilitated by an understanding of the nature of concepts.

There has been a great deal of research and theory on the nature of concepts (Klausmeier, 1980; Smith & Medin, 1981; Tennyson & Cocchiarella, 1986). Virtually all of the research and theory on concepts acknowledge the role of semantic features. Ironically, to exemplify semantic features as they relate to concepts, we must use words which, of course, are not the concepts themselves, only symbols for the concepts. With this in mind, consider Fig. 5.5, which illustrates the role of semantic features in defining concepts. The words in set

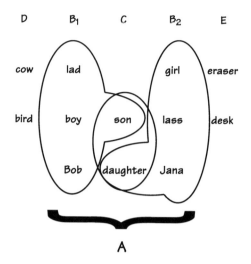

FIG. 5.5. Semantic features. From *A Cluster Approach to Elementary Vocabulary Instruction* (p. 37) by R. J. Marzano and J. S. Marzano, 1988, Newark, DE: International Reading Association. Copyright 1988 by International Reading Association. Reprinted by permission.

A all represent concepts with the semantic features human, animal, and two-legged. The words in B1 and B2 represent concepts that are differentiated by the fact that all B1 concepts contain the added semantic feature of male, all B2 words represent concepts with the added semantic feature of female. The concepts represented by words in set C do not share a male–female distinction, but they do share a semantic feature that might be called *siblings*.

Semantic-feature theory, then, asserts that concepts are defined by sets of semantic characteristics. The concept represented by the word *cow* is defined by semantic features such as animate, concrete, four-legged, milk-producing, and so on. The concept represented by the word *desk* is defined by semantic features such as inanimate, concrete, four-legged, used for paperwork, and so on. Actual words are symbols or tokens for concepts you have stored in your long-term memory.

One of the most striking features of a skillful reader is the ease and speed with which they are able to recognize these symbols or tokens. Skillful readers can course through text at rates of upward of 300 words per minute—upward of 5 words per second. Indeed, Adams (1990) explained that skillful readers can perceive whole words as quickly and accurately as single letters. Although the process of recognizing words is probably best described as a set of related subprocesses, one of the primary methods is through spelling patterns. Adams illustrates how we use spelling patterns via the following words:

hypermetropical
hackmatack
thigmotaxis

She explained:

> If the above words are new to you, then you could only have read them one way: by decoding them. Yet, for skillful readers of English, decoding such words is easy—so easy in fact, that if you had known the meanings of these words and if they had appeared in meaningful connected text, you might have sped right through them without even noticing whether you had ever seen them before. (1992, p. 54)

In contrast to the ease with which the words above are decoded, Adams offered the following:

Karivaradharajan
Bydgoszcz
Shihkiachwag
Verkhneudinsk

Adams posed the question: Why are these words much more difficult to read? She provided the following answer:

> The answer, of course, relates to their spelling patterns. These words are not English. Their spelling patterns are unfamiliar. You, as a skillful reader, are very good at decoding, but you do not read from single letters to sounds. Instead you have learned to recognize whole spelling patterns at once ... fluent word recognition does not proceed letter by letter; the fluent reader eventually comes to recognize frequent words and spelling patterns at a glance. (1992, p. 54)

The word processor, then, uses spelling patterns to identify words that are the tokens or symbols for concepts you have learned. But what happens if you do not know the word in the text? Most theorists now believe that you make an initial determination of whether the word is important to the overall meaning of the text. If your determination is that the word is not important, then you skip it. However, if you determine that the unknown word is important, then you try to determine the meaning of the word. You might reread the sentence in which it appeared, looking for clues to its meaning. You might even stop to look up the word in a glossary or a dictionary.

In summary, the word processor facilitates the recognition of words that are tokens for concepts. This is done primarily through common spelling patterns. If the decoded word is not known, the word processor makes a determination of its importance to the overall meaning of the text. If the word is considered key to the meaning of the text, then attempts are made to figure out the meaning of the word.

***Mediating the Word Processor.*** It is usually fairly obvious when students are not processing effectively at the word level. The basic evidence is that students have difficulty recognizing the words in the text. They skip words, they mispronounce words, they replace words. If too many words are skipped, comprehension breaks down quickly. Again, when this cognitive process goes awry, metacognitive attention must be paid to it.

Given that the primary way we recognize words is through spelling patterns, a useful, mediational technique is to help students use one of many decoding strategies that have been recommended (see Marzano, Hagerty, Valencia, & DiStefano, 1987). Virtually all of these strategies instruct students to break an unrecognized word into parts that represent syllables, figure out the sounds of the parts, and then blend the parts together.

At a more self-regulatory level, students might be provided with an explicit strategy for dealing with words they cannot recognize. Following is a four-step strategy:

1. Skip the word and read to the end of the sentence.
2. Go back to the word and ask, "What word would make sense here and begins with this letter or letters?"
3. If unable to determine the unknown word, reread the previous sentence or continue reading the next sentence and try Steps 1 and 2 again.
4. If still unable to recognize the word, identify a word that would make sense and continue reading. (Marzano et al., 1987, p. 153)

The techniques described above are effective mediational devices if students are simply having difficulty decoding the orthographic representation for words for which they have internalized concepts. However, students who have difficulty recognizing words may be doing so because they have not developed the concepts that the words represent. This is a much more serious issue. In such a situation, helping students is a matter of increasing their sight vocabulary. Recent research by Nagy and his colleagues (Nagy, 1988; Nagy & Anderson, 1984; Nagy, Anderson, & Herman, 1987; Nagy & Herman, 1987; Nagy, Herman, & Anderson, 1985) indicated that wide reading is one of the best ways of increasing one's vocabulary. Specifically, Nagy estimates that if students spend 20 minutes per day reading at a rate of 200 words per minute for 200 days of the year, they would read 1 million words of text annually. Given this amount of reading, children would encounter 15,000 to 30,000 unfamiliar words and would learn between 750 and 1,500 of them. "A period of sustained silent reading could lead to substantial yearly gains in vocabulary, probably much larger than could be achieved by spending the same amount of time on instruction specifically devoted to vocabulary" (Nagy & Herman, 1987, p. 26).

In summary, the word-processing component of reading can be enhanced by providing students with specific decoding strategies. In a more generic sense, word processing is enhanced by developing a student's base of concepts, the tokens for which are easily recognized by sight, through extended wide reading.

### The Macrostructure Generator

The ultimate product of the reading process is a *macrostructure*. Psychologists such as Walter Kintsch and Teun van Dijk explain that a macrostructure contains the "gist" of what is read (Kintsch, 1974, 1979; Kintsch & van Dijk, 1978; van Dijk, 1977, 1980; van Dijk & Kintsch, 1983). In Fig. 5.1, this is represented as occurring after the other processes. In fact, the creation of a macrostructure occurs throughout the reading process. That is, as you read something, you are constructing your own representation of the basic gist of that information. That representation is formed via the use of what van Dijk and Kintsch (1983) refer to as *macrorules* that are applied in a highly metacognitive fashion. Specifically, they identify three basic macrorules, which can be described in the following way:

1. *Deletion*—Given a sequence of propositions, delete any proposition that is not directly related to the other propositions in the sequence.
2. *Generalization*—Replace any proposition by one that includes the information in a more general form.
3. *Construction*—Replace any set of propositions by one or more that include the information in the set stated in more general terms. (p. 190)

According to these rules, when you create a macrostructure you construct a parsimonious representation of the information that does not include specific details about what you read, but includes the general outline of the information. This explains why you usually do not remember the specific facts in an interesting story that you read, but you do tend to recall the general flow of information and events (e.g., "There was this boy and girl from different sides of the town. One was very rich and one was very poor. The rich one met the poor one . . .").

*Mediating the Macrostructure Generator.*   Again, it is fairly clear when the student is not processing information effectively at the macrostructure level. The student might be able to provide specific details contained in the text, but cannot articulate the overall structure and intent of the text. For example, the student might be able to provide you with specific names, facts, and events about a story, or even specific episodes, but cannot articulate the general flow of action and the plot.

To mediate the macrostructure generator, a teacher might provide students with techniques for organizing large blocks of information. Many of these involve the use of graphic organizers like those in Fig. 5.6. Specifically, a teacher might first cue a student to use graphic representations like those in Fig. 5.6 to organize information in a text. In general, students will use more than one graphic organizer to represent all the important information in a text (Marzano, 1992). Once the

Descriptive Pattern

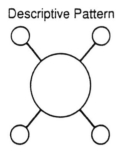

Sequence Pattern

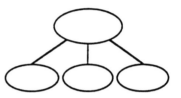

Process/Cause Pattern

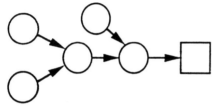

Problem/Solution Pattern

Generalization Pattern

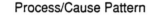

Concept Pattern

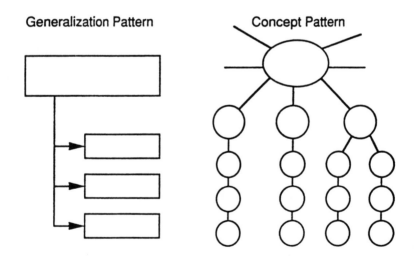

FIG. 5.6. Six types of graphic organizers. From *A Different Kind of Classroom: Teaching with Dimensions of Learning* (p. 45) by R. J. Marzano, 1992, Alexandria, VA: ASCD. Copyright Association for Supervision and Curriculum Development. Adapted by permission.

information is represented graphically, students would then be asked to state the information verbally.

At a more self-regulatory level, Brown and her colleagues (Brown & Day, 1983) have identified a process that mirrors the steps in macrostructure construction:

1. Delete trivial material that is unnecessary to understanding.
2. Delete redundant material.
3. Substitute superordinate terms for lists (e.g., "flowers" for "daisies, tulips, and roses").
4. Select a topic sentence, or invent one if it is missing. (p. 10)

According to Brown, this strategy requires time and attention to be used effectively. As we have seen, learners must shape a strategy to meet their style and needs and then practice it to a point at which it could be applied with relative ease.

## CONCLUSION

The basic premise of this chapter is that thinking and reasoning within a given domain can be enhanced only within the context of the salient mental processes for that domain. Additionally, the component parts of those mental processes cannot be detached from the overall process and enhanced in isolation. Rather, they must be fostered through the interaction of a skilled teacher with a learner who is actively engaged in the target process. This is referred to as *mediated instruction*. Unfortunately, to engage in such instruction, a teacher must have a thorough understanding of the targeted process.

In this chapter, I have presented a top-down parallel-processing model of reading involving five components. Additionally, I have described mediational techniques and strategies for each processing component. Ideally, educators, researchers, and theorists in the English language arts will construct useful models of the many other mental processes important to the language arts (i.e., writing, speaking, and listening) and identify mediational techniques for the various processing components specific to those models.

Finally, this chapter serves as a graphic illustration of the fact that there are no easy ways to enhance thinking and reasoning within any domain. The lofty goals regarding enhanced thinking and reasoning, articulated in many national reports, will be reached only through a concentrated effort to better understand the situated thinking and reasoning within the various content domains American students must master to be effective members of a complex, information-based society.

## ACKNOWLEDGMENT

Portions of this chapter are based on *New Approaches to Literacy: Helping Students Develop Reading and Writing Skills* by R. J. Marzano and D. E. Paynter. © Copyright 1994 by the American Psychological Association. Adapted with permission.

## REFERENCES

Adams, M. J. (1990). *Beginning to read: Thinking and learning about reading.* Cambridge, MA: MIT Press.

Adams, M. J. (1992). Word recognition and reading. In C. J. Gordon, G. D. Labercane, & W. R. McEachern (Eds.), *Elementary reading instruction* (pp. 45–67). Needham Heights, MA: Ginn Press.

American Federation of Teachers (1985, September). Critical thinking: It's a basic. *American Teacher*, p. 21.

Anderson, J. (1982). Acquisition of cognitive skills. *Psychological Review, 89,* 369–406.

Anderson, J. (1983). *The architecture of cognition.* Cambridge, MA: Harvard University Press.

Anderson, J. (1990). *Cognitive psychology and its implications.* New York: Freeman.

Anderson, P. M., & Rubino, G. (1991). *Enhancing aesthetic reading and response.* Urbana, IL: National Council of Teachers of English.

Beyer, B. K. (1988). *Developing a thinking skills program.* Boston, MA: Allyn & Bacon.

Brown, A. L., Campione, J. C., & Day, J. (1981, April). Learning to learn: On training students to learn from texts. *Educational Researcher, 10,* 14–24.

Brown, A. L., & Day, J. (1983). Macrorules for summarizing texts: The development of expertise. *Journal of Verbal Learning and Verbal Behavior, 22,* 1–14.

Clark, H. H., & Clark, E. V. (1977). *Psychology and language.* San Diego: Harcourt Brace.

College Entrance Examination Board (1983). *Academic preparation for college: What students need to know and be able to do.* New York: Author.

Copi, I. M. (1972). *Introduction to logic.* New York: Macmillan.

Costa, A. (1991). *Developing minds: Programs for teaching thinking.* Alexandria, VA: Association for Supervision and Curriculum Development.

de Bono, E. (1985). The CoRT thinking program. In J. W. Segal, S. F. Chipman, & R. Glaser (Eds.), *Thinking and learning skills: Vol. 1. Relating instruction to research* (pp. 363–388). Hillsdale, NJ: Lawrence Erlbaum Associates.

de Beaugrande, R. (1980). *Text, discourse and process: Toward a multidisciplinary science of text.* Norwood, NJ: Ablex.

Farrell, E. J. (1991). Instructional models for English language arts, K–12. In J. Flood, J. M. Jensen, D. Lapp, & J. R. Squire (Eds.), *Handbook of research on teaching the English language arts* (pp. 63–84). New York: Macmillan.

Feuerstein, R. (1980). *Instrumental enrichment: An intervention program for cognitive modifiability.* Baltimore, MD: University Park Press.

Feuerstein, R., Rand, Y., Hoffman, M. B., & Miller, R. (1980). *Instrumental enrichment.* Baltimore, MD: University Park Press.

Fitts, P. M., & Posner, M. I. (1967). *Human performance.* Belmont, CA: Brooks Cole.

Flavell, J. H. (1977). *Cognitive development.* Englewood Cliffs, NJ: Prentice-Hall.

Flavell, J. H. (1981). *Cognitive monitoring.* In W. P. Dickson (Ed.), *Children's oral communication skill* (pp. 35–60). New York: Academic Press.

Futrell, M. H. (1987, December 9). A message long overdue. *Education Week, 7*(14), 9.

Glaser, R. (1984). Education and thinking: The role of knowledge. *American Psychologist, 39*, 93–104.

Glaser, R. (1985). Learning and instructions: A letter for a time capsule. In S. F. Chipman, J. W. Segal, & R. Glaser (Eds.), *Thinking and learning skills* (Vol. 2, pp. 609–618). Hillsdale, NJ: Lawrence Erlbaum Associates.

Glasser, W. (1981). *Stations of the mind.* New York: Harper & Row.

Goodman, K. S. (1967, February). *Reading: A psycholinguistic guessing game.* Paper presented at the annual meeting of the American Educational Research Association, New York.

Gough, P. B. (1972). One second of reading. In J. F. Kavana & I. G. Mattingly (Eds.), *Language by ear and by eye* (pp. 331–358). Cambridge, MA: MIT Press.

Graesser, A. C., & Bower, G. H. (Eds.). (1990). *Inferences and text comprehension.* San Diego, CA: Academic Press.

Hansen, J., & Graves, D. H. (1992). Unifying the English language arts curriculum. In J. Flood, J. M. Jensen, D. Lapp, & J. R. Squire (Eds.), *Handbook of research on teaching the English language arts* (pp. 805–819). New York: Macmillan.

Hayes, J. R. (1981). *The complete problem solver.* Philadelphia, PA: The Franklin Institute.

Huey, E. B. (1974). *The psychology and pedagogy of reading.* Boston, MA: MIT Press. (Original work published 1915)

Johnson-Laird, P. N. (1983). *Mental models.* Cambridge, MA: Harvard University Press.

Johnson-Laird, P. N. (1985). Logical thinking: Does it occur in daily life? In S. F. Chipman, J. W. Segal, & R. Glaser (Eds.), *Thinking and learning skills: Vol. 2. Research and open questions* (pp. 293–318). Hillsdale, NJ: Lawrence Erlbaum Associates.

Just, M. A., & Carpenter, P. A. (1987). *The psychology of reading and language comprehension.* Newton, MA: Allyn & Bacon.

Kintsch, W. (1974). *The representation of meaning in memory.* Hillsdale, NJ: Lawrence Erlbaum Associates.

Kintsch, W. (1979). On modeling comprehension. *Educational Psychologist, 14*, 3–14.

Kintsch, W., & van Dijk, T. A. (1978). Toward a model of text comprehension and production. *Psychological Review, 85*, 363–394.

Klausmeier, H. J. (1980). *Learning and teaching concepts.* New York: Academic Press.

Klenk, V. (1983). *Understanding symbolic logic.* Englewood Cliffs, NJ: Prentice-Hall.

Kosslyn, S. M. (1980). *Image and mind.* Cambridge, MA: Harvard University Press.

LaBerge, D., & Samuels, S. J. (1976). Toward a theory of automatic information processing in reading. In H. Singer & R. B. Riddell (Eds.), *Theoretical models and processes of reading* (pp. 548–579). Newark, DE: International Reading Association.

Lehn, K. V. (1983). On the representation of procedures in repair theory. In H. P. Ginsburg (Ed.), *The development of mathematical thinking* (pp. 201–253). New York: Academic Press.

Marzano, R. J. (1992). *A different kind of classroom: Teaching with dimensions of learning.* Alexandria, VA: Association for Supervision and Curriculum Development.

Marzano, R. J., Hagerty, P. J., Valencia, S. W., & DiStefano, P. P. (1987). *Reading diagnosis and instruction: Theory into practice.* Englewood Cliffs, NJ: Prentice-Hall.

Marzano, R. J., & Paynter, D. E. (1994). *New approaches to literacy: Helping students develop reading and writing skills.* Washington, DC: American Psychological Association.

Nagy, W. E. (1988). *Teaching vocabulary to improve reading comprehension.* Newark, DE: International Reading Association.

Nagy, W. E., & Anderson, R. C. (1984). How many words are there in printed school English? *Reading Research Quarterly, 19*, 303–330.

Nagy, W. E., Anderson, R. C., & Herman, P. A. (1987). Learning word meanings from context during normal reading. *American Education Research Journal, 24*, 237–270.

Nagy, W. E., & Herman, P. A. (1987). Breadth and depth of vocabulary knowledge: Implications for acquisition and instruction. In M. G. McKeown & M. E. Curtis (Eds.), *The nature of vocabulary acquisition* (pp. 19–35). Hillsdale, NJ: Lawrence Erlbaum Associates.

Nagy, W. E., Herman, P. A., & Anderson, R. C. (1985). Learning words from context. *Reading Research Quarterly, 20*, 233–253.

National Science Board Commission on Precollege Education in Mathematics, Science and Technology (1983). *Educating Americans for the 21st century.* Washington, DC: Author.

Paivio, A. (1971). *Imagery and verbal processing.* New York: Holt, Rinehart & Winston.

Paris, S. G., & Lindauer, B. K. (1982). The development of cognitive skills during childhood. In B. W. Wolman (Ed.), *Handbook of developmental psychology* (pp. 333–349). Englewood Cliffs, NJ: Prentice-Hall.

Paris, S. G., Lipson, M. Y., & Wixson, K. K. (1983). Becoming a strategic reader. *Contemporary Educational Psychology, 8*, 293–316.

Powers, W. T. (1973). *Behavior: The control of perception.* Chicago: Aldine.

Resnick, L. B. (1987). *Education and learning to think.* Washington, DC: National Academy Press.

Rumelhart, D. E. (1989). The architecture of mind: A connectionist approach. In M. I. Posner (Ed.), *Foundations of cognitive science* (pp. 133–159). Cambridge, MA: MIT Press.

Simon, H. A., & Kaplan, C. A. (1989). Foundations of cognitive science. In M. I. Posner (Ed.), *Foundations of cognitive science* (pp. 1–47). Cambridge, MA: MIT Press.

Smith, E. E., & Medin, D. L. (1981). *Categories and concepts.* Cambridge, MA: Harvard University Press.

Sternberg, R. J. (1984). *Beyond IQ: A triarchic theory of human intelligence.* New York: Cambridge University Press.

Sternberg, R. J. (1988). *The triarchic mind: A new theory of human intelligence.* Middlesex, England: Penguin Books.

Tennyson, R. D., & Cocchiarella, M. J. (1986). An empirically based instructional design theory for teaching concepts. *Review of Educational Research, 56*(1), 40–71.

Toulmin, S. (1958). *The uses of argument.* Cambridge, England: Cambridge University Press.

Toulmin, S., Rieke, R., & Janik, A. (1981). *An introduction to reasoning.* New York: Macmillan.

Tulving, E. (1972). Episodic and semantic memory. In E. Tulving & W. Donaldson (Eds.), *Organization of memory* (pp. 185–191). New York: Academic Press.

Turner, A., & Greene, E. (1977). *The construction of a propositional text base.* Boulder: Institute for the Study of Intellectual Behavior, The University of Colorado at Boulder.

van Dijk, T. A. (1977). *Text and context.* London: Longman.

van Dijk, T. A. (1980). *Macrostructures.* Hillsdale, NJ: Lawrence Erlbaum Associates.

van Dijk, T. A., & Kintsch, W. (1983). *Strategies of discourse comprehension.* Hillsdale, NJ: Lawrence Erlbaum Associates.

Vygotsky, L. S. (1962). *Thought and language.* Cambridge, MA: MIT Press.

# Chapter 6

# Television and the American Child

George Comstock
*Syracuse University*

The statistics are familiar. By the estimates of the A. C. Neilsen Company, children 2–11 years of age watch almost 30 hours of television a week; the figure for teenagers is about 25 hours (Comstock, 1991a). This is not undivided attention, of course, for television viewing is "a discontinuous, often interrupted, and frequently nonexclusive activity for which a measure in hours and minutes serves only as the outer boundary of possible attention" (Comstock, Chaffee, Katzman, McCombs, & Roberts, 1978, pp. 146–147). These are also averages, and individuals vary widely in amount of viewing. Nevertheless, any viewing places some limits on the quantity and quality of attention that can be given to other activities.

What are the implications of television viewing for intellectual development and scholastic achievement? These have been persistent questions since the introduction of the medium in the United States on a widespread basis in the late 1940s and early 1950s, and enough data have been accumulated—primarily in the past decade—to make answers possible. The necessary analytic journey will have three stages:

1. An examination of the direction and degree of any association between viewing and achievement
2. An evaluation of the evidence in behalf of various hypothesized effects of viewing on traits and abilities related to achievement
3. An attempt to explain—based on this and other evidence—why there is any association.

These stages can be rephrased as questions: Are viewing and achievement related? Are traits and abilities on which achievement might depend affected by viewing? What is the best explanation of any association between viewing and achievement?

## ASSOCIATION

Amount of time spent viewing television by American children and teenagers is negatively associated with their academic performance. There are five major sources of evidence:

1. The 1980 California Assessment Program (CAP) data and successive follow-ups (1980, 1982, 1988)
2. The 1980 High School and Beyond (HSB) data collected by the National Center for Educational Statistics (Keith, Reimers, Fehrman, Pottebaum, & Aubey, 1986)
3. The 1983–1984 National Assessment of Educational Progress (NAEP) data collected by the Educational Testing Service (ETS) under support of the Office of Education (B. Anderson, Mead, & Sullivan, 1986)
4. The Eight State Assessment (ESA) data synthesis representing more than 1 million children and teenagers (Neuman, 1988)
5. A sample of several thousand sophomores, drawn from the 1980 HSB data, from whom data were obtained 2 years later when they were seniors (Gaddy, 1986).

The quality of measurement, the size and comprehensiveness of the samples, and the consistency of the results make such a conclusion irrefutable.

Most attention will go to the California data because of (a) the extremely large sample size, and (b) the representation of the greatest variety of achievement. In the spring of 1980, the state-run CAP obtained data on mathematics, reading, and writing achievement and television exposure for everyone present in the 6th and 12th grades on the day of testing. For the 6th grade, this was 282,000; for the 12th grade, 227,000. This represented 99% of the enrolled population. Later follow-ups included other subjects.

It is not only data-set size that promises quality. It is also sponsorship—any such nationally visible endeavor sponsored by a department of education of a large state would represent the scientific norm of highest achievable quality, or reliability and validity.

The combination—two grades and three kinds of achievement—leads to six sets of data. At both grade levels and for each of the three kinds of achievement (Figs. 6.1 and 6.2), there was a negative association between amount of television

**ACHIEVEMENT IN THREE SUBJECTS**

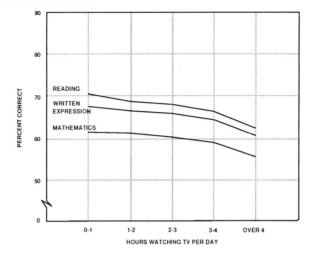

**READING ACHIEVEMENT BY HOUSEHOLD SOCIOECONOMIC STATUS**

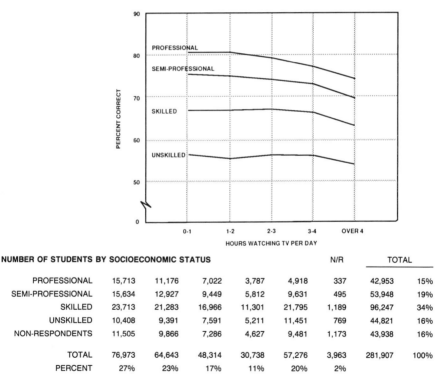

| NUMBER OF STUDENTS BY SOCIOECONOMIC STATUS | | | | | | N/R | TOTAL | |
|---|---|---|---|---|---|---|---|---|
| PROFESSIONAL | 15,713 | 11,176 | 7,022 | 3,787 | 4,918 | 337 | 42,953 | 15% |
| SEMI-PROFESSIONAL | 15,634 | 12,927 | 9,449 | 5,812 | 9,631 | 495 | 53,948 | 19% |
| SKILLED | 23,713 | 21,283 | 16,966 | 11,301 | 21,795 | 1,189 | 96,247 | 34% |
| UNSKILLED | 10,408 | 9,391 | 7,591 | 5,211 | 11,451 | 769 | 44,821 | 16% |
| NON-RESPONDENTS | 11,505 | 9,866 | 7,286 | 4,627 | 9,481 | 1,173 | 43,938 | 16% |
| TOTAL | 76,973 | 64,643 | 48,314 | 30,738 | 57,276 | 3,963 | 281,907 | 100% |
| PERCENT | 27% | 23% | 17% | 11% | 20% | 2% | | |

FIG. 6.1. Television, Achievement, and Socioeconomic Status: Sixth Grade. From California Assessment Program. *Student achievement in California Schools. 1979–1980 annual report: Television and student achievement.* © 1980 by California State Department of Education. Adapted with permission.

**ACHIEVEMENT IN THREE SUBJECTS**

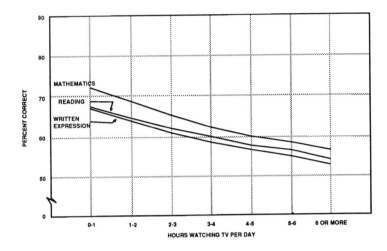

**READING ACHIEVEMENT BY EDUCATIONAL LEVEL OF HEAD OF HOUSEHOLD**

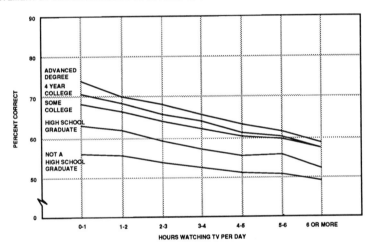

| NUMBER OF STUDENTS BY EDUCATIONAL LEVEL OF HEAD OF HOUSEHOLD | | | | | | | TOTAL | |
|---|---|---|---|---|---|---|---|---|
| ADVANCED DEGREE | 16,923 | 9,244 | 6,128 | 3,424 | 1,730 | 818 | 1,323 | 39,590 | 17.4% |
| 4 YEAR COLLEGE | 14,928 | 10,097 | 7,725 | 4,613 | 2,425 | 1,127 | 1,656 | 42,571 | 18.7% |
| SOME COLLEGE | 17,679 | 14,017 | 12,305 | 8,149 | 4,491 | 2,233 | 3,366 | 62,240 | 27.3% |
| HIGH SCHOOL GRADUATE | 13,090 | 11,885 | 11,850 | 8,822 | 5,294 | 2,714 | 4,101 | 57,756 | 25.4% |
| NOT A HIGH SCHOOL GRADUATE | 5,097 | 4,968 | 5,074 | 4,127 | 2,462 | 1,403 | 2,261 | 25,392 | 11.2% |
| TOTAL | 67,717 | 50,211 | 43,082 | 29,135 | 16,402 | 8,295 | 12,707 | 227,549 | |
| PERCENT | 29.8% | 22.1% | 18.9% | 12.8% | 7.2% | 3.7% | 5.5% | | 100% |

FIG. 6.2. Television, Achievement, and Socioeconomic Status: 12th Grade. From California Assessment Program. *Student achievement in California Schools. 1979–1980 annual report: Television and student achievement.* © 1980 by California State Department of Education. Adapted with permission.

104

viewed and achievement. As exemplified by reading (Figs. 6.1 and 6.2), on which we focus because it has been the subject of more inquiry in regard to television than other subjects (Neuman, 1988) and because the patterns are essentially the same regardless of subject, for each level of family socioeconomic status there was a negative association with viewing for each of the types of achievement.

In contrast (Fig. 6.3), among pupils whose English fluency was limited, amount of viewing was positively associated with achievement. Even a downturn at the level of greatest viewing did not produce an overall downward curve.

There are five important qualifications:

1. Family socioeconomic status is positively associated with achievement, and this relationship is far stronger than the negative one between achievement and amount of viewing.

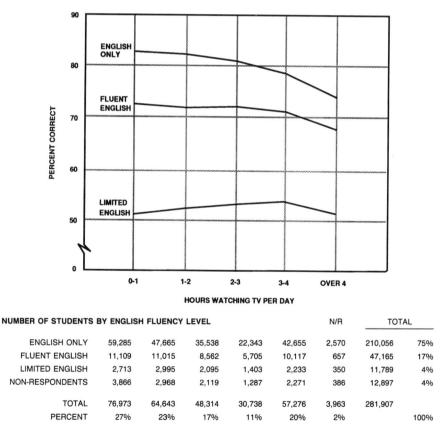

| NUMBER OF STUDENTS BY ENGLISH FLUENCY LEVEL | | | | | N/R | TOTAL | |
|---|---|---|---|---|---|---|---|
| ENGLISH ONLY | 59,285 | 47,665 | 35,538 | 22,343 | 42,655 | 2,570 | 210,056 | 75% |
| FLUENT ENGLISH | 11,109 | 11,015 | 8,562 | 5,705 | 10,117 | 657 | 47,165 | 17% |
| LIMITED ENGLISH | 2,713 | 2,995 | 2,095 | 1,403 | 2,233 | 350 | 11,789 | 4% |
| NON-RESPONDENTS | 3,866 | 2,968 | 2,119 | 1,287 | 2,271 | 386 | 12,897 | 4% |
| TOTAL | 76,973 | 64,643 | 48,314 | 30,738 | 57,276 | 3,963 | 281,907 | |
| PERCENT | 27% | 23% | 17% | 11% | 20% | 2% | | 100% |

FIG. 6.3. Language Proficiency, Television, and Reading Achievement: Sixth Grade. From California Assessment Program. *Student achievement in California Schools. 1979–1980 annual report: Television and student achievement.* © 1980 by California State Department of Education. Adapted with permission.

2. The inverse association between amount of television viewing and achievement increases as family socioeconomic status rises.
3. The inverse relationship between amount of television viewing and achievement is stronger at the 12th-grade than at the 6th-grade level.
4. For the lowest level of family socioeconomic status, the inverse relationship
   is sometimes barely observable, and occasionally there is a rise in achievement with greater viewing before the decline appears at the lower grade
   level.
5. The numbers in the highest viewing categories, where declines in achievement are sharpest, are sizable, with about 30% in both grades reporting
   that they watch 3 or more hours a day.

Although narrowly defined subgroups certainly might differ, few would argue
on the grounds of California deviance that data from such mammoth samples
would not apply to American children and teenagers generally. However, in this
instance the corroborating data are extraordinary in quantity and quality.

Keith et al. (1986) reported on the relationship between television viewing
and achievement scores equally weighted between mathematics and reading of
more than 28,000 seniors in the HSB data. B. Anderson et al. (1986) described
the relationship between viewing and reading among about 100,000 4th, 8th, and
11th graders in 30 states in the NAEP data. Neuman (1988) aggregated the
outcomes for viewing and reading, vocabulary, and study skills from eight state-
wide evaluations (California, Connecticut, Maine, Illinois, Michigan, Pennsylvania, Rhode Island, and Texas), using samples of 18,000 when the numbers were
in the hundred thousands (California and Michigan) to make the task feasible
on contemporary computers, with a representative, weighted total sample of about
173,6000. Gaddy (1986) examined the outcomes for viewing and reading, vocabulary, and mathematics for samples of about 2,400 and 5,000 from the HSB
data for students who were high school sophomores in 1982 and seniors in 1984.

In every instance, the CAP outcomes were confirmed. For example, the NAEP
data parallels the CAP pattern at all three grades for socioeconomic status, viewing, and reading (Table 6.1), whereas the HSB sophomore–senior panel does so
at both grade levels. The latter also provides direct evidence that the degree of
inverse association increases with household educational resources that would
be expected to be more frequent the higher the level of socioeconomic status,
such as number of books, having an encyclopedia, or subscribing to a newspaper
(Table 6.2). If the African-American samples are taken as surrogates for groups
of lower average socioeconomic status than their White counterparts, both the
NAEP and HSB data further confirm that the prominence of a negative association
increases with socioeconomic status—for it is less pronounced among African
Americans than among Whites.

A CAP follow-up (1988) indicates that the viewing-lower-achievement phenomenon is not confined to basic skills (Table 6.3). Data representing every

TABLE 6.1
Reading Proficiency (0–500) and TV Viewing
by Ethnicity and Parental Education

|  | Hours of TV viewing per day | | |
|---|---|---|---|
|  | 0–2 | 3–5 | 6 or more |
| Ethnicity |  |  |  |
| Grade 4 |  |  |  |
| White | 232 | 228 | 213 |
| Black | 200 | 201 | 190 |
| Hispanic | 208 | 204 | 193 |
| Grade 5 |  |  |  |
| White | 274 | 268 | 253 |
| Black | 246 | 248 | 236 |
| Hispanic | 249 | 249 | 238 |
| Grade 11 |  |  |  |
| White | 301 | 291 | 275 |
| Black | 272 | 267 | 262 |
| Hispanic | 277 | 268 | 254 |
| Parental education |  |  |  |
| Grade 4 |  |  |  |
| No high school diploma | 201 | 207 | 195 |
| High school graduate | 220 | 220 | 206 |
| Post High school | 237 | 231 | 210 |
| Grade 8 |  |  |  |
| No high school diploma | 247 | 252 | 236 |
| High school graduate | 262 | 259 | 246 |
| Post High school | 279 | 271 | 255 |
| Grade 11 |  |  |  |
| No high school diploma | 274 | 272 | 260 |
| High school graduate | 287 | 279 | 268 |
| Post High school | 305 | 295 | 279 |

From Anderson, B., Mead, N., & Sullivan, S. *Television: What do National Assessment results tell us?* © 1986 by Educational Testing Service. Adapted with permission.

student available for testing (more than a quarter of a million) in the eighth grade documents that amount of viewing was inversely associated with achievement in science, history, and social science, as well as in reading, writing, and mathematics.

There have been some claims of curvilinearity (Fetler, 1984; Neuman, 1988), with achievement rising and then falling as viewing increases. The 1980 CAP data, the largest and most comprehensive by grade and subject matter, give only the slightest hint of such a shape among the comparatively flat 6th-grade curves for those from households of the lowest socioeconomic status, although it is visible for those with limited fluency in English (Fig. 6.3). The 8th-grade curves for all five subjects similarly are essentially flat among those reporting viewing 2 or fewer hours a day. Fetler (1984), in his analysis of a sample of 10,000 6th

## TABLE 6.2
### Correlations Between Media Use and Achievement Variables[a]

| Achievement measure | All Students | | Blacks | | Females | |
|---|---|---|---|---|---|---|
| | Sophomore | Senior | Sophomore | Senior | Sophomore | Senior |
| | *n = 5074* | | *n = 2365* | | *n = 4997* | |
| Vocabulary | -.158 | -.176 | -.031 | -.023 | -.177 | -.186 |
| Reading | -.160 | -.155 | -.042 | -.011 | -.168 | -.160 |
| Math Level 1 | -.173 | -.188 | -.008 | -.011 | -.202 | -.196 |
| Math Level 2 | -.157 | -.169 | -.021 | -.030 | -.159 | -.176 |
| Grades | -.128 | -.127 | -.032 | .021 | -.146 | -.136 |

| | High resource | | Medium resource | | Low resource | |
|---|---|---|---|---|---|---|
| | Sophomore | Senior | Sophomore | Senior | Sophomore | Senior |
| | *n = 2974* | | *n = 3960* | | *n = 3112* | |
| Vocabulary | -.241 | -.220 | -.076 | -.121 | -.037 | -.094 |
| Reading | -.226 | -.174 | -.064 | -.089 | -.064 | -.086 |
| Math Level 1 | -.211 | -.204 | -.105 | -.122 | -.084 | -.109 |
| Math Level 2 | -.171 | -.175 | -.097 | -.110 | -.073 | -.113 |
| Grades | -.189 | -.148 | -.080 | -.089 | -.051 | -.074 |

[a]Smallest significant correlation (one-tailed alpha = .05, corrected for design effect) for all students is .032; for blacks, .047; for females, .032; for high-resource group, .042; medium-resource group, .036; and for low-resource group, .041. Calculated using Fisher's *r* to *Z* transformation.

*Note.* From G. D. Gaddy. Television's impact on high school achievement. *Public Opinion Quarterly, 50,* 340–359. © 1986 by American Association for Public Opinion Research. Adapted with permission.

TABLE 6.3

Television Viewing and Achievement in Five Areas (Eighth Grade)

| Amount of TV Viewing (Hours) | Percentage of Students | Percentage Correct Scores | | | | |
|---|---|---|---|---|---|---|
| | | Reading | Written Expression | Mathematics | History– Social Science | Science |
| 0 | 2 | 68.1 | 63.6 | 59.0 | 58.2 | 61.8 |
| 0–½ | 4 | 67.7 | 64.0 | 59.1 | 57.9 | 61.6 |
| ½–1 | 9 | 67.4 | 63.5 | 58.7 | 57.4 | 61.0 |
| 1–2 | 19 | 67.6 | 63.7 | 58.7 | 57.4 | 60.9 |
| 2–3 | 22 | 66.4 | 62.5 | 57.0 | 56.1 | 59.7 |
| 3–4 | 17 | 65.0 | 61.0 | 55.2 | 54.7 | 58.7 |
| 4–5 | 11 | 63.6 | 59.5 | 53.4 | 53.3 | 57.2 |
| 5+ | 17 | 58.3 | 54.6 | 48.8 | 49.3 | 53.7 |
| $N = 285{,}743$ | | | | | | |

Note. From California Assessment Program. *Annual report 1985–1986.* © 1986 by California State Department of Education. Adapted with permission.

graders in one of the CAP follow-ups again covering reading, writing, and mathematics, concluded there was some evidence of curvilinearity. Inspection of the data (Fig. 6.1) presented here suggests that any such trend is confined to the two lowest socioeconomic strata, and that otherwise, the shapes are either almost wholly or wholly downward. Potter (1987), among about 550 pupils in the 8th and 12th grades, found a threshold of about 10 hours of viewing per week before amount of viewing became negatively associated with a composite measure of varied scholastic achievement, and concluded that there might be some curvilinearity. Neuman (1988) concluded from her ESA aggregation that there was a comparable threshold. She also found in the eight-state pooled data a modest curvilinearity that was most visible at the intermediate, less so at the elementary, and not at all at the high school level, which essentially parallels the CAP data, where any such sign is confined to the earlier 6th grade (Fig. 6.4). Keith and colleagues (1986), in the very large HSB sample, found no evidence of curvilinearity for mathematics and reading achievement.

Thus, there is no case for universal curvilinearity, and none at the high school level. There is a good case at the intermediate level, and a fair one at the elementary level. It is also more likely to appear among those not fluent in English or from households lower in socioeconomic status. This pattern suggests

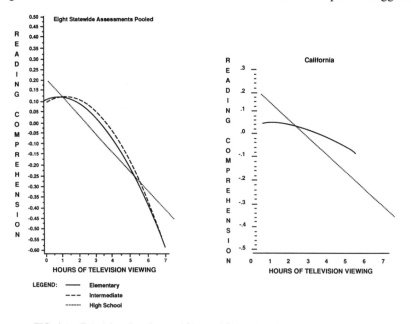

FIG. 6.4. Television, Reading, and Shape of Slope (Best Fit Regression Equation Lines). From S. B. Neuman. The displacement effect: Assessing the relation between television viewing and reading performance. *Reading Research Quarterly, 23*(4), 414–440. © 1988 by International Reading Association. Adapted with permission.

that for those younger or disadvantaged economically or linguistically, a little viewing may be a correlate of achievement. However, the important point is that except perhaps for those so disadvantaged, any curvilinearity at the intermediate and elementary levels is a quantitatively trivial anomaly (Fig. 6.4) in curves whose shapes are decidedly downward.

## TRAITS AND ABILITIES

Television viewing variously has been said to enhance or impede scholastic achievement. When the hypothesized effects are positive, such outcomes would mitigate any negative effects of viewing and might themselves be masked in the data just examined by whatever other than viewing is causally responsible for its inverse association with achievement. When the hypothesized effects are negative, they may also offer at least a partial explanation for the inverse association, although other factors also may be involved. Seven topics require discussion: cognitive skills, vocabulary, interests, impulse control, perceptual and spatial responses, imaginativeness, and creativity.

### Cognitive Skills

"Sesame Street" exemplifies the use of television to intervene developmentally in behalf of cognitive skills (Cook & Curtin, 1986). The model calls for the extensive use of research to produce programming that is both entertaining and educationally effective for preschool children between the ages of 2 and 5. It has had continuing national success in viewership and critical esteem since it was introduced in the United States more than 20 years ago, and has been "adopted and adapted" (Cook & Curtin, 1986) in numerous other countries (for example, "Plaza Sesamo" in Mexico). It teaches signs, numbers, and letters effectively, but is less effective at cognitive and reasoning skills, and although viewing such programs may leave children better prepared for the immediate tasks of initial school, there is no evidence that those who view regularly are better off in knowledge or skills in a later grade (Ball & Bogatz, 1970; Bogatz & Ball, 1971; Cook, Appleton, Conner, Shaffer, Tomkin, & Weber, 1975; Comstock, 1991a). This is hardly an indictment of "Sesame Street," for as Gerald Lesser (1974), the Harvard professor of education who had a major role in designing the series, wrote, "Sadly, we have not been able to show in any conclusive way that any program of early education has definite or lasting effects on children" (p. 15). However, it does mean that we must reject the hypothesis that the widespread viewing of this series—which is watched regularly by between 50% and 60% of the preschool target group—has increased scholastic achievement in later years.

## Vocabulary

Extensive early research on the effects of the introduction of television indicated that it increased the vocabulary of children and teenagers, but this increase was largely confined to the nomenclature of commercials, news, and entertainment (Schramm, Lyle, & Parker, 1961). The implication was that general vocabulary was not much benefited, although young people became newly familiar with names, phrases, and terms in which the medium specializes. This interpretation was compellingly confirmed in a three-community experiment in British Columbia (Williams, 1986) in which a community newly introduced to television was compared with two other communities, one with long-term access to a single Canadian channel and another with long-term access to several additional channels, including the American networks. Although before–after measures from the same persons (*longitudinal research*) and comparisons between those of the same age before and after (*cross-sectional analysis*) pointed to numerous effects of television, there was no hint that scores on a standardized measure of vocabulary were affected. This does not mean that the vocabularies of children and teenagers today are not larger than they were four or five decades ago as a result of the pervasiveness of the media, the proliferation of technological innovations, and widespread adoption of new or unfamiliar terminology. It means that the hypothesis that television viewing specifically has had the effect of increasing general vocabulary and thereby aids in achievement must be rejected, although it remains plausible that it teaches names, phrases, and terms special to it.

## Interests

It is contemporary folklore that television can incite public interest in various topics, and this is indeed so from art gallery openings, sporting events, works of literature, and popular writings to, historically speaking, the National Football League and the television-created holiday, Super Bowl Sunday (Comstock, 1991b; Comstock et al., 1978; Belson, 1959). However, persisting effects on interests pertinent to scholastic achievement are another matter. Himmelweit, Oppenheim, and Vince (1958), as part of an extensive examination of the effects of the introduction of television on children and teenagers in Great Britain, found scant evidence of any influence of the medium on participation in cultural or intellectual pursuits—visiting museums or art galleries; going to a concert, play, or ballet; discussing politics; reading books; or writing a play, poem, or story. In one instance, they interviewed young persons visiting a museum before and after a British Broadcasting Corporation report on a special exhibit, and found no difference in the number of visitors, only about 10% in the "after" period who had seen the program, and of those not all were there to see the featured exhibit. They note with disappointment, "Television stimulates interests, but only fleetingly" (p. 47). They acknowledge the perennially obvious, that young people sometimes seek out dramatized works. However, it is important to recognize this for a phenomenon largely confined to directionality of interests and experience rather than increasing the number of readers or the amount of reading done, because those so affected for the most part will be able readers alert for circumstances that would merit such activity. The hypothesis that television viewing to a widespread degree stimulates interests in a way that further scholastic achievement must be rejected.

## Impulse Control

Hornik (1981) has pooled a number of hypothesized outcomes of television that would adversely affect achievement—hyperactivity, reduced attention span, failure to control impulses, perseverance (Halpern, 1975; Swerdlow, 1981; Winn, 1977)—as an intolerance for the pace of schooling. Because the focus is the pace and not the schooling, *impulse control* seems the more appropriate common element.

One of the supposed villains among television's repertoire has been the fast pace of programs directed at or favored by children, which presumably would overstimulate them or leave them dissatisfied with the pace of ordinary events. However, D. Anderson, Levin, and Lorch (1977) found no difference in task performance among preschool children who saw "Sesame Street" episodes edited to be extremely slow or fast in pace. One investigator has reported that "Sesame Street" decreased perseverance compared to entertainment and nature films (Salomon, 1979), while several others have found that educational programming such as "Sesame Street" has beneficial effects compared to entertainment (Gadberry, 1980; Tower, D. Singer, J. Singer, & Biggs, 1979). The most consistent finding is that violent programming contributes to diminished impulse control among both preschool and elementary school-age children (Desmond, J. Singer, & D. Singer, 1990; Freidrich & Stein, 1975; Gadberry, 1980; J. Singer, D. Singer, Desmond, Hirsch, & Nichol, 1988; Stein & Friedrich, 1972). The positive findings mean that the hypothesis of a detrimental effect on impulse control cannot be rejected, with the evidence strongest for the violent programming that makes up so much of the schedule for both children's and more general audience programming.

## Perceptual and Spatial Responses

There has been speculation that television has improved children's perceptual and spatial skills because of the increased decoding of visual imagery required by viewing (Greenfield, 1984). In turn, such enhanced ability would contribute to scholastic achievement in some areas (art, drawing, geography, form recognition) while arguably compensating for deficits in other skills that might be attributable to television.

The evidence is fairly straightforward. The ability of children to recall details from a complex visual display (such as a painting by Brueghel), transform three-dimensional objects into two-dimensional plans, recognize an object from a different perspective, discern a figure in a pattern, order objects serially by some rule (such as size, height, or width), or identify an object seen from different perspectives as the same may be enhanced by exposure to television (Henderson & Rankin, 1986; Rovet, 1983; Salomon, 1974, 1979). However, the episodes for which such effects have been consistently demonstrated are essentially instructional videos that thoroughly and carefully demonstrate the particular visual process in question. The major exception is the report by Salomon (1979) that exposure to "Sesame Street" enhanced the ability to order pictures logically and discern an embedded figure, but again the stimulus was educational and not everyday entertainment, news, and sports programming. In the three-community British Columbia experiment, Williams (1986) and colleagues administered a standardized and widely accepted measure of spatial ability as part of a package measuring cognitive skills, and found no evidence that television increased such ability.

This pattern should not be surprising. Videos can be quite effective teachers when they are attended to, and especially when the skills involved benefit from visual presentation. Ordinary television, whether public or commercial, is hardly designed to be pedagogic in regard to visual and spatial skills, and any incidental contribution would occur early and quickly when its visual elements were novel to the preschool viewer. The hypothesis that ordinary television viewing has enhanced the visual and spatial abilities of the young must be rejected.

## Imaginativeness

It has been argued that television impedes elaboration and invention (J. Singer & D. Singer, 1981, 1983) by "visual images that are self-sufficient, occur at a predetermined pace, and are continuous" (Comstock, 1991a, p. 114). Reading and radio listening elicit more from the consumer, leading Greenfield and Beagles-Roos (1988) among others to speculate that historically "the growing importance of television means that children socialized by this medium may have more information but be less imaginative" (p. 88).

Again, the evidence is fairly straightforward. Television frequently provides depictions that serve as the basis for imaginative play (Alexander, Ryan, & Munoz, 1984; James & McCain, 1982; Lyle & Hofman, 1972; Reid & Frazer, 1980), although it may somewhat constrain its variety by offering the same examples to so many. The reported inverse correlations between imaginativeness and amount of television exposure are small (C. Peterson, J. Peterson, & Carroll, 1987; J. Singer, D. Singer, & Rapaczynski, 1984; Tucker, 1987), and ambiguous as to the direction of causality. Weigel and Jessor (1973) found that among teenagers conventionality of values and attitudes and viewing were positively correlated, but it would be quite plausible that less imaginative young people allocate somewhat more time to the medium, for viewing by definition is a conventional and unimaginative pursuit. In experiments it has been repeatedly found—for those ranging in age from preschool to adult—that recall of principal story elements is greater from television than radio (Barrow & Westley, 1959; Gunter, 1979, 1980; Hayes, Kelly, & Mandel, 1986; Siegel, 1973; Vig, 1980; Waite, 1976). This was in part the basis for the speculation of Greenfield and Beagles-Roos. Also, in experiments it has been found consistently among children in the first through the fourth grades that imaginativeness in completing partially told stories is greater for radio than television (Greenfield, Farrar, & Beagles-Roos, 1986; Greenfield & Beagles-Roos, 1988). Meanwhile, McIlwraith, Schallow, and Josephson (McIlwraith & Josephson, 1985; McIlwraith & Schallow, 1982–1983; Schallow & McIlwraith, 1986–1987) in a series of surveys typically found no associations, positive or negative, between amount of television viewing and constructive fantasizing, defined as "vivid" and "considered to be pleasant or useful."

As a trait, imaginativeness is quite stable and not open to influence from transient factors (Comstock, 1991a). The findings, then, suggest that media differ in the amount of imaginative activity they provoke but do not affect imaginative ability. The hypothesis that viewing suppresses achievement by reducing imaginative ability must be rejected.

## Creativity

Creativity is defined as "the ability to produce something new, such as a new idea . . . a new solution . . . a piece of art . . . painting . . . or . . . film, drama, music, or ballet" (p. 79) by the *Dictionary of Behavioral Science* (Wolman, 1989). As with imaginativeness, inverse correlations with television viewing have been reported (Peirce, 1983) but they are small and by the same rationale those less creative might be expected to allocate more time to television. Unlike imaginativeness, performance after exposure to radio and television stories on measures of *divergent thinking* (originality) and *idea fluency* (new ideas) did not differ among third- and sixth-grade children (Runco & Pedzek, 1984). In contrast, Watkins (1988) found that when asked to write stories about "real life" or for "television," young persons in the third through eighth grades wrote more complicated stories for television, and he concluded that the conventions of television storytelling influenced all the stories. This hardly suggests a negative contribution by television, except in the sense of narrowing options. On the other hand, Williams (1986) and colleagues in the three-community experiment in British Columbia found in both the cross-sectional and longitudinal analyses that the introduction of television reduced scores on a standard measure of divergent thinking, although it did not affect those for ideational fluency. However, more important, they found scant sign that amount of contemporary viewing was associated, positively or negatively, with either measure of creativity.

In summary, the introduction of the medium may have depressed performance on tests of divergent thinking, but there is no evidence that contemporary amount of viewing affects creativity. The hypothesis that viewing negatively affects achievement by interfering with creativity must be rejected.


## EXPLANATION

The examination of the varied hypotheses about the effects of television on achievement-related traits and abilities did not help in the explanation of the negative association between amount of viewing and achievement, except for eliminating some possibilities. There is no evidence that television contributes to such attributes on a widespread basis, and thus no reason to think that the negative associations mask a positive influence. The only evidence of a negative influence occurs for impulse control, and this surely is insufficient for the shape of the recorded associations—which are negatively more severe for those older, although one would expect impulse control to be more affected the younger the viewer.

The one instance in which the effects of television on achievement were examined on a large scale by experimental design, which means that causal interpretation would be justified if those receiving the television treatment declined in achievement, was the three-community British Columbia study. Williams (1986) and colleagues concluded that introduction of the medium into the site they call "Notel" (but which would have been better labeled "Nutel") decreased reading achievement between the 2nd–3rd and 8th–10th grades, but another analysis of the same data held that the data were inconclusive because there were as many contrary as there were supportive trends (Comstock, 1991b). The less direct approach of examining correlational studies that record associations but do not permit straightforward causal inference (Burton, Calonico, & McSeveney, 1979; Fetler, 1984; Gaddy, 1986; Keith et al., 1986; Morgan & Gross, 1980; Potter, 1987; Ridley-Johnson, Cooper, & Chance, 1983; Roberts, Bachen, Hornby, & Hernandez-Ramos, 1984; Walberg & Tsai, 1984–1985) for the extent to which negative associations survive the control (statistically) of other variables (representing alternatives to a causal link between viewing and achievement) "modestly but importantly support a causal interpretation" (Comstock, 1991a). This is because the associations survive in the largest samples, those where the most variables are controlled, and at all ages, and the specific study (Gaddy, 1986) sometimes cited as documenting that the association proves spurious when sufficient variables are controlled, in fact is so limited by its operationalizations of viewing and achievement that it does not address the question (Comstock, 1991a).

The remaining option, then, is to assemble from the available findings the most plausible picture possible of why there is a negative association. The result is a mock path analysis (Fig. 6.5). The one available path analysis (Keith et al., 1986) won't do because it includes too few variables. The paths, direction, and strength of association represent a subjective weighting of the sample sizes, quality of measure, and frequency of outcome across pertinent situations (Comstock, 1991a).

Background factors are paramount. Higher family socioeconomic status predicts (++) greater mental ability (IQ) on the part of a young person, a wider range of in-home educational resources represented in the model by print availability (++), and greater parental involvement (++) with schooling and other activity. Greater parental involvement, in turn, predicts greater amounts of time spent on homework (+) and on homework in conjunction with television viewing (+). Higher socioeconomic status also predicts lower centrality of television in the household (−−−), the degree to which it is used heavily, without rules, and is the mass medium relied upon almost exclusively. Mental ability predicts achievement (+++). It also predicts ability to read (+++), which is positively related to a favorable attitude toward learning (+) and negatively related to amount of viewing (−−). Availability of print and other resources is negatively (−) associated, while household centrality of television is positively (+++) associated with amount of viewing. Parental involvement is positively associated with both time spent on homework (+) and, because of this, time spent doing homework while watching television (+). Ability to read predicts achievement (++). So does a favorable attitude toward learning (++). Amount of viewing is a negative predictor of reading outside of assignments (−), which is a positive predictor (++) of achievement. Amount of viewing is a predictor of doing homework with television (+), which modestly assists achievement (+), and a negative predictor of time spent on homework (−), which is a strong predictor (+++) of achievement. Amount of viewing is negatively associated with instrumental viewing (−), which is marked by selective use of the medium and particularly with use of it for information. It is a positive predictor of ritualistic viewing (++), which is marked by heavier use of the medium, low use for information, and high use for light entertainment and action–adventure. Ritualistic viewing, in turn, probably neither helps nor hurts achievement (0), whereas instrumental modestly (+) helps.

Although it is not perhaps unambiguously clear visually, the model partitions the variance in lower achievement among nontelevision and television factors, with somewhat more assigned to the former than to the latter. The negative association in part is attributable to those of lesser ability and less-advantaged backgrounds watching more television. However, the data also support an independent, causal contribution by television. It occurs through the displacement of time spent acquiring the basic skills of reading, writing, and arithmetic during the early critical elementary school years (Williams, 1986) and through the displacement of time spent maintaining these skills. These are represented in the

118

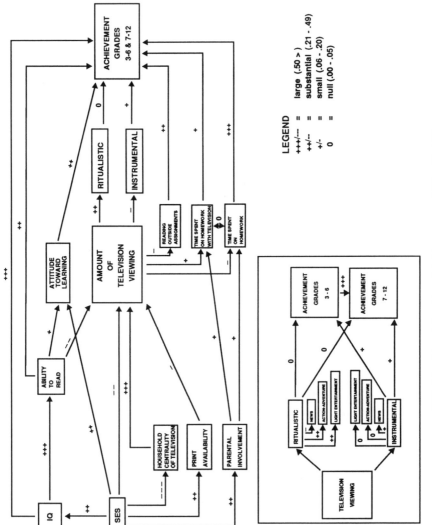

FIG. 6.5. Interrelationships of Achievement and Other Variables.

model by the negative association between amount of viewing and total home-work and reading outside of assignments. It also occurs through the lowering of the quality of study engaged in jointly with viewing. This is represented in the model by the positive association between amount of viewing and homework with television.

The greater the amount of viewing, the less likely it is that activities that promote achievement will be engaged in. At the same time, many of the predictors of greater viewing are also predictors of lower achievement. The data presented at the outset described the negative association between achievement and amount of viewing as greatest for those from the most advantaged backgrounds and those in the higher grades where scholastic demands are greater and positive for those with limited skills in English. This pattern is analogous to that found by Schramm et al. (1961) in their large-scale examination of the effects of the introduction of television on children and teenagers: Heavy viewing by the less bright was associated with higher achievement whereas heavy viewing by the mentally most able was associated with lower achievement. The most plausible explanation is that the role of television depends on what it displaces. When it brings to the child experiences, stimuli, and information equivalent or superior educationally to that in the environment, its effect is positive or null. When it fails to match the environment, its effect is negative. The greater emphasis on diversion in all forms of television—entertainment, news, sports—in American culture (and in most other cultures as well; Comstock, 1991b) ensures that as amount of viewing increases a negative effect on achievement becomes more likely.

## CONCLUSION

By the time they graduate from high school, children and teenagers typically will have spent more time with television than in the classroom (Fosarelli, 1986), although individuals vary widely in amount of viewing. Data from the past few years make it possible to address the implications of this phenomenon for scho-lastic achievement. Evidence extraordinary in quantity, quality, and consistency indicate that the two are negatively associated, with achievement declining as amount of viewing increases. This holds for all social strata and for all subjects, including subjects such as science and history and social studies, as well as the basic skills of reading, writing, and mathematics. The degree of negative asso-ciation increases with household socioeconomic status and is more pronounced in the higher grades where academic demands are greater. Examining support for hypothesized effects of television exposure on cognitive skills, vocabulary, interests, impulse control, perceptual and spatial responses, imaginativeness, and creativity offered little in the way of explanation. The correlational data repre-senting additional variables offered some support for a causal influence of viewing by the survival of the negative association when other variables were controlled (statistically) in the largest samples with greatest number of additional variables and for the full range of ages, because the control of these variables could have indicted the original negative association as spurious and attributable to the newly controlled variables. Based on data from a variety of sources, a mock path model is presented in which various background factors, such as socioeconomic status and mental ability, are shown to predict both achievement and greater viewing, so that in part the negative association is explained by those less likely to perform well viewing greater amounts of television. However, in addition, the data indicate that viewing has an independent, causal influence primarily through displacing time spent acquiring the basic skills and later maintaining them, and by diminishing the quality of time spent on homework when it is done in conjunction with viewing. It is proposed that the role of the former is somewhat greater than the latter, but that the evidence supports this dual process rather than one or the other alone. It is also proposed that the influence of television in this sphere depends on whether what it presents and what is selected for viewing is educationally superior or inferior to alternative experiences, and that the emphasis of American television on diversion makes certain a negative association between viewing and scholastic achievement.

## REFERENCES

Alexander, A., Ryan, M., & Munoz, P. (1984). Creating a learning context: Investigations on the interactions of siblings during television viewing. *Critical Studies in Mass Communication, 1*, 345–364.

Anderson, B., Mead, N., & Sullivan, S. (1986). *Television: What do National Assessment results tell us?* Princeton, NJ: Educational Testing Service.

Anderson, C., & McGuire, T. (1978). The effect of TV viewing on the educational performance of 13 elementary school children. *The Alberta Journal of Educational Research, 24*, 156–163.

Anderson, D. R., Levin, S., & Lorch, E. (1977). The effects of TV program pace on the behavior of preschool children. *AV Communication Review, 25*, 159–166.

Ball, S., & Bogatz, G. A. (1970). *The first year of "Sesame Street": An evaluation*. Princeton, NJ: Educational Testing Service.

Barrow, L. C., & Westley, B. H. (1959). Comparative teaching effectiveness of radio and television. *AV Communication Review*, entire.

Belson, W. A. (1959). Effects of television on the interests and initiative of adult viewers in Greater London. *British Journal of Psychology, 50*, 145–158.

Bogatz, G. A., & Ball, S. (1971). *The second year of "Sesame Street": A continuing evaluation* (Vols. 1 & 2). Princeton, NJ: Educational Testing Service.

Burton, S., Calonico, J., & McSeveney, D. (1979). Growing up with television: Effects of preschool television watching on first-grade children. *Journal of Communication, 30*, 164–170.

California Assessment Program. (1980). *Student achievement in California schools. 1979–1980 annual report: Television and student achievement*. Sacramento: California State Department of Education.

California Assessment Program. (1982). *Survey of sixth-grade school achievement and television viewing patterns*. Sacramento: California State Department of Education.

California Assessment Program. (1988). *Annual report, 1985–1986.* Sacramento: California State Department of Education.

Comstock, G. (1991a). *Television and the American child.* San Diego: Academic Press.

Comstock, G. (1991b). *Television in America* (2nd ed.). Newbury Park, CA: Sage.

Comstock, G., Chaffee, S., Katzman, N., McCombs, M., & Roberts, D. (1978). *Television and human behavior.* New York: Columbia University Press.

Cook, T. D., Appleton, H., Conner, R., Shaffer, A., Tamkin, G., & Weber, S. J. (1975). *"Sesame Street" revisited: A study in evaluation research.* New York: Russell Sage Foundation.

Cook, T. D., & Curtin, T. R. (1986). An evaluation of the models used to evaluate television series. In G. Comstock (Ed.), *Public communication and behavior* (Vol. 1, pp. 1–64). San Diego: Academic Press.

Desmond, R. J., Singer, J. L., & Singer, D. G. (1990). Family mediation: Parental communication patterns and the influences of television on children. In J. Bryant (Ed.), *Television and the American family* (pp. 293–310). Hillsdale, NJ: Lawrence Erlbaum Associates.

Fetler, M. (1984). Television viewing and school achievement. *Journal of Communication, 34,* 104–118.

Fosarelli, P. (1986). In my opinion . . . Advocacy for children's appropriate viewing of television: What can we do? *CHC, 15*(2), 79–80.

Freidrich, L., & Stein, A. H. (1975). Aggressive and prosocial television programs and the natural behavior of preschool children. *Monographs of the Society for Research in Child Development, 38*(4, Serial No. 151).

Gadberry, S. (1980). Effects of restricting first graders' TV viewing on leisure time use, IQ change, and cognitive style. *Journal of Applied Developmental Psychology, 1,* 161–176.

Gaddy, G. D. (1986). Television's impact on high school achievement. *Public Opinion Quarterly, 50,* 340–359.

Greenfield, P. (1984). *Mind and media: The effects of television, video games, and computers.* Cambridge, MA: Harvard University Press.

Greenfield, P., & Beagles-Roos, J. (1988). Television versus radio: The cognitive impact on different socioeconomic and ethnic groups. *Journal of Communication, 38*(2), 71–92.

Greenfield, P., Farrar, D., & Beagles-Roos, J. (1986). Is the medium the message?: An experimental comparison of the effects of radio and television on imagination. *Journal of Applied Developmental Psychology, 7,* 201–218.

Gunter, B. (1979). Recall of brief television news items. *Journal of Educational Television and Other Media, 5,* 57–61.

Gunter, B. (1980). Remembering television news: Effects of picture content. *Journal of General Psychology, 102,* 127–133.

Halpern, W. (1975). Turned-on toddlers. *Journal of Communication, 25*(4), 66–70.

Hayes, D. S., Kelly, S. B., & Mandel, M. (1986). Media differences in children's story synopses: Radio and television contrasted. *Journal of Educational Psychology, 78,* 341–347.

Henderson, R. W., & Rankin, R. J. (1986). Preschooler's viewing of instructional television. *Journal of Educational Psychology, 78,* 44–51.

Himmelweit, H., Oppenheim, A. N., & Vince, P. (1958). *Television and the child.* London: Oxford University Press.

Hornik, R. (1981). Out-of-school television and schooling: Hypotheses and methods. *Review of Educational Research, 51*(2), 193–214.

James, N. C., & McCain, T. A. (1982). Television games preschool children play: Patterns, themes and uses. *Journal of Broadcasting, 26*(4), 783–800.

Keith, T. Z., Reimers, T. M., Fehrman, P. G., Pottebaum, S. M., & Aubey, L. W. (1986). Parental involvement, homework, and TV time: Direct and indirect effects on high school achievement. *Journal of Educational Psychology, 78*(5), 373–380.

Lesser, G. S. (1974). *Children and television: Lessons from "Sesame Street."* New York: Random House.

Lyle, J., & Hoffman, H. R. (1972). Children's use of television and other media. In E. A. Rubinstein, G. A. Comstock, & J. P. Murray (Eds.), *Television and social behavior: Vol. 4, Television in day-to-day life: Patterns of use* (pp. 257–273). Washington, DC: U.S. Government Printing Office.

McIlwraith, R. D., & Josephson, W. L. (1985). Movies, books, music, and adult fantasy life. *Journal of Communication, 35*(2), 167–179.

McIlwraith, R. D., & Schallow, J. (1982–1983). Adult fantasy life and patterns of media use. *Journal of Communication, 33*(1), 78–91.

Morgan, M., & Gross, L. (1980). Television viewing, IQ, and academic achievement. *Journal of Broadcasting, 24,* 117–133.

Neuman, S. (1988). The displacement effect: Assessing the relation between television viewing and reading performance. *Reading Research Quarterly, 23*(4), 414–440.

Peirce, K. (1983). Relation between time spent viewing television and children's writing skills. *Journalism Quarterly, 60,* 445–448.

Peterson, C. C., Peterson, J. L., & Carroll, J. (1987). Television viewing and imaginative problem solving during preadolescence. *The Journal of Genetic Psychology, 147*(1), 61–67.

Potter, W. J. (1987). Does television viewing hinder academic achievement among adolescents? *Human Communication Research, 14*(1), 27–46.

Reid, L. N., & Frazer, C. F. (1980). Children's use of television commercials to initiate social interaction in family viewing situations. *Journal of Broadcasting, 24*(2), 149–158.

Ridley-Johnson, R., Cooper, H., & Chance, J. (1983). The relation of children's television viewing to school achievement and IQ. *Journal of Educational Research, 76,* 294–297.

Roberts, D. F., Bachen, C. M., Hornby, M. C., & Hernandez-Ramos, P. (1984). Reading and television: Predictors of reading achievement at different age levels. *Communication Research, 11*(1), 9–49.

Rovet, J. (1983). The education of spatial transformations. In D. R. Olson, & E. Bialystok (Eds.), *Spatial cognition: The structures and development of mental representations of spatial relations* (pp. 164–181). Hillsdale, NJ: Lawrence Erlbaum Associates.

Runco, M., & Pezdek, K. (1984). The effect of television and radio on children's creativity. *Human Communication Research, 11,* 109–120.

Salomon, G. (1974). Internalization of filmic schematic operations in interaction with learner's aptitudes. *Journal of Educational Psychology, 66*(4), 499–511.

Salomon, G. (1979). *Interaction of media, cognition, and learning.* San Francisco: Jossey-Bass.

Schallow, J. R., & McIlwraith, R. D. (1986–1987). Is television viewing really bad for your imagination? Content and process of TV viewing and imaginal styles. *Imagination, Cognition, and Personality, 6*(1), 25–42.

Schramm, W., Lyle, J., & Parker, E. B. (1961). *Television in the lives of our children.* Stanford, CA: Stanford University Press.

Siegel, H. (1973). McLuhan, mass media, and education. *Journal of Experimental Education, 41,* 68–70.

Singer, J. L., & Singer, D. G. (1981). *Television, imagination, and aggression: A study of preschoolers.* Hillsdale, NJ: Lawrence Erlbaum Associates.

Singer, J. L., & Singer, D. G. (1983). Psychologists look at television: Cognitive, developmental, personality, and social-policy implications. *American Psychologist, 38,* 826–834.

Singer, J. L., Singer, D. G., Desmond, R., Hirsch, B., & Nichol, A. (1988). Family mediation and children's cognition, aggression, and comprehension of television: A longitudinal study. *Journal of Applied Developmental Psychology, 9,* 329–347.

Singer, J. L., Singer, D. G., & Rapaczynski, W. S. (1984). Family patterns and television viewing as predictors of children's beliefs and aggression. *Journal of Communication, 34*(2), 73–89.

Stein, A. H., & Friedrich, L. K. (1972). Television content and young children's behavior. In J. P. Murray, E. A. Rubinstein, & G. A. Comstock (Eds.), *Television and social behavior: Vol. 2. Television and social learning* (pp. 202–317). Washington, DC: U.S. Government Printing Office.

Swerdlow, J. (1981). What is television doing to real people? *Today's Education, 70,* 50–57.

Tower, R., Singer, D., Singer, J., & Biggs, A. (1979). Differential effects of television programming on preschoolers' cognition, imagination and social play. *American Journal of Orthopsychiatry, 49*, 265–281.

Tucker, L. A. (1987). Television, teenagers, and health. *Journal of Youth and Adolescence, 16*(5), 415–425.

Vig, S. R. (1980). The role of visual elements in the learning of television news by adolescents. *Dissertation Abstracts International, 40*(5-B), 1957–1958.

Waite, C. H. (1976). The effects of pictorial, audio, and print television news messages on undergraduate students as measured by output, recall, error, and equivocation. *Dissertation Abstracts International, 36*(8-A), 4833.

Walberg, H. J., & Tsai, S. (1984–1985). Correlates of reading achievement and attitude: A national assessment study. *Journal of Educational Research, 78*(3), 159–167.

Watkins, B. (1988). Children's representations of television and real-life stories. *Communication Research, 15*(2), 159–184.

Weigel, R. H., & Jessor, R. (1973). Television and adolescent conventionality: An exploratory study. *Public Opinion Quarterly, 37*(1), 76–90.

Williams, T. M. (Ed.). (1986). *The impact of television: A natural experiment in three communities.* New York: Academic Press.

Winn, M. (1977). *The plug-in drug.* New York: Viking.

Wolman, B. B. (1989). *Dictionary of behavioral science.* New York: Academic Press.

# Part II

# LITERACY LEARNING

# Chapter 7

# Rembrandt at the Sixteenth Chapel: Demystifying Language Acquisition

Naomi S. Baron
*The American University*

## CRACKING THE LANGUAGE CODE

Recently I had some painting done in my house. While the crew seemed willing enough, they turned out to be less than the professionals I thought I had hired. One afternoon I came home to find the lead painter standing back and admiring the ceiling he had just completed. The man, who was in his 30s, was wearing a tee shirt from the local community college he had attended. Always eager to display his knowledge, he mused, "I feel like Rembrandt at the Sixteenth Chapel."

After a long, puzzling moment, I finally conjured up the intended image of Michelangelo painstakingly covering the ceiling of the Sistine Chapel at the Vatican. My first thought: A little learning is a dangerous thing. But my second was how the pronouncement of this would-be savant epitomized the process by which language users try to make sense—to crack the code—of language they don't understand.

Children learning their native tongue spend their earliest years working intently to crack the language code. With time, in literate societies, they expand their cryptographic horizons from spoken language to include reading and writing as well. As we will see, the challenges (and the strategies) for making sense of language continue into our adult lives.

How do children manage, in just half a dozen years, to make such remarkable headway, having entered a world whose linguistic codes are so radically unintelligible? In this chapter, we will begin to demystify the process. Before we begin, though, we need some background.

## Major Theories of Language Acquisition

Since the 1950s, linguists, psychologists, and students of child development have proposed three basic models of how young children learn to talk. The first model, building on the ideas of earlier behavioral psychologists, was articulated by B. F. Skinner (1957), who argued that children learn language through a process of stimulus, response, and reward. The child sees a cat (stimulus), says "cat" (response), and is praised by the approving parent for uttering the correct name. Underlying the Skinnerian model are a number of important assumptions about the acquisition process, including:

1. Human language acquisition differs little from acquisition of trained behaviors in other species (e.g., parrots learning to talk, rats learning to run mazes).
2. Children imitate a lot of adult speech, and these imitations are a critical component of language learning.
3. Adults correct their children's mistakes (and children learn through these corrections).
4. Much of the language children use is formulaic (rather than directly "created" by the children themselves).

The second model, proposed by linguist Noam Chomsky (1959, 1965), looks upon children not as trainable animals but as problem-solving, miniature grammarians. The task at hand is so difficult, says Chomsky, that success cannot be explained through external modeling. The only reasonable explanation for how language is learned (so the argument continues) is that children are already born, innately endowed, with the rudiments of human language structure. Among the presuppositions underlying the Chomskian perspective are these:

1. Language learning by (human) children is unique in the animal kingdom.
2. Children engage in little if any imitation of the language of others.
3. Adult attempts to correct children's errors do not facilitate language development, and few such attempts are made anyway.
4. Most of children's utterances are novel, not formulaic.

The third model reflects the perspectives of sociolinguists and specialists in child development who focus on adult–child interaction (see, e.g., Bruner, 1975, 1983; Gleason, 1993; Gleason & Weintraub, 1978; Nelson, 1973). The sociolinguistic model sees language acquisition as a mix of essential biological predispositions—chimps, after all, don't really learn human language (see, e.g., Terrace, 1979)—and a strong guiding influence from the social community. Among the presuppositions of the sociolinguistic model are these:

1. Whereas language learning in human children is unique (given our biological inheritance), the process of acquiring actual sounds, words, sentences, and conversational skills is highly influenced by the language—and people—surrounding growing children.
2. Language acquisition is a combination of creativity and imitation.
3. Adults do correct children's linguistic mistakes, and children do learn in the process.
4. Language learning grows out of children's needs for communication in a social context. Social contexts provide a scaffolding upon which to hang specific linguistic structures.

All three of these models attempt to explain the mechanisms by which children manage to crack the language code. The Chomskian model invokes innatism, the Skinnerian model begins with trial and error, and the sociolinguistic model focuses on parent–child interaction.

Over the past 20 years, I have wrestled with these models, finding useful (or at least provocative) threads in all three, but still being left with some basic questions:

1. *Why* do children put forth the enormous effort necessary to crack the language code?
2. *How* do children actually *do* it?
3. Do they all do it the same way?
4. Are the mechanisms and strategies children learn in mastering spoken language related to other language puzzles (including literacy, second-language acquisition, and cognitive/linguistic challenges later in life)?

In my attempts to grapple with these lingering questions, I have constructed a simple schema in terms of which to think about language acquisition (see Baron, 1992, for a more detailed analysis of the issues). Although the schema draws heavily upon the sociolinguistic model, it goes beyond that model in trying to resolve my concerns.

## A Schema for Language Acquisition

To understand how and why children learn language, we begin with four basic observations:

1. Language learning is functional and social.
2. Language learning is explicable (demystifiable).
3. Language learning is variable.
4. Language learning is coherent.

Let's look at each of these in turn.

*Language Learning is Functional and Social.*  Growing children need to make sense of the conversational stream into which they are born. The reasons are twofold: to satisfy their material needs—procuring a bottle, not a diaper, or vice versa (*functional needs*) and to establish and maintain social rapport (*social needs*). The material drive is intuitively obvious. The social pressure to crack the code is less so.

Children learn to talk for much the same reason that adults chat with their dogs, strangers strike up conversations on long-distance trips, and foreigners persist in addressing one another in mutually unintelligible tongues. This motivation is the *conversational imperative.* By virtue of the conversational imperative, we tend (at least in the United States) to talk when in the presence of other sentient beings, regardless of whether we make ourselves understood. Our impetus for conversation may be a desire for social companionship, the practical need to convey information, or both.

One favorite example of the conversational imperative at work in children comes from a 4-year-old English-speaking boy, Alex, who found himself briefly hospitalized in French-speaking Canada. Knowing only a few words of French (including that he was a *petit garçon*) and recognizing quickly that the other children in his room understood no English, Alex hit upon a clever strategy. Sitting up in bed and turning to address the 5-year-old girl on his right, he articulately inquired, "Aga doodoo bubu *petit garçon?*"

Alex's *petit garçon* got a rise from his would-be playmate, so he continued: "Mugu gugu wugu *petit garçon?*" Throughout his stay in Canada, a string of babbling ending in *petit garçon* became Alex's method of "conversing in French."

Adults sometimes engage in equally ingenious behavior, also driven by the conversational imperative. The anthropological linguist Kenneth Pike regularly begins speaking Quechua with informants whose language he is trying to decipher, simply to maintain some semblance of "conversational" normalcy with a person whose language he does not understand. And adults learning a third language report anecdotally that they sometimes fall back upon their second language when they feel at a loss for words in their new tongue.

*Language Learning is Explicable (Demystifiable).*  If the conversational imperative is the critical force behind cracking the language code, the most important mechanism for doing so is *language orienteering.* Through language orienteering, children actively construct strategies (the way pioneers construct pathways) for making sense of the language stream around them. In the next section, we will look at language orienteering in some detail.

By recognizing and understanding the role of language orienteering in language learning, we free ourselves from having to rely, like the Chomskyites, on innatism as a fallback explanation for how children learn language. We also avoid the Skinnerian position, which unrealistically roots most learning in trial and error coupled with adult rewards. In a word, understanding language orienteering enables us to demystify the language-acquisition process.

*Language Learning is Variable.* Do children all learn language the same way? While admitting some variance in the speed with which children pass through developmental stages, acquisition theorists during the 1960s and 1970s clearly implied that all children follow the same basic path (see, e.g., Brown, 1973; Slobin, 1973). We now recognize—aided by the observations of more socially oriented psychologists and linguists (e.g., Goldfield & Snow, 1989; Nelson, 1973; Wells, 1986) as well as by commonsensical parents—that children vary considerably in both the rate and style of their early language acquisition. Such factors as the child's sex, birth order, and personality, along with parental age and level of education, help explain much of the natural variation that occurs in children's linguistic odysseys.

*Language Learning is Coherent.* Finally, language learning is a coherent process. Most acquisition strategies are not limited to a single age group, a specific language, or even a particular channel of linguistic expression. Rather, language orienteerers of all ilk use remarkably similar approaches in working to break the language code.

Examples from a range of language-decipherment contexts illustrate the similarities in strategies, particularly when the strategizer doesn't know the "correct" language form:

### Across Ages (Child, Adult)

*Child:* A 6-year-old boy, explaining to his father why he was carrying a water pitcher outside, commented,
"Mama wants it brungen out."

*Adult:* A customer in a Rand-McNally store came in requesting
"a globe of Texas."
And my erstwhile painter likened himself to
"Rembrandt at the Sixteenth Chapel."

### Across Languages (First, Second Language)

*First Language:* A 7-year-old, complaining that his mother was taking too long combing his hair, mumbled,
"All that will do is just dawdle us."

*Second Language:* The menu in a small restaurant in Athens listed the speciality of the house:
"lamp shops."

Although rarely yielding such humorous examples, the strategies learners use in deciphering spoken and written language also have strong similarities:

### Across Modalities (Spoken, Written)

*Spoken Language:*   Children (or foreigners) need to memorize the routines used in American telephone conversations (e.g., who says hello first, how to take turns, how to terminate the conversation).

*Written Language:*   As we learn to decipher print, we also need to master the "routines" of books (e.g., in English, as opposed to Hebrew, we read from front to back; in English, as opposed to French, the table of contents appears in the beginning rather than the end).

Using this four-part schema for language acquisition as a backdrop, we now direct our focus to language orienteering—the major strategy children use to crack the language code. In the next section, we look at orienteering in early spoken-language acquisition; in the following section, we turn to orienteering during the early stages of literacy. The final section considers the question of variation in children with respect to orienteering strategies.

## LANGUAGE ORIENTEERING:
## THE SPOKEN LANGUAGE

In the sport of orienteering, adventurers set out into the woods (armed with some basic tools, e.g., matches, an initial food supply) to fend for themselves and find their way to an appointed spot. No path is inherently right or wrong. Participants may reach dead ends, go hungry, or become frustrated. Individual paths share many similarities. But in the end, each forager charts a unique path.

Language acquisition is fundamentally language orienteering. Each participant sets out with an essential tool: a genetic endowment for language learning. The natural environment through which learners blaze a trail is the social community. The goal is to join the group as a full-fledged member—to become linguistically *saturated*, that is, to reach a plateau in learning when adult members of the language community no longer find need to correct what you say.

To get a sense of the orienteering process in children, consider how Sara, Ryan, and Alex (each a composite of children I have observed) struggle to talk about notions of similarity or comparison. These notions can be expressed in English through such phrases as:

*Similarity*
    These two things are *like* each other.
    These two things are *similar to* each other.
    These two things are *the same as* each other.

*Comparison*
> This thing is *bigger than* that thing.
> This thing is *as big as* that thing.

For a young child, the concepts of likeness and comparison may be clear long before the grammar falls into line. Alex (age 4) struggled with the linguistic markers for over a year, coming out with questions such as:

> "Are these two like the same?"

Sara (also age 4), standing on a chair and beaming across the room at her mother, declared,

> "I'll be so big than you."

Ryan (age 4 as well), in a foot race with his older sister, called out,

> "I can run so faster than you!"

Labeling Alex or Sara or Ryan's syntax *wrong* assumes a model of language acquisition in which a priori rules of comparison exist that none of the children has yet mastered. To say, alternatively, that Alex, Sara, or Ryan consistently constructs independent grammatical rules of comparison (later to be replaced by normative adult versions) reads too much into many such utterances. A number of children's novel words and grammatical attempts are as ephemeral as this afternoon's playdough construction. Children use the material at hand to fashion an edifice that satisfies their immediate interests and needs. When they are done, they mush the raw materials back into the can so a new sculpture can be created the next time.

Language-orienteering strategies run the gamut from stable rules to playdough. The spectrum is divisible into *analogies, scissors-and-paste*, and *potshots*.

## Orienteering in Spoken Language:
## Analogies, Scissors-and-Paste, Potshots

*Analogies in Spoken Language.*  Children striving for grammatical saturation seek out regularity. Learners' success at identifying regularity and making analogies with similar constructions in their repertoires generally goes unheralded (e.g., 3-year-old Sara correctly using *pans* as the plural of *pan*). Yet when Sara speaks of "two *mans*," we delight in her creative use of analogy (or, depending upon your linguistic model, of an *overgeneralization* or *rule*).

What do children's analogies look like? Ryan's aunt had sent him a splendid Mickey Mouse tee shirt. William, Ryan's best friend, already sported the same model. When their nursery-school teacher commented on their shared couture, Ryan (age 3;6) responded,

> "I'll wear mine, and William is going to wear hims."
> (By analogy, *her : hers = him : hims*)

What do we know about children's analogies? First, grammatical analogies by young language learners represent thoughtful attempts to forge language enabling them to communicate. Some of the analogies (e.g., *boy : boys = pan : pans*) yield grammatical results and others don't, although the working principles behind both are the same. Second, children's grammatical analogies have staying power. The same child who worked out:

> "William is going to wear hims."

articulated *hims* for several months before the possessive finally yielded to *his*. And third, grammatical analogies in which children have a "stake" (i.e., in the creation and use of which they have exerted effort) are generally resistant to adult correction. When Ryan's teacher pursued Ryan's malapropism with

> "Oh, so William is going to wear *his*?"

Ryan confirmed,

> "That's right, William will wear hims!"

*Scissors-and-Paste in Spoken Language.*    The second language-orienteering strategy is scissors-and-paste. Like analogies, scissors-and-paste strategies reveal principled attempts at language. Yet scissors-and-paste strategies are not direct analogues of grammatical constructions. Rather, they are intelligent attempts to cut and paste together words and phrases to express meanings, when the child does not yet have a grasp of the conventional adult grammar.

A query from 3-year-old Sara:

> "Why you don't like my chooses?"

illustrates the strategy. Not yet knowing how to form *wh-* questions in English (i.e., that following the question word, an auxiliary verb—here, *do*—must be inserted before the subject, yielding "Why don't you like my chooses?"), Sara concocted her own reasonable principle: Stick the *wh-* word (*Why*) in front of the declarative sentence ("You don't like my chooses"). As Klima and Bellugi (1966) showed long ago, many children pass through this stage in the formation of questions, and the innovation is easily describable through transformational-style rules (i.e., S $\Rightarrow$ Q + Sentence Nucleus).

Yet a large number of children's scissors-and-paste creations would require curious ad hoc rules to describe the idiosyncratic regularities that individual children come up with. What is more, such "Rube Goldberg rules" camouflage the active process of children groping with language constructions. Consider a request from Sara at age 3;2:

> "Would-you-please don't do that?"
> (pasting together the memorized phrase "Would-you-please"
> with the request "Don't do that")

or her query at age 3;6:

> "Where is it can be?"
> (a melange of "Where is it" and "Where can it be?")

In each case, Sara's "gluing" strategy is essentially the same. The importance of this simple principle is lost if we preoccupy ourselves with devising rules for each grammatical neologism.

Because scissors-and-paste constructions are never direct copies of grammatical utterances, these neologisms are never grammatically correct. However, because, like analogies, they result from concerted effort, scissors-and-paste constructions also have longevity (a few days, weeks, or longer). And as constructions in which the child has some "stake," scissors-and-paste utterances are, like analogies, generally resistant to adult correction.

***Potshots in Spoken Language.*** Potshots are ungrammatical, one-time attempts to construct language on the fly. The conversational imperative to take part in the language duet yields such grammatical hodge podges as:

> "Are you still have any of these candies before?"
> (said by a 4-year-old to a friend, upon encountering a strangely shaped piece of candy)
>
> "Wait *until* [ = for] me!" (Sara at 3;6)
>
> "Where *were* [ = have] we been?" (Alex at 3;8)

Potshots are evanescent—especially the longer ones. Describing them with formal rules is inappropriate, yet dismissing them ignores a vital process by which children bootstrap their way into linguistic competence. Because children have no "stake" in these utterances, potshots are likely candidates for successful parental correction.

## LANGUAGE ORIENTEERING:
## THE WRITTEN LANGUAGE

As we watch infants become toddlers and preschoolers, it is clear that orienteering through spoken language is a gradual process. Careful observers can actually see it happen, like a flower unfolding in slow-motion time-lapse photography.

But what about the acquisition of literacy skills? The popular lore—and pedagogy—that many of us grew up with suggested that children (in literate societies) remain blissfully nonliterate until age 5 or 6, at which time adults immerse them in basal readers and penmanship drills, and the new generation suddenly becomes literate.

These days, we know better. Just as spoken-language skills gradually emerge from the continuing communication efforts of parents and children, we now speak of *emergent literacy* (e.g., Teale & Sulzby, 1986) as the multiyear process by which children become "saturated" in written language.

Acquiring literacy in any language is hard work, but in a language such as English, whose orthographic system is hardly user-friendly, the challenges are particularly acute. At the same time, of course, the opportunities for orienteering abound.

### Written Orienteering: Analogies, Scissors-and-Paste, Potshots

*Analogies in Written Language.* The English spelling system is the patchwork product of military conquests, friendly borrowings, historical sound shifts, and prescriptive normalization. Since young learners are not privy to all this language history, they rely heavily upon logical strategies in reading and spelling until such time as we adults drill them into memorizing all the exceptions.

In reading, for example, consider the challenge a 5-year-old has upon encountering the word *put*. Logic—analogy—says it might be pronounced *putt* (as in "putt-putt golf," rhyming with *cut*). Why, indeed, should it rhyme with *foot*? And so children who can pronounce *put* perfectly well in speech sometimes end up reading it as *putt*.

A similar orthographic dilemma afflicts children learning to write, and analogy is again a reasonable orienteering response. Consider the words *speech* and *speak*. Since the vowels are pronounced the same way, many a child reasons, by analogy, that they should be spelled (written) the same way. Hence, we find *s-p-e-a-c-h* or *s-p-e-e-k*.

As I tell my 8-year-old son, English spelling isn't fair.

*Scissors-and-Paste in Written Language.* Newcomers to literacy sometimes piece together strategies that (nearly) inevitably yield incorrect results. In reading, a good example is the rule of thumb that one kindergartner adopted for dealing with words beginning with the letters *th-*. Continually having problems in reading such words as *they, the, them,* and *thank,* he sensibly decided to simplify the task: Pronounce them all *they,* regardless of the ending of the word or what part of speech the sentence called for.

In early writing, many children initially write words using only consonants. *Walk* becomes *w-l-k, come* turns into *c-m,* and so on. Experts in literacy (and, following their lead, classroom teachers) wax eloquent about the importance of encouraging this kind of "magic spelling" in children just learning writing. Whatever the merits of fostering such independence, we should at least be aware that children's orthographic omissions (and commissions) are generally driven by cogent scissors-and-paste strategies. Given the relatively close match between consonantal sounds and letters (exceptions like *k, c,* and *s* and *t* notwithstanding), children quite reasonably give an honest stab at representing the consonants in a word. As for the omitted vowels? It's not that 5-, 6-, or 7-year-olds are unaware that words have vowels as well. Rather, using the commonsense strategy "when in doubt, leave it out," such children paste together the consonantal frame with . . . nothing.

***Potshots in Written Language.***   Finally, just as with spoken language, young readers and writers sometimes resort to out-and-out potshots. A good example in reading is picking out a few letters in a difficult word and then guessing at the rest, rather than troubling to sound out the word phonetically. Interestingly, the words children come up with are oftentimes more complex than the target words written before them. I have, for example, heard 6- and 7-year-olds offer the following renditions:

> *manages* read as *manipulates*
> *secret* as *secluded*

and

> *nicely* as *necessarily.*

What makes these renderings potshots? The next time the same children encountered the same words, the words came out as *miniscule, secondly,* and *nevertheless,* respectively.

What about potshots in writing? Here, too, children new to literacy often grab at what first comes to mind, rather than thinking through the letter they really are looking for. Confusions between visually similar letters such as *p, b,* and *d* are common (in both reading and writing). Children write *pan* as *b-a-n* (and read *pot* as *d-o-t*). Whereas developmental experts speak of children not yet being "ready" to make the distinctions between these letters, we can reasonably ask wherein does their unreadiness lie? For many children, the answer is not in being able to distinguish the letters, but rather in having the patience each and every time to attend carefully to individual letters and not jump to snap conclusions.

## ORIENTEERING AND VARIATION

If language orienteering is the major strategy by which children decipher the spoken—and written—language code, we might reasonably expect all language learners to be active language orienteerers. But is this so?

The traditional language-acquisition literature implies the answer is "yes." Researchers and commentators have long spoken of toddlers' and preschoolers' *overgeneralizations* of morphology (e.g., *hims* instead of *his*; *brungen* instead of *brought*; *sheeps* instead of *sheep*) as an inevitable stage in language development. (Recall that in our schema, overgeneralizations are equivalent to analogies.) But *do* all children actually overgeneralize, much less use scissors-and-paste strategies or potshots?

Previously, we observed that language learning is variable—that children differ not only in their rate but also in their style of early acquisition. In introducing the notion of language orienteering, we described orienteering as a highly individual venture. And so it is, for not all children are linguistic innovators.

Consider children who are late talkers—a group often composed of shy children, second-born children, and, more often than not, boys. Late talkers are frequently prone to imitate language they hear from others rather than coming up with novel constructions of their own. As a 3-year-old, Alex was more likely to imitate the speech of adults and other children around him than to create his own multiword utterances. Oftentimes, such imitations provide a linguistic stepping-stone for launching into independent constructions later on.

Many children who are initially shy or linguistically cautious reach a takeoff point between ages 3 and 4, when they cease being heavy imitators and begin launching into analogies and scissors-and-paste strategies (along with potshots). Yet some cautious starters never reach takeoff in orienteering.

Why?

Continuing shyness may be the explanation. Lack of such creativity may also be a sign of slow (though normal) language development. And with yet other children, the problem is a genuine developmental language disorder.

In his landmark study of language acquisition, Roger Brown (1973) and his colleagues at Harvard University described the syntactic and morphological development of three children, code-named Adam, Eve, and Sarah. Although Adam and Eve commonly coined analogies in their uses of past tense and plural (*goed* for *went, mans* for *men*), Sarah—who was the slowest to learn grammar—did not.

Curiously, I had once before encountered children who failed to try out such basic orienteering. As a graduate student, I had done a close grammatical analysis of the spontaneous productions of a group of 4-, 5-, and 6-year-old children with specific language impairment. (Though physically, intellectually, and emotionally normal, they were abnormally slow in their language development.) Although these children sometimes had appreciable vocabularies and did combine words into phrases and sentences, none of them ever produced a morphological overgeneralization.

Subsequent study of children with specific language impairment may well show that these children represent one end of an acquisition spectrum, with highly adventuresome orienteerers at the other end. Brown's Sarah, for example, was not language-impaired. She was simply linguistically conservative. Students of second-language acquisition (e.g., Ehrman & Oxford, 1989) report similar variation in strategies (and perhaps aptitudes) for learning a second language. Some learners won't utter a word or phrase unless they can say it correctly, while others bound ahead as second-language orienteerers, coming up with the same sorts of analogies, scissors-and-paste constructions, and potshots we see in many—but not all—children.

At my son's school, *tae kwon do* is offered in the after-school program. In addition to teaching his students how to punch, kick, and block, the instructor works to instill mental and spiritual qualities as well. At each session, the children are taught about the four tenets of this style of *tae kwon do*: integrity, self-control, perseverance, and indomitable spirit.

Several times a year, belt tests are held. The students are put through their paces in performing their *kata* (forms) and, for the older children, sparring. But the children are also examined on their understanding of the tenets of the sport.

During my son's yellow-belt test, three other students were also being tested. Each of the four candidates was asked to identify one of the four tenets. The first one came up with "integrity." The next two children remembered "self-control" and "perseverance." When it came time for the fourth child—a slightly nervous 9-year-old—there was a silence. Gently, the instructor asked once more for the last tenet. After staring down at his still-white belt, the child ventured, "abdominable spirit?"

Children have an abdominable spirit to develop communication skills—in understanding and speaking, reading and writing. Our responsibility as adults is to offer rich linguistic models and to nourish children's attempts to crack the language code.

# REFERENCES

Baron, N. S. (1992). *Growing up with language.* Reading, MA: Addison-Wesley.

Brown, R. (1973). *A first language.* Cambridge, MA: Harvard University Press.

Bruner, J. (1975). The ontogenesis of speech acts. *Journal of Child Language, 2,* 1–19.

Bruner, J. (1983). *Child's talk.* New York: Norton.

Chomsky, N. (1959). Review of B. F. Skinner's *Verbal behavior* (New York: Appleton-Century-Crofts, 1957) in *Language, 35,* 26–58.

Chomsky, N. (1965). *Aspects of the theory of syntax.* Cambridge, MA: MIT Press.

Ehrman, M., & Oxford, R. (1989). Effects of sex differences, career choice, and psychological type on adult language-learning strategies. *Modern Language Journal, 73*, 1–13.

Gleason, J. B. (Ed.) (1993). *The development of language* (3rd ed.). New York: Macmillan.

Gleason, J. B., & Weintraub, S. (1978). Input language and the acquisition of communicative competence. In K. Nelson (Ed.), *Children's language* (Vol. 1, pp. 171–222). New York: Gardner Press.

Goldfield, B. A., & Snow, C. E. (1989). Individual differences in language acquisition. In J. B. Gleason (Ed.), *The development of language* (2nd ed., pp. 303–325). Columbus, OH: Merrill.

Klima, E., & Bellugi, U. (1966). Syntactic regularities in the speech of children. In J. Lyons & R. J. Wales (Eds.), *Psycholinguistic papers* (pp. 183–208). Edinburgh: Edinburgh University Press.

Nelson, K. (1973). Structure and strategy in learning to talk. *Monographs of the Society for Research in Child Development, 38* (1–2, Serial No. 149).

Skinner, B. F. (1957). *Verbal behavior.* New York: Appleton-Century-Crofts.

Slobin, D. I. (1973). Cognitive prerequisites for the development of grammar. In C. A. Ferguson & D. I. Slobin (Eds.), *Studies of child language development* (pp. 175–208). New York: Holt, Rinehart & Winston.

Teale, W. H., & Sulzby, E. (Eds.). (1986). *Emergent literacy: Writing and reading.* Norwood, NJ: Ablex.

Terrace, H. (1979). *Nim: A chimpanzee who learned sign language.* New York: Knopf.

Wells, G. (1986). Variation in child language. In P. Fletcher & M. Garman (Eds.), *Language acquisition* (2nd ed., pp. 109–139). Cambridge, England: Cambridge University Press.

# Chapter 8

# SIVL: The Instructional Design Underlying a Foreign Language Vocabulary Tutor

Mitchell Rabinowitz
Regina Steinfeld
*Fordham University*

Recently, I (Rabinowitz) had the opportunity to spend a month during each of three consecutive summers at the Max-Planck Institute for Psychological Research in Munich, Germany. I was excited by this opportunity and each summer, prior to my trip, I set many goals that I hoped to accomplish during my visit. One goal was to learn to speak German.

I never had much success in learning a foreign language. In high school, I studied French and just barely passed. Retrospectively, not believing much in innate aptitudes, I reasoned that my problems with language learning were probably related more to method of instruction than to personal competence. I contrasted the textbook, memorization, and practice orientation I experienced in school with the type of opportunities I would have to learn German while actually living in Germany. I would be able to learn German in a realistic context where there is actually a real consequence for becoming competent in the language. I would be able to try some of the language-learning strategies described by Naomi Baron (chapter 7, this volume). I wouldn't have to do the rote memorization and drill that I remembered so well from my school days. I had a reason and an opportunity. I would finally learn a second language! I was excited; yet, I failed miserably.

There were probably many reasons for my failure but I know it wasn't for lack of trying. Whenever anyone spoke in German, whether to me or to someone else, I listened very attentively to see if I could induce the grammar and the meaning of the words. The problem I experienced was that I couldn't even make out the words. I heard a steady stream of sounds with the end of one word blending into the beginning of another. I couldn't figure out where one word stopped and the next began. I remembered from my readings in psycholinguistics that this is actually a good description of how people speak (H. Clark & E. Clark, 1977). I asked a few Germans I knew to speak slowly and enunciate each word, but this was effortful for them and it took the language out of the context I so valued. It also reminded me of the school-based learning in which I didn't want to engage. I could go through a listing of the other contextual activities I tried, but the point is that none of them worked.

The realization I came to during the end of my third month in Germany was that I needed to learn some of the basics of the language (like vocabulary and verb conjugation) if I were going to be able to take advantage of the context. For example, knowledge of the vocabulary beforehand would have helped me pick out the words in conversation. At least I would have some knowledge that I could apply in a top-down fashion to provide me with some idea of what to search for auditorily. What I learned too late was that *context wasn't everything.* I needed the memorization and practice to provide the prerequisite knowledge to take advantage of context, and I needed the context to make the memorization and practice meaningful. Most foreign-language teachers probably would have told me this from the start (Barnett, 1986; Halverson, 1985; Koda, 1989; Laufer, 1990).

Having convinced myself of the need for some rote memorization and practice, I then asked myself why did this component of learning have to be so difficult and why were so many people not able to master it? I was now in an area I knew something about. Keeping with the task of memorizing vocabulary, I knew that, left to their own resources, different people would use different strategies to memorize vocabulary (Schneider & Pressley, 1989). I also knew that success in memorization would vary depending on the specific strategy (or strategies) used (Rabinowitz, Freeman, & Cohen, 1992; Siegler, 1987). This brought me back to the strategy-instruction literature and the realization that I knew what the good strategies were for this task, and if we taught students to use these strategies, we would make the acquisition process much more successful (Borkowski, Carr, & Pressley, 1987; Pressley, Cariglia-Bull, Deane, & Schneider, 1987; Rabinowitz, 1984).

For example, for memorizing vocabulary there is the keyword mnemonic (Atkinson, 1975; Yates, 1966). The method involves a two-step process. The first is forming an association between the foreign-language word and an English word that sounds like it. The acoustically similar word is the keyword. The next step involves forming an interactive image to connect the keyword with the foreign word's English translation. For example, the Spanish word for *letter* is *carta.* An English word that sounds like *carta* is *cart. Cart* is the keyword for *carta.* An interactive image, which connects the keyword and its Spanish-word translation, is that of a cart being used to haul a huge letter. To remember the

Spanish word, given the English equivalent, you remember the sentence, which provides you with the keyword. This then provides you with a cue for the Spanish word. The effective use of the keyword method in learning vocabulary has been repeatedly demonstrated across different languages and with varied populations (Atkinson & Raugh, 1975; J. Levin, Johnson, Pittleman, K. Levin, Shriberg, Toms-Bronowski, & Hayes, 1984; J. Levin, Dretzke, Pressley, & McGivern, 1985; Mastropieri, Scruggs, & J. Levin, 1985; Raugh & Atkinson, 1975).

In addition, J. Levin and M. Levin (1989) developed a component that can be added to the keyword mnemonic to help people learn the gender that is associated with nouns in some languages. For example, feminine nouns in Spanish are preceded by the article *la* and masculine nouns are preceded by *el*. To help remember which article goes with which noun, J. Levin and M. Levin suggest that before beginning to memorize, students should choose two people—one male and one female—that they are familiar with and can easily image. When the keyword mnemonic is constructed, if the noun is feminine, preface the image with "Imagine the woman you chose . . ." So in the example using *letter*, the keyword mnemonic would be "Imagine your woman pushing a cart being used to haul a big letter." The woman in the mnemonic signifies that the article should be *la*. If the gender of the noun were masculine, use "Imagine the man you chose . . ." as part of the keyword mnemonic.

Let's teach more people to use the keyword mnemonic!

Unfortunately, I also realized that this solution would not work. Here I was in Germany, trying to memorize foreign vocabulary, and I know the keyword mnemonic. I taught many courses on memory and mnemonics. Was I using the mnemonic to help me memorize the vocabulary? No, I was relying on all the strategies that I knew were less effective. Why was I doing this? Because I was lazy and I knew that it would require a lot more immediate effort on my part to construct the keywords and use the mnemonic. Knowing about the strategy is only one part of the problem. Being willing to apply the necessary effort is the other.

The final phase of this story involved the wishful thinking on my part that if someone constructed the keyword mnemonics for a set of vocabulary words, then other people would be able to take advantage of this effortful work. The memorization portion of the language-learning process could be made much less difficult and learners would be able to devote their attentional resources to learning the other components of language with a more solid base of knowledge to build upon. This reasoning led to the development of the SIVL (*S*trategic *I*nstruction for *V*ocabulary *L*earning) tutor.

In the following section, we will describe the SIVL tutor. All examples will be made in reference to learning Spanish vocabulary. The tutor itself, however, is a shell, in that the data files are external to the program, and with the appropriate mnemonics, it can be easily adapted for other languages.

## THE SIVL TUTOR

SIVL is a computer-based tutor developed by Mitchell Rabinowitz and Haresh Sabnani.[1] The goals embodied in the tutor are twofold. The first is to facilitate the acquisition of foreign vocabulary by providing students with keyword mnemonics for each word. The second is to provide a context in which to wean students from relying on the mnemonic and to promote speedy and accurate retrieval. We felt that ultimately, when students needed to retrieve the Spanish word for a word like *letter*, we did not want them to have to go through the following process:

1. Think of the English word.
2. Think of the interactive image that involves the English word and the keyword.
3. Retrieve the keyword.
4. Use the keyword to retrieve the foreign vocabulary word.
5. Finally say the foreign vocabulary word.

We felt that having to engage in this type of slow, elaborate process would disrupt the other components of language learning. Rather, with our second goal, we wanted to move the student from initially having to rely on the keyword mnemonic to generate the Spanish word, to simply knowing the Spanish word when presented with its English equivalent. We feel that it is this second goal that distinguishes the SIVL tutor from others that are available (e.g., Gruneberg, 1992; J. Levin & M. Levin, 1989).

### Using SIVL

When the student first starts SIVL, the tutor first asks for the student's name. This is so the tutor can start to build a data file stored with information specific to that student. The purpose is so that the tutor can provide specific feedback regarding the student's own performance. Also, if this is not the first time the student has used the tutor, it allows the tutor to access previous data relevant to the student.

The student then chooses a list of words to study. This list could be one that is precompiled or the student can select specific words from the sample of possible words to be included in the list. This option allows the student (or teacher) to

---

[1]This program requires a DOS operating system, 64 K of RAM, graphics capability, and a color monitor. Requests for information on obtaining a copy of the tutor should be addressed to Mitchell Rabinowitz, Graduate School of Education, Fordham University.

F9 - Word + Sentence     Esc - Exit

The English word: letter

Tell me the Spanish word:

\>\>

FIG. 8.1.   Tutor screen during Trial 1.

customize the lists to meet his or her specific needs. Each list consists of 20 words that are randomly presented.

Before beginning the first trial, the student is presented a set of instructions that explain the goals of the tutor and how it works. The student is told that the first time through the list the primary goal is to memorize the words. Students are told about the keyword mnemonic, how it works, and are given an example.

### Initial Goal: Memorize the Word

Our initial goal for students who are just beginning to learn a list of words is for them to make use of and rely on the keyword mnemonics we prepared[2] to memorize the words. As a consequence, many of the instructional-design principles that characterize the tutor are omitted from the first learning trial with a list.

On Trial 1, students are presented with a screen that is similar to that depicted in Fig. 8.1. They are presented with an English word and their goal is to type in the Spanish equivalent. There are two options at this point. If the student knows the Spanish word, he or she can immediately type in the answer and press the return key. For nouns, the associated article must be included and, for all words, spelling must be correct. The tutor provides immediate feedback regarding accuracy of the response.

If the student does not know the answer, he or she can press the F9 key. The student is then presented with a window similar to the one presented in Fig. 8.2.

---

[2]Some of the mnemonics were adopted from the set provided by J. Levin and M. Levin (1989) with permission from the authors.

The Spanish word and keyword plus sentence are:

la carta

Imagine your woman pushing a **cart** being used to haul a big letter.

DON'T WORRY ABOUT TIME!

FIG. 8.2.   F9 hint window.

In this window, the correct answer and the mnemonic with the highlighted key-word are presented. As described earlier, the mnemonic hint entails the presentation of a sentence that depicts the keyword and the English word in some interactive context. For nouns, the additional mnemonic of "imagine your man or woman" is included to give a clue regarding gender. Students are encouraged to take their time and study the mnemonic so they won't need to look at the hint again. When the student is ready, he or she types in the answer and immediate feedback regarding accuracy is presented.

*Feedback.*   If the student types in the wrong answer, he or she is presented with a window similar to that presented in Fig. 8.3. The orientation we took toward accuracy feedback is that if the student gets the word wrong, we would present the correct answer along with the full mnemonic hint. We would provide the student with as many opportunities as possible to study the mnemonic. Students are allowed as much time as they want to study the words in this context.

Trial 1 involves going through the list of 20 words. After Trial 1, the character of the tutor changes dramatically.

### Weaning Off Strategy Use

At the start of Trial 2, the tutor is designed to present the full mnemonic if needed, but also to encourage quick and accurate retrieval of the foreign word without the use of the mnemonic. Two mechanisms are incorporated into the tutor to support this goal: (1) hints with diminished contextual support and (2) a scoring system to motivate retrieval. After completion of the first trial, students are presented with a second set of instructions detailing the additional components of the tutor.

At this point, the tutor becomes a game. The goal for the student is to obtain a high score. The student starts out the game with 0 points. Each word has a

Didn't get it.        Correct answer is: la carta

                      The keyword is: cart

The keyword plus sentence is:

Imagine your woman pushing a cart being used to haul a big letter.

Press any key to continue or Escape to quit.

FIG. 8.3.   Error window.

maximum credit of 20 points associated with it and the total number of points one can receive per list is 400. The scoring system is described later. The first screen of Trial 2 is depicted in Fig. 8.4. The words on a list are presented in a different random order for each trial. The objective of the game is for the student to repeat the list over and over again until a score of 400 is obtained.

The game is designed so that the student is constantly competing against him- or herself to achieve a better score. As will be demonstrated, the orientation to try and improve performance is involved with the students' responses to individual words as well as their performance across the entire list. The game was

F1 - Sentence    F5 - Keyword + Sentence    F9 - Word + Sentence    Esc - Exit

The English word: letter

Tell me the Spanish word:

>>

Score:

FIG. 8.4.   Tutor screen for trials after Trial 1.

designed so that students compete against themselves in order to encourage the development of attributions regarding effort (Ames, 1984).

## Diminished Contextual Support

On the first trial, when students ask for a hint, they are presented the answer and the keyword in an interactive sentence. At this point students are provided with three hint options. These three hints vary in terms of the contextual support provided to the student and the amount of the cognitive load the student has to assume. The F9 key still presents the hint that is shown in Fig. 8.2; all components of the hint are provided to the student, so that all the student has to do is study and rehearse. The other two hints are accessed by hitting either the F5 or the F1 key. With these hints, parts of the context are removed so that students have to do more of the cognitive work to generate the answer. The windows associated with these two keys are presented in Fig. 8.5.

The hint associated with the F5 key provides the student with the English word presented in the context of the keyword mnemonic. However, the foreign word (the answer) is *not* provided, thereby encouraging the student to retrieve it using the mnemonic clue. The hint associated with the F1 key provides the English word in the interactive sentence from which the keyword has been omitted. With this hint, the student needs to recall the keyword and also then use the keyword as a prompt to retrieve the foreign vocabulary word.

## Scoring System

Scoring is manipulated to encourage students to use the hints with less contextual support. Using the hint with the most contextual support (F9 key) yields the least number of points. As contextual support is decreased, the number of points associated with the hint increases. Retrieval without the use of hints is, in most instances, associated with the greatest number of points.

Response options are summarized as follows:

F9—Spanish word, keyword, interactive-image sentence 5 points
F5—Keyword and interactive-image sentence 10 points
F1—Interactive-image sentence without keyword 15 points

Of course, for any word, students can choose not to use a hint at all and simply type in the foreign vocabulary word. If correct, the number of points earned is equivalent to 20 points minus the reaction time for the student's response—the faster the response, the more points are awarded.

It is important to point out that students accrue no points for an incorrect answer. This is done to try to inhibit guessing. Students can hit the F9 key and be presented with the answer and earn 5 points or they can guess, and possibly

**F5 window**

The Spanish word and keyword plus sentence are:

Imagine your woman pushing a **cart** being used to haul a big letter.

**F1 window**

The Spanish word and keyword plus sentence are:

Imagine your woman pushing a **xxxx** being used to haul a big letter.

FIG. 8.5.   F5 and F1 hint windows.

get it wrong, and earn 0 points. The rationale, once again, is to inhibit students from building associations to incorrect responses.

**Feedback**

During the initial trial, students receive feedback only concerning the accuracy of their responses. No score is provided and no measure of reaction time is given. After the initial learning trial, students' responses are timed, response times are presented to the students, and scoring is recorded. If the answer is incorrect, the students are presented with the error window (Fig. 8.3).

### Reaction Times

For each response, the student's reaction time is presented in contrast with this student's fastest reaction time for that word. To determine reaction time, two values are computed from the beginning of the presentation of the word. The first is how long it takes to start typing. The second is the time it takes to hit the return key. The reaction time is the average of these two values. This information is presented in the form of a bar graph that shows the student's current reaction time and his or her fastest reaction time for that word. Over trials, then, students are constantly prompted to beat their fastest time for a specific word, thereby increasing speed and making it less appealing to ask for hints. This feedback is not presented, however, when students hit the F9 key. In this context we wanted students to spend as much time as they needed to study the mnemonic and not to concentrate on time.

### Scoring

The score at the bottom of the screen is revised after each response. At the end of a trial, the student is presented with his or her current score and the best score of that list. Thus, students are encouraged to improve on their own best score.

## Motivation

Obviously, no instructional material is useful unless students actually make use of it. Memorizing foreign vocabulary words is not a task that many students are eager to engage in. In designing the tutor, we tried to make it more likely that students would engage in the activities that would lead to memorization of vocabulary. First, to increase the probability that students would use the tutor, we designed the program to try to take advantage of the inherent motivational value of that medium (Lepper, 1985). Second, we designed the tutor as a game, so that students would be motivated to beat their best performances and provided feedback for them to monitor their own performance.

Third, to reduce boredom while playing the game, we provided a mechanism whereby students did not have to respond continually to words that they had mastered from the list. At the start of the game, a criterion reaction-time level is set. Students are informed that if they are able to retrieve the word three trials in a row with reaction times under the criterion level, they will receive credit for the word and the word will be removed from the list. Three comments need to be made regarding this criterion value. First, the default criterion level is set at 3 seconds. This criterion, however, is a variable that can be modified to be faster or slower to suit each individual's goals and typing skill. Second, because words are removed from the list, students receive more massed practice with words that they are slower to learn. Third, when a word is removed from the list, the student is given 20 points for having mastered that word. When the student starts the next trial, his or her score will start out with the number of points credited. Thus, as the student goes through a number of trials on the same list, the number of words presented will decrease and the points at the beginning of the trial will increase. Ultimately, when the student has mastered all the words, the tutor will inform the student that he or she has 400 points and no words will be presented.

## EPILOGUE

Our goal in this chapter was to present the SIVL tutor and the instructional design principles underlying its development. Obviously, the next step is to assess whether the tutor succeeds in meeting the goals that were set. Steinfeld, in her dissertation, is currently evaluating the efficacy of the tutor.

In her study, she provided a sample of first-year high-school students who were taking their first course in Spanish an opportunity to use the tutor. She arranged with the classroom teacher that over a period of 6 weeks, students would be asked to learn 20 new vocabulary words per week. For the first 2 weeks, students were brought into the school's computer room for one period during each week to use the tutor. For the next 2 weeks, the tutor was not made available and the students were once again left to their own devices to memorize the words for those weeks. For the last 2 weeks, they were once again provided access to the tutor for one period during each week.

The observational results so far are that students appeared to be very eager to go to the computer room to use the tutor and they often complained when the period was over. Many students had not yet obtained a score of 400 and wanted to continue until they succeeded. Thus, at least informally, it seems that the tutor was meeting the goal of maintaining motivation in the students.

In terms of memorization performance, 6 weeks after the learning opportunity the teacher gave a cumulative vocabulary test for the words assigned during the 6 weeks of training. One of the groups that participated in the study was homogeneously grouped as "average" students. Their performance on the cumulative test for the words that they were asked to learn during the weeks that they had access to the tutor was 45% correct. Their recall level for the words that they were asked to learn during the 2 weeks when the tutor was not made available was 17% correct. Clearly, using the tutor seems to help these students learn the vocabulary. It is important to realize that this result was obtained under conditions in which the students only had one opportunity per week for approximately 40 minutes to use the tutor.

Obviously, this is preliminary data and much more analyses and assessment need to be carried out. However, the initial data looks very promising. We look forward to the opportunity to present a more detailed analysis of the efficacy of the tutor.

# REFERENCES

Ames, C. (1984). Competitive, cooperative, and individualistic goal structures: A motivational analysis. In R. Ames & C. Ames (Eds.), *Research on motivation in education: Student motivation* (Vol. 1, pp. 177–207). New York: Academic Press.

Atkinson, R. C. (1975). Mnemotechnics in second-language learning. *American Psychologist, 30,* 821–826.

Atkinson, R. C., & Raugh, M. R. (1975). An application of the mnemonic keyword method to the acquisition of a Russian vocabulary. *Journal of Experimental Psychology, 104,* 126–133.

Barnett, M. A. (1986). Syntactic and lexical/semantic skill in foreign-language reading: Importance and interaction. *Modern Language Journal, 70,* 343–349.

Borkowski, J. G., Carr, M., & Pressley, M. (1987). "Spontaneous" strategy use: Perspectives from metacognitive theory. *Intelligence, 11,* 61–75.

Clark, H. H., & Clark, E. V. (1977). *Psychology and language.* New York: Harcourt Brace Jovanovich.

Gruneberg, M. (1992). *Linkword language series.* Penfield, NY: Artworx Software.

Halverson, R. J. (1985). Culture and vocabulary acquisition: A proposal. *Foreign Language Annals, 18,* 327–330.

Koda, K. (1989). The effects of transferred vocabulary knowledge on the development of L2 reading proficiency. *Foreign Language Annals, 22,* 529–540.

Laufer, B. (1990). Ease and difficulty in vocabulary learning: Some teaching implications. *Foreign Language Annals, 23,* 147–155.

Lepper, M. R. (1985). Microcomputers in education: Motivational and social issues. *American Psychologist, 40,* 1–18.

Levin, J. R., Dretzke, B. J., Pressley, M., & McGivern, J. E. (1985). In search of the keyword method/vocabulary comprehension link. *Contemporary Educational Psychology, 13,* 191–205.

Levin, J. R., Johnson, D. D., Pittleman, S. D., Levin, K. M., Shriberg, L. K., Toms-Bronowski, D., & Hayes, B. L. (1984). A comparison of semantic- and mnemonic-based vocabulary-learning strategies. *Reading Psychology: An International Quarterly, 5,* 1–15.

Levin, J. R., & Levin, M. E. (1989). *Improving the foreign language vocabulary learning of "at risk" minority students.* Undergraduate Teaching Improvement Grant, University of Wisconsin, Madison.

Mastropieri, M. A., Scruggs, T. E., & Levin, J. R. (1985). Mnemonic strategy instruction with learning-disabled adolescents. *Journal of Learning Disabilities, 18,* 94–100.

Pressley, M., Cariglia-Bull, T., Deane, L., & Schneider, W. (1987). Short-term memory, verbal competence, and age as predictors of imagery instructional effectiveness. *Journal of Experimental Child Psychology, 43,* 194–211.

Rabinowitz, M. (1984). The use of categorical organization: Not an all-or-none situation. *Journal of Experimental Child Psychology, 38,* 338–351.

Rabinowitz, M., Freeman, K., & Cohen, S. (1992). Use and maintenance of strategies: The influence of accessibility to knowledge. *Journal of Educational Psychology, 84,* 211–218.

Raugh, M. R., & Atkinson, R. C. (1975). A mnemonic method for learning a second-language vocabulary. *Journal of Educational Psychology, 67,* 1–16.

Schneider, W., & Pressley, M. (1989). *Memory development between 2 and 20.* New York: Springer-Verlag.

Siegler, R. S. (1987). Some general conclusions about children's strategy-choice procedures. *International Journal of Psychology, 22,* 729–749.

Yates, F. A. (1966). *The art of memory.* London: Routledge & Kegan Paul.

# Chapter 9

# Integration of the Abilities That Foster Emerging Literacy

Theresa M. Bologna
*Fordham University*

Discussion at a Screening for Kindergarten conference:

*How many children will we screen this year?*

*We expect about 75 children at this school alone. With this new protocol the districtwide committee developed, each child should take about 15 minutes with another 15–20 minutes with the parents.*

*Ideally we'll have a better picture of who these kids are. Last year was a disaster. Too many kids couldn't handle the curriculum. What's going on?*

*The kindergarten curriculum doesn't cover enough basics. The kids we're getting now are younger. Even though most of them have had preschool experience they just don't seem to be ready to focus on the prereading lessons.*

*Not all of them are younger. We're also seeing greater numbers of kids, particularly boys, who come to us as they are turning 6. The funny thing is some of these kids have trouble, too.*

*Maybe the problem is not in the kids. The curriculum committee decided last spring to spend this year examining the usefulness of the present kindergarten curriculum. We seem to refer more and more kindergartners for some type of remediation yet the number who still need remediation in the upper grades has not changed over the same period of time.*

This discussion could take place at any school regardless of descriptors: urban/suburban/rural, culturally heterogeneous or homogeneous, white-collar/blue-collar/working-class/poverty-level family configurations. Despite all the research to date intended to facilitate the planning of effective instructional environments for young children, one thing remains clear. There are no simple, clear directives (Adams, 1992; Durkin, 1987). Many children show signs of literacy before any formal instruction. Others have difficulty with extensive, even individualized, formal instruction. The extent of this concern reached the policymakers on a federal level and has been included as the first goal in the proposed federal legislation, Education 2000. *All children will enter school ready to learn.*

The role of school is to teach. The responsibility of the early-childhood specialist is to design instructional environments that meet the needs of the breadth of young children who enter the classroom. The discussion that follows examines the characteristics that young children bring to learning. When teachers design instructional environments based upon these characteristics, the premise is that children can, want to, and will learn.

Early-childhood settings include any learning environment for children age birth through 8 years old. The National Association for the Education of Young Children (NAEYC), the Council for Exceptional Children, Division for Early Childhood (CEC/DEC), and the Association for Childhood Education International (ACEI), recognize this range as inclusive of the early developmental stages that mark the beginnings of learning. The learning environment includes the totality of influences external to the child that one uses to design an atmosphere in which the child can, wants to, and will learn (e.g., space planning, activity selection, instructional strategies, modes of adult interaction, conversational tones, time frames, staffing patterns, expectations, and all that these factors encompass). It is during this early development that young children move toward the ability to interpret written language and, in turn, use written language to communicate wants, needs, interests, and information. This latter ability has come to be known as *emerging literacy.*

## CHARACTERISTICS OF YOUNG CHILDREN
## AND THE LEARNING ENVIRONMENT

Three major characteristics describe the makeup of young children: *They are movers, they are curious, and they are emotional.* Young children remind us quickly of their presence by the almost constant motion of at least one part of their bodies, by their incessant quest for knowing what is going on, and by their outbursts of joy, sadness, love, and hate. Their behavior is typically holistic. They respond to a situation in observable actions that include language and represent feelings.

An effective learning environment for young children involves designing opportunities for experiences that recognize this holistic mode. Such an environment relies upon perceptual development that matches the ability to maneuver one's body in a way that facilitates interaction with people and objects. The child exhibits curiosity through movement and language. Language grows with the ability of the child to think about the environment. Therefore, cognition and language are also integral to developing effective learning environments. Young children feel the reaction of and from the environment. They have not yet learned to put feelings in perspective in relation to the concepts that define the situation. The favorite teddy bear gets hungry, sleepy, feels pain, and so on. The exceptional popularity of Barney, the large purple dinosaur, attests to this strong connection between feelings and the reality of concepts. The affective tone of the environment as it nurtures social competence and affective development in general completes the picture. Table 9.1 displays overlapping characteristics of the young, developing child and the learning environment.

## Movers and Perceptual Development

Attaining a still environment with young children is near impossible, as those working in early childhood settings agree. Picture the class sitting quietly: One child's tongue licks the side of the lips on a face in deep concentration; others tap rhythmically with their fingers; knees pump up and down to an internal beat; a few reposition themselves periodically as they work; at least one is up and down repeatedly. From birth, children use all their senses along with body movements to explore and keep in touch with their environment. They sense pressure on their bodies—a warm hug versus a tight squeeze, the heat steaming from the classroom radiator versus the cold, hard floor under their feet, the sound of the pencil as it moves across the paper versus the hum of voices from the class across the hall. They sense changes within their bodies: hunger, pain, the movement of joints and muscles as they move around, sitting and standing, walking and running, and everything in between. They sense all this. They remember these experiences and then recall them in order to repeat or avoid a situation.

Children's abilities grow from gross attempts to accomplish a task to finer and finer differentiations of movements. They continually work at integrating all the senses, sensations, and body movements to better define their level of achievement. Adults are amazed at the number of times a child will repeat the same task. The young child appears to know that this repetition will lead to mastery

TABLE 9.1
Integration of the Abilities That Foster Emerging Literacy

| *Characteristics That Identify Young Children* | *Factors That Influence Designing Learning Environments* |
| --- | --- |
| THEY ARE MOVERS! | Perceptual development |
| THEY ARE CURIOUS! | Cognition and language |
| THEY ARE EMOTIONAL! | Social competence and affective development |

of the task at hand and often to the discovery of an additional step that expands on the task.

Neuroscience has vastly expanded our understanding of the workings of the brain and the mind (Damasio & Damasio, 1992; Goldman-Rakic, 1992; Kandel & Hawkins, 1992; Shatz, 1992). Scientists can isolate areas of the brain that affect language usage, retrieval of words, visual orientation, monocular and binocular vision, and the ability to control body movements. Flowers, Wood, and Naylor (1991) have detected differences in brain function during reading between children considered good readers and those labeled dyslexic. Galabruda (1988) detected structural differences in the temporal region of the brains of adults considered dyslexic. The integration of the abilities that make up human action and interaction continues to generate hypotheses and research.

The era of training specifically for perceptual abilities passed as educators and psychologists realized that focusing on this area did not lead to more effective outcomes, that is, children could not learn to read any better than they did prior to such training (Arter & Jenkins, 1979). Isolating perceptual abilities is not the answer to fostering emerging literacy. Young children use body movement and sensation not merely to expend energy. They punctuate their learning by movement and sensation: tongue extension when concentrating, hair twirling, squirming, moving up and down, tapping, shouting, whispering to themselves (and to others!), and whatever else suits their fancy. Movement and sensation are integral to the developing child. Based upon this, inclusion of perception as evidenced in movement and sensation necessarily becomes a part of designing instructional environments in early-childhood settings.

**Curiosity and Cognition and Language**

Young children are naturally curious. For what seems to be every waking moment, they explore. We've already noticed how much they move. Exploration provides young children with a breadth of information about their environment: what the world looks like from under tables, how they feel if they stick their hand in the potatoes or the pudding, what their parents do when they (the children) stick their hands in the potatoes or pudding, how hard they have to swing to hit the ball with the bat in their hands, what Mom and Dad look like and say when they (the children) hit the ball with the bat. Each experience becomes part of the child's memory. As experiences are repeated and expanded, information is stored that can be recalled at a later time. All this occurs in what seems to be a natural sequence with some direct, but primarily incidental instruction.

This is what we know: There is an integral relationship between thinking and language about which Chomsky (1980), Vygotsky (1977, 1978), Bruner (1978), and Bloom (1970) theorized. In very young children, as we try to assess their abilities, we attempt to separate functioning into those abilities that represent cognition and those that represent language. We are rarely, if ever, successful in isolating one from the other in the very young. Developers of domain-referenced assessment tools struggle with this issue each time an instrument is revised or reviewed.

From the child's perspective, is there indeed a difference? As the young children attempt to define the world they explore, they acquire the sounds they hear around them to put a name to what they know. Animals are named for the sounds they make. Objects that represent the animals have the same name. A swing that looks like a duck becomes the *gaak-gaak* swing (*quack-quack* swing). The sound of an object becomes its name. For example, a car becomes "brmmmmm" and any vehicle that can move the child around is called "brmmmmm." Acquiring language becomes the child's entree into the community culture. By combining what one knows with the community's use of sounds to describe what one knows, children begin to communicate verbally with the people around them, both adults and peers. As children mature within their culture, they learn more about their world and simultaneously use their existing language and expand upon it to further define what they know and don't know.

Preschoolers are notorious for the famous question: *Why?* Adults are notorious for getting tired of answering all the questions, especially the same one 100 times over a morning. Why do children keep asking the same question? Do they hear? Do they listen? Do they comprehend? The answers are "yes" and "no" to all of these. Piaget (1954, 1962) proposed that young children assimilate what appears to be a new piece of information and consider its relationship to other pieces of information already in memory (*accommodation*). If the information is integrated into their body of knowledge, it becomes observable in language usage and behavior as an adaptation of a previous use of language and/or behavior.

Accomplishing each of these (*assimilation, accommodation,* and *adaptation*) involves perception, memory, cognition, and language. Again, the child must integrate a wealth of input from a wealth of resources and try to make sense of it. An awesome task! Yet, this is one that most children accomplish with relative ease and aplomb.

## Emotions and Affective Development

Young children are full of emotion. They often react to the tone of a situation rather than to the words. They are the first ones to notice that we are tired, angry, sad, and happy. They have not yet developed the social skill to hide what they feel from others around them, nor do they protect themselves from noticing what others are feeling.

Developing social competence provides young children with a basis for comprehension of the written word. Even with this knowledge we tend to delegate the development of social competence to a lower rung on the ladder of learning. The early-childhood professional is generally viewed as "one who plays with children." No matter how sophisticated we become in understanding the concept of play and its role in learning, we still view play and learning to socialize with the adults and peers in the environment as simple and basic: simple—no, basic—yes. From the adult perspective, play is synonymous with recreation. From the child's perspective, play is the means to construct meaning from experiences and imaginary manipulations of experiences. Children use play to construct meaning from and about their environment (DeVries & Kohlberg, 1987).

In order to make sense of what is going on in their environment, children physically explore, ask questions, incorporate the information into the knowledge base, and eventually interact with people and things based on all the above. One of the methods used to remember all these parts is *scripts and schemata*. Young children accumulate a repertoire of situations from their experience. Based upon this repertoire they act out what they perceive to have occurred. In their play they expand upon and manipulate the experience to explore and clarify for themselves the reality of these situations (Anisfeld, 1984; Kagan, 1984).

Scripts and schemata provide a culture with a shared basis for recognizing what one means when one says, "How are you today?" Usually the questioner is not looking for a detailed description of what your physical well-being is like, or your psyche, but just means to greet you. The expected response, "Fine, thanks," often has nothing to do with the reality of the circumstances. But, how does the young child make sense of this? Often they do not, and many funny stories result because of a young child's unsocialized perspective on a socialized interaction. For example, an adult might say to a child who is visiting the classroom for the first time "We are happy that you could come today." The child responds with "Why?"—wondering how it matters to this adult, who is a stranger to them.

In order for young children to become literate they must first recognize the verbal and nonverbal cues of their community. As they develop a working knowledge of these cues, they simultaneously absorb the multiple ways that these cues are exhibited. Gradually, toddlers and preschoolers come to understand that graphics (pictures and symbols) can represent the words in their language. A second part of the comprehension process that makes up literacy is the recognition that the language itself represents chunks of information and socially agreed-upon ways of sharing information, for example, asking and responding to questions. Young children must learn the scripts and schemata that make their community unique, that make it a social unit and them a part of it.

As children learn scripts and schemata, they are also learning how to share their emotions and how to keep them private. They are learning the socially accepted ways to express anger, happiness, sadness, frustration, and the like. The guidelines of social behavior enable the child to continue to explore the environment without being either trampled upon or trampling someone else. Understanding these guidelines also helps children as they attempt to interpret written communication. For example, the young child learns the family routine that occurs at dinnertime. Although there are similarities from family to family, the schema with its related script is unique to the child's family. Certain behaviors are routine and expected. Conversations have a familiar flow. As children begin to read and interpret the meaning of the printed word, they rely on these schemata and scripts to help them understand the story line. Familiar schemata and scripts provide the "information between the lines" that allow the child to interpret what is written along with what is implied.

Children learn those things that are interesting to them. Educators have known this and theorists discussed this long before most of the readers of this text could think or read. Dewey (1938) reminded educators to value the quality of the experiences they provided. Piaget (1954, 1962) observed the natural wanderings of children as they explored and interacted with the people and things in their environment. Montessori (1964) recognized this with the young children for which she developed the Children's House in Italy a century ago. Head Start replicates her intent to provide an interesting and enriching environment for young children at risk for learning effectively.

Katz and Chard (1991) articulated the need to provide an interesting learning environment in their recommendation to engage children in their learning through active involvement in self-initiated and self-actualized projects. In their examination of such an approach they described the dispositions for learning that a teacher needs to foster to facilitate learning. "Broadly defined, dispositions are relatively enduring habits of mind and action, or tendencies to respond to categories of experience across classes of situations" (Katz & Chard, 1991, p. 31). The disposition to participate in learning forms alongside young children's experience with this endeavor. Learning experiences that maintain interest and encourage continued quest for information nurture the development of positive attitudes and productive dispositions. Those experiences or activities that become drudgery, leading to boredom, nurture attitudes and behavior problems that plague children, their teachers, their families, and the larger community in which they live.

## IMPLICATIONS FOR DESIGNING ENVIRONMENTS THAT FOSTER EMERGING LITERACY

### Using the Existing Knowledge Base

In our attempts to understand young children, theorists and researchers tend to isolate areas of functioning so that they may be examined in depth with minimal interference from other factors. Examination of discrete factors is manifested in two ways: *research* and *assessment*.

*Quantitative* research, also called experimental and quasi-experimental research, examines independent and dependent variables in controlled situations. The variables that represent characteristics the researcher proposes to investigate must be clearly defined and discrete by necessity. They must be independent of other confounding variables or factors that could affect the outcome of the research. In contrast to this, *qualitative* research, also called ethnographic research, proposes to examine a situation as it exists in its typical, holistic mode. To put this in the context of the abilities that foster emerging literacy, researchers have studied perceptual abilities (Arter & Jenkins, 1979; Tarver & Dawson, 1988); the impact of language, literacy, and social structure (Heath, 1983); discrete areas of investigations, such as the work of Ehri (1983, 1990), which focuses on the young child's emerging ability to recognize written words, along with examining the young child's phonological awareness (Clay, 1985; Torgesen, Morgan, & Davis, 1992) and the usefulness of incorporating this aspect of learning into instructional planning.

Efforts to assess young children follow parallel attempts to collect information about the discrete factors that can help and hinder a child's ability to participate effectively in learning. Historically, developmental assessment that entails some form of norm-referenced testing includes the collection of information about children based upon preconceived domains. The child's movement patterns, perceptual abilities, cognitive and language base, and social–emotional development are observed, recorded, analyzed, and subsequently matched to what is considered typical development. Based upon this collection of information, the teacher proposes to develop an instructional environment that will foster learning. Significant discussion continues as researchers, theorists, and practitioners expand upon and even replace norm-referenced, standardized measures with assessment methods considered more authentic to the characteristics of young children (Kamii, 1990; Roderick, 1991).

The value of examining the discrete characteristics that young children bring to learning rests in the premise that teachers can plan effective instructional environments if they know for whom they are planning. The problem stems from planning that recognizes the unique nature of the characteristics but apparently disregards the overlap between these characteristics.

Two modes of practice that significantly impact on young children are *whole language* instruction that grew out of the work of the Commission on Reading at the National Institute of Education (Anderson, Hiebert, Scott, & Wilkinson, 1985) and the work of the National Association for the Education of Young Children (NAEYC) that proposes *developmentally appropriate practice* in early-childhood settings (Bredekamp, 1987). The similarity between the two approaches is the recognition that learning is an integrated process relying on all the characteristics that young children bring to learning. In support of a whole-language approach the Commission stated that "all of the uses of language—listening, speaking, reading, and writing—are interrelated and mutually supportive. It follows therefore that school activities that foster one of the language arts will benefit the others as well" (Anderson et al., 1985, p. 79). Adams (1992), a strong proponent of phonics instruction, particularly as the child is beginning to read, simultaneously urges an awareness of the pitfalls in generalizing about "whole language."

> To some, the very term "whole language" instruction is translated to mean an uninformed and irresponsible effort to finesse necessary instruction with "touchy-feely" classroom gratification—and worse. . . . By misinterpreting each other, we prolong a fruitless debate, and worse, we do so at the cost of precious progress and of our school children's potential reading achievement. (pp. 24–25)

Developmentally appropriate practice in early-childhood settings has been equally misinterpreted.

## Developmentally Appropriate Practice (DAP)

Educators who consider themselves early-childhood specialists continue to stand defensively in response to the rhetoric about the field: "Play is the work of young children"; "Early-childhood teachers need to be warm and nurturing"; "Anyone can teach in an early-childhood setting." The latter truisms are barriers to those lobbying for certification requirements that validate the unique aspects of early-childhood education (Association of Teacher Educators and National Association for the Education of Young Children, 1991).

DAP, as proposed by NAEYC (Bredekamp & Rosengrant, 1992), represents the efforts of the largest professional organization lobbying for the educational needs of young children to define parameters of practice. It represents an organized, well-thought-out effort to pool the resources available in child development and learning to validate recommended practice. The national conference yearly draws approximately 25,000 of its total membership together to share ideas. A national-level committee, representing the membership that includes all levels of participation (paraprofessional to assistant teacher through to higher education faculty) developed the guidelines, which were initially published in 1986. At each yearly conference, the membership continues to reflect on the written statement. This approach makes DAP an evolving mode of operation as opposed to a static set of rules for early childhood professionals. These guidelines attempt to synthesize and build upon the knowledge we have about the way young children develop and learn. Two elements characterize DAP: selection of activities that match the interests and abilities of the child coupled with individualized instruction. These elements are crucial to the development of instructional environments that foster emerging literacy.

Young children are as much alike as they are different. Theorists such as Piaget (1954, 1962), Erikson (1963), and Gesell, Ilg, and Ames (1974) proposed stages of development whereas Vygotsky (1978) proposed developmental growth along paths that spiral and intertwine. The one aspect of agreement is the wide range of variability within typical growth patterns. Selection of activities that match abilities and interests implies that the person(s) designing the instructional environment understands the abilities and interests of the age group for which they are planning. This requires a working knowledge of the age group from the perspective of the child. What indeed can the *child* accomplish? What is the *child* interested in pursuing?

The task of selection of activities is complicated by multiple factors epitomized by the working philosophy of the planner. "Designing a curriculum for young children includes deciding what knowledge they should acquire. One basis upon which to make decisions is what the adults in the children's culture believe is important for them to know" (Katz & Chard, 1991, p. 21). A second part of this is observable in the types of strategies that the teacher employs. If the teacher believes that children are constructing knowledge through self-initiated and self-directed projects, the role of the teacher becomes one of facilitator, guide, and resource person. If the teacher believes that young children's spontaneous activity is typically haphazard, the instructional mode will be more directive.

The task of individualizing instruction is equally complicated, yet is one that occurs in many classrooms over and over during any single aspect of instruction. Individualizing may appear to be as simple as slowing the pace of the activity, simplifying the language, using manipulative or facilitating cooperative learning and peer tutoring. In order to individualize, the teacher must develop a keen sense of the children as they propose and respond to the existing mode of instruction. A teacher who has prepared extensively for the reading of a new and special storybook to her young charges must be ready to cope with the number of children who lose interest quickly despite the preparation. The immediate task is to change the mode of instruction so that the children can actively engage in the learning process. The long-term task is to determine why that mode did not work with that group at that point in time. Just as there is a wide range of variability of interests and abilities in any particular age range of the group we include in the early-childhood years (birth to about 8 years old), there is a wide range of responses to instruction and receptiveness to types of instruction:

> Our goal is not that children become alike in all respects; differences in abilities and talents are valued in most communities. But many outcomes with respect to knowledge, skills, dispositions, and feelings should be homogeneous, that is we want those outcomes for all children. That all children should have the disposition to be readers, for example, requires heterogenous treatments. In other words to achieve the same objectives with diverse children *different* teaching strategies and curriculum elements are called for. (Katz & Chard, 1991, p. 45)

Selection of activities that are interesting, that match the abilities of the age group, that meet the individual needs of the class group, and that foster emerging literacy should be the goal of those responsible for designing early-childhood settings. "Early literacy development does not simply happen; rather, it is part of a social process, embedded in children's relationships with parents, siblings, grand-parents, friends, caretakers, and teachers" (McLane & McNamee, 1991, p. 4).

## DAP and Emerging Literacy

By recognizing the unique learning style of each young child, DAP provides an environment that nurtures the child's development in the three areas noted earlier: perception, language and cognition, and affective development. When the guidelines for DAP are employed to frame the planning for an early-childhood setting, young children find themselves free to move about, explore, and react to and with their environment. While recognizing the child's unique interests and abilities, the teacher plans instructional opportunities that build upon the child's natural inclination to move about, explore, and react to and with the environment. Such a learning environment fosters the development of a proactive disposition to learn.

The content of a curriculum consists of the knowledge base and skills that one proposes for a particular age range of children or grade. Kindergarten and first-grade curricula content have changed in the last 20 years as we have learned more about what children can learn at earlier ages. This change has also affected the content in programs for infants, toddlers, and preschoolers. As the needs of our society have changed with technology and speed of communication, the content of instruction changes. We are preparing young children to live in a community that will function quite differently from the one in which their parents grew up. Can we see the day when all mail is electronically delivered? Our E-mail number could become as important as our social security number and street address.

For children to become literate, the content in early-childhood settings must reflect the knowledge base and skills that we already know lead to good readers (Adams, 1992; Durkin, 1987). How this knowledge base and skill acquisition is imparted becomes equally important. Developmentally appropriate practice consciously blends the characteristics that portray young children into the reality of designing an instructional environment exemplified by movement, exploration, and reactions that occur simultaneously.

For all the debate about Chall's work (Carbo, 1988; Chall, 1967, 1983, 1989; Stahl, 1988), one aspect remains clear. Children achieved progress in learning to read directly in relation to the motivation level generated by the teacher's interest in the program used, regardless of the program. This leads to strong implications for planning early-childhood settings that support emerging literacy. Young children engage in learning that interests them. When teachers design instructional environments based upon the characteristics that portray young children, the premise is that they can, they want to, and they will learn.

## REFERENCES

Adams, M. J. (1992). *Beginning to read: Thinking and learning about print.* Cambridge, MA: MIT Press.

Anderson, R. C., Hiebert, E. H., Scott, J. A., & Wilkinson, I. A. G. (1985). *Becoming a nation of readers.* Washington, DC: National Institute of Education.

Anisfeld, M. (1984). *Language development from birth to three.* Hillsdale, NJ: Lawrence Erlbaum Associates.

Arter, J. A., & Jenkins, J. R. (1979). Differential diagnosis: prescriptive teaching: A critical appraisal. *Review of Educational Research, 49,* 517–555.

Association of Teacher Educators and National Association for the Education of Young Children. (1991). Early childhood teacher certification. *Young Children, 47*(1), 16–21.

Bloom, L. (1970). *Language development: Form and function in emerging grammars.* Cambridge, MA: MIT Press.

Bredekamp, S. (1987). *Developmentally appropriate practice in early childhood programs serving children from birth to 8.* Washington, DC: National Association for the Education of Young Children (NAEYC).

Bredekamp, S., & Rosengrant, T. (1992). *Reaching potentials: Appropriate curriculum and assessment for young children* (Vol. 1). Washington, DC: National Association for the Education of Young Children.

Bruner, J. S. (1978). From communication to language: A psychological perspective. In I. Markova (Ed.), *The social context of language* (pp. 17–48). New York: Wiley.

Carbo, M. (1988). Debunking the great phonics myth. *Phi Delta Kappan, 70,* 226–240.

Chall, J. S. (1967). *Learning to read: The great debate.* New York: McGraw-Hill.

Chall, J. S. (1983). *Stages of reading development.* New York: McGraw-Hill.

Chall, J. S. (1989). Learning to read: The great debate 20 years later. *Phi Delta Kappan, 71,* 521–538.

Chomsky, N. (1980). On cognitive structures and their development: A reply to Piaget. In M. Piatelli-Palmarini (Ed.), *Language and learning: The debate between Jean Piaget and Noam Chomsky* (pp. 35–42). Cambridge, MA: Harvard University Press.

Clay, M. M. (1985). *The early detection of reading difficulties.* Portsmouth, NH: Heinemann.

Damasio, A. R., & Damasio, H. (1992). Brain and language. *Scientific American, 267*(3), 88–95.

DeVries, R., & Kohlberg, L. (1987). *Constructivist early education: Overview and comparison with other programs.* Washington, DC: National Association for the Education of Young Children.

Dewey, J. (1938). *Experience and education.* New York: Collier.

Durkin, D. (1987). *Teaching young children to read* (4th ed.). Boston, MA: Allyn & Bacon.

Ehri, L. C. (1983). Summaries and a critique of five studies related to letter-name knowledge and learning to read. In L. Gentile, M. Kamii, & J. Blanchard (Eds.), *Reading research revisited* (pp. 131–153). Columbus, OH: Merrill.

Ehri, L. C. (1990). Development of the ability to read words. In R. Barr, M. L. Kamii, P. B. Mosenthal, & P. D. Pearson (Eds.), *Handbook of reading research* (Vol. 2, pp. 383–417). New York: Longman.

Erikson, E. H. (1963). *Childhood and society* (rev. ed.). New York: Norton.

Flowers, D. J., Wood, F. B., & Naylor, C. E. (1991). Regional cerebral blood flow correlates of language processes in reading disabilities. *Archives of Neurology, 48,* 637–643.

Galabruda, A. M. (1988). The pathogenesis of childhood dyslexia. In F. Plum (Ed.), *Language, communication, and the brain* (pp. 127–137). New York: Raven.

Gesell, A., Ilg, F. L., & Ames, L. B. (1974). *Infant and child in the culture of today.* New York: Harper & Row.

Goldman-Rakic, P. S. (1992). Working memory and the mind. *Scientific American, 267*(3), 110–117.

Heath, S. B. (1983). *Ways with words: Language, life and work in communities and classrooms.* Cambridge, England: Cambridge University Press.

Kagan, J. (1984). *The nature of the child.* New York: Basic Books.

Kamii, C. (Ed.). (1990). *Achievement testing in the early grades.* Washington, DC: National Association for the Education of Young Children.

Kandel, E. R., & Hawkins, R. D. (1992). The biological basis of learning and individuality. *Scientific American, 267*(3), 78–86.

Katz, L. G., & Chard, S. C. (1991). *Engaging children's minds: The project approach.* Norwood, NJ: Ablex.

McLane, J. B., & McNamee, G. D. (1991). The beginnings of literacy. *Zero to Three, 12*(1), 1–8.

Montessori, M. (1964). *The Montessori method.* New York: Schocken.

Piaget, J. (1954). *The construction of reality in the child.* New York: Ballantine.

Piaget, J. (1962). *Play, dreams, and imitation in childhood.* New York: Norton.

Roderick, J. A. (1991). *Context-responsive approaches to assessing children's language.* Urbana, IL: National Conference on Research in English.

Shatz, C. J. (1992). The developing brain. *Scientific American, 267*(3), 60–67.

Stahl, S. A. (1988). Is there evidence to support matching reading styles and initial reading methods? A reply to Carbo. *Phi Delta Kappan, 70,* 317–322.

Tarver, S., & Dawson, M. M. (1988). Modality preference and the teaching of reading. *Journal of Learning Disabilities, 11,* 17–29.

Torgesen, J. K., Morgan, S., & Davis, C. (1992). The effects of two types of phonological awareness training on word learning in kindergarten children. *Journal of Educational Psychology, 84,* 364–370.

Vygotsky, L. S. (1977). *Thought and language.* Cambridge, MA: MIT Press.

Vygotsky, L. S. (1978). *Mind in society.* Cambridge, MA: MIT Press.

# Chapter 10

# Teachers Need to Know How Word Reading Processes Develop to Teach Reading Effectively to Beginners

Linnea C. Ehri
*City University of New York Graduate School*

Whole-language instruction has gained a strong following among primary-grade teachers in today's schools (Gursky, 1991). One feature making whole-language instruction attractive is that the reading and writing activities are meaningful and interesting not only to students but also to teachers. However, a weakness of this approach is the absence of systematic phonics instruction[1] during the first year of reading instruction. Some attention is paid to letter–sound relationships as students attempt to invent spellings during journal writing and as teachers read big books and stop to point out initial letters and sounds in salient words. However, care is not taken to ensure that each student masters the alphabetic system by learning all the letter shapes and names, learning which sounds they typically symbolize in words, learning how to segment words into sounds, and learning how to blend the sounds of letters to form words. Studies indicate that students who fall behind in learning to read do so because they have not acquired sufficient, working knowledge of the alphabetic system. Because this learning is difficult for them, they do not pick it up simply by being exposed to print (Juel,

---

[1]By systematic phonics instruction, I mean instruction that follows a plan and is effective in providing students with working knowledge of the alphabetic system as it symbolizes speech so that students' word-reading competencies develop and mature. I am not subscribing to any particular way of teaching phonics. Rather, in this chapter I attempt to specify the various graphophonic processes that students must be enabled to acquire in order to develop into mature readers. Systematic instruction may not be needed for students who enter school already knowing how to read, but it must be provided to students who enter school with little of this knowledge, and teachers of beginning reading must know how to provide this instruction.

1988; Juel, Gough, & Griffith, 1986; Stanovich, 1986; Wagner & Torgeson, 1987).

In this chapter, I suggest that, to become effective instructors of beginning reading, kindergarten and first-grade teachers need to understand the course of development that beginners follow when they learn to read, and how to assess whether these processes are developing adequately in individual students. With this knowledge, teachers are in a better position to make instructional decisions. Very recently our knowledge about reading processes and their development has advanced significantly as a result of research investigating these processes. (For summaries of this research, see Adams, 1990; Anderson, Heibert, Scott, & Wilkinson, 1985; Barr, Kamil, Mosenthal, & Pearson, 1991; Brady & Shankweiler, 1991; Gough, Ehri, & Treiman, 1992). In the following, I review what we have learned from research about the development of reading processes, including the various ways that words are read, how word-reading fits into text-reading, and what processes are needed in order for novices to make progress in learning to read.

One all-too-common approach to educating teachers about how to teach reading is to give them a list of dos and don'ts. For example, whole-language advocates tell teachers that instruction in reading should be meaning-based, students should write daily in journals, and they should do lots of silent and oral reading of real literature. Students should not read words in isolation on flash cards, and they should never read nonwords. Also prohibited are worksheets, phonics drills, memorization, direct instruction and practice on component processes of reading, and tests given to see what students have learned about reading and its components. Likewise, advocates of phonics instruction offer lists of dos and don'ts. They may tell teachers that students should never hear letter–sound relations pronounced in isolation but only in the context of words. Or they may assert that students should not be allowed to guess words they are reading in text but should always stop and sound them out. Typically prescriptions and proscriptions are presented dogmatically without a full explanation of how these practices are related to the development of reading processes and without any research evidence. This do–don't approach makes teachers heavily dependent on authority for making instructional decisions, and it discourages them from relying on their own knowledge, experience, and judgment.

A better approach to educating teachers of reading is to help them acquire working knowledge about many aspects of reading acquisition. This knowledge should include processes that develop in learners, informal tests to observe whether these processes are developing in individual students, various instructional approaches, methods, and activities, and how they promote the development of processes (Ehri & Williams, in press). Teachers who have extensive knowledge about reading have a much greater chance of success. Moreover, teaching becomes a highly interesting challenge when you know what to expect from learners as they make progress, what problems might develop, and the best ways to fix them. In this chapter, I discuss some of the processes that I think teachers should know indicate ways to assess their development in readers, and offer a sam instructional activities that hold promise of promoting their development.

## READING PROCESSES AND THEIR DEVELOPMENT

When skilled readers read and understand text, many cognitive and linguistic processes operate concurrently and automatically in synchrony. The interactive model presented in Fig. 10.1, adapted from Rumelhart (1977), depicts these mental processes. The center box represents a central processor that receives and interprets information coming in from readers' eyes as lines of text are scanned. The boxes around the center depict the various sources of information that are stored in readers' memory and enable them to recognize and interpret text.

Knowledge of language enables readers to process sentences and their meanings. Knowledge of the world, including both encyclopedic and experiential knowledge, supplies readers with the background for understanding ideas and filling in parts that are left implicit and assumed known rather than stated explicitly in the text. Readers use their metacognitive knowledge to monitor the quality of their comprehension and to verify that the information makes sense and meets specific purposes. If problems are detected, corrective strategies may be implemented, such as rereading or self-questioning (Baker & Brown, 1984). Memory of the text read up to that point enables readers to interpret incoming text in terms of previously processed meanings. Lexical knowledge refers to the reader's dictionary of words held in memory, those known in speech, and those

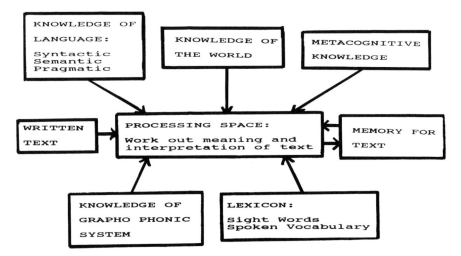

FIG. 10.1. Interactive model that depicts the various knowledge sources operating in parallel as readers process and comprehend text.

known in print by sight (Ehri, 1991, 1992). Accessing sight words in lexical memory is the principal way that readers recognize most words in text. Knowledge of the graphophonic system involves knowing how the spelling system symbolizes speech, including how letters can be transformed into blends of sounds to approximate known words (Venezky, 1970). Readers use sounding out and blending processes to decode unfamiliar words.

Knowledge of language and the world begins to develop during the preschool years before children move into independent reading (Goelman, Oberg, & Smith, 1984; McGee & Richgels, 1990). The experience of listening to storybooks enables children to practice and become familiar with several reading processes, including the process of applying their linguistic knowledge and their world knowledge to understand text, and the process of retaining text meanings in memory and drawing from this to interpret subsequent text. For books heard many times, children may learn to pretend-read the stories by memorizing the text and using pictures as prompts to recall text on each page (Sulzby, 1985). This may teach them about the structure of sentences that appear more frequently in text than in speech. There is evidence that young children's vocabularies grow from listening to storybooks (Robbins & Ehri, 1994). The development of meta-cognitive strategies is apparent when children ask questions to clarify the meanings of stories being read to them. It is important to recognize that even though preschoolers cannot read print on their own, the experience of listening to storybooks allows them to practice many of the processes that they will need in the future when they do learn to read print independently.

Various experiences may acquaint preschoolers with the squiggles constituting written language. When adults read books to children, they may slide their finger under the lines of print they are reading, and they may explain how print is structured. This shows children where book language comes from, and it corrects the misconception that adults are reading the pictures. Another source for learning about written language comes from environmental print. As preschoolers travel with parents to supermarkets, shopping malls, and restaurants, labels and signs that distinguish stores and products may be pointed out, helping children learn what written forms of words look like (Mason, 1980; Masonheimer, Drum, & Ehri, 1984). Letter knowledge emerges as adults name and point to alphabet letters in storybooks, alphabet books, and signs, and as they have children practice naming plastic magnetic letters clinging to the doors of their refrigerators and writing their own names (Mason, 1980).

Although bits and pieces of reading may appear in preschoolers, the bulk of reading skill of the sort that involves reading print independently emerges when reading is taught formally in the primary grades. By independent reading, I mean the ability to read words and text from written forms without the aid of pictures or other nonalphabetic prompts. This involves acquiring the two knowledge sources depicted at the bottom of Fig. 10.1, and learning to integrate all the knowledge sources in Fig. 10.1 to read text fluently (Chall, 1983).

## Ways to Read Words

When beginners learn to read English, their eyes encounter three types of structural units that make contact with their knowledge of language: letters, words, and sentences. During the course of learning to read, the eyes come to favor written words. The advantage of words over sentences is that words can be assimilated in one glance. The advantage of words over letters is that written words correspond more reliably to spoken words than letters correspond to sounds. Many years ago, Cattell (1886) found that skilled readers can recognize a whole word as quickly as they can recognize a single letter, and, in fact, they can name a word faster than a letter. Because words are the primary units of written language for learners, it is essential for teachers to understand how words are read and how word-reading skill develops.

At least five ways to read words can be distinguished: by sight, by sounding out and blending letters, by analogizing to known words, by pronouncing common spelling patterns, and by using context cues. In each case the processes differ (Ehri, 1991, 1994). As readers attain skill, they learn to read words in all five ways.

When readers read words *by sight* they access information about the words stored in lexical memory from previous experiences reading the words. This process is used to read words that have been read several times before. Sight of the written word triggers its spelling, pronunciation, and meaning immediately in memory without any sounding out or blending required. Reitsma (1983) found that beginning readers in first grade needed four experiences reading the words to store them as sight words in memory. You can tell when readers are reading words by sight because they read the words as whole units, with no pauses between sounds, and they read the words within one second of seeing them.

In my research I have found that the traditional way of viewing sight-word learning, as rote memorization of the visual forms of words, is incorrect (Ehri & Wilce, 1979, 1980b, 1983, 1985, 1987a, 1987b). Skilled readers do not read sight words by memorizing associations between the shapes of words and their meanings. This view is incapable of explaining how skilled readers can recognize in an instant any one of the thousands of words that they know by sight and how they can learn to read new sight words with very little practice (Ehri, 1992).

My findings indicate that sight words are secured in memory through the application of letter–sound knowledge. The process of learning individual sight words involves forming associations between particular spellings of words and their pronunciation/meaning amalgams by applying knowledge of letter–sound relations. Readers remember how to read a specific word by interpreting letters they see in the spelling as symbols for sounds they detect in the pronunciation of the word. For example, the initial letter *g* in *giggle* gets remembered as the sound /g/[2] rather than /j/ because the pronunciation of the word specifies /g/; *i*

---

[2] I designate sounds in words by placing lower-case letters between slash marks. I represent spellings of words by placing letters and words in italics.

is remembered as /i/, *gg* as /g/, *le* as /ul/. In this way, the spelling is bonded to a pronunciation/meaning amalgam[3] and stored in memory. The next time the reader sees the word, he or she can retrieve the spelling/pronunciation/meaning amalgam from memory to read it. Knowledge of letter–sound relations provides the powerful mnemonic system that bonds the written forms of specific words to their pronunciations in memory. Once the system is known, readers can learn to read words and build a lexicon of sight words easily.

Adams and Huggins (1985) studied sight-word reading by selecting 50 words that had to be known by sight to be read correctly, words such as *ocean, bouquet, aisle,* and *busy,* which could not be sounded out because of their irregular spellings. The words were ordered by frequency of occurrence in text so that easier words preceded harder words. Examples of the words are listed in the first column in Table 10.1. Adams and Huggins found that students in grades 2–5 typically read words accurately until they reached a point in the list where the words became unfamiliar (i.e., not in their sight vocabularies). At this point readers shifted from sight-word reading to sounding out and blending, which caused them to hesitate and often misread the words (e.g., pronouncing *tongue* as /ton/-/gyu/). These findings document the process of sight-word reading. Readers use this approach to read not just irregular words but all words that have been practiced sufficiently to become established in their lexical memory. Assessing readers' store of sight words can be used to decide whether a specific text is within their reading ability. Texts that contain at least 90% sight words can be read by children independently (Johns, 1978).

Another way to read words is *by sounding out letters and blending them into pronunciations that approximate real words* (also referred to as *phonological recoding*) (Beck, 1981; Ehri, 1991; Marsh, Freidman, Welch, & Desberg, 1981; Venezky, 1970; Venezky & Johnson, 1973). This is a strategy that readers can employ to read words they have never seen before. To use this strategy requires knowing how letters typically symbolize sounds in words, not only single letters but digraphs such as *th, sh, ea, ou.* Phonological recoding is a slower way of reading words than sight-word reading and tends to emerge later during development (Ehri & Wilce, 1983), although this may depend upon how reading is taught (Wimmer & Hummer, 1990). Disabled readers have special difficulty learning to phonologically recode words (Ehri & Wilce, 1983; Rack, Snowling, & Olson, 1992). The best way to assess readers' recoding ability is to have them read pseudowords that cannot be read by sight because they have never been

---

[3]It is necessary to refer to pronunciation/meaning amalgams rather than just pronunciations here. This is because the meaning dictates the pronunciation that is bonded to a spelling. To illustrate the problem, there are spellings that are pronounced in more than one way: *wind, lead, affect.* Two separate sight words are established in memory in each case to represent the two different pronunciation/meaning amalgams. For example, the sight word *wind* meaning "encircling" consists of a spelling–pronunciation bond that includes *i*—/iy/ (long-i sound). The sight word *wind* meaning "moving air" consists of a bond that includes *i*—/i/ (short-i sound).

TABLE 10.1
Ways That Words and Pseudowords Might Be Read by Readers

| By Sight[a] | By Sounding Out/Blending[b] | By Analogy[c] | By Spelling Pattern[d] |
|---|---|---|---|
| break | goan | greak | tain |
| busy | taich | fusy | goach |
| sugar | soag | tugar | joal |
| none | vep | jone | sug |
| prove | fiss | brove | vess |
| yacht | jul | bacht | fip |
| calf | paig | dalf | chail |
| suede | chol | nuede | pog |
| react | leck | leact | juck |
| island | juf | disland | lef |
| tongue | choub | fongue | foud |
| depot | fod | nepot | chob |
| bouquet | paf | souquet | vag |
| fiance | veeg | riance | peef |
| guitar | haip | fuitar | hain |
| chauffeur | foon | mauffeur | foop |
| rhythm | vud | chythm | jub |
| heights | jeeb | beights | veed |

[a]Words from Adams & Huggins (1985) list.
[b]Pseudowords with uncommon spelling patterns (Treiman et al., 1990).
[c]Pseudowords created by changing the initial letter of sight words in column 1. Analogy and sounding out strategies yield different pronunciations.
[d]Pseudowords with common spelling patterns (Treiman et al., 1990).

read before. In Table 10.1 are listed pseudowords with uncommon spelling patterns taken from a study by Treiman, Goswami, and Bruck (1990).

An alternative way to read unfamiliar words is to read them *by analogy to known words*, that is, by recognizing spelling similarities between new and known words (Goswami, 1986; Goswami & Bryant, 1990; Marsh et al., 1981). In looking at a word never read before, readers may notice that a part of it resembles a known sight word. They access the similar sight word in their lexicons and then adjust the pronunciation to accommodate the new word, for example, reading "peak" by analogy to "beak" or "fight" by analogy to "night." This is an easier way for beginners to read words than phonological recoding because it requires blending fewer subword units to make the word, *p* plus *-eak*, rather than *p* + *ea* + *k*.

To read words by analogy to known sight words requires that beginners have some rudimentary decoding skill (Ehri & Robbins, 1992). They have to have enough knowledge so that they can recognize how letters correspond to sounds in the known and new words and how to blend the subunits (e.g., *p* + *eak*). Also they need sufficient letter–sound knowledge to be able to store the sight words in memory by bonding spellings to pronunciations in the way I described previously.

In the third column of Table 10.1 is a list of pseudowords that if read by analogy to real words are pronounced one way and if read by sounding out and blending are pronounced another way. Read them to see which way you pronounce them. The footnote in the table explains the two solutions.

Another way to read unfamiliar words is *by detecting and pronouncing familiar spelling patterns*. This process is later to emerge, after readers have learned a number of sight words. To establish spelling patterns as familiar units in memory, readers must first acquire a sight vocabulary consisting of several words exhibiting the same spelling patterns (e.g., words sharing stems such as -*ick*, -*ank*, -*ine*), and they must recognize how the common letter sequences are pronounced as single blends. Treiman et al. (1990) found that beginners were more accurate in reading nonwords with stems common to several other words than nonwords with uncommon stems. Examples of their common-stem nonwords are listed in the last column in Table 10.1. Stahl, Osborn, and Lehr (1990) list 37 rime stems that have stable pronunciations across words and can be used to derive nearly 500 primary-grade words. These are listed in Table 10.2.

One final way to read words is *by using context cues to guess words* (Goodman, 1965, 1976). As portrayed in Fig. 10.1, readers can use their knowledge about language, their knowledge of the world, and their memory for the text already read, to guess the identity of some words as they read text. You can experience the value of context cues by attempting to read the words that are missing in the text (Robinson, Monroe, Artley, Huck, & Jenkins, 1965), displayed in Fig. 10.2. It is easy to guess function words such as *to* and *the* but hard to guess content words unless they have appeared in prior text, for example, *Farmer* and *truck*. This way of reading words is evident in the oral-reading errors (miscues) that readers produce when they read text aloud (Allington, 1984; Biemiller, 1970; Goodman, 1976; Leu, 1982; Weber, 1970). When words are misread, the words substituted will often fit the sentence structure and meaning, indicating that context influenced how the words were read. This approach may be used mainly to read unfamiliar words (L. Carnine, D. Carnine, & Gersten, 1984). Familiar words are recognized so quickly

TABLE 10.2
Set of Rime Spellings That Can Be Used to Derive Nearly
500 Primary Grade Words[a]

| -ack | -all | -ain | -ake | -ale | -ame | -an |
|------|------|------|------|------|------|-----|
| -ank | -ap | -ash | -at | -ate | -aw | -ay |
| -eat | -ell | -est | -ice | -ick | -ide | -ight |
| -ill | -in | -ine | -ing | -ink | -ip | -ir |
| -ock | -oke | -op | -ore | -or | -uck | -ug |
| -ump | -unk | | | | | |

[a]These were taken from Stahl et al. (1990). These authors in turn took the list from Wylie & Durrell (1970).

### The Little Gray Truck

It was time for ▇▇▇ Field to pick the ▇▇ on his farm.

With ▇ bang and a bump ▇▇ big ears of corn ▇▇ into his little gray ▇▇▇. At last there was ▇ more room in it. ▇ Farmer Field started off ▇ town with his corn.

▇▇ little gray truck was ▇ a hurry. It went ▇▇▇ down the old farm ▇▇ just as fast as ▇▇ wheels could turn.

FIG. 10.2. Page from a basal text in which every fifth word has been deleted to illustrate processes involved in guessing words based on context cues. Illustration from *Friends Old and New* (p. 190) by H. Robinson, M. Monroe, A. Artley, C. Huck, & W. Jenkins. Copyright 1965 by Scott, Foresman. Reprinted by permission. Text from *The Christian Science Monitor*. Copyright 1961 by The Christian Science Publishing Society. All rights reserved. Reprinted by permission.

and automatically by sight that contextual expectations do not have time to facilitate the process (Perfetti, 1985; Stanovich, 1980).

To summarize, there are several ways to read words: by sight, by sounding out and blending, by analogy to known sight words, by pronouncing familiar spelling patterns, and by guessing from context. Which process is the primary one for any particular word depends upon whether readers have practiced reading that word. Words sufficiently familiar in print are read by sight. Words unfamiliar in print are read using the other strategies.

## Reading Words in Text

Contextual guessing does not account for the way that readers read most words in text. Studies of the predictability of words in text indicate that on average 25% to 30% of the words can be guessed correctly. However, the most important content words are the least predictable, only 10% correct (Gough & Walsh, 1991). Thus, to guess words effectively, most of the surrounding words in a text must be known. To read these accurately, a reader must use processes other than contextual guessing. Hence, this is not the major way that words are identified.

During text reading, all of these ways of reading words may contribute (Ehri, 1987; Perfetti, 1985). In the skilled reader, several different processes are thought to operate together in parallel. As readers' eyes fixate on words known by sight, the first process to fire is lexical access that happens quickly and automatically. This yields recognition of the word's meaning and pronunciation. Other processes do not lie dormant, however, but are activated as well and perform a confirmatory function. Knowledge of the graphophonic system confirms that the pronunciation, derived from lexical access, does fit the spelling pattern on the page. Knowledge sources involving language, the world, and text memory confirm that the meaning of the word fits into the sentence and is consistent with the text's meaning up to that point. The redundancy in the system that arises from several knowledge sources operating in parallel serves to maintain highly accurate reading, to make the reader sensitive to errors, and to provide a means of self-correction when errors disrupt comprehension.

Whereas skilled readers have operational use of all these processes during text reading, disabled readers do not. They are most apt to be weak in their knowledge of the graphophonic system and in their sight vocabulary (Ehri, 1989; Juel, Griffith, & Gough, 1986; Liberman & Shankweiler, 1979; Perfetti, 1985; Stanovich, 1986). As a result, their reading is not fully supported by all the knowledge sources. Stanovich (1980) provides evidence that disabled readers *compensate* for inadequate decoding and sight-word reading by relying more heavily on word-guessing strategies. It is important for teachers to ensure that beginners learn to use all of these sources adequately so their text reading is fully supported.

Currently, educators who advocate a whole-language approach to teach reading (K. Goodman & Y. Goodman, 1979) claim that use of context is the major way that readers read words in text and that this is what they should be taught to do skillfully. These educators ignore and do not provide instruction for the other ways to read words. In fact, K. Goodman (1976) claims that readers do not read individual words when they read text, but rather use context cues and guess words. Only when they cannot guess a word do readers attend to letter cues in words. According to Goodman, having to attend to individual words to read them requires too much time and effort and subtracts attention from the processing of meaning.

Results of several studies reveal that this view is flawed because it fails to consider the process of reading words by sight (Ehri, 1991; Perfetti, 1985; Stanovich, 1980, 1986). Studies show that by the end of first grade, readers can recognize words by sight automatically without expending attention or effort. Beginners can look at a word and recognize its meaning instantly, even under conditions in which they try to ignore the word (Golinkoff & Rosinski, 1976; Guttentag & Haith, 1978).

To experience automatic word recognition, look at Fig. 10.3 and try labeling the pictures from left to right as rapidly as you can while ignoring the words printed on the pictures. You will find that you cannot ignore the words, indicating that your mind is processing them automatically. Reading words automatically by sight is much faster and more accurate than reading words by sampling letter cues and guessing. Also, it is much less time-consuming and involves much less conscious attention. Findings of several studies (Stanovich, 1980, 1986) indicate that effective sight-word reading, not effective use of context cues to guess words, lies behind effective text reading.

## The Development of Word Reading

Suppose you measured various capabilities and experiences of children entering kindergarten without any reading ability, for example, their knowledge of vocabulary words, their IQs, the number of books read to them by parents, the education level and socioeconomic status of parents, their knowledge of nursery rhymes, the number of hours spent watching TV each week, their knowledge of letter names, and their ability to segment spoken words into sounds. You waited for 2 years while they acquired reading skill in school, and then you measured their reading ability. Which of the capabilities would best predict their reading achievement? Various researchers have done this and found that letter-name knowledge and sound-segmentation skill are the best predictors, better than all the others (Chall, 1967; Share, Jorm, Maclean, & Matthews, 1984). These capabilities stand at the gate of reading acquisition and screen who is admitted and who is not. Although other capabilities may contribute to reading skill as well, they do not have a chance to exert an impact if beginners cannot get through the gate by knowing letters and how to segment. The reason that these two capabilities are so important is that they are needed for learning to read words in the various ways described earlier (Ehri, 1992).

Ehri (1991, 1994) divides the course of development of word-reading processes into four phases: (a) a visual cue phase, (b) a rudimentary alphabetic phase, (c) a mature alphabetic phase, and (d) a spelling pattern phase. During the *visual cue phase*, readers memorize visual, contextual, or graphic features of words to remember how to read them. They do not use letter–sound relations. During the two *alphabetic phases*, readers use letter–sound correspondences to read words. Alphabetic processing is considered *rudimentary* when readers process only some of the letters and sounds in words, for example, initial and final letters. Alphabetic

FIG. 10.3. The reader's task is to ignore the words and name the pictures from left to right as rapidly as possible. Use of this task in research studies has shown that readers who know the written words by sight cannot ignore them. The words are processed inadvertently and slow them down in naming the pictures, indicating that readers process the words automatically without attention or effort. From "Learning to Read and Spell Words" by L. C. Ehri, *Journal of Reading Behavior, 19,* 5–31. Copyright 1987 by National Reading Conference. Reprinted by permission.

processing is considered *mature* when readers process all of the letters and sounds in words. The *spelling pattern phase* emerges after readers have had sufficient experience processing words alphabetically to learn which letters combine frequently in different words and how they are pronounced. In this phase, familiar spelling patterns along with letter–sound knowledge are used to read words.

Visual-cue reading portrays how emergent readers process words. It is an immature process adopted by children who know little about letter–sound relations and how to segment words into sounds (Byrne, 1992). Lacking letter knowledge, they use whatever cues are visually salient in or around words to remember how to read them, for example, the golden arches behind the sign saying "McDonald's," the two tall posts in the middle of the spelling of "yellow," the tail at the end of the spelling of "dog." If they remember any letters in words, it is not because they interpret the letters as symbolizing sounds in the words. Masonheimer, Drum, and Ehri (1984) examined visual-cue readers' awareness of letters in environmental print they could read. They found that when the youngsters were shown familiar signs with one of the letters altered (e.g., *XEPSI* for *PEPSI*), they read them as if nothing had changed. This indicates that visual-cue readers do not use letter cues to remember how to read environmental print.

Studies of visual-cue reading reveal that the associations remembered are between print and meanings rather than between print and specific pronunciations. *Crest* might be read as "toothpaste" or "brush teeth," indicating that letter–sound ties in the spelling do not constrain the word accessed in memory (Harste, Burke, & Woodward, 1982). Studies also indicate that visual-cue readers have trouble remembering how to read words for any length of time when the words lack distinctive context cues and are read from alphabetic print alone (Mason, 1980). When presented with words they have never read before, visual-cue readers have no way of reading them except by guessing the words from context cues. For example, if shown a picture of a car drawn above the word *tire*, visual-cue readers will guess that the word says "car" and remain oblivious to the letter discrepancy. Visual-cue readers know how to read too few words to be able to read text other than by pretend-reading through memorization.

The rudimentary alphabetic phase becomes possible when beginners learn about letter–name or letter–sound relations and about how to segment initial sounds in words. With this knowledge, they can use partial alphabetic cues to remember how to read words by sight. I have called this *phonetic-cue reading.* For example, they might remember how to read "milk" by bonding the initial and final letters *m* and *k* to the beginning and ending sounds /m/ and /k/ in the pronunciation. In several studies (Ehri & Wilce, 1985; Scott & Ehri, 1989) we showed that whereas visual-cue readers learn to read words most easily when they contain salient visual cues, phonetic-cue readers learn to read words most easily when letters symbolize salient sounds in the words. In one study, we taught beginners visually salient spellings (e.g., *wBc* to stand for "giraffe") and phoneti-cally salient spellings (e.g., *LFT* for "elephant"). We found that the former type was easier for visual-cue readers to learn to read, whereas the latter type was easier for phonetic-cue readers to learn.

Mason (1980) showed that phonetic-cue readers can remember how to read words when the words lack any context and must be read from their alphabetic forms alone. If shown words they have never read before, phonetic-cue readers may mistake the new words for known sight words if the words share some of the same letters (Ehri & Wilce, 1987a, 1987b). Phonetic-cue readers can build a sight vocabulary that is sufficient to support the reading of text composed of those words. However, unfamiliar words must be guessed from context because phonetic-cue readers lack the sounding-out and blending skill needed to figure out unknown words. In recent studies, we have found that older disabled readers exhibit characteristics of phonetic-cue reading (Ehri & Saltmarsh, 1991).

When beginners acquire more complete knowledge about how the alphabetic system symbolizes speech, including how the vowel spelling system works and how digraphs such as *ch, th,* and *ea* symbolize sounds, they advance to the mature alphabetic phase of reading words (Ehri, 1991). They become skilled at sounding out and blending unfamiliar words. They add words to their sight vocabulary by processing and remembering how all of the letters in a word's spelling symbolize sounds detected in the word's pronunciation. For example, *milk* is fully analyzed as *m*-/m/, *i*-/i/, *l*-/l/, and *k*-/k/ when the spelling is bonded to the pronunciation in memory.

The process of bonding spellings to pronunciations of specific words may influence the sounds that mature alphabetic readers believe constitute words (Ehri & Wilce, 1980b, 1986). For example, the spelling of *pitch* may cause readers to conceptualize a /t/ sound in the pronunciation that is not thought of as being present in *rich*. Learning the spelling of *family* may induce readers to believe that the pronunciation consists of three syllables, /fam/-/i/-/ly/ rather than two, /fam/-/ly/. To the extent that readers can justify the presence of letters in spellings by recognizing how they symbolize sounds in the word's pronunciation, they can bond the full spelling to the pronunciation and retain letter information in memory as they learn to read words by sight (Ehri, 1992).

The sight vocabulary of mature alphabetic readers grows rapidly as readers process new words in their reading. Their word reading is highly accurate and they do not often mistake similarly spelled words, unlike phonetic-cue readers. This is because fairly complete letter-based representations of the sight words are bonded to pronunciations in memory.

As more words are added to the sight vocabularies of mature alphabetic readers and as they practice sounding out and blending letter combinations, the spelling-pattern phase of word reading emerges. Pronunciations of common letter sequences become known as *units*. These units make the task of reading unfamiliar words easier, particularly multisyllabic words. For example, fewer subunits must be blended to read the word *infuriate* if readers recognize familiar spelling patterns within the word, such as *in, fur*, and *ate*, and how to pronounce them, than if each letter must be sounded out and blended. Also, fewer units are required to bond spellings to pronunciations in learning to read multisyllabic words by sight.

During this phase, readers may learn to associate some spelling patterns with meanings, for example, *un-, -tion, -ed, -ing, -able*. Instruction that teaches readers about roots of words, prefixes and suffixes, and that distinguishes patterns in terms of language origins (e.g., Greek, Latin, and Anglo–Saxon), serves to enhance the learning of spelling patterns and their utility for reading words (Henry, 1989; Templeton, 1992).

## IMPLICATIONS FOR TEACHING READING

The four phases described above are useful for characterizing the development of word-reading processes. Knowing about these can tell teachers what to look for as signs of development and what processes need to be in place before others can be expected to emerge. In considering what teachers might do to insure that word-reading processes develop, I can suggest various activities. However, this should not be construed as a prescription for teaching reading. These activities illustrate some ways that objectives might be accomplished. There are other ways as well. Moreover, learning to read skillfully involves more than learning to read words.

To prepare students for the rudimentary alphabetic phase of reading, they need to learn how to name and to write letters. During the preschool years, parents can contribute by reading alphabet books to children, pointing out letters in environmental print, singing the alphabet song, teaching children to name the letters and to write their own names, and so forth. Also, adults can engage children in playing sound games that involve finding rhyming words, finding words that begin with the same sounds, and dividing words into sounds. In this way adults can help children learn to detach the form of language from its meaning and to focus on sounds. To the extent that such informal preschool experiences provide children with letter knowledge and sound-segmentation ability, they will be better prepared for learning to read independently when they begin formal instruction in school.

During the preschool years, it is important for children to experience reading in various contexts, for example, identifying environmental print, listening to storybooks, hearing letters sent by relatives. In this way, children become aware of the act of reading; they learn about its purposes; they observe what people do when they read, and so forth. These experiences serve to orient children so that when they receive formal instruction in school, they know where they are headed and what to expect (Dyson, 1984).

Activities performed during shared book reading (Holdaway, 1979) can introduce preschoolers to the structure of print and how spoken language is represented in print. Once children are familiar with a storybook, adults can slow down their reading of the story enough to fingerpoint-read the lines of text. This involves pointing to each word as it is read. Such a procedure supplemented by explanations can reveal many things to beginners: where the text begins and ends on a page; how lines of text run from left to right; how meaningful speech can be analyzed into words, syllables, and punctuation marks. As a result, preschoolers may begin to grasp how written language corresponds to spoken language. However, studies show that preschoolers who have memorized a text cannot learn to fingerpoint-read that text themselves simply by watching someone else do it. In order to track speech in print at the level of words, they need to know how to segment initial sounds in words and how to represent the sounds with letters (Ehri & Sweet, 1991; Morris, 1992).

Because letter knowledge and sound awareness are so important for learning to read, kindergarten and first-grade teachers need to identify and work with those children who lack this knowledge. Letter mnemonics are useful for helping children learn the shapes of letters and how to associate them with sounds. We showed this in a study where we taught children to associate each letter shape with the name of an object that was shaped like the letter and had a name beginning with that letter's sound (e.g., *s* drawn like "snake" beginning with /s/, *t* drawn like "table" beginning with /t/) (Ehri, Deffner, & Wilce, 1984). We found that this procedure taught letter–sound associations more effectively than other procedures, such as learning pictures unrelated to the shapes of letters, or simply rehearsing the letter–sound associations. A very popular program to teach letters in British kindergartens is "Letterland" (Wendon, 1990, 1992), which makes extensive use of mnemonics.

It is important to recognize that if students already know the names of letters, it is easy to teach them the letter–sound relations that are present in the names, for example, /b/ in *b* (bee), /j/ in *j* (jay), /m/ in *m* (em). Most letters, in fact, have a relevant sound in their names. Mnemonics would not be needed to teach these associations.

Once children learn the names or sounds of several letters, then they can begin to use their letter knowledge to invent spellings of words for the purpose of conveying meaning in print (Read, 1971). Teachers can use the task of inventing spellings to get children analyzing sounds in words and finding letters to symbolize those sounds. It is important for teachers to intervene and help students detect all of the sounds in words and to pick appropriate letters for those sounds. Sounds needing special attention are consonant blends, for example, /bl/, /st/, /str/, which are difficult to separate because they are pronounced together so quickly.

Children having trouble learning to read find the task of segmenting sounds in words especially difficult. One way to ease the task is to teach students how to monitor the articulatory movements occurring in their mouths when they pronounce words, for example, recognizing that there are three mouth positions involved in saying "bad": (1) lips closed for /b/, (2) mouth open for /a/, (3) tongue touching the roof of the mouth for /d/ (C. Lindamood & P. Lindamood, 1975). By locating the sounds of words in their mouths, beginners are provided with a basis that is more tangible and easier to scrutinize than that coming into their ears. Acoustic features of speech are ephemeral and disappear quickly.

Various researchers such as Henderson (1985) and Treiman (1993) have studied the course of development of invented spellings. In spelling the sounds they hear in words, children progress from representing only some of the sounds (e.g., *yl* for "while," *jrf* for "giraffe") to representing all the sounds (e.g., *wil, jeraf*). The letters they choose progress from nonconventional symbols for sounds (e.g., *jrem* for "dream," *sgat* for "skate") to more conventional symbols (e.g., *drem, scat*). When children learn the regularities of the spelling system, they have a much easier time remembering the correct spellings of individual words (Ehri, 1986).

Once children have some knowledge of letter–sound relations, they can begin to build a sight vocabulary. This is done mainly by reading meaningful text that is written at their level (i.e., about 90% sight words, 10% unfamiliar words). As readers encounter new words in text, as they pronounce them and recognize their meanings, and as they analyze how the spellings match up to the pronunciations so that the two become bonded, they begin to establish the new words as sight words in memory. At the outset, this learning may be helped by having students keep a set of cards printed with the words they have learned to read in the text. The cards can be reviewed, combined to form sentences, analyzed and sorted for letter–sound similarities, and so forth. One technique used in the Reading Recovery program (Clay, 1979, 1991) is to take selected words from stories just read and have children segment the letters to discover how they correspond to sounds in the words. Studying newly learned words in these ways may make beginners more aware of constituent letters and may speed up sight-word learning.

Teaching children the strategy of sounding out and blending words may be easier once they know how letters symbolize sounds, particularly vowel letters, and once they have learned a number of words by sight. This strategy is important for directing their attention to letter–sound relations within words. However, decoding English in this way may involve some trial and error and may not result in a recognizable word (e.g., the irregularly spelled sight words in Table 10.1). However, it is still a useful strategy to know. One trick readers must learn is how to blend consonants so that the vocalic element present when the sound is pronounced in isolation is deleted when it is blended with other sounds (e.g., pronouncing *b* as "buh" in isolation vs. /b/ in "blue").

Another strategy for reading words never read before is to teach children to look for familiar parts in the words, parts they know how to pronounce, for example, "in," "at," "on." A program used at the Benchmark School in Pennsylvania teaches children several key words that are especially useful for decoding unknown words. These words are posted on the wall and become familiar sight words to the children (Gaskins et al., 1988). Teachers can learn more about this approach by viewing a videotape obtainable from the Center for the Study of Reading at the University of Illinois.

Once beginners acquire working knowledge of the alphabetic system and once their sight-word lexicons begin to grow, then the best thing they can do to become more fluent readers is to practice reading and rereading lots of stories and books that are appropriate for their sight-word level (Chall, 1983; Stanovich & Cunningham, 1992; Stanovich & West, 1989). Practice is also important for strengthening the strategies of sounding out/blending and reading by analogy so that both develop as effective ways to read unfamiliar words.

Assessing the various capabilities that are involved in reading words can be done with informal tests administered to individual students. In the Reading Recovery program (Clay, 1979, 1991), informal assessment is considered an essential first step in working with a child and is called "roaming around the known." Periodic assessment is also important to verify that students are making the progress expected. The advantage of individual over group-administered tests is that teachers can observe processes and strategies as well as products.

One important capability for teachers to examine in novices is their letter knowledge, that is, their ability to write and name both upper- and lower-case letters.

Whereas letter names can be elicited by presenting randomly ordered letters one at a time, this is not the best way to assess beginners' knowledge of letter–sound relations. Beginners are more apt to reveal what they know about letter–sounds in an invented spelling task. In this task, the teacher pronounces words whose spellings are unfamiliar and asks students to write the sounds they hear in the words. The maturity of their invented spellings can be interpreted by comparing inventions to developmental examples given in Henderson (1985), Gentry (1981), and Morris and Perney (1984). This task also reveals students' ability to segment words into constituent sounds.

To test children's sight vocabulary, teachers can use lists of words that are organized by grade level (Harris & Jacobson, 1972), or words that their students have been exposed to in text. Words read within 1 second of seeing them are considered to be known by sight (Boder & Jarrico, 1982). Teachers can determine whether a book is within a child's reading capability by pointing to individual words selected at random on various pages and making sure that the child can read 90% of the sampled words by sight.

It may be especially important to check children's ability to read high-frequency function words by sight, words such as the following: *was, the, which, that, from, and, are, did, do, for, get, have, here, it, she, not, said, that, the, this, to, what, who, with.* These words are crucial for reading and comprehending sentences in text. In one study (Ehri & Wilce, 1980a), we found that students needed to practice reading function words in meaningful text rather than in isolation on flash cards to learn to process their meanings.

Children's ability to use sounding out and analogy strategies can be assessed by giving them pseudowords containing letter–sound relations or letter parts that they are expected to know. Teachers who have not had their students practice reading words in isolation or reading pseudowords may be surprised at their students' success. This is because students do not have to practice word and pseudoword reading in isolation to develop these capabilities.

To conclude, I have provided a cursory look at how word-reading processes develop during kindergarten and first grade and what this might mean for the teaching of reading. Much more could be said, not only about reading but also about spelling processes and how they contribute. In discussing how to teach reading, I have adhered to neither a whole-language nor a phonics list of dos and don'ts. Both lists oversimplify the solution to the problem of teaching reading effectively to all beginners, and both lists fall short in specifying how to teach all of the major processes involved in learning to read. It is important for teachers to move beyond lists and to acquire their own practice-based understanding of how reading processes develop and which instructional procedures are effective for developing which processes. I hope that teachers will become interested in the processes I have discussed, that they will look further for additional information (Adams, 1990; Balmuth, 1982; Cunningham, 1991; Feitelson, 1988), and that they will not be put off by the technical language and jargon used in some research papers and books. Also, I hope they will try out some of the informal assessment tasks I have suggested in order to learn more about the extent of development of individual students and to detect those lagging behind and needing special help. By knowing what to expect regarding the course of development in beginners, by having tools to see whether individual readers are developing as expected, and by accumulating a repertoire of effective instructional procedures to move learners forward, teachers can achieve much success in fostering the growth of independent reading skill in beginners.

## REFERENCES

Adams, M. (1990). *Beginning to read: Thinking and learning about print.* Cambridge, MA: MIT Press.

Adams, M., & Huggins, A. (1985). The growth of children's sight vocabulary: A quick text with educational and theoretical implications. *Reading Research Quarterly, 20*, 262–281.

Allington, R. (1984). Oral reading. In P. D. Pearson (Ed.), *Handbook of reading research* (pp. 829–864). New York: Longman.

Anderson, R., Heibert, F., Scott, J., & Wilkinson, I. (1985). *Becoming a nation of readers.* Washington, DC: The National Institute of Education.

Baker, L., & Brown, A. (1984). Cognitive monitoring in reading. In J. Flood (Ed.), *Understanding reading comprehension* (pp. 21–144). Newark, DE: International Reading Association.

Balmuth, M. (1982). *The roots of phonics.* New York: Teachers College Press.

Barr, R., Kamil, M., Mosenthal, P., & Pearson, P. (Eds.). (1991). *Handbook of reading research* (Vol. 2). New York: Longman.

Beck, I. (1981). Reading problems and instructional practices. In G. Mackinnon & T. G. Waller (Eds.), *Reading research: Advances in theory and practice* (Vol. 2, pp. 55–95). New York: Academic Press.

Biemiller, A. (1970). The development of the use of graphic and contextual information as children learn to read. *Reading Research Quarterly, 6*, 75–96.

Boder, E., & Jarrico, S. (1982). *The Boder test of reading-spelling patterns.* New York: Grune & Stratton.

Brady, S., & Shankweiler, D. (1991). *Phonological processes in literacy: A tribute to Isabelle Y. Liberman.* Hillsdale, NJ: Lawrence Erlbaum Associates.

Byrne, B. (1992). Studies in the acquisition procedure for reading: Rationale, hypotheses and data. In P. Gough, L. Ehri, & R. Treiman (Eds.), *Reading acquisition* (pp. 1–34). Hillsdale, NJ: Lawrence Erlbaum Associates.

Carnine, L., Carnine, D., & Gersten, R. (1984). Analysis of oral-reading errors made by economically disadvantaged students taught with a synthetic-phonics approach. *Reading Research Quarterly, 19*(3), 343–356.

Cattell, J. M. (1886). The time it takes to see and name objects. *Mind, 11*, 63–65.

Clay, M. (1979). *The early detection of reading difficulties.* Auckland, NZ: Heinemann.

Clay, M. (1991). *Becoming literate: The construction of inner control.* Auckland, NZ: Heinemann.

Chall, J. S. (1967). *Learning to read: The great debate.* New York: McGraw-Hill.

Chall, J. S. (1983). *Stages of reading development.* New York: McGraw-Hill.

Cunningham, P. (1991). *Phonics they use: Words for reading and writing.* New York: HarperCollins.

Dyson, A. H. (1984). Learning to write/learning to do school: Emergent writers' interpretations of school literacy tasks. *Research in the Teaching of English, 18*, 233–264.

Ehri, L. C. (1986). Sources of difficulty in learning to spell and read. In M. L. Wolraich & D. Routh (Eds.), *Advances in developmental and behavioral pediatrics* (pp. 121–195). Greenwich, CT: JAI.

Ehri, L. C. (1987). Learning to read and spell words. *Journal of Reading Behavior, 19*, 5–31.

Ehri, L. C. (1989). The development of spelling knowledge and its role in reading acquisition and reading disability. *Journal of Learning Disabilities, 22*, 356–365.

Ehri, L. C. (1991). Development of the ability to read words. In R. Barr, M. Kamil, P. Mosenthal, & P. Pearson (Eds.), *Handbook of reading research* (Vol. 2, pp. 383–417). New York: Longman.

Ehri, L. C. (1992). Reconceptualizing the development of sight-word reading and its relationship to recoding. In P. Gough, L. C. Ehri, & R. Treiman (Eds.), *Reading acquisition* (pp. 107–143). Hillsdale, NJ: Lawrence Erlbaum Associates.

Ehri, L. C. (1994). Development of the ability to read words: Update. In R. Ruddell, M. Ruddell, & H. Singer (Eds.), *Theoretical models and processes of reading* (4th ed., pp. 323–358). Newark, DE: International Reading Association.

Ehri, L. C., Deffner, N. D., & Wilce, L. S. (1984). Pictorial mnemonics for phonics. *Journal of Educational Psychology, 76*, 880–893.

Ehri, L. C., & Robbins, C. (1992). Beginners need some decoding skill to read words by analogy. *Reading Research Quarterly, 27*, 12–26.

Ehri, L., & Saltmarsh, J. (1991, October). *Do beginning and disabled readers remember the letters in words they have learned to read?* Paper presented at the NATO Advanced Study Institute on Differential Diagnoses and Treatments of Reading and Writing Disorders, Chateau de Bonas, France.

Ehri, L., & Sweet, J. (1991). Fingerpoint reading of memorized text: What enables beginners to process the print? *Reading Research Quarterly, 26*, 442–462.

Ehri, L. C., & Wilce, L. S. (1979). The mnemonic value of orthography among beginning readers. *Journal of Educational Psychology, 71*, 26–40.

Ehri, L. C., & Wilce, L. S. (1980a). Do beginners learn to read function words better in sentences or in lists? *Reading Research Quarterly, 15*, 451–476.

Ehri, L. C., & Wilce, L. S. (1980b). The influence of orthography on readers' conceptualization of the phonemic structure of words. *Applied Psycholinguistics, 1*, 371–385.

Ehri, L. C., & Wilce, L. S. (1983). Development of word identification speed in skilled and less skilled beginning readers. *Journal of Educational Psychology, 75*, 3–18.

Ehri, L. C., & Wilce, L. S. (1985). Movement into reading: Is the first stage of printed word learning visual or phonetic? *Reading Research Quarterly, 20*, 163–179.

Ehri, L. C., & Wilce, L. S. (1986). The influence of spellings on speech: Are alveolar flaps /d/ or /t/? In D. Yaden & S. Templeton (Eds.), *Metalinguistic awareness and beginning literacy* (pp. 101–114). Portsmouth, NH: Heinemann.

Ehri, L. C., & Wilce, L. S. (1987a). Cipher versus cue reading: An experiment in decoding acquisition. *Journal of Educational Psychology, 79*, 3–13.

Ehri, L. C., & Wilce, L. S. (1987b). Does learning to spell help beginners learn to read words? *Reading Research Quarterly, 22*, 47–65.

Ehri, L. C., & Williams, J. P. (in press). Learning to read and learning to teach reading are both developmental processes. In F. B. Murray & C. Smith (Eds.), *A knowledge base for teacher education.* San Francisco: Jossey-Bass.

Feitelson, D. (1988). *Facts and fads in beginning reading: A cross-language perspective.* Norwood, NJ: Ablex.

Gaskins, I., Downer, M., Anderson, R., Cunningham, P., Gaskins, R., Schommer, M., & The Teachers of Benchmark School. (1988). A metacognitive approach to phonics: Using what you know to decode what you don't know. *Remedial and Special Education, 9*, 36–41.

Gentry, R. (1981). Learning to spell developmentally. *Reading Teacher, 34*, 378–381.

Goelman, H., Oberg, A., & Smith, F. (1984). *Awakening to literacy.* London: Heinemann.

Golinkoff, R., & Rosinski, R. (1976). Decoding, semantic processing and reading comprehension skill. *Child Development, 47*, 252–258.

Goodman, K. (1965). A linguistic study of cues and miscues in reading. *Elementary English, 42*, 639–643.

Goodman, K. (1976). Reading: A psycholinguistic guessing game. In H. Singer & R. Ruddell (Eds.), *Theoretical models and processes of reading* (2nd ed., pp. 497–508). Newark, DE: International Reading Association.

Goodman, K., & Goodman, Y. (1979). Learning to read is natural. In L. Resnick & P. Weaver (Eds.), *Theory and practice of early reading* (Vol. 1, pp. 137–154). Hillsdale, NJ: Lawrence Erlbaum Associates.

Goswami, U. (1986). Children's use of analogy in learning to read: A developmental study. *Journal of Experimental Child Psychology, 42*, 73–83.

Goswami, U., & Bryant, P. (1990). *Phonological skills and learning to read.* Hillsdale, NJ: Lawrence Erlbaum Associates.

Gough, P. B., Ehri, L. C., & Treiman, R. (Eds.). (1992). *Reading acquisition.* Hillsdale, NJ: Lawrence Erlbaum Associates.

Gough, P., & Walsh, S. (1991). Chinese, Phoenicians, and the orthographic cipher of English. In S. Brady & D. Shankweiler (Eds.), *Phonological processes in literacy: A tribute to Isabelle Y. Liberman* (pp. 199–209). Hillsdale, NJ: Lawrence Erlbaum Associates.

Gursky, D. (1991). Whole language: A special report. *Teacher Magazine, 2*, 20–47.

Guttentag, R., & Haith, M. (1978). Automatic processing as a function of age and reading ability. *Child Development, 49*, 707–716.

Harris, A. J., & Jacobson, M. D. (1972). *Basic elementary reading vocabularies.* New York: Macmillan.

Harste, J., Burke, C., & Woodward, V. (1982). Children's language and world: Initial encounters with print. In J. Langer & M. Smith-Burke (Eds.), *Bridging the gap: Reader meets author* (pp. 105–131). Newark, DE: International Reading Association.

Henderson, E. (1985). *Teaching spelling.* Boston, MA: Houghton Mifflin.

Henry, M. K. (1989). Children's word structure knowledge: Implications for decoding and spelling instruction. *Reading and Writing: An Interdisciplinary Journal, 2*, 135–152.

Holdaway, D. (1979). *The foundations of literacy.* Sydney, Australia: Ashton Scholastic.

Johns, J. L. (1978). *Basic reading inventory.* Dubuque, IA: Kendall/Hunt.

Juel, C. (1988). Learning to read and write: A longitudinal study of 54 children from first through fourth grades. *Journal of Educational Psychology, 80*, 437–447.

Juel, C., Griffith, P., & Gough, P. (1986). Acquisition of literacy: A longitudinal study of children in first and second grade. *Journal of Educational Psychology, 78*(4), 243–255.

Leu, D. (1982). Oral reading error analysis: A critical review of research and application. *Reading Research Quarterly, 17*, 420–437.

Liberman, I., & Shankweiler, D. (1979). Speech, the alphabet, and teaching to read. In L. Resnick & P. Weaver (Eds.), *Theory and practice of early reading* (Vol. 2, pp. 109–132). Hillsdale, NJ: Lawrence Erlbaum Associates.

Lindamood, C., & Lindamood, P. (1975). *Auditory discrimination in depth.* Boston: Teaching Resources Corporation.

Marsh, G., Freidman, M., Welch, V., & Desberg, P. (1981). A cognitive-developmental theory of reading acquisition. In G. Mackinnon & T. G. Waller (Eds.), *Reading research: Advances in theory and practice* (Vol. 3, pp. 199–221). New York: Academic Press.

Mason, J. (1980). When *do* children begin to read: An exploration of four-year-old children's letter and word reading competencies. *Reading Research Quarterly, 15*, 203–227.

Masonheimer, P. E., Drum, P. A., & Ehri, L. C. (1984). Does environmental print identification lead children into word reading? *Journal of Reading Behavior, 16*, 257–272.

McGee, L., & Richgels, D. (1990). *Literacy's beginnings.* Boston, MA: Allyn & Bacon.

Morris, D. (1992). Concept of word: A pivotal understanding in the learning-to-read process. In S. Templeton & D. Bear (Eds.), *Development of orthographic knowledge: The foundations of literacy* (pp. 53–77). Hillsdale, NJ: Lawrence Erlbaum Associates.

Morris, D., & Perney, J. (1984). Developmental spelling as a predictor of first-grade reading achievement. *Elementary School Journal, 84,* 441–457.

Perfetti, C. (1985). *Reading ability.* New York: Oxford University Press.

Rack, J., Snowling, M., & Olson, R. (1992). The nonword reading deficit in developmental dyslexia: A review. *Reading Research Quarterly, 27,* 28–53.

Read, C. (1971). Preschool children's knowledge of English phonology. *Harvard Educational Review, 41,* 1–34.

Reitsma, P. (1983). Printed word learning in beginning readers. *Journal of Experimental Child Psychology, 75,* 321–339.

Robbins, C., & Ehri, L. (1994). Reading storybooks to kindergartners helps them learn new vocabulary words. *Journal of Educational Psychology, 86,* 54–64.

Robinson, H., Monroe, M., Artley, A. S., Huck, C., & Jenkins, W. (1965). *Friends old and new.* Chicago, IL: Scott, Foresman.

Rumelhart, D. (1977). Toward an interactive model of reading. In S. Dornic (Ed.), *Attention and performance VI.* Hillsdale, NJ: Lawrence Erlbaum Associates.

Scott, J. A., & Ehri, L. C. (1989). Sight word reading in prereaders: Use of logographic vs. alphabetic access routes. *Journal of Reading Behavior, 22,* 149–166.

Share, D., Jorm, A., Maclean, R., & Matthews, R. (1984). Sources of individual differences in reading acquisition. *Journal of Educational Psychology, 76,* 1309–1324.

Stahl, S., Osborn, J., & Lehr, F. (1990). *Beginning to read: Thinking and learning about print by Marilyn Jager Adams: A summary.* Urbana-Champaign, IL: Center for the Study of Reading.

Stanovich, K. E. (1980). Toward an interactive-compensatory model of individual differences in the development of reading fluency. *Reading Research Quarterly, 16,* 32–71.

Stanovich, K. E. (1986). Matthew effects in reading: Some consequences of individual differences in the acquisition of literacy. *Reading Research Quarterly, 21,* 360–406.

Stanovich, K., & Cunningham, A. (1992). Studying the consequences of literacy within a literate society: The cognitive correlates of print exposure. *Memory and Cognition, 20,* 51–68.

Stanovich, K., & West, R. (1989). Exposure to print and orthographic processing. *Reading Research Quarterly, 24,* 402–433.

Sulzby, E. (1985). Children's emergent reading of favorite storybooks: A developmental study. *Reading Research Quarterly, 20,* 458–481.

Templeton, S. (1992). Theory, nature and pedagogy of higher-order orthographic development in older students. In S. Templeton & D. Bear (Eds.), *Development of orthographic knowledge: The foundations of literacy* (pp. 253–277). Hillsdale, NJ: Lawrence Erlbaum Associates.

Treiman, R. (1993). *Beginning to spell: A study of first-grade children.* New York: Oxford University Press.

Treiman, R., Goswami, U., & Bruck, M. (1990). Not all nonwords are alike: Implications for reading development and theory. *Memory and Cognition, 18,* 559–567.

Venezky, R. (1970). *The structure of English orthography.* The Hague, Netherlands: Mouton.

Venezky, R., & Johnson, D. (1973). Development of two letter–sound patterns in grades one through three. *Journal of Educational Psychology, 64,* 109–115.

Wagner, R., & Torgeson, J. (1987). The nature of phonological processing and its causal role in the acquisition of reading skills. *Psychological Bulletin, 101,* 192–212.

Weber, R. (1970). A linguistic analysis of first-grade reading errors. *Reading Research Quarterly, 5,* 427–451.

Wendon, L. (1990). Synthesis in Letterland: Reinstating phonics in a "whole language" setting. *Early Childhood Development & Care, 61,* 139–148.

Wendon, L. (1992). *First steps in Letterland.* Cambridge, England: Letterland Ltd.

Wimmer, H., & Hummer, P. (1990). How German-speaking first graders read and spell: Doubts on the importance of the logographic stage. *Applied Psycholinguistics, 11,* 349–368.

Wylie, R., & Durrell, D. (1970). Teaching vowels through phonograms. *Elementary English, 47,* 787–791.

# Part III

# CREATING CONTEXTS
# FOR THINKING
# AND LITERACY

# Chapter 11

# The Case for Multiculturalism in Transforming Education

Clement B. G. London
*Fordham University*

It is a fair assumption to suggest that multiculturalism and the transformation of education have garnered much attention in recent years. However, because these issues are so encompassing, albeit substantive areas of academic discourse, there is no simple manner in which justice may be accorded them. Certainly, they require more than superficial examination. In the context of educational dynamics, the issue of multiculturalism has already spawned national debate among scholars, educators, and politicians in very much the same way that *A Nation at Risk* and subsequent documents have prodded the public's conscience regarding schooling and teachers' education, all issues of education reform.

We note with respect that Lawrence Cremin (1964), president of Teachers College, Columbia University, authored a scholarly volume of more than 400 pages that examined the transformation of schools for the extended period, 1876–1957. We recall that 1957, the year of Sputnik, stands out as one of, if not the single most dynamic watershed in the pantheon of U.S. educational transformation. The changes following this dynamic year have been phenomenal. Obviously, the challenge implicit in taking Cremin's work up to contemporary times would be an extraordinary one (a reasonable dissertation challenge, if you will).

The aim of this chapter is to offer a call to dialogue about the debates that are now going on about multiculturalism and the transformation of education, a call to try and understand the linkage between the two concepts as well as with the still larger issue of why we educate. It is, above all, to see the dialogue as conversations that may assist the process of explication and meaning-making, such that our understanding of these issues may transcend the ideational level of our thinking and reach the possibility of becoming actualized.

Conversations (Bleich, 1988; Rosen, 1992) mean that the texts of others live on in ours and that they have both connections and edges. The presence of connections or linkages means that the thinking of others lives on in our own; and the presence of edges means that something new or different has been added. However, it is the edges that keep conversations going. It is also true that it is the differences and conversations about differences that keep the discourse on multiculturalism and the transformation of education alive, as the search for compromises arising out of coalitions continues.

It is in the process of cross-cross-fertilization that coalition germinate and create conditions under which new conversations, needed in education, will forever be forthcoming. Therefore, connections and edges will generate further conversations and create more meaning-making, knowledge, and inquiry: altogether, the prime movers of change. Bateson (1972) reasoned that a theory of difference is a theory of learning. Therefore, from this perspective, difference becomes a resource as well as a potential. Thus, conversations, connections, tensions, and anomalies, all supporters of difference, become propellers of inquiry into strategies, procedures, and principles, as well as collaborative efforts at linking multiculturalism and education reform.

## EDUCATION AS MORAL RESPONSIBILITY

The thesis begins with the assertion that the heart of educational decision making and change resides in a corpus of moral responsibilities which, in turn, derive their sustenance from values. If education is intended to serve the polity, then it follows that the knowledgeable must be vigorously engaged in shaping public values. Teaching, therefore, becomes more precisely relevant because it presupposes that something of value must be transmitted. Similarly, educating the individual citizen is inherently moral, because the inequality of status between teacher and student suggests that one has the obligation to help in promulgating the developmental enculturation of the other through a system of sophisticated pedagogical procedures.

Philosophically speaking, schooling requires specific strategies of educational initiation that will facilitate access into the larger social domain. This is an educational act, a rite of passage that encompasses responsibilities. A cardinal step toward this undertaking would suggest that a consensus must be built around a set of goals and policies that are representative of all the diverse groups within the polity. A healthy society has the responsibility for securing the future of its young, who must be oriented with the skills, understandings of the accumulated wisdom or the civilization of what defines the rational life. But, of course, this cannot happen unless the nation acts as if it truly believes that all children and youth, the nation's next generation, are equally valuable as persons, whatever their circumstances. In other words, the nation must find ways to express convictions of meaningfulness of the moral, ethical values implicit and explicit, and thus reflected in the educational goods and services as the best available, and offered as part of a comprehensive curriculum in schools everywhere, equitably (Ryan, 1988).

Education is the basis of the orientation and socialization processes. It provides the determinants, the underpinnings of development, encompassing vital issues of values, the prime movers of what evoke and give sustenance to attitudes, lifestyles, belief systems, understandings of the symbolic universe, as well as networks of individuals and groups, all of which subscribe to the meaning of life. In essence, these characteristics, these essentials are all associated with the fundamental act of change, of transformation in education.

Education institutions must receive the affirmation and support of the larger society in taking the initiative to exercise and champion moral judgment. Human conduct should be grounded in moral responsibility that relates to the commonweal or good of the culture. To be moral is to respect the personality in ourselves and in others, to be understanding, to be social-minded and intelligent in the venture of living. It implies the exercise of wholesome living, and includes such universals as friendship, honesty, courage, justice, truth, and self-control. To share in these characteristics is to approximate experience in health, happiness, and human fulfillment, all common human aspirations.

Integrating moral judgment and responsibility with teaching and learning is an imperative. Morality in education provides rational bases that ultimately reflect what knowledge is of most worth. It is the centrality of a larger dynamic that determines the purpose of education. Morality helps to define curriculum in its noblest sense, and likewise affirms unique qualities of the human personality. Hence, helping an individual to confront life situations through the making of ethical judgments and moral decision making, must indeed remain a responsibility of education. Comfort is reasonable, but life is about its challenges. Therefore, schooling must morally assist in the preparation.

Because education takes its cue from the larger ecological environment it assumes the awesome responsibility of preparing the young to make critical judgments derived from critical skills used both for survival and for posterity. Part of this responsibility is to help learners recognize and incorporate ethical codes of values; to use skills of decision making in both academic and nonacademic settings. Learners need to know how to think clearly, choose wisely, and act responsibly for their own individual, group, and societal good. They need, also, to be helped in developing moral-ethical standards with which to evaluate problems and solutions that they are likely to face as adults. Educational leadership must strive to affirm this.

It should be clear that because a vital end product of education involves passing on the social heritage along with the development of individual talents, a concomitant concern should be that of finding and applying grounded educational theory that would sharpen, clarify, and thus facilitate rather than confuse. Theory of educational decisions inevitably involves conflicting ideals and viewpoints that require reasonable dialogue for compromise and consensus. These processes undergird the serious business of educational transformation.

Communication between and among participating groups is necessary. Dialogue about educational theory permits participants to examine the positions they share, and eventually, this leads to further understanding. In this way, each participant or group can become helpful in shedding light on the conversations regarding conceptualization, organization, presentation, and evaluation procedures of education. Moreover, a combination of views can be helpful in the development of new perspectives and positions based on practical realities and in renewed efforts to promote genuine improvement, not merely change. But, because various participants enter the conversations with different expertise and from varying perspectives, and also because educational issues are complex, collaboration often presents itself as a viable strategy of operation.

## TRANSFORMATION

The strategy of collaboration means several things to different persons. It may mean using oneself and others to outgrow ourselves. It implies using the process of incrementing our knowledge through the involvement of others in our inquiry, or the search for improved performance. More profoundly, it is a questioning of the ways in which we make meaning out of our world. In these relationships and conversations, collaboration is vitally linked to the concept of transformation.

Transformation is the ability to take a situation and recast, review, reorganize, or restructure it, at the same time giving credence to improvement. In operation, transformation demands of us to seriously rethink our notions of values, including the conceptualization of knowledge as a dynamic relationship among people, disciplines, and systems. Transformation, in its democratic frame of reference, accommodates the consideration of different views of knowledge about how learners organize themselves according to their own cognitive styles; how the sources of authority shift and change as functions of experience; and, how these, when taken together, become topics of conceptual and curricular interests.

## EDUCATIONAL TRANSFORMATION
## AS CURRICULAR TRANSFORMATION

Posited here for consideration is the view that educational transformation is indeed curricular transformation. This view derives its legitimacy from the rationale that in placing emphasis on the concerns of students, parents, teachers, faculty, or community member–participants, the consensus invariably seems to be about what schools are, how they function, and what they should teach. In short, all of these several publics involved in the conversations about schools and schooling, pay attention to the fundamental issue, curriculum: the essence of what could make a significant difference between what ought to be and what exists.

From a philosophical stance, curriculum may be perceived as a metaphor for the lives we wish to see lived in the classroom; it is that which permeates the kinds of lives we choose to live and which get played out in the classrooms. It is the source of meaning-making and inquiry, motivated by conversations between and among disciplines, systems of communication, and personalized knowledge that provides teachers with a reference for planning, teaching, and learning.

How we conceptualize curriculum affects roles for handling emerging issues such as the influx of new, non-White immigrants in schools across the nation, the roles we play, as well as the criteria employed for judging our students' inquiry. Curriculum is therefore a prediction that allows us to learn, to grow, and to revise our plans about schools and schooling. These are decisions derived from conversations resulting in planned, moral activity, involving commitments to, and beliefs in, people and the roles we envision that schools, colleges, and universities should play in a democracy.

Curriculum is the heart of every school's program, and therefore remains essentially the most cogent concern of a culture's philosophy of education. As such, curriculum is a public issue. Because the general public uses the results of curricular processes, public policy cannot be avoided or obscured, because the compelling concerns always surround the questions of what is being taught, how well it is being taught, and what should be adopted, deleted, modified, or adapted. It follows, therefore, that any approach to curricular design or redesign, in particular, creative curriculum, must eschew haphazard, fragmentary approaches, and instead must encompass systematic, developmental planning. Indeed, it would become virtually impossible for creative programs to command academic respect if their formulations ignore acceptable principles of design that are grounded in sound theory and practice. Without such critical, pedagogical concerns, the acceptability of curricular programs within educational communities is diminished considerably, and rightly so. Likewise, a systematic procedure of well-defined sequential steps, derived from substantive deliberations, should help to make the product–outcome generically and universally applicable. These are prerequisites for change. They facilitate transformation.

All change is stressful for education, precisely because schools are universal institutions charged with the service of both those who want change and those who resist it. Still, curricula of education are traditionally known to have been in the fundamental process of change. In this context, new content has been added, some old materials have been modified or altogether discarded. But, more often than not, many new programs or portions thereof have emerged looking very much like their predecessors. At the same time, however, the gradual process of curricular change has tended to reflect the relatively gradual evolution of society itself.

The launching of Sputnik in 1957 became a direct cause of vastly accelerated curricular revision. A major educational movement got under way, most notably in mathematics and the physical sciences. But it must be noted that the first round of school curricular reform then was both an upper- and middle-class affair that embraced primarily college-bound students. The cry of the poor and disadvantaged ethnic minorities was then only a whisper. Today, there are very compelling situations of urgency that transcend national interest. There is tension within as well as between and among nation-states. There are rapid political changes; instability in economic, political, and social conditions; ever-changing circumstances affecting the human condition alongside advances in technological progress; greater intolerance and misunderstanding—all of which have heightened the need to change the emphasis on some aspects of curriculum theory, structure, content, and methodology in light of the need to address these deepening human problems.

But, in order to make substantive change regarding these identifiable human concerns, transformation will have to mean more than superficial appearances. It must mean addressing aspects of the educational order to include attention to traditional practices and customs that are integrated with sound theoretical and practical pedagogical concepts and ideas. Such change must consider social, political, and economic processes as acts of faith, transcending the mere appeasement of special-interest groups, and instead minister to the needs of the larger ecological environment. For here the purpose should be to make the citizenry more cognizant, more culturally conscious, more socially understanding and tolerant of outcomes that speak to the needs of the commonweal or good.

Curricular change requires effort and time, often scarce commodities in schools, colleges, and universities. It also requires a certain level of commitment and security as underpinnings for the taking of educational risks, if only because fear of the unknown and the urge to maintain the status quo become impediments to educational change. It is not enough for leaders to make high-minded speeches, or to employ irrational, defensive rhetoric that stymies efforts, but rather, there is need for orientation, compromise, openness, flexibility, and honest dialogue that will allow issues to be fairly articulated in conversations.

Such overriding considerations suggest that the nation owes it to itself to ensure that no one should be denied the opportunity to share in comprehensive curricular and instructional practices, that understanding the human condition should not necessarily be reflected as a chronological perspective of only economic, political, and military events. It is not simply using events that are articulated in textbooks driven by marketing and profit matrices, not only events that feature a strictly Eurocentric grounding by White males who merely add insights to those same economic, political, and military events, but a comprehensive set of offerings that reflect and benefit all concerns of all the people.

The nation deserves an education that is shared in the context of keeping alive the philosophical commitment to the creation and maintenance of a literate society. And literacy must mean more than segmented and disproportionate offerings. Parity and equity of service must serve the larger, national purpose.

## MULTICULTURALISM, ITS PHILOSOPHY
## AND PEDAGOGY IN THE CONTEXT
## OF EDUCATIONAL TRANSFORMATION

Diversity among the population and the promulgation of public education have been traditional strengths of the United States, but are also sources of conflict. In the context of diversity, the word *multiculturalism* has become one of the most debated in recent educational literature. Multicultural education is one of the most recent manifestations of conflict over educational values; it emerges among other issues of race, religion, and ethnicity which have traditionally occupied conversations about the role of schools in addressing such issues. Multiculturalism has almost replaced race as a major concern, despite the fact that race-related issues were supposed to be resolved with the Supreme Court decision of 1954. This shift in emphasis, although it recognizes the nation's unique diversity, still remains a burning problem, particularly because it is reasoned to be related to African Americans as well as to their special historical circumstances, including their status as involuntary immigrants to this land.

As a consequence, the most misunderstood construct in the dynamics of multiculturalism is the *multicultural curriculum*, which has come to be designated the "Curriculum of Inclusion." In many ways, the concept is mired in much rhetoric and abuse, precisely because it has become associated with what Schlesinger (1992) calls "the curse of racism, the great failure of the American experiment, the glaring contradiction of American ideals . . . and the still crippling disease of American life" (p. 14). Unfortunately, too many persons tend to see the efficaciousness of multicultural education as being about African Americans. The inference of racial antagonism gets mixed in with otherwise strong pedagogical constructs. For example, while on the one hand the New York State Department of Education endorses a Curriculum of Inclusion the New York City public school system remains unalterably opposed to this idea. And the matter has become so volatile, with serious social, political, and educational ramifications.

In fact, multiculturalism can have several definitions. One generic, philosophical view avers that ethnic diversity, cultural pluralism, and linguistic multiplicity are essential ingredients of its characteristics (Banks, 1989; Gold, Grant, & Rivlin, 1977; Hale-Benson, 1988). Another popular position regards multiculturalism as being concerned with the modification of the total school environment, so that children from all ethnic groups may share in the equality of educational opportunity. This notion encompasses references to the pluralistic nature and possibilities of a democratic society, and it infers that the values implicit in a multicultural/pluralistic educational model will flourish when programs offer breadth of study that transcends the ordinary order of things.

One dynamic perception of the mission of a multicultural education program is to promote the development and implementation of a structured, integrated curriculum that is designed to foster knowledge, understanding, and constructive intergroup relations, as well as improved, qualitative academic preparation. As a process, it requires the full participation of all school personnel, families, and the school's community; it speaks to the incorporation of the notions of equity with regard to gender, age, race, disability, or sexual orientation. It also suggests the equitable distribution of knowledge, instructional resources, and financial school support, irrespective of school-district tax bases. These are all basic value underpinnings of a democratic society.

Indeed, theories of multiculturalism turn on the logical assumption that people living in a multiethnic society need to have a greater understanding of their own history and that of others; that shared knowledge will contribute to a more harmonious, patriotic, and committed polity; and that all persons in a nation's educational institutions should have an opportunity to learn about the differing and unique contributions to the national heritage. This altogether reflects the actualization of democracy (Ponterotto, 1993).

According to Banks (1989), culture consists of behavior patterns, symbols, institutions, all values, and other man-made components of society. It is the unique achievement of a human group or constellation that distinguishes it from other human aggregates. Whereas cultures are in many ways similar, a particular one constitutes a unique whole. Thus, *culture* is a generic concept with wide boundaries. As a consequence, one may describe the United States' macroculture as well as the microculture within it to include the culture of poverty, popular culture, youth culture, the Southern culture, the Appalachian culture, and the culture of the intellectual community, or the literati. Values are culture-based.

Because culture is the root of multicultural and multiethnic studies, education suggests a kind of structure that is related in some way to a range of cultural groups. But the concept itself implies much more than education related to many cultures. In fact, a major aim of multicultural education is one of educating students so that they will acquire knowledge about a range of cultural groups while they develop attitudes, skills, and abilities that are needed to function at some level of competency within different cultural environments, locally, nationally, and internationally. Such cultures may be social-class cultures, regional cultures, religious cultures, or national cultures (e.g., the national culture of Japan). Another appropriate goal of multicultural education is to facilitate reform of the total school environment, so that students from the various cultural groups, reflected in the larger ecological environment and the classroom, will be able to experience equal educational opportunities.

Multicultural education implies a form of education that is related in some ways to a range of ethnic groups. Multiethnic education should help students develop knowledge, skills, attitudes, and abilities that are needed in order to relate to a range of ethnic groups and to function in ethnic-group cultures within some level of competency. Another appropriate goal of multiethnic education is leverage, the change of the total environment so that it will respond to ethnic students more positively and therefore enable them to experience education equity. As such, multiethnic education is essential to, although not a total part of, the more global concept of multicultural education. Multicultural education programs should include participation of ethnic and racial minorities. It should never be relegated to the simplistic idea of "feeling good," as some detractors are often inclined to assert.

As in the case of any emerging field, there are some telling concerns that confront educators as they attempt to organize and implement sound programs of multicultural education. Some of these concerns may include conceptual confusion and philosophical conflicts, as well as widespread disagreements regarding what should be the proper role of public schools and institutions of higher learning in handling innovative conceptualizations in terms of their adoption and/or adaptation. As has happened over time with debate on educational change generally, current discourse on multiculturalism, multicultural education, multiethnic education, and their corollary, the Curriculum of Inclusion, continues among educators, politicians, and social scientists, with diverse and often conflicting ideological positions being advanced. In an educational, albeit a curricular sense, however, this is healthy. It is essentially what conversations ought to do, especially in the case of a nation attempting to answer its own question: What knowledge is of most worth for the young who must be duly acculturated into the awesome responsibility of assuming the mantle of the nation's legacy of civilization?

It is in the process of conversating that a curriculum comes into being after interested and competent publics adopt a set of recurring responses to a set of evolving circumstances. But, quite apart from the complex and continuous task of curriculum development, there is also added difficulty when a discipline or subject area, relatively new or still in the process of becoming, presents a philosophical articulation that requires further refinement and clarification. Such is the case of multiculturalism, of multicultural education. But, this kind of exercise is a critical and fundamental part of a larger educational dynamic that is altogether a buttress of the nation's educational philosophy, its values, or whatever sustains it. Now the nation needs to act with deliberation.

A cue may be taken from the post-Sputnik educational era. A cursory examination of this epoch of history will show that the educational reaction was exceedingly dramatic. It took the culture into a quantum leap of a postindustrial, high technological, information-processing whirl that enabled the nation to take charge of change in a manner that was not contemplated, but which in hindsight, clearly demonstrates the nation's unquestioned need to meet compelling exigencies head-on.

A similar set of needs exists requiring contemporary educational transformation, that educational change agents and change facilitators take charge of change, not in a clichéd sense of maintaining the "way things have always been" (Apple, 1990), but by the investiture of plans born of conversations and collaborative participation, precisely because the truth of our history and unique world leadership demand it (Sobol, 1990).

Because curriculum is defined as a mechanism by which a culture performs the socialization of its young, there is general acceptance that education and educational transformation are accorded the quality of comprehensive undertakings. All that is conceptualized, organized, and taught reflects the philosophical position of a given culture regarding the status of its citizenry. The constructs that constitute a culture's curriculum must speak to the needs of the entire polity, must be comprehensive in scope and sequence, must be inclusive of the values of all members of society, must reflect its diversity and democratic principles, and above all provide the underpinnings of freedom in all of its ramifications. The necessity for the inclusion of multiculturalism in the dynamics of educational transformation must derive its legitimacy from these perspectives, outcomes of continuing conversations.

## CONCLUSION

The mind at work in the classroom calls attention to the need to encourage learners to become independent thinking, learning, and communicating participants in home, school, and community. It is also a call for learners to become interactive, reflective, and informed, that they would characterize or epitomize citizens who, as individuals, are communicative, concerned as well as sharing in the social freedoms and obligations. Students, the young, the nation's future must be prepared to communicate in a world that is becoming increasingly smaller and within a society that is becoming increasingly diverse. Survival as a nation and as a planet requires that we all must be willing and able to accept the challenges of the 21st century and be actively involved in change.

Solving current and future problems requires that we be able to communicate with others within our own society and throughout the world (Powell, 1992). Helping students to become effective problem solvers is crucial. Thus helping students become effective thinkers is increasingly recognized as a primary goal of education. Rapid expansion of knowledge points to the importance of curricula that empower students to locate and process knowledge, rather than simply to memorize facts. It is also about developing the ability to think creatively, objectively, and analytically (Hughes, 1985). In essence, students must be cogently nurtured in their understanding of the dynamics of the world around them. But such nurturance, while deriving its impetus from school, home, and community, must gain its overriding sustenance from those persons whose awesome responsibility lies in the realm of teaching and learning in the classroom. These persons are our teachers.

Teaching is a very complex undertaking. Neither research and theory, nor practical experience can provide all the answers to instructional problems. Because of this fact, judgment remains one of the most fundamental abilities a teacher must have. Reflection improves a teacher's ability to make rational, well-founded judgments. Through reflection, a teacher is able to make tacit beliefs explicit and thus available for examination and revision, if necessary. Through reflection, a teacher is able to make and assess decisions about the application of theory and research within specific, practical settings. Most important, reflection helps teachers to assess their ongoing efforts to empower children and youth to become full participants within a democratic society. This means that through reflection, teachers can examine students' perspectives and assess the impact of decisions on the learning and behavior of students. And through reflection, teachers can constantly reevaluate their ability to fulfill their ethical commitments to children, youth, and society.

But becoming a reflective teacher means, among other things, assuming the role, and the responsibility, for transforming the school in such a way as to empower students to become actively productive participants within a school and its community. Put simply, this implies that teachers must help students become motivated and successful learners, participate productively in society, determine their own futures, and play an active role in making society a better place for all.

According to Goodman (1984), Ross (1987), and Zeichner and Liston (1987), a reflective teacher makes rational and ethical choices about what to do and how to teach, and assumes responsibility for those choices. In this manner, such a teacher must continually answer important questions. Such questions may include: What do children need to know and be able to do in society? Which teaching strategies are most likely to result in this learning? Are my teaching practices on ethical commitments to children and youth? Do my practices address caring and other abstractions as justice, honesty, and fairplay? What evidence have I that I am accomplishing my goals? In other words, a reflective teacher must be very thoughtful and responsible. Essential characteristics should always form the values which undergird the teaching–learning transaction, as well as the behavior and performance of the teacher (Ross, Bondy, & Kyle, 1993) in the classroom.

The mind at work in the classroom means in this context, employing to the fullest all of the innate possibilities of both teacher and taught, utilizing the support from the larger ecological environment.

## REFERENCES

Apple, M. (1990). *Ideology and curriculum* (rev. ed.). New York: Routledge.

Banks, J. A. (1989). *Multicultural education: Issues and perspectives*. Boston, MA: Allyn & Bacon.

Bateson, G. (1972). *Steps to an ecology of mind*. New York: Ballantine.

Bleich, D. (1988). *The double perspective: Language, literacy, and social relations*. New York: Oxford University Press.

Cremin, L. A. (1964). *The transformation of the school*. New York: Random House.

Gold, M. J., Grant, C. A., & Rivlin, H. A. (1977). *In praise of diversity: A resource book for multicultural education*. Washington, DC: Teacher Corps, Association of Teacher Educators.

Goodman, J. (1984). Reflection and teacher education: A case study and theoretical analysis. *Interchange, 15*(3), 9–26.

Hale-Benson, J. E. (1988). *Black children: Their roots, culture, and learning styles*. Baltimore, MD: Johns Hopkins University Press.

Hughes, C. S. (1985). Foreword. In A. L. Costa (Ed.), *Developing minds: A resource book for teaching thinking* (pp. ix–x). Alexandria, VA: Association for Supervision and Curriculum Development.

National Commission on Excellence in Education (1983). *A nation at risk: The imperative for educational reform*. Washington, DC: U.S. Department of Education.

Ponterotto, J. G. (1993, Spring). A multicultural school of education. *Cultural Vision, 2*, 2–3.

Powell, R. E. (1992, September). Goals for the language arts program: Toward a democratic vision. *Language Arts, 69*, 342–349.

Rosen, H. (1992). *Personal communication*. Bloomington: Indiana University Press.

Ross, D. D. (1987). *Reflective teaching: Meaning and implications for preservice teacher educators*. Paper presented at the Reflective Inquiry Conference, Houston, Texas.

Ross, D. D., Bondy, E., & Kyle, D. W. (1993). *Reflective teaching for student empowerment: Elementary curriculum and methods*. New York: Macmillan.

Ryan, K. (1988, May). Moral education in the life of the school. *Educational Leadership, 45*(8), 4–8.

Schlesinger, A. M. (1992). *The disuniting of America*. New York: Norton.

Sobol, T. (1990). Understanding diversity. *Educational Leadership, 48*(3), 27–30.

Zeichner, K. M., & Liston, D. P. (1987). Teaching student teachers to reflect. *Harvard Educational Review, 57*, 23–48.

# Chapter 12

# Cognitive Apprenticeships: Putting Theory into Practice on a Large Scale

Sharon M. Carver
*Carnegie Mellon University*

In keeping with the theme of this volume, the goal of the Year of Discovery collaboration was to involve researchers, teachers, and students in developing high-level thinking skills useful for learning and communication across the curriculum. Furthermore, our goal was for students' increased independence in thinking and learning to improve their participation in their families and communities as well. Because the latter contexts make few distinctions between subject areas and encourage involvement of diverse individuals, we focus on integrated learning in a context of inclusion. The apprenticeship model described and demonstrated in the Year of Discovery program is an age-old approach whose possibilities are only beginning to be explored in public education.

## THE COGNITIVE-APPRENTICESHIP APPROACH

During the recent decade of educational reform, researchers have refocused their attention on methods for teaching a craft through apprenticeship as opposed to the lecture-style transmission and rote learning of facts and algorithms (Carver, Lehrer, Connell, & Erickson, 1992; Palincsar & Brown, 1984; Rogoff, 1990; Resnick, 1987; Schoenfeld, 1985). Basing a school-learning environment on an apprenticeship model implies several assumptions about the nature of the teacher–pupil and pupil–pupil interactions. The teachers must indeed be "masters" or experts in the field(s) relevant to the content to be learned as well as in the means for training novices, who are typically at varied levels of mastery. Apprenticeship also implies that learning relationships last for a significant period of time and represent an important context for the present and future well-being of both the master and the apprentice. For example, apprentice tailors spend years of full days working with a few experts and more advanced apprentices in one limited domain that will be the key to their lifelong ability to survive and support a family (Lave, 1988).

Extending the model from physical skills to the cognitive domains involved in contemporary schooling (Collins, Brown, & Newman, 1989) complicates the teaching and learning processes because the relevant processes are typically invisible, cannot be described by vocabulary shared by all the participants, and are not represented in standard form. Furthermore, in some cases, there are social or cultural constraints that limit the acceptability of verbalizing thoughts, debating approaches, and acknowledging misunderstanding, all of which are central to effective high-level thinking.

The Year of Discovery learning environment was created to implement and evaluate a cognitive-apprenticeship approach in an urban middle school in Rochester, New York. The particular design described in this chapter is the sixth qualitatively different design developed during a 4-year collaboration between the University of Rochester and the Rochester City School District. (Carver, in press, describes the initial project development and the first five designs.)

During the 1992–1993 school year, 120 seventh-grade students participated in the Year of Discovery project. Sixty percent of the students were African-American, 25% were White, 10% were Hispanic, and 5% were from other minority groups. Seventy percent of the students qualified for free or reduced-cost lunches based on their family income. More than 25% of the students were labeled as being at moderate-to-high academic risk based on excessive absences, retention in a grade, multiple failing marks, poor standardized test scores, or suspensions. The general focus of the school leadership was on transmission of knowledge and behavior control, and the school as a whole had little history of innovation prior to our involvement with them.

We designed our learning environment to meet the apprenticeship assumptions in the following ways. We formed a teaching team with experienced teachers from varied disciplines (math, science, English, social studies, reading, Spanish, and special education), and these teachers collaborated with technology consultants and a mentor teacher familiar with apprenticeship methods from the University of Rochester Graduate School of Education and Human Development. The heterogeneity of each class included ability levels ranging from *Option 1 Special Education* students to *Major Achievement Program* students, as well as racial diversity and roughly even numbers of male and female students. Our design involved each teacher working with one class of students on extended interdisciplinary research and communication projects for a significant portion of the academic year, specifically, a 2-hour block of time each morning, all year. In contrast to the continuity of having the same teacher for each of these "project" blocks, we arranged afternoon classes such that each student would have one afternoon with each of the subject-area experts. Our focus on research projects with formal presentations (given both orally and via HyperCard on Macintosh computers) was the result of community and school-district emphasis on students' need for greater skill in independent learning and communication in preparation for entering the workforce.

## PRINCIPLES FOR COGNITIVE APPRENTICESHIP ENVIRONMENTS

The Year of Discovery learning environment was designed according to the 17 principles for cognitive-apprenticeship environments (Table 12.1) discussed by Collins, Hawkins, and Carver (1991).

### Principles for Curriculum Content

According to the cognitive-apprenticeship model, curriculum objectives should address four types of knowledge: (a) *subject-matter-specific knowledge* made explicit in most standard curricula, (b) *generally applicable strategies* for using domain knowledge to solve problems, (c) *control strategies* for making decisions among available options and monitoring progress, and (d) *learning strategies* relevant to the other three types of knowledge. As far as domain knowledge is concerned, the Year of Discovery curriculum is aligned with the state-mandated seventh-grade academic content, although we did focus our attention on the most central aspects of the curriculum to allow time for learning to use the computers and for in-depth work on projects.

Our major emphasis was on heuristic strategies for moving beyond the typical student approach to research (Table 12.2a) to an approach that we labeled the *Steps to Discovery* (Table 12.2b). We developed a cognitive model that explicitly identifies 16 substeps associated with the five steps listed in Table 12.2b, along with multiple strategies for accomplishing each substep. This model then served as the basis for our instruction and assessment of student learning.

Though we had a less explicit model for both control and learning strategies, we did talk explicitly with students about their choices of general strategies according to particular project assignments and about how to allocate their limited time and effort to best meet the project requirements.

### Principles for Instructional Methods

Apprenticeship instruction in the Year of Discovery curriculum focused primarily on the Steps to Discovery. We began on the first day of school with *modeling* the five steps in contexts that were both familiar and highly motivating for the

TABLE 12.1
Design Principles for Cognitive Apprenticeship Environments

---

*Content:*  Types of knowledge required for expertise
　Domain knowledge
　　subject-matter-specific concepts, facts, and procedures
　Heuristic strategies
　　generally applicable techniques for accomplishing tasks
　Control strategies
　　general approaches for directing one's solution process
　Learning strategies
　　knowledge about how to learn new concepts, facts, and procedures

*Method:*  Ways to promote the development of expertise
　Modeling
　　teacher performs a task so students can observe
　Coaching
　　teacher observes and facilitates while students perform a task
　Scaffolding
　　teacher provides supports to help the student perform a task
　Articulation
　　teacher encourages students to verbalize their knowledge and thinking
　Reflection
　　teacher enables students to compare their performance with that of others
　Exploration
　　teacher invites students to pose and solve their own problems

*Sequencing:*  Keys to ordering learning activities
　Global to local skills
　　focus on conceptualizing the whole task before executing the parts
　Increasing complexity
　　meaningful tasks gradually increasing in complexity
　Increasing diversity
　　practice in a variety of situations to emphasize broad application

*Sociology:*  Social characteristics of learning environments
　Situated learning
　　students learn in the context of working on realistic tasks
　Community of practice
　　communication about different ways to accomplish meaningful tasks
　Intrinsic motivation
　　students set personal goals to seek skills and solutions
　Cooperation
　　students work together to accomplish their goals

---

*Note.* From A. Collins, J. Hawkins, and S. M. Carver, 1991. In *Teaching Advanced Skills to At-Risk Students: Views from Research and Practice* (B. Means, C. Chelemer, & M. S. Knapp, Eds.). Copyright © 1991 by Jossey-Bass. Adapted with permission.

TABLE 12.2a
Typical Approach to Research

| *Steps to Getting an A* |
|---|
| Get topic |
| What does the teacher want? |
| Find encyclopedia |
| What volume do I need? |
| Copy information |
| How many paragraphs do I need? |
| Recopy neatly |
| How many pages have I filled? |
| Get a grade |
| Did the teacher like what s/he read? |

TABLE 12.2b
Research and Communication Model

| *The Steps to Discovery* |
|---|
| Ask |
| What do I want to know? |
| Find |
| Where can I find information? |
| Organize |
| How does that information answer my question? |
| Present |
| How can I best share what I've learned with others? |
| Reflect |
| How can I improve my presentation? |

students. For example, we introduced the project at a seventh-grade assembly during which our research team acted out the five steps for answering the question "Who are the seventh graders?" We showed that we found two pages of data per student in the counselor's office, reduced and sorted it using a spreadsheet, presented interesting highlights (e.g., the most common girl's name, the most frequent birthday, etc.), and reflected on ways we could have done each of the steps in a more effective or interesting manner.

The introduction continued during the next 5 weeks with teachers demonstrating and *coaching* the students through week-long projects (e.g., an autobiography, a travel advertisement for a state, etc.). In theory, coaching involves the teacher keeping tabs on students as they work independently, so that guidance, redirection, and correction can be provided as necessary. In practice, the teachers were not yet skilled in monitoring students' process, especially with class sizes over 30. Practice improved with the help of researchers and Kodak volunteers, because of both their familiarity with the research process and the increased adult–student ratio.

After the introductory projects, the curriculum included five major units, each focusing on a period in history covered in the seventh-grade curriculum. The lead teacher for each unit designed the unit project to require incorporation of information from each of the academic disciplines. During these units, the teachers continued to coach students, providing progressively less *scaffolding*, meaning support and guidance, as the students gained in proficiency.

During these units, the teachers and researchers also encouraged students to *articulate* their research and communication processes, so that the classroom discourse could focus on the curriculum objectives. *Reflection* on the Steps to Discovery process is built into the last step, but the key is to focus student reflection on all phases of the process, not just the final presentation. Finally, the broad scope of the project assignments invited student *exploration* of the research and communication process; there were always many paths to effective presentations and creativity was encouraged.

## Principles for Instructional Sequencing

The sequencing principles specified by the cognitive-apprenticeship model relate closely to the methods described previously. We progress from a *global to a local understanding* of the Steps to Discovery so that students get a clear overview of the process and the rationale for it before learning individual components. In the early stages, students experienced the entire five steps within one period, 1 day, or 1 week. Later, as we began to focus on the details of each step, they spent 5 weeks going through the process.

This progression also allowed us to gradually increase the *complexity* of the project requirements, both in terms of the number of parts in a project and in terms of the standards of excellence. For example, later projects required Hyper-Card stacks and one other form of visual presentation (poster, skit, etc.), whereas initial projects only required HyperCard. Also, students were allowed to sit down and read oral reports during the early phases, but they had to stand and only refer to notes in the end. As student skills improved, we also increased the *diversity* of the projects so that students became familiar with varied sources of information (e.g., texts, people, media, etc.), approaches to organization (e.g., compare/contrast, pros/cons, timelines, etc.), presentation formats and audiences, and evaluation criteria.

## Principles for the Sociology of the Classroom

In order to *situate the students' learning* in a realistic context, our initial goal was to have them create museum exhibits to teach others in the community about topics of mutual interest. Although several museums in Rochester offered to participate in and support the project, we only produced one exhibit that was sufficiently professional to display for the public (an exhibit about Rochester displayed via HyperCard at the Rochester Museum and Science Center). In this case, we were working with only one class of students intensively, as opposed to the 120 students who participated in the 1992–1993 implementation. Because of the time constraints involved in working with so many students, we modified our goal to teaching other students in the school. That way, the students still needed to focus on accuracy and richness of presentation, but did not need to spend so much time on refinement and glitz.

The *community of practice* developed naturally because we involved all students and teachers in the project. As students became interested, they began spending lunch periods and other free time working and began to spend more time communicating about academic topics and strategies. The most dramatic effects of this discourse occurred when small groups of students learned new features of HyperCard and were then sought by their peers for tutoring. We encouraged this phenomenon by purposely teaching some new techniques to only a few students in each class (e.g., how to use the scanner to digitize images).

Developing a community of practice leads to both *intrinsic motivation* and to *cooperation*. Students want to contribute to the group product and are encouraged to help each other with ideas and strategies. The project objectives were also broad enough to allow students to set their own agendas and choose their own methods much of the time. The difficulty in these areas arises when resources are scarce and when conflicts arise. The students need to be taught strategies for maintaining their interest when they have to wait and for resolving conflicts constructively.

## ASSESSMENT IN AN APPRENTICESHIP ENVIRONMENT

The cognitive apprenticeship model does not include principles for assessment because the goal of traditional apprenticeship is mastery learning. Students keep working until they have sufficient skills to establish a shop of their own, and diversity in the length of an apprenticeship is commonly accepted. Furthermore, mastery is easier to determine because of the physical product being constructed (e.g., a garment has to be appealing, serviceable, durable, etc.). But the complications of moving to *cognitive* apprenticeship, mentioned previously, affect assessment as well as instruction. The lack of a common vocabulary and standard representations for invisible cognitive processes hinders the evaluation of student progress.

In order to assess the general heuristics specified by our model of the Steps to Discovery, we rely on inferences made from both product and process evaluations. For each research project, the students actually produce a visible product, usually a HyperCard stack, which can be evaluated for its quality of content, layout, interest, and so on. To get more information about the process, we have also collected the students' intermediate products so that we can evaluate the order in which they create the cards in the stack and the ways in which they change them over time. We also gave written midterm and final examinations that required students to describe the approach they would take to a hypothetical project. The questions progressed from general overviews of the whole process to specific questions about each step. For example, we asked, "What are the most important questions to ask about the Civil War?" and "Where would you find information?"

Even though these written evaluations target the Steps to Discovery directly, they cannot assess students' ability to actually use the skills independently, to make appropriate decisions about how to frame their research and communication, or about how much effort students are putting into the project. Our central assessment aims to document these processes. Each student participated in two miniproject assessments during the year, once between November and February, and then again between March and May. For each assessment, the researchers worked with 15 students at a time for 4 consecutive days on a research project requiring a HyperCard product (thus it took 8 weeks to complete one round of assessment for all 120 students). During the 8 hours that each group of students worked on the assessment, researchers rated each student's level of independent execution of 16 substeps of the Steps to Discovery model, took videotaped snapshots of key points in the process (the initial brainstorming session, the organization session, and the presentation/reflection session), and wrote qualitative descriptions of each student's participation, effort, and motivation. (See Carver et al., 1992, for details of the assessment design.)

## PROMISING RESULTS OF COGNITIVE APPRENTICESHIP

To demonstrate the gains that students made in acquiring the Steps to Discovery, I present quantitative summary data for the whole group of subjects and then discuss two sample cases in detail.

Table 12.3 shows the gains that the four classes of students participating in the project made on the written exam between the first and second semester. The increasing scores reflect greater familiarity with the five steps, both in general descriptions and in response to specific queries. For example, half of the students who took both tests (41/82) generated more open-ended questions on the final than the midterm and only 7 had fewer. Similarly, half of the students cited more diverse resources on the final than on the midterm and only 3 cited fewer. Samples of improved answers are included in the cases that follow.

TABLE 12.3
Improvement in Written Exam Scores

|  | Midterm | | | Final | | |
|---|---|---|---|---|---|---|
|  | (30 Pts) January | | | (31 Pts) June | | |
| Group A | 21.44 | (71%) | N = 17 | 24.92 | (80%) | N = 21 |
| Group B | 19.21 | (64%) | N = 24 | 24.80 | (80%) | N = 25 |
| Group C | 20.13 | (67%) | N = 23 | 27.41 | (88%) | N = 22 |
| Group D | 21.57 | (72%) | N = 28 | 29.07 | (94%) | N = 28 |
| Overall | 20.86 | (70%) | N = 92 | 27.19 | (88%) | N = 96 |

During the process assessment, each student's ability to execute each of the Steps to Discovery substeps was rated as: 1—Able to do the step when the name is suggested, 2—Needs a substantial hint, or 3—Needs detailed instruction. Table 12.4 shows the overall improvement across the 16 substeps for each class. The basic improvement is from needing hints or detailed instruction on each step to being able to do some steps independently and needing hints on others. The sample cases include data for each substep separately.

The two sample cases are included in the Appendix. EM was a white, female student with high ability but extremely low engagement, partially as a result of conflicts at home. She developed a positive rapport with one of the teachers and several of the researchers and was discovered to have a talent for both conducting research and creating HyperCard stacks. MR was a Hispanic, male student with lower ability and inconsistent engagement in school. The use of computers interested him, and he responded well to the extra attention provided by the researchers.

The case data presented in the Appendix includes the checklist scores for both assessments, summaries of the notes each student took in the assessment packets provided by the researchers, the qualitative descriptions of the student's engagement during each phase of the project, and the stacks produced. The final entries for each case include contrasting answers from the written midterm and final exams. Although the reader is encouraged to review these cases carefully, I will highlight several key features of each.

TABLE 12.4
Improvement in Independent Skill Use

|  | Assessment 1 | | Assessment 2 | |
|---|---|---|---|---|
| Group A | 2.11 | N = 17 | 1.59 | N = 15 |
| Group B | 2.26 | N = 19 | 1.65 | N = 22 |
| Group C | 2.05 | N = 20 | 1.62 | N = 17 |
| Group D | 1.99 | N = 18 | 1.37 | N = 22 |
| Overall | 2.10 | N = 74 | 1.56 | N = 76 |

EM proved to be familiar with the ASK and FIND stages early in the year, so her major improvement between assessments was in the latter steps to discovery. Similarly, the biggest change in her assessment packet was in the drawing of an appropriate stack diagram during the organizing session. The improvement in her motivation, if somewhat inconsistent, is evident from the qualitative descriptions. The resulting improvement in her stacks can be seen in the increasing relevance of the graphics, descriptiveness of the button names, and the amount of important information conveyed. Her answers to the opinion questions on the final indicate that she was aware of her progress and her need for engagement in the learning process.

MR began with lower scores on the first assessment checklist, so he had greater room for improvement in all areas. These improvements are clear from the additional questions he generated in his assessment packet and in the nature of his card plan. The fact that the computer would serve as a hook for MR is evident early in the first assessment when the promise of working on them motivated him to finish gathering his information. The graphics in his first stack and the descriptiveness of his buttons further indicate his interest and capability in that area. MR's need for continual support and encouragement from the researchers continues on the second assessment. He has also managed to get past the graphics "bug" to focus more of his attention on including information relevant to his topic on the second stack. MR's overview of the research process is substantially deeper on the final, although some of his other answers still reflect less than desirable depth.

In both cases, the students improved dramatically during the Year of Discovery program. They became interested in the project work, particularly in using HyperCard as a medium. At the same time, they both still have considerable room for improvement.

The positive group and individual data even after an intervention of only 1 year, together with the experience collaborating with committed teachers in the school, have convinced me that the potential for the effective use of cognitive-apprenticeship approaches in public schools is real, even on a large scale. At the same time, suggesting extended application of cognitive-apprenticeship principles requires evaluation of the extent to which the principles were actually followed in the Year of Discovery program and specification of ways to follow them more closely.

## VIOLATING APPRENTICESHIP ASSUMPTIONS

Many of the problems we encountered while implementing cognitive-apprenticeship principles in the Year of Discovery program can be traced to violations of the basic apprenticeship assumptions. Though we composed an implementation team of experienced teachers and consultants, the Year of Discovery design required them to teach across disciplines, use new technology, and use new apprenticeship methods. In other words, they were not actually experts in all of the relevant aspects of teaching. In many of the educational reforms, the teachers are, in fact, apprentices of mentor teachers as they learn to teach in more effective ways. This problem was exaggerated by the high teacher mobility; only one of the seven teachers currently teaching in our project was among the eight teachers participating when I last spoke at Fordham in November 1991.

Viewing the students as apprentices has similar problems to viewing the teachers as experts. We were asking the students to learn new domain knowledge, new heuristics, and new technology all at once, which means that they didn't get to focus enough on any one aspect. Creating large classes with students ranging from those needing special education services to those qualifying for the Major Achievement Program was an impractical way to provide heterogeneity because the teachers could not handle the diversity in addition to the new project approach. We also began to have difficulty maintaining the heterogeneity of the class once advanced course options became available. For example, more advanced students can take foreign language class instead of reading, but it is only offered during certain periods.

In order to maximize the time each student spent with the project teacher, we created daily blocks of project time in the morning. But the students' high mobility and low attendance rates reduced the amount of actual time available for the project. Of the 130 students on the roster at the beginning of the year, we lost 21 and gained 10 within the first month of school. We lost another 10 and gained 5 during the rest of the year, and we had 3 truants. Even for the students on the books and attending school throughout the year, we had only 48 students present for both written exams and both process assessments. Those with high attendance are disproportionately from the higher ability groups, which makes it even more difficult to help engage lower ability students enough to help them progress significantly.

Finally, we focused our curriculum on developing independent learning and communication skills in the hopes of linking with areas that students could both relate to their current lives and find useful in their future jobs. Unfortunately, the students were still required to take final exams focusing on pure domain knowledge (despite waivers we had initially secured from the school district), so they felt pressure to turn their attention to memorization in preparation for the immediate exams rather than the long-term goals. Also, the district policy of social promotion, whereby students progress to ninth grade at age 16 regardless of earning passing grades in eighth grade, serves to decrease motivation to engage in school for students who have already repeated one or two grades and are therefore older than the rest (one third of our students in the 1992–1993 academic year).

## MAKING COGNITIVE APPRENTICESHIP WORK

Given the many ways in which even the highly supported and well-funded Year of Discovery project compromised the basic assumptions of the apprenticeship model, how can the model be implemented more fully so that the potentials evident in the data presented here can be maximized?

- Invest in Teacher Training. Both practicing teachers and student teachers need to be taught about apprenticeship by apprenticeship. In other words, we need to change both the content and the methods of teachers' education and professional development.

- Allow Choices/Specialization for Students. Because knowledge is expanding so rapidly, educators cannot keep using the strategy of simply expanding the curriculum, and selection of a standard set of content appropriate for all students becomes inappropriate. Broad coverage of basics could be the standard for some period of time or for specific areas, yet students could progressively narrow their choice of specialty areas as they develop clearer interests and deeper knowledge and skills. Breadth in areas like current events, health, and so on, might continue throughout the required schooling period.

- Promote Long-Term Affiliation. There are many ways that students can get the benefit of continuity even when individual teachers make transitions. Link students with a group of teachers for several years at a time. For example, in our middle school, students now stay with the same teaching team (one teacher from each subject area) for all 3 years in the school. This system allows teachers to develop relationships with both the students and their families. Another possibility for establishing long-term affiliation is to involve individuals and businesses from the local community. As schools become more effective, they can also attract families in their community to keep their children in the local school rather than busing them across town.

- Align Assessments with Priorities. When establishing curriculum priorities according to the apprenticeship model, the focus moves away from pure content knowledge, so assessments must shift as well. The content, format, and scoring of individual exams must reflect the learning environment that the students experience. At the same time, the policies for larger scale assessment and promotion must be consistent with the mastery learning goal.

Take heart! The possibility of designing effective cognitive apprenticeship environments is within our reach. Many of the contributors to this volume have developed instructional methods that can be used within the cognitive-apprenticeship framework and have provided pointers for implementing them in typical school settings. Reaching the goal of facilitating students' thinking in the classroom is well worth the time and effort of the talented teachers, researchers, parents, and administrators currently involved in implementation projects. As in many of these efforts, the students in the Year of Discovery program have begun setting their minds to work in the classroom and their clear progress motivates future implementation initiatives.

## ACKNOWLEDGMENTS

This research was supported by grants from the James S. McDonnell Foundation, Cognitive Studies in Educational Practice Program; Apple Computer, Inc., Crossroads Program; and a subcontract from the Center For Technology in Education. I acknowledge the following staff and graduate students for their important contributions to site design and development, model building, and data collection and analysis: Pamela Asquith, Deborah Essley, Paula Jones, Margaret Mukooza, Doug Renz, Myunghee Ryu, and Stan Swiercz. I thank the students, teachers, and administrators of the Charlotte Middle School for their cooperation and participation in this project.

## APPENDIX:
### Data From Two Cases

### D2-EM ASSESSMENT CHECKLIST SCORES

|                                  | 1st | 2nd |
|----------------------------------|-----|-----|
| Ask                              |     |     |
| Generate ideas                   | 1   | 1   |
| Form questions                   | 1   | 1   |
| Select questions                 | 2   | 1   |
| Generate resources               | 1   | 1   |
| Select resources if too many     | 1   | 1   |
| Ask average                      | 1.2 | 1.0 |
| Find                             |     |     |
| Access resource                  | 1   | 1   |
| Access info within resource      | 2   | 1   |
| Summarize info                   | 3   | 2   |
| Find average                     | 2.0 | 1.3 |
| Organize                         |     |     |
| Organize info in some way        | 2   | 2   |
| Represent info to fit the format | 2   | 1   |
| Plan the entire presentation     | 2   | 1   |
| Organize average                 | 2.0 | 1.3 |
| Present                          |     |     |
| Present the product              | 2   | 2   |
| Clarify the info                 | 3   | 2   |
| Explain how it's done            | 3   | 1   |
| Present average                  | 2.7 | 1.7 |

Reflect

| | | |
|---|---|---|
| Evaluate own presentation | 3 | 2 |
| Evaluate peer presentation | 3 | 1 |
| Reflect average | 3.0 | 1.5 |

| | | |
|---|---|---|
| Overall Average | 2.0 | 1.3 |

## D2-EM ASSESSMENT PACKET COMPARISON

### 1st Assessment—Civil Rights

Subtopic—Susan B. Anthony
Ask
Generated 7 questions (4 open-ended) plus 3 follow-ups
Ask–Find
Generated all three types of resources (people, written, visual)
Selected library books and Mr. Allen (SS teacher)
Scattered notes, copying evident
Relevant info, clear source
Organize
No stack diagram
Card plan: intro-family life-middle-pictures-her picture-end of her life-end

### 2nd Assessment—Future Plans

Subtopic—Doctor
Ask
Generated 8 questions (6 open-ended) [note form not full questions]
Ask–Find
Generated all three types of resources (people, written, visual)
Selected library, assessment library, T.V.
Notes in paragraph form, some copying evident
Relevant info, clear source
Organize
Stack Diagram (drawn): intro → index → [types or ed or salary or pictures]
     all of which → end → intro
Card Plan: intro-index-types of doctors-education-salary-end

## EM—1ST ASSESSMENT

### Ask

EM did well in this session, in spite of MH's disruptions. MH specifically directed taunts at EM. Over time, EM gained control of herself, and handled MH's taunts with maturity by ignoring and disregarding them. This proved effective, and

MH's attempts to aggravate EM diminished. EM was quite upset that MH was allowed to choose another topic after throwing a tantrum because he did not want to research woman's suffrage. She viewed this as MH receiving special privilege because of his sex. In spite of all the distractions, EM was very involved in the brainstorming, and she produced some questions that were a level deeper than those produced by the majority of the students. Overall, EM appears to be quite intelligent as well as personable, although she does not think of herself as very smart. With encouragement, she could be very successful in the future.

### Find

At the beginning of the session, EM was well-behaved and receptive to the assessor's suggestions. But her work habit was not consistent. The second day of the project, she was disruptive and unmotivated; as a result, she refused to attain enough information to answer any of her questions, or summarize the data.

### Organize

EM came late to the organize session because she had gone to one of the classrooms to talk to her friends. It was difficult to get her to take the work seriously. She was restless and started playing with the videocamera and looking out the window to see other students. At the end she did discuss her plans with the assessor but she did not put much effort into it.

### HyperCard Work (see Fig. 12.1)

EM was next to impossible to motivate during computer time. Even with the assessor's full attention, she refused to work until threatened with a referral to the house office. When I asked her what the problem was, she explained that she and her mother had a "big fight" that she was very upset about. The next day her mother was in school and confirmed that they were having a difficult time dealing with each other and that EM was going to be spending some time living with Mrs. M (her project teacher).

### Present/Reflect

Consistent with her behavior during the entire assessment, EM was not interested in participating and interrupted conversations between myself and the other group members. EM chose to complain about the project rather than take part in the activity.

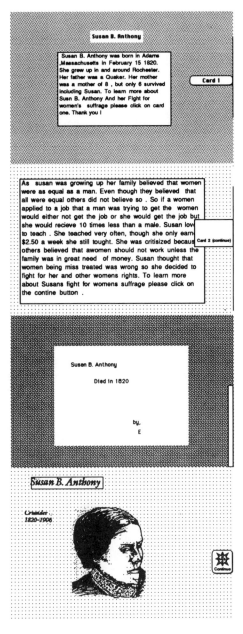

FIG. 12.1. HyperCard work on 1st assessment by EM.

## EM—2ND ASSESSMENT

### Ask

EM did the bulk of the work in this session. She was attentive and engaged throughout our time, and produced a good number of questions and resources. EM seems to want to succeed, but also seems to be unsure of herself and uncomfortable with her role in school. EM's motivation is tentative, and she may lack self-confidence in her ability to succeed. She seems to have ambivalent expectations about her future. She does seem to have the ability to be successful, but not the belief in herself.

### Find

EM was not quite motivated to work on finding information. She was very passive and did not accomplish much work the first day. However, her work attitude changed positively the next day. She took the initiative to find information on her own, and caught up from the previous day's lack of work. She summarized a great deal of information about becoming a doctor; her summary was relevant to her questions.

### Organize

EM was not disruptive but she did not take any initiative to start working on her organization plan. She needed coaching and direction from me to fill out the plan, but then drew her diagram on her own.

### HyperCard Work (see Fig. 12.2)

EM did much better this assessment compared to last. She stayed focused on the computers even though she claims not to like them, and completed a nice stack. The improvement in her attitude and effort were notable.

### Present/Reflect

EM's stack had a lot of detailed information but she could have spent more time proofreading as there were several spelling and grammatical errors. EM was restless during much of the activity and wanted to get finished as soon as possible, which meant that she didn't give much thought to some of the reflection questions. EM made it clear that she doesn't like doing the assessment project.

### D2:EM WRITTEN EXAM (10/30 → 31/31)

List the Steps
    Midterm:   "Ask, Find, Organize, Present, Reflect"
    Final:       "Ask, Find, Organize, Present, Reflect"

FIG. 12.2.   HyperCard work on 2nd assessment by EM.

Process Overview

Midterm:   "I would ask myself the questions needed. Then I'd go to the library or other sources and find the info needed. Then I'd gather my info, put it on the computer. Finally I'd present. But after I'd look at my presentation and think about what would make it better so I know next time"

Final:   "First I would find out what part of the Civil War I had to work on. And then make a list of questions. Next I would find the information from the library. After that I would organize the info. The next step would be to put it on the computer and present it. Finally I would look back and see what I could have done to improve."

Best Questions

Midterm:   no answer

Final:   "Where did the war take place? What year was it? What were some causes for war? Who? __ vs. __ What is the civil war? Who won?"

Where to Look
  Midterm:   no answer
  Final:     "Library, encyclopedia, magazines, T.V., movies, assessment library"

Ways to Organize
  Midterm:   no answer
  Final:     "It could be organized in an oral presentation or in HyperCard"

Show HyperCard
  Midterm:   no answer
  Final:     (drawn) intro → end/index → [who? where? famous people and marks, etc.] all of which → end/index

HyperCard vs. Essay/Oral
  Midterm:   no answer
  Final:     Better:  "It looks neater, helps learn more about the computer, fun"
             Worse:   "a lot of work"

Good Presentation
  Midterm:   no answer
  Final:     "alot of pictures and effects but still having a lot of information"

Opinion Questions
  Midterm:   "At first when you begin the program it's a little difficult, but with the help of Mrs. Jones, Mrs. Wssly, and all the others it's like fun."
  Final:     "Always listen to the teachers. If you don't listen you will find out the hard way like I did."
             "I liked the Colonial Day project. Because it challenged me but at the same time I was learning and having fun."
             "I am going to start fresh in September. I will listen more."

## C1-MR ASSESSMENT CHECKLIST SCORES

|                              | 1st | 2nd |
|------------------------------|-----|-----|
| Ask                          |     |     |
| Generate ideas               | 3   | 3   |
| Form questions               | 2   | 2   |
| Select questions             | 2   | 2   |
| Generate resources           | 2   | 3   |
| Select resources if too many | 2   | 1   |
| Ask average                  | 2.2 | 2.2 |
| Find                         |     |     |
| Access resource              | 3   | 1   |
| Access info within resource  | 3   | 1   |

| | | |
|---|---|---|
| Summarize info | 2 | 2 |
| Find average | 2.7 | 1.3 |
| Organize | | |
| Organize info in some way | 3 | 2 |
| Represent info to fit the format | 3 | 1 |
| Plan the entire presentation | 3 | 1 |
| Organize average | 3.0 | 1.3 |
| Present | | |
| Present the product | 3 | 2 |
| Clarify the info | 3 | 2 |
| Explain how it's done | 3 | 1 |
| Present average | 3.0 | 1.7 |
| Reflect | | |
| Evaluate own presentation | 3 | 2 |
| Evaluate peer presentation | 3 | 1 |
| Reflect average | 3.0 | 1.5 |
| Overall Average | 2.7 | 1.7 |

## C1-MR ASSESSMENT PACKET COMPARISON

### 1st Assessment—Future Plans

Subtopic—Basketball Career
Ask
   Generated 1 question (1 open-ended)
Ask–Find
   Generated all three types of resources (people, written, visual)
   Selected library books and encyclopedia
   Notes in list form
   Relevant info, source unclear
Organize
   Linear stack diagram: introduction → index → nutrition → exercise → training → skill
   Card plan: introduction-index[nutrition,exercise,training,skills]-nutrition-exercise-training-skills

### 2nd Assessment—AIDS

Ask
   Generated 9 questions (5 open-ended)
   Selected 3 questions
Ask–Find
   Generated all three types of resources (people, written, visual)

Selected library
Notes in paragraph form, some copying evident
Notes relevant, organized by question, clear source
Organize
Stack Diagram (drawn): intro → index → [subtopics or end] → intro
{some was drawn by experimenter}
Card Plan: what is going to be about-index-what does aids come from-is
there a cure-how long can you live if you have aids-what I learn, end

## MR—1ST ASSESSMENT

### Ask

MR was quiet through most of the session. He suggested only one research topic and one resource. Efforts to try to get more involvement from him were unsuccessful.

### Find

On the first day of the assessment project, he was not motivated to read articles, instead, he was more interested in fellow students' HC activities. I had to keep an eye on him and push him on task all the time. Therefore, the process of finding information was slow. Yet, he did not interrupt other students. At the end of the second day of the assessment project, he was speedy to finish up summarizing information since he realized that most students were working on the computers.

### Organize

MR was very quiet during this session. He was not disruptive or distracted by others. But he was not participating very actively, either. When given individual attention and help, however, he became responsive and discussed his plan with the instructor to get it done. With such a close environment with much personal attention, MR could concentrate himself more than he could in the classroom. His work attitude was generally quite positive.

### HyperCard Work (see Fig. 12.3)

He worked quietly and independently. He concentrated on his work all the time.

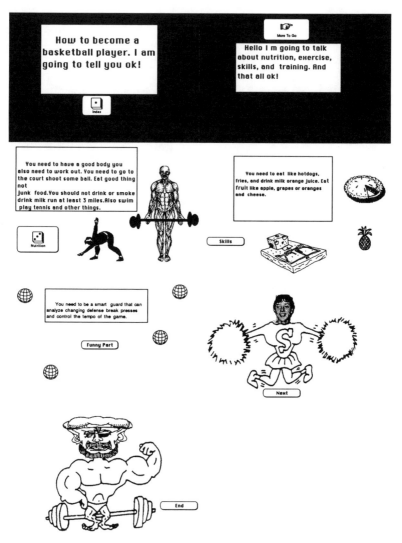

FIG. 12.3. HyperCard work on 1st assessment by MR.

## Present/Reflect

MR seemed very bored and was reluctant to participate during our present/reflect session. He offered very few comments about his group members' work even when I asked him directly. Regarding his own work, he commented that he needed to add more pictures and planned to do that when he returned to the classroom. However, MR would not comment further on any of the other evaluation questions I asked him. Regarding what he liked best about the project, he said, "Nothing." This remark did not really agree with what I observed of him while working on his stack. I think he did like doing the project, but over time MR seems to get restless and loses his motivation to continue working.

## MR—2ND ASSESSMENT

### Ask

MR was quiet through most of the session. He made very few contributions, either to the list of questions, or to the list of resources. Attempts to draw him into the activity were unsuccessful. His few contributions hint that he may not be comfortable with the ASK process, and may lack some of the needed subskills. He did pay attention, and recorded the ideas that the other students were generating throughout the session.

### Find

MR was quiet and well-behaved through the session. He devoted himself to finding information, although he needed help from the assessor to access the materials. He had almost finished taking notes the first day of the project, which gave him a good sense of accomplishment. His summaries were relevant to his questions.

### Organize

MR was a little reluctant at first to get involved. He complained about having to come to the office again. After he saw the rest of his group members working, he became more involved. MR needed some guidance from Ms. A to get his plan organized, but drew the map of his stack on his own.

### HyperCard Work (see Fig. 12.4)

MR was a little slow on the computers but seems to enjoy them. He was much more focused this assessment compared to the last and stayed on task nicely. His HyperCard skills were poorly developed.

### Present/Reflect

At first MR seemed reluctant to participate but as the activity progressed he became more involved and thought seriously about how he could improve his stack. He seemed very proud of his work ("I was really into this, man," he said to John).

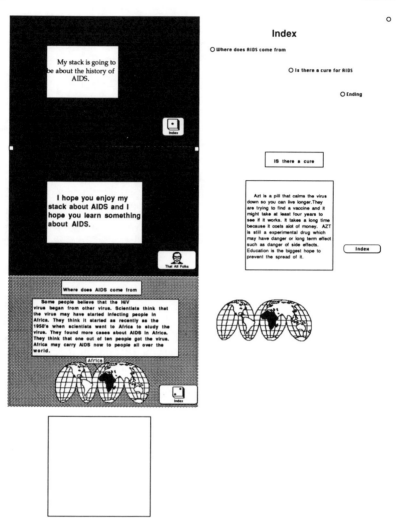

FIG. 12.4.   HyperCard work on 2nd assessment by MR.

## C1-MR WRITTEN EXAM (12/30 → 26/31)

List the Steps
    Midterm:  "Think, Recognize, Ask, Find, Look"
    Final:      "Find, Organize, Present, Reflect, Define"

Process Overview
    Midterm:  "Go to the libray and get the good infomation about Vietnam War"
    Final:      "I will first find out what are the questions And then I will find
                information on the civil war. And then get some answer how it

started And then write down the important thing down in sheet paper then go over it then copy in the compter."

Best Questions

Midterm: "How did it started?"

Final: "How the civil war started Why where they fighting How long it took to finish the civil war."

Where to Look

Midterm: "The libray and local libray"

Final: "I will go to the library and find book of the civil war"

Ways to Organize

Midterm: no answer

Final: "First you go over it and see how it start the civil war And then you kept on going"

Show HyperCard

Midterm: no answer

Final: "I will open it and write my work and put diagram in it so look beter."

HyperCard vs. Essay/Oral

Midterm: no answer

Final: "For me HyperCard is better because it's more quicker And more least work the writing again."

Good Presentation

Midterm: "Good information, pictures of war"

Final: "If you have any picture in stack If you have good information."

Opinion Questions

Midterm: "I will tell him to study when he got test."

"I like this semester because it was fun, we work together alot"

Final: "To work hard if he do he past."

"I like the canning one because it was fun and you work with other people."

"I will do alot of my work. Pay attention to class."

## REFERENCES

Carver, S. M. (in press). The Discover Rochester Design Experiment: Collaborative change through five designs. In J. Hawkins & A. Collins (Eds.), *Design experiments: Integrating technology into schools*. Cambridge: Cambridge University Press.

Carver, S. M., Lehrer, R., Connell, T., & Erickson, J. (1992). Learning by hypermedia design: Issues of assessment and implementation. *Educational Psychologist, 27*(3), 385–404.

Collins, A., Brown, J. S., & Newman, S. E. (1989). Cognitive apprenticeship: Teaching the craft of reading, writing, and mathematics. In L. B. Resnick (Ed.), *Knowing, learning, and instruction: Essays in honor of Robert Glaser* (pp. 453–494). Hillsdale, NJ: Lawrence Erlbaum Associates.

Collins, A., Hawkins, J., & Carver, S. M. (1991). A cognitive apprenticeship for disadvantaged students. In B. Means, C. Chelemer, & M. S. Knapp (Eds.), *Teaching advanced skills to at-risk students: Views from research and practice* (pp. 216–243). San Francisco, CA: Jossey-Bass.

Lave, J. (1988). *The culture of acquisition and the practice of understanding* (Rep. No. IRL88-0007). Palo Alto, CA: Institute for Research on Learning.

Palincsar, A. S., & Brown, A. L. (1984). Reciprocal teaching of comprehension-fostering and monitoring activities. *Cognition and Instruction, 1*, 117–175.

Resnick, L. B. (1987). Learning in school and out. *Educational Researcher, 16*(9), 13–20.

Rogoff, B. (1990). *Apprenticeship in thinking: Cognitive development in social context.* New York: Oxford University Press.

Schoenfeld, A. H. (1985). *Mathematical problem solving.* Orlando, FL: Academic Press.

# Chapter 13

# Cooperative Learning in Reading and Language Arts

Edythe J. Holubec
David W. Johnson
Roger T. Johnson
*University of Minnesota*

"I certainly am enjoying teaching a lot more now that I am using cooperative learning," one teacher says to another.

"Cooperative learning? That's just group work with another name, isn't it?" the teacher responds.

"Not at all. With group work, you put students in groups and give very little direction. With cooperative learning, you start out with a great deal of structure for short periods of time and teach your students how to work together."

"That sounds interesting. Tell me more."

Cooperative learning is an effective way to help students learn, but many teachers do not realize that cooperative learning is not the same as group work. These teachers put students in groups, tell them to work together, and then are disappointed with the results. They may make the groups too large, use group grades to try and force students to work together, and give low grades to those who do not succeed. When students and parents complain, the teacher may decide that "cooperative learning" does not work and discontinues group work.

However, teachers who learn the differences between group work and cooperative learning find vast differences. They learn how to determine an effective group size, how to use methods other than grades to help students work together, and how to teach students to work with others effectively. It usually takes several years to become adept at structuring cooperative learning, but teachers find that teaching becomes easier and more effective when they have learned how to do it. Cooperative learning works well in the areas of reading and language arts.

## COOPERATIVE LEARNING IS DIFFERENT
## FROM GROUP WORK

In traditional classroom learning groups, members may see little benefit from working together. Interdependence and a sense of teamwork is usually low. Often, very little joint work is required and members do not take responsibility for others' learning. Members may work on their own, interacting primarily to clarify assignments and share information. Achievement may be individually recognized and rewarded. Often an appointed group leader is in charge of directing members' participation. Groups are not taught social skills or how to process the quality of the group's efforts. A group grade may be given to reward or punish the group for its work.

A cooperative learning group, however, is a team. As seen in Table 13.1, students work together to accomplish shared goals. Students are responsible for all group members' learning and are not finished with the work until every group member has learned. Group members hold themselves and each other accountable for producing high quality work and achieving the group's goals. The work is structured so that it is meaningful and each member is needed. Members provide both academic and personal support based on being committed to and caring about each other. Students are taught the appropriate taskwork and teamwork skills needed to be successful, and teachers hold students accountable for using these skills to coordinate the group's efforts and achieve the group's goals. All members

TABLE 13.1
Traditional Learning Groups Versus Cooperative Learning Groups

| Traditional Groups | Cooperative Groups |
|---|---|
| Low interdependence. Members take responsibility only for self. Focus is on individual performance only. | High positive interdependence. Members are responsible for own and each other's learning. Focus is on joint performance. |
| Individual accountability only. | Both group and individual accountability. Members hold self and others accountable for high quality work. |
| Assignments are discussed with little commitment to each other's learning. | Members promote each other's success, doing real work together, helping and supporting each other's efforts to learn. |
| Teamwork skills are ignored. Leader is appointed to direct members' participation. | Teamwork skills are emphasized. Members are taught and expected to use social skills. Leadership shared by all members. |
| No group processing of the quality of its work. Individual accomplishments are rewarded. | Groups process quality of work and how effectively members work together. Continuous improvement is emphasized. |

are responsible for group leadership, and groups routinely analyze their effectiveness in achieving their goals and in working together. The emphasis is on continuously improving the quality of the learning and the quality of the teamwork.

Teachers doing group work may use it only during a special project or lesson. Teachers doing cooperative learning use it daily. They know how to use cooperative learning effectively for as briefly as 3 minutes or for a whole period. They can use it to appropriately reinforce previously learned material or skills. They can use it to introduce new material. They can use it with the anticipatory set, guided practice, peer assessment of individual work, discussion, drill, or closure. They can use it to teach reading, writing, speaking, listening, and thinking.


## THE FIVE ESSENTIAL ELEMENTS

Teachers who master cooperative learning learn how to apply the five essential elements of cooperative learning. Why? Because this puts teachers, not books or curriculum, in control of directing the classroom learning. This allows teachers to tailor cooperative learning to their unique instructional needs. This allows teachers to diagnose the problems some students may have in working together and to intervene in order to increase student and group effectiveness.

However, learning how to use the five elements in classrooms is not easy. Like learning to play a sport or a musical instrument, it does not happen overnight. It takes continued training and practice. Is it worth it? Research and classroom practitioners have indicated that when these elements are carefully structured into a lesson, effective learning takes place. Cooperative learning improves student learning and retention, promotes higher level understandings, self-esteem, motivation, acceptance of self and others, and improves attendance and behavior. What educator could argue with that? However, teachers must learn to effectively implement the strategies that make it work in their classrooms.

### Element 1: Positive Interdependence

The heart of cooperative learning is positive interdependence. Teachers structure this by giving students the goal of learning the assigned material *and* making certain that all members of the cooperative group learn it. Students are not considered finished until all group members learn the material at a preset level (mastery), until every member improves, or until an acceptable group product is completed, one which every member helped with and can explain. Positive goal interdependence can be strengthened with a reward for successful groups (such as bonus points or time to play a learning game), divided resources (each group member is given a part of the total information required to complete an assignment), and/or with everyone being assigned a needed job or role (such as reader, recorder, checker, encourager, elaborator, summarizer, and question-asker).

### Element 2: Face-to-Face Promotive Interaction

Once positive interdependence is established, the teacher must ensure that students interact in a positive way to help each other accomplish the task and promote each other's success. *When students explain their learning to others, they learn more.* So, teachers make certain that students explain their learning and thinking to other students often during a session in order to enhance learning. Students are taught to listen to others with care and to provide each other with the help, assistance, support, and encouragement needed for good learning.

### Element 3: Individual Accountability

Students learn together so that they can subsequently perform better as individuals. *The purpose of cooperative learning groups is to make each member individually stronger.* To ensure that each member is involved, a small group size (two or three members) is best. Individual members must learn that they cannot "hitchhike" on the work of others. Teachers hold students accountable for their share of the work by making certain that individuals contribute to their group, by informally quizzing students at random, or by giving everyone individual tests or assignments over material the group is asked to master. Results are shared with both the individual and the group, so that group members know who needs more assistance, support, and encouragement.

### Element 4: Social Skills

Contributing to the success of a cooperative effort requires interpersonal and small-group skills. Placing socially unskilled individuals in a group and telling them to cooperate is a formula for failure. Students must be taught the appropriate communication, leadership, decision-making, trust-building, and conflict-management skills. The teacher directly teaches students such skills as *checking for understanding, encouraging others to contribute,* or *summarizing the group's ideas so far,* then encourages practice until students do them automatically.

### Element 5: Group Processing

When students in cooperative learning groups regularly discuss how well they are learning and working together and make plans to excel, it should not surprise anyone that achievement and effective group skills improve. Teachers should carefully structure the time and procedures for students to reflect, share, and plan for academic and group improvement. Groups should answer questions such as "What specific things are you doing that helps your group learn the material?" and "What specific things are you doing that helps your group work together effectively?" This helps students learn to value their positive actions and make a commitment to continue them. Questions such as "What is one challenge that would make your group even better?" and "What is your plan for doing it?" then help students make a commitment to improve. When members work *and* reflect on their work together on a regular basis, the group gradually and continually improves.

Cooperative learning groups may be used to ensure active cognitive processing of information and ideas with *informal cooperative learning*, to teach specific content and lessons with *formal cooperative learning*, or to provide long-term support and assistance for academic progress with *cooperative base groups*.

## START WITH INFORMAL COOPERATIVE LEARNING

Teachers often find it easiest to begin with *informal cooperative learning*. Informal cooperative learning is a strategy for getting all students to cognitively process material in a short time. Learning is enhanced when students explain their learning and ideas *out loud* to another student, a method that can be used with *any* lesson. How is it done? Teachers assign students a partner and, at various places in the lesson, have the students explain and listen to their partners explain their learning so far. Teachers selectively listen during this time to check student comprehension and determine if corrective feedback is needed. The cognitive processing involved produces greater student understanding and retention. The short amount of time involved (1–2 minutes) and the highly structured format help students keep focused on the task.

Any direct instruction, discussion, or learning experience can be transformed into an active-learning experience with full classroom participation using informal cooperative learning.

### Direct Instruction

Before a lecture, teachers can involve every student in contributing what they already know about the subject if they have partners talk together to determine what they know. Teachers listen and encourage both partners to share. They correct misconceptions, if necessary. Then teachers give information at the level needed for their students. The stop every 10 minutes or so and ask their students to discuss with their partner what they are learning. Again, teachers listen to determine if students are participating and comprehending. Teachers proceed through the information in this manner until they have finished, then have students summarize their overall learning together.

### Reading to the Class

Before reading a story to the class, teachers may read the title and show the picture to the students, then tell students to ask their partner to tell them what they think this book will be about. If previous knowledge is needed for understanding, teachers can have the children ask their partners questions to determine if they have the prerequisite knowledge (e.g., "What is an island?"). As the children ask and answer each other, teachers listen carefully and give more explanation if needed. Teachers read a portion of the story and then stop for a comprehension check. Again, students are told to ask their partners questions that will check comprehension and perhaps predict or elaborate on the material covered so far. Teachers proceed in this way through the story. At the end, students are asked to tell their partners how they liked the reading and to thank their partners for helping them learn. With a bit of forethought, a system such as Bloom's Taxonomy (Bloom, 1956) can be used to induce thinking on all levels: knowledge, understanding, application, analysis, synthesis, and evaluation.

**Sustained Silent Reading**

In sustained silent reading, students choose books on their reading and interest levels to read alone for a prolonged period of time. Although reading is done individually, getting students ready to comprehend and teaching them to analyze and summarize their reading make good cooperative bookends. Before reading, teachers have students explain to their partners what they read in their book last time and predict what they will read about today. After reading, students summarize what they read and tell their partners what they liked about it. Again, Bloom's Taxonomy can be useful to generate deeper levels of thinking. Such sharing enhances the pleasure of reading, as well as teaching students important skills such as summarizing. Students also get oral reading practice by reading favorite books or sections to their partners. When teachers unobtrusively listen in, they gain an understanding of the individual student's reading preferences and strengths.

**Oral Reading**

Instead of tedious, teacher-directed "round-robin" readings at the instructional reading level, teachers should have students read orally with their partners. Partners can decide how they will divide up the reading material (alternating paragraphs? reading half?). They help each other with difficult words and with understanding what they are reading. Teachers circulate to give additional help and encouragement. If partners are reading from different books, this is no problem: they can read their books to each other. Students thus gain maximum oral reading (and listening) practice with an interested audience in a safe reading environment. No seatwork is needed to keep those not reading busy because every student in the classroom is reading or listening to a partner. Again, teachers unobtrusively listen to gain information about an individual student's reading strengths and weaknesses for future reference.

## GET SERIOUS WITH FORMAL COOPERATIVE LEARNING

When teachers are accustomed to informal cooperative learning, then they should begin to use *formal cooperative learning* to teach specific content and appropriate social skills. The same partners can again be used, as in the informal cooperative learning groups because the best group size is usually two or three members. Groups may last from a single class period to several weeks. Any assignment in any curriculum for any age student can be assigned to formal groups; teachers may best wish to start with guided practice. In planning, teachers should do the following:

1. *Specify the objectives for the lesson.* In every lesson there should be an academic objective specifying the material or concepts to be learned and a social-skills objective specifying the interpersonal or small-group skill to be used and mastered during the lesson.

2. *Make a number of preinstructional decisions.* Teachers should decide on the size of the group (two or three members), how they will assign students to groups (heterogeneous), the roles students will be assigned (such as reader, recorder, encourager), the materials needed to conduct the lesson, and the way the room will be arranged (group members close together).

3. *Explain the task and positive interdependence.* Teachers must clearly define the assignment, explain the required academic concepts and strategies, specify the positive interdependence (such as group goal, shared material, and roles) and maintain individual accountability (through methods such as random checking, quizzes, and roles), give the criteria for success, and explain the social skills in which students will be expected to engage. A group social skill list can be posted in the classroom and emphasized for each cooperative lesson. It may spell out a word (e.g., *groups*) as in the following example:

Give your ideas.
Reach for everyone's best.
Orally explain and listen.
Use quiet voices.
Praise good ideas.
Stay on task.

4. *Monitor the groups.* Teachers always circulate among the groups while they work to observe and monitor student learning and interactions. They intervene when necessary to teach needed academic or social skills. They systematically observe and collect data on each group in order to give positive feedback and help groups set goals for improvement.

5. *Evaluate student learning and social-skill effectiveness.* Student learning is carefully assessed, so that both teachers and students know what has been learned. This can be as simple as having students tell or write what they learned, or may be more formal, with a quiz or assignment. In addition, students evaluate how well they worked as a group and plan for continued improvement. Efforts to learn are celebrated and teachers have students congratulate their group-mates for their hard work.

## Formal Cooperative Learning and Reading/Language Arts

Formal cooperative learning is used to enable all students to master material and learn the necessary language arts and reading skills being taught. Any or all guided practices should be structured in formal cooperative learning lessons. Formal cooperative learning can be used in many ways.

*Reading.*    Teachers can have students work cooperatively together to answer comprehension questions about a reading, to learn to locate information, or to study new vocabulary. Groups can answer questions about such things as theme, plot, and characterizations used in the story; they can write or draw alternative endings to a story. Teachers monitor to make certain every student learns, helps, and explains the work and the material.

*Spelling or Vocabulary Building.*    On the first day, group members divide up the words to learn, then teach their words to the group. The next day, the group writes the words in sentences that illustrate their meaning. The third day, students drill each other, rotating the roles of "teacher" and "student" and help each other think of ways to remember words missed. The fourth day, the teacher gives a practice test and group members grade each other's papers and help one other with needed learning. The fifth day, the teacher gives an individual quiz for an individual grade. Group members encourage each other to do their best and then congratulate each other afterward for their efforts. Bonus points or some other reward may be awarded to groups that improve their work, or when everyone scores above a predetermined criterion.

*Writing Types.*    Before students can manage particular types of writing (e.g., letters, poems, narratives, critiques) they may need experience learning how to write that form in cooperative groups. For example, teaching students to write a comparison–contrast paper starts with direct instruction, with the groups engaging in a guided practice of identifying comparison–contrast paragraphs, then group-writing comparison–contrast paragraphs until every member knows how. Teachers have groups exchange paragraphs and learn to apply criteria for judging the writing, then have students write one individually. Group members check individual papers to determine if members have succeeded in meeting the criteria and congratulate each other on effort and success. During this exercise, teachers circulate, give feedback, point out possible problems, encourage success, and check off each group when members show mastery. Groups discuss what helped them do well and plan for improving their future writing and cooperative interactions.

*Writing Correctly.* As students write, teachers notice areas that need improvement if students are to write more accurately or precisely (i.e., vocabulary, spelling, capitalization, punctuation, transition, characterization, tone). Teaching areas such as these may involve some direct instruction, group-guided practice, independent practice, and individual assessment. It is the group's job to help every member learn the skills being taught, although not everyone in the group has to learn the same material in order for the group to help them meet their learning goals.

*Prewriting and Response Groups.* Students often need help in coming up with a writing topic and seeing it through to fruition. Groups are responsible for helping members find satisfactory topics that fit the assignment. Students orally shape their pieces by explaining what they will write about while group members take notes for them; students use these notes to help in the writing. Since opening paragraphs are often difficult, groups can help members write a good beginning. Writing is individual, but group members assist each other with such elements as staying motivated, getting unblocked, and thinking of better wording. Group members read and respond to the initial drafts: Do they understand it all? Any brilliant parts? Any confusing parts? Does it flow appropriately? Is it effectively paragraphed? Are the beginnings and endings clear? Are transitions in place? Is the tone consistent? Does it fit the assignment? Students then rewrite as needed. In the second draft, group members edit for correctness: punctuation, capitalization, spelling, and usage. This may necessitate another rewriting, after which members will proofread for final corrections. The paper is finally ready either for a wider audience, for a portfolio, or for grading. During this process, teachers circulate and listen, help, encourage, correct, and celebrate interesting ideas and new understandings, and group members congratulate each other on their efforts and successes.

Trust and good relationships are essential for genuine sharing and editing among students. Trust is built *only* over time as students regularly work together and learn that others will respond in a positive, beneficial way to their ideas and writings. The more that teachers have students work together for the good of group members and the more teachers teach students how to be encouraging and positive with each other, the greater the trust and the more genuine the writing and editing. Also, teachers must model trust behaviors by monitoring in a positive, encouraging, and helpful way.

*Speaking, Listening, and Thinking.*   As teachers teach students cooperative skills, they are also directly teaching students to be better communicators, listeners, and thinkers. The list of cooperative skills includes such *speaking skills* as summarizing out loud, extending other's answers, and generating further answers. *Listening skills* include paraphrasing other's work, encouraging participation by all, and asking other members to plan out loud. *Thinking skills* involve seeking accuracy by correcting and/or adding to summaries, seeking elaboration, and integrating ideas into a single position. As students learn these and other cooperative skills, they are also learning language arts. The practice that students receive while working consistently in cooperative groups ensure that they will develop these skills past the superficial level.

*Oral Presentations.*   Anytime teachers wish to teach or prepare students to give oral presentations, cooperative learning can help. Group members prepare each other by helping members come up with topics, helping each other gather information, helping to prepare the oral presentation, then being a practice audience. Members coach each other on appropriate presentation skills and help others manage the nervousness involved in speaking to a larger group. Presentations are made either to the whole class or to another group. Partners also learn to give joint speeches, because students should be able to do both.

*Structured Controversy.*   Teachers help engage students in learning and promote effective conflict skills by using structured-controversy groups. Any issue in reading or language arts that has two sides can be used (e.g., preservation of rain forest vs. development of resources, Edgar Allan Poe vs. Walt Whitman as the better writer, the Puritans' too restrictive life vs. their creating a solid foundation for moral living). Students are assigned to groups of four and each pair in the group takes a side. The pairs do research to gather facts and opinions, then each pair gets 5 minutes to explain and defend their side while the other pair listens, asks questions, and takes notes. Ten minutes of open discussion follow, with each pair trying to convince the other. Then, pairs switch sides and, from their notes and from memory, argue the opposite side using the same time frame. Afterward, students are taught to drop sides and write a concensus position with which all members in the group agree.

*Group Projects.*   Group projects are done only *after* students have learned the appropriate cooperative skills, because coordinating individual efforts involves quite complex interaction skills. When students have internalized the five basic elements, and know how to work successfully, positively, and thoughtfully with each other, managing conflict successfully, then they are ready for longer, cooperative group projects. Group projects vary from computer simulations to formal research papers. Students need to agree on a topic to explore, divide up the research, and teach each other what they have learned individually. Teachers should regularly check on individual contributions and understanding of the processes involved by giving individual quizzes or requiring individual feedback. Students may jointly write their learnings in a prescribed format and/or give a presentation to the class or other groups. When students are effective group members, joint projects can be a rewarding learning experience for all.

## ONE STEP FURTHER WITH BASE GROUPS

When teachers become adept with formal cooperative learning, they may wish to go one step further with cooperative learning and develop *base groups* in their classrooms and school.

Cooperative base groups are long-term, heterogeneous, cooperative learning groups with stable membership. Members are taught to give each other the support, encouragement, and assistance needed for members to attend class, complete assignments, learn, and develop cognitively and socially in healthy ways. Because they are permanent, lasting from 1 to several years, they provide students with long-term caring peer relationships. They meet regularly to discuss each member's academic progress, to provide assistance and support to each other, and to help each other succeed. Base groups help members when they miss school and support each other in stressful times.

Base groups are a school family. Such groups help students learn how to be part of caring friendships built around important work. Students learn how to be helpful to others on a long-term basis and how to accept help when needed. Students need these long-term relationships to feel a sense of belonging and self-esteem. The groups' heterogeneity helps students learn empathy and the perspectives of different others. In addition to enriching students' lives and developing the school community, base groups relate directly to reading and language arts' goals by helping students more fully understand a wide variety of perspectives, empathize with a wider range of characters, and see many points of view. In addition to deepening students' comprehension and writing, such understandings enrich their world outlook and help them make wise and ethical decisions.

## SUMMARY

Cooperative learning is very different from group work. Cooperative learning is carefully structured with five essential elements in order to promote student success. Teachers who learn how to use cooperative learning find that it is a natural way to teach language arts and reading. These teachers use informal cooperative learning partners to promote cognitive rehearsal and get students accustomed to communicating with and listening to each other. They use carefully planned formal cooperative learning groups to teach specific content, academic skills, and social skills. They develop a cooperative classroom community by building base groups in which students give each other academic and social support. When these groups are an integral part of reading and language arts, students' skills and attitudes in reading, writing, speaking, listening, and thinking improve. What could be better?

## BIBLIOGRAPHY

Bloom, B. (Ed.). (1956). *Taxonomy of educational objectives handbook I: Cognitive domain.* New York: McKay.

Holubec, E. (1980). Vocabulary lesson. In V. Lyons (Ed.), *Structuring cooperative learning: The 1980 handbook* (pp. 155–166). Edina, MN: Interaction.

Holubec, E. (1983). Don't reinvent the wheel: Use cooperative learning to structure student–student interaction in writing classes. *Proceedings of the Conference of College Teachers of English in Texas, 48,* 35–39.

Holubec, E. (1985). High school English poetry lesson. In R. Johnson, & D. Johnson (Eds.), *Cooperation in the classroom* (pp. 281–287). Edina, MN: Interaction.

Holubec, E. (1987). Cooperative poetry: I, too. In R. Johnson, D. Johnson, & E. Holubec (Eds.), *Structuring cooperative learning: Lesson plans for teachers* (pp. 195–200). Edina, MN: Interaction Book Company.

Holubec, E. (1992). How do you get there from here? Getting started with cooperative learning. *Contemporary Education, 63*(3), 181–184.

Holubec, E., Johnson, D., & Johnson, R. (1992). Dealing with conflict: A structured cooperative controversy procedure. In C. M. Hurlbert & S. Totten (Eds.), *Social issues in the English classroom: Theory and practice* (pp. 76–89). Urbana, IL: National Council of the Teachers of English.

Holubec, E., Johnson, D., & Johnson, R. (1993). Impact of cooperative learning on naval air traffic controller training. *The Journal of Social Psychology, 133*(3), 337–346.

Johnson, D., & Johnson, R. (1989). *Cooperation and competition: Theory and research.* Edina, MN: Interaction.

Johnson, D., & Johnson, R. (1991). *Learning together and alone: Cooperative, competitive, and individualistic learning* (3rd ed.). Englewood Cliffs, NJ: Prentice-Hall.

Johnson, D., & Johnson, R. (1992). *Creative controversy: Intellectual challenge in the classroom.* Edina, MN: Interaction.

Johnson, D., Johnson, R., & Holubec, E. (1987). *Structuring cooperative learning: Lesson plans for teachers.* Edina, MN: Interaction.

Johnson, D., Johnson, R., & Holubec, E. (1992). *Advanced cooperative learning* (2nd ed.). Edina, MN: Interaction.

Johnson, D., Johnson, R., & Holubec, E. (1993a). *Circles of learning: Cooperation in the classroom* (4th ed.). Edina, MN: Interaction.

Johnson, D., Johnson, R., & Holubec, E. (1993b). *Cooperation in the classroom* (5th ed.). Edina, MN: Interaction.

Johnson, D., Johnson, R., & Holubec, E. (1994). *The nuts and bolts of cooperative learning.* Edina, MN: Interaction.

# Chapter 14

# In Search of Thinking Environments

Regis Bernhardt
Patricia Antonacci
*Fordham University*

There is an excitement about walking into a school where you have never been. As you enter the school lobby, you view the students' triumphs and victories behind glass showcases; walking farther down the corridor, you are surrounded by large bulletin boards displaying the children's work, their art, stories, and projects. Indeed, you have gained entrance into the world of school where the story only begins to unfold. It is, however, not until you go beyond the walls of the classroom that the most profound narratives are told through the lives of the children who interact together within their social worlds.

Each classroom declares a singular culture, maintained through the interactions of the unique individuals within the community of learners. It is through each child's distinct participation within the group that the authoring of stories begins. Children come together at the beginning of the school year, and at once they are "differentiating and negotiating among their intersecting social worlds" (Dyson, 1993, p. 3). Within this school context they think, learn, and use language in a variety of social worlds. Dyson (1993) described the classroom as a complex social place with a number of social worlds, including the official school world.

An effective method to learn about most aspects of classroom environments is to enter during the school day as an ethnographer and bear witness to the numerous social interactions engaged in by both the children and the children with their teacher. Social researchers know that this is best achieved through their active participation in the students' lives, observing and recording their stories. Indeed, it leads to what Ryle calls "thick descriptions" (cited in Geertz, 1973, p. 6) of the cultural environments. It is what Dyson (1993) did in her

2-year study of Louise's class, which led her to describe classroom life as "a complex social place, one in which a number of worlds coexisted and intersected" (p. 2). As an ethnographer, Dyson became part of the children's lives in the classroom where she observed how the teacher worked to foster relationships between children to form a community of learners. In addition to this "official school world," she learned about the "unofficial" social worlds of children, both worlds wherein children learn and use language. It is indeed through such research that the influences within classroom environments on children's thinking and learning are made most explicit.

There are other aspects of the cultural environment of the classroom to study, and along with these various facets are different methodologies. Therefore, what we present here is not an alternative approach to ethnography, but one that may be used to augment the social researcher's information. We will yield testimony about classroom environments that have been deliberately designed by teachers for the members of the learning community. By entering the social worlds of two first-grade classrooms to conduct a "dig" of the materials that were left behind after a full day of school, we draw conclusions about the kinds of thinking that are fostered within these two classrooms. Learning environments will be reconstructed from the artifacts that remain in the classroom after the teacher and the children leave for their homes. The artifacts within a class are related to the work of the children; the artifacts can, therefore, tell a story about how the children learn, how they use language to think and to construct knowledge. Thus, our focus is on the materials found in each classroom as they relate to literacy instruction.

The purpose of this chapter is to provide a description of one aspect of the classroom environment. We are in search of ways to uncover how official school worlds might enhance or diminish thoughtful learning. That is, we want to unearth how children are developing ways of thinking by the kinds literate opportunities that are designed for them by the materials they use in their designated official school worlds, deliberately selected and arranged by their teachers.

## THE PHYSICAL WORLD OF THE CLASSROOM

It is true that a "dig" will not allow you to listen in on the children as they interact with each other, as they work with print to construct meaning the way Dyson (1993) and others have done. However, the kinds of print that were left behind by the children, the kinds of texts they used to read during the day, the bulletin-board displays, the teacher's professional books, supplementary materials to support the literate communities of classrooms, the arrangement of the room with respect to learning centers, and the contents of the desks provide the setting of a story to be told. The study of the materials in the classroom used to teach and learn about literacy is the study about the ways thinking is encouraged and promoted in the official school world. In short, we sought to answer the question: What do the materials, selected and arranged by the teacher, tell about the classroom environment?

What follows is a recounting of our explorations of the treasures within two divergent classrooms; it is the accounts of our archaeological dig! Imagine the excitement that overcame Howard Carter in 1929 when he entered the tomb of Tutankhamen, making his singular discovery causing him to declare:

> The next day was . . . the day of days, the most wonderful that I have ever lived through. Darkness and blank space, as far as an iron testing-rod could reach, showed that whatever lay beyond was empty. Widening the hole a little, I inserted the candle and peered in. . . . At first I could see nothing, the hot air escaping from the chamber causing the candle flame to flicker, but presently, as my eyes grew accustomed to the light, details of the room within emerged slowly from the mist, strange animals, statues, and gold—everywhere the glint of gold. . . . "Can you see anything?" It was all I could do to get out the words, "Yes, wonderful things . . ." (quoted in Edwards, 1976, p. 13)

Sharing Carter's excitement, we, too, entered into the classroom environment in search of *the* prized treasure—a thoughtful environment. We sought to determine the extent that thinking is promoted through the deliberate selection and arrangement of materials within two different first-grade classrooms.

## Background of Two First-Grade Classrooms

Two first-grade classrooms that were studied are located in a small urban school. One first-grade class was housed in the same room with the same teacher for more than 15 years. The second first-grade classroom was added because there was a reorganization within the school district. For this class, the teacher was new to the school, but not to the teaching profession. Both teachers had more than 15 years of experience in the teaching profession, and they both spent considerable time in the primary grades.

At the time of the study, both teachers were given a set of basal readers. Within this school it was expected, and even mandated, that reading instruction be delivered through a basal reading program that was used throughout the school. Furthermore, it was the major tool for the entire language-arts program within the first grade. Any deviation was taken through the initiative of the classroom teacher.

## Blueprints of Classroom Environments

Before we entered the classroom to conduct our "dig," it was necessary to create blueprints for classroom environments. The blueprints would serve as templates to be used when we categorized the artifacts that we found. The categories would also permit us to infer the philosophies of the teachers and the kinds of activities the children would be engaged in.

### Blueprint of a Thinking Environment

The set blueprints for a classroom environment that promotes thinking in primary grades is detailed yet not prescriptive. The child is the curriculum who, in a sense, is responsible for designing the instructional agenda.

In a classroom that promotes thinking, students would be placed in a mindful state that "results from drawing novel distinctions, examining information from new perspectives, and being sensitive to context. It is an open, creative, probabilistic state of mind in which the individual might be led to finding differences among things thought similar and similarities among things thought different" (Langer, 1993, p. 44).

Included in the blueprint for a thinking environment are the components of the metacurriculum that Perkins (1992) described as an essential part of his *Smart School*. Without describing the metacurriculum in detail, its components ensure the use of literacy materials that develops thinking. For example, such a curriculum has *levels of understanding* that assist in thinking across the content areas. Moreover, fundamental to the metacurriculum is the development of *intellectual passions*. Consider the print materials that are used in the first grade, or any grade in the elementary schools. When a teacher uses children's literature, which contains the best models of language and offers stories that incite the imagination to teach reading, children cannot help but develop a passion for reading. In all areas of learning and assessment, students are engaged in *learning to learn*; their metacognitive strategies are developed.

We cannot leave Perkins' idea of metacurriculum without turning to the component of *languages of thinking*, which indeed is essential to our blueprint of a thinking environment. We need to ask: "What kind of language supports thinking?" The answer to this very question provides the foundation of the whole-language movement. Becoming literate in a whole-language environment is synonymous with learning in a thinking environment. Cambourne's (1988) Model of Learning, as it applies to literacy learning, provides the essential elements of the whole-language philosophy. A brief summary of the key features of his model follows:

> *Immersion:* Students are immersed in a variety of texts. They read a variety of good children's literature; they also read stories composed by their peers.
>
> *Demonstration:* Modeling and demonstrating of how text works is the key to good teaching. They watch others, both teachers and students, as they compose texts and read texts.
>
> *Engagement:* While students are immersed in reading and writing texts, and as they observe others, they are active learners. Immersion and demonstration demand engagement by the students.

*Expectation:* Learners are part of the community of learners where there is an expectation of success. The expectations are powerful coercers of behaviors. Expectations are, however, in step with the child's literacy development; in other words, they are realistic.

*Responsibility:* Students become empowered, because they gradually share in the responsibility for their own learning. They begin to make their own decisions about the learning process.

*Use:* When students practice, they become proficient. Unlike the kinds of practice associated with reading workbooks, children use their newly acquired concepts and skills in more purposeful ways, with material that is constructed on authentic language models. They also engage in writing text similar to the kinds that they read.

*Approximation:* An approximation is a mistake which is essential for learning to occur. When students begin to "try on" their language, they oftentimes approximate its use until they reach the desired model. Within a thinking environment, risk taking is encouraged because it is a prerequisite for learning. Children are applauded for trying something new.

*Response:* The response given to students learning in a thinking environment occurs in natural contexts, where feedback and help come from the experts within the community of learners, that is, from both teachers and students. The purpose of response is to inform the learner, rather than to pass harsh judgment on her. Feedback provides the assistance to the learner until she can perform the task independently.

To summarize, a blueprint for a thinking environment places the child as learner at the heart of the curriculum, who is actively engaged in tasks that are relevant to him. The child's work, both his oral and written texts, are viewed as significant. Children are immersed in print, and in the words of Andrea Butler, "The walls are dripping with print!" Such print is varied, and it is displayed for numerous reasons. The language that is used in written as well as spoken texts is never decontextualized. Children become skilled by using print purposefully. The texts selected for literacy instruction are the best models of language and of stories, and they are numerous and varied. Language that occurs in variety of contexts, including personal communication, content-area language, language "to get things done," is viewed by students as important. Such language becomes "literacy events," a basis for instruction. It is indeed easy to understand how literacy learning is purposeful and authentic.

### Blueprint of a Thoughtless Environment

Such is not the case in a thoughtless environment, where thinking about text is not demanded. In this section, we describe a classroom where literacy is both taught and learned with little thought.

In describing a blueprint for thoughtful environments, we equated the whole-language practice with one that demanded active learners who quickly develop dispositions of thought. A parallel practice to whole language is the basal-reading program. A reliance on this program to teach literacy results in a thoughtless environment for both the teacher and the students. Just how does a daily consistent use of the basal reader and workbooks lead the teachers and students to a mindless state? A brief description of the basal-reading program and how it is used will demonstrate how it frees its users up from thinking.

The basal-reading program is a comprehensive, systematic, and sequential syllabus. A prominent feature is the Teacher's Guide, which is used as a lesson plan for the teacher who delivers the predesigned instruction to a group of students. The program is constructed with a scope and a sequence of skills to be presented in a very systematic approach, where skills are taught sequentially in the order in which they occur. The stories in the basal reader are short, and they, too, are constructed on the skill that is being learned. To reinforce and to strengthen the skill, the students are provided with practice in their workbooks. Why does this approach fail to promote thinking?

A major criticism of basal programs is in the story. In the preprimers and primers, the stories are very short, and they are constructed on a formula. Their purpose is to teach decoding early on so the children will get a sense of success. However, the results are deleterious. These are the stories with which children have their first experiences in learning how to read. While the language of each story should be rich, it is contrived. The short stories lack the elements of a good story, and therefore fail to hold the child's interest. In this environment, because reading is perceived primarily as decoding, the child is exposed to stories that simply induce decoding; thinking about the story is deemphasized, probably because there is little to think about.

A second major criticism of the basal-reading program is the workbook. The workbook is a management tool used by the teacher to keep busy those children who are not receiving direct instruction within the small group. Workbook pages also provide the practice for the skill that the child was taught for the day. Workbooks include pages of questions that children answer by filling in the blank spaces, which supposedly affords them the use of the language skill that is being developed in learning to read. There are several reasons why the work-book is a major contributor to a thoughtless environment. This type of repetitious exercise leads to automatic behavior and is at the roots of mindlessness (Langer, 1989). Another issue is that whether students need the practice or have mastered the skill, they are expected to complete the workbook pages. Such time could indeed be used more efficaciously.

The third criticism of the basal program is its major selling point, the Teacher's Guidebook: Teachers do not have to make the critical decisions about the literacy instruction of the child when they employ the manual as directed. Shannon (1989) calls this the *reification* of the basal program, when both the teachers and the administrators look to this program as one designed by experts. The teachers need only apply the program the way it was intended, and the children will learn to read. Indeed this lets the teacher off the "thinking hook." Furthermore, the assumption is that when the child does not learn, it is the fault of the child and not the program that has been designed by the experts.

The final escape from thinking comes from the perception of writing. As a language form, it is perceived to develop separate and apart from reading. So for classrooms where there is a heavy reliance on basal materials, children compose their own texts only after they have learned to read. Children do not write in response to what they have read. The kinds of writing that children do is filling in the blanks on worksheets. This type of writing does not demand critical thinking, nor does it engage the child in the composing process that facilitates thinking as it supports learning how to read.

When basal-reading programs are in use as they were proposed by the publishers, and when there is an absolute confidence in their performance, the responsibility for literacy learning lies not with the teachers or with the students, but in the materials. The demands on thinking for both the teacher and the students are limited, for they work in a thoughtless environment.

## THE ARTIFACTS LEFT BEHIND

### Methods for Studying Culture

Qualitative methods were used to determine whether the instructional materials within environments of two first-grade classrooms promote thinking and learning. The artifacts found in a classroom provide another window to examine the kinds of learning in which students are engaged. How could culture be studied without analyzing social interactions of the children and teacher?

Artifacts provide the anthropologist with the *physical culture* to study. Therefore, analyzing the artifacts within the classrooms allows us to infer the teachers' philosophies, values, and beliefs related to literacy learning and instruction. More specifically, the arrangement of classroom furniture, the kinds of materials used for language-arts instruction, the methods of storing and displaying materials, the bulletin boards, the accessibility to print and materials for writing by children are the *trail of objects* that describes an important element of the story, the setting of the story. These artifacts make a statement about the kinds of learning that occurred in this classroom. From the study of the classroom environment, inferences may be drawn about a teacher's philosophy, values, and beliefs underlying her literacy instruction. From each set of inferences drawn from the classroom's physical culture and associated with literacy instruction, it is quite possible to determine if such an environment promotes or restricts thinking.

Anthropologists commonly focus on the physical culture or the artifacts associated with various groups (Deetz, 1977). In the past decade, an increasing number of social scientists have accepted the idea that everyday objects have important meanings and are worthy of study. Adopting an anthropological frame of reference, the assumption is that *material culture makes culture material* (Czikszenlmihalyi & Rochberg-Halton, 1981). Lawton and Scane (1991) analyzed the physical culture of the offices of CEOs and used the data to infer values. They found, for example, that offices of CEOs expressed conservative values as well as a desire for change and a strong commitment to children and education. Evidence suggests that people in their selection of clothes, furniture, decoration, books, and their arrangement of objects are sending messages about who they are, who they would like to be, and what is important to them (McCracken, 1988). Because certain objects possess special meaning to individuals, they commit energy and time to their care (Czikszentmihalyi & Rochberg-Halton, 1981). Finally, Campbell (1987) punctuates the impact of studying workplaces to understand values by explaining that "a man's (woman's) work space isn't just about his (her) job. It is a kind of Rorschach test, psychologists say, communicating everything from a love of power to a desire to create an impression or simply feel at home" (p. 66).

When it was time to enter the two classrooms, we kept in mind that we were searching for a thoughtful environment. We entered each room with our blueprints; each blueprint was a template to use in collecting and categorizing the artifacts for literacy learning.

## PROCEDURES FOR ANALYZING THE PHYSICAL CULTURE OF A CLASSROOM

The procedures we use to interpret the physical culture in each of the classrooms in order to determine how they reflect the teachers' philosophies, values, and beliefs related to literacy instruction were adapted from the methods used by Lawton and Scane (1992). Only the materials related to literacy instruction were included in our "dig"; these were counted and categorized. We also included the arrangement of the materials, as well as the classroom furniture.

The materials were indexed using the following categories: print materials, teacher's professional materials, and instructional aids and equipment. Table 14.1 itemizes the materials and their frequency found in each room, Classroom A and Classroom B. This is followed by a descriptive account of their accessibility and the arrangement of the furniture within each classroom.

Using the blueprint of environments, the physical culture, that is, the trail of objects that remained in each classroom and their placement in the classroom were analyzed. Their analysis may be found in the discussion that follows.

TABLE 14.1
Literacy Instructional Materials

| PRINT MATERIALS | CLASSROOMS | |
| --- | --- | --- |
| | A | B |
| Basal Readers | 1 Set | 4 Sets |
| Basal Workbooks | 1 Set | 1 Set |
| Children's Journals | 27 | 0 |
| Children's Literature | 392 | 121 |
| Big Books | 27 | 2 |
| Published Children's Stories | 17 | 0 |
| Library Books | 125 | 29 |
| *TEACHERS' PROFESSIONAL MATERIALS* | | |
| Books | 7 | 0 |
| Journals | 0 | 0 |
| *INSTRUCTIONAL AIDS AND EQUIPMENT* | | |
| Video | 8 | 2 |
| Audio Tapes | 10 | 4 |
| Computer Software | 8 | 0 |
| Charts | 8 | 5 |
| Puppets | 13 | 2 |
| Flannel Board Sets | 12 | 0 |
| Television/VCR | Shared | Shared |
| Computer | 2 | 0 |
| Tape Recorder & Listening Center | 1 | 0 |
| Flannel Board | 1 | 0 |

## Print Materials

***Classroom A.*** In Classroom A, we found one set of basal readers stored on the lowest shelf of the classroom. The basal readers did not comprise a complete set, and they were not arranged in an orderly way. From appearances, in this classroom the basal reading program did not assume much, if any, prominence as part of the literacy instructional program.

We found over 300 pieces of outstanding children's literature. In some cases, there were multiple copies of a book with an accompanying big book, as in the case of *Good Night, Moon.* There was an open bookshelf, where copies of children's literature were displayed. The rest of the books were arranged on bookshelves that were accessible to the students. There were 28 copies of enlarged editions of the small pieces of literature. Big books are large versions of select children's literature. Their purpose is to provide demonstrations of "how print works" through shared-book experience and modeling by the teacher of good reading.

In this classroom, there were no traces of workbooks, nor were there worksheets. Rather, children's writing consisted of composed text, such as stories written in their journals in response to stories they read. An example of one such story was the one written by Curtis in response to having read or heard *Good Night, Moon*. Books written, illustrated, and published by the children themselves were part of the children's library, and one was featured, displayed on the open bookshelf. Each child's desk contained a journal in which there were indications that writing in the journal was a daily practice. On one table were learning logs, near an incubator that housed duck eggs. The learning logs were day-to-day accounts of how the inside of the egg looked to the children. In some learning logs were pictures and stories; in some were pictures accompanied by single words; in others were pictures and no words.

A simple analysis of the print materials found in Classroom A led us to conclude that reading and writing were taught together, composed text was perceived as writing, reading instruction included whole pieces of children's literature, writing was a daily practice, and, finally, but very important, value was placed on students' work.

*Classroom B.*   What we saw when we ventured into classroom B, was indeed less promising. There we found three complete sets of basal readers. Two sets were neatly arranged on the top shelf, close to the reading table for easy accessibility. In each child's desk was a basal reader, one of the preprimers or a primer, depending on the students' reading level. There was also a workbook to accompany the reader. The workbook pages that were completed were marked with correct (C) or incorrect (X) symbols.

There were approximately 100 books classified as children's literature. They were stored on the bottom shelf against the window in the back of the room, which was inaccessible to the children. There were no open book cases where books could be displayed. Additionally, only two big books were found in the corner of the room with signs that they were unused.

In this class, there were no indications of text composed by students. There were no journals in sight, nor were there any books written and published by the children. The predominant kind of writing we found was in the workbooks. A second kind of writing was copying; the daily message that was composed by the teacher was copied off the board by students on large sheets of yellow-lined paper. It was clear that care was taken by the children to form letters perfectly and to leave the appropriate spacing between words.

A simple analysis of the print materials found in Classroom B was that there was a heavy reliance on the basal reading program that directed the literacy program. There was little, if any, evidence that children's literature was part of literacy instruction. Indeed, writing was not perceived as composing text; writing was perceived as copying from the board. The kinds of writing activities that were assigned to children were paltry.

## Teachers' Professional Materials

*Classroom A.* In Classroom A there were professional books and journals in a small bookstand on the teacher's desk. Left open on the teacher's desk was a professional journal, which indicated that the teacher was in the middle of reading an article. Seven books, six on whole language and one on science in the primary grade, were in the bookstand. In addition to the books, there were two professional journals and two magazines written for children, one on science and the other on literature.

The evidence here showed us that the teacher in this classroom engages in reading current professional books and journals. This may account for her using the current practices related to literacy learning.

*Classroom B.* There were no indications that this teacher engaged in reading journals and books related to the teaching profession, since we found none in the classroom. On the teacher's desk were the accompanying teacher guides, one for each of the basal readers that were used by the teacher in this classroom.

There is a simple conclusion drawn from examining the teacher's professional books. This teacher is directed by the basal reader: it is the publisher, in effect, who teaches reading (Shannon, 1989). The teacher has withdrawn from making any critical decisions about instruction, since they have been prepackaged by the publisher of the basal-reading program that is in use.

## Instructional Aids and Equipment

*Classroom A.* In Classroom A there were numerous videos of classical children's literature, with titles of corresponding books used in the reading instructional program. The VCR was shared with other teachers. There were two computers with software that included several word processing programs and a graphics program, as well as additional software for science and math. The computers were found near the writing center, and it was obvious that they were used to publish children's written work from the story that was found in the printer. Near the library was a listening center where five children could listen to the audio tapes of books.

There were four bulletin boards that displayed the children's artwork and stories. One bulletin that was accessible to the children was a message board that was functional. The children's names were neatly printed with a push pin under the name and space around it. Some children's names had messages under them, pinned with the tack. A set of printed rules that the children followed when writing messages was displayed above the message board. For example, one rule stated, "Always sign your name."

In addition to the bulletin board, there were charts, many of which were made by the teacher. One chart that was made by a child appeared above the incubator.

The chart listed rules that explained how to turn the duck eggs. One rule stated: "Wash your hands first."

There was a wall story that hung across a large portion of the wall and was signed by nearly all of the children in the classroom. A flannel board, with pictures of the characters of a folk tale, was on display. This was used as a prop for retelling. Nine different kinds of puppets were nestled on a rug in the reading corner. Their most obvious use was for creative dramatics and for reenacting a story that was read.

From the kinds of instructional aids and equipment that we found in this class, it was clear that literacy was a central part of the lives of the community of workers. The message board indicated that literacy was developed in many different and meaningful ways. Creative dramatics and retelling were used to engage children in making different responses to stories, demonstrating that creative thinking was encouraged.

*Classroom B.* In Classroom B, we found two videos of Disney movies. There were four audiotapes of songs for primary grades, and no computer software. There were five charts found in this classroom, and they were commercially prepared: one was a color chart; one was a set of the alphabet, upper- and lowercase; one was a calendar chart; one a number-concept chart with the spelling of each number from 1 through 10; and the last was a science chart on basic food groups.

There was one bulletin board displaying children's work. The work on the bulletin board was artwork, pictures showing seasonal changes. There were no stories written by children displayed on bulletin boards.

Our analysis of this category of materials of Classroom B led us to findings that are consistent with our previous results related to the artifacts within the two other categories. The entire literacy-instructional program is directed by the basal-reading program, with very little, if any, divergence from it. The paucity of additional instructional aids and equipment confirmed this finding. There was a tight control of literacy instruction by the publisher, as well as a rigidity with no flexibility, shown by this teacher's strict adherence to the prescriptive lessons. Furthermore, it was not clear whether children's work was valued. From the bulletin-board display, it was apparent that children were not recognized for their abilities to construct a story.

## Arrangement of Materials

*Classroom A.* In this classroom the desks were arranged in worktables to accommodate small groups of four children. With this arrangement, collaborative talk is facilitated. Small-group activities, which invite talk, are the underlying principle of a transactional classroom. In such classrooms, children are active learners, engaged in small groups on authentic tasks, where group talk is encouraged "to construct knowledge and meaning" (Wells & Chang-Wells, 1992, p. 59).

We found five centers for learning throughout the room: The writing center and the library corner were adjacent to each other; the science center and math center stood side by side; and the art center was in close proximity to the writing center. The story center looked enticing: It was set apart from the mainstream of classroom activity; brightly colored pillows were scattered about; books for reading were on display; and above the corner were illustrations of the rules for using the library corner, such as, "No talking," and "Four at a time." The writing center was organized so that the writing paper and other materials were easily accessible to the students. Its organization deliberately solicited students to engage in writing. The teacher's desk was obscure, in the corner and out of the way. Its position did not command the attention of the students.

The arrangement of furniture and materials provides further insight into a teacher's instructional philosophy. In the case of Classroom A, the furniture was found arranged for active engagement by students for working in small groups. Materials for work were made accessible to students, indicating that options were given to them. The centers also indicated a choice, but along with the freedom to choose came a set of student expectations to assume certain responsibilities, as shown by the list of rules above each center. The placement of the teacher's desk, in an out-of-the-way area, was in alignment with the room arrangement: The teacher led from behind, she was the facilitator who encouraged the children to work together to construct meaning. It was clear from the room arrangement that the teacher did not believe in the transmission of knowledge, as when lessons are conducted from the front of the room to the whole class. Rather from this classroom arrangement, we inferred that the teacher believed in a transactional model of instruction, where the emphasis is placed on the construction of knowledge through active participation by the children.

***Classroom B.***    The desks in this classroom were arranged in single groupings, with one child at a desk. The organization indicated that students work alone in this classroom; such an arrangement does not encourage collaborative talk, rather it encourages competition and independence in completing assignments.

In Classroom B, we found no centers for writing, art, quiet and shared reading, science, or math. Rather the materials for writing were stored in an area close to the teacher's closet. The books for independent reading were shelved in a place that was inaccessible to the children. Math and science materials and books occupied separate shelves. This type of storage of instructional materials indicated a tight control of the materials by the teacher. Clearly, children could not make an independent decision to write or read without a request to the teacher. It was the teacher who decided when such activities could be engaged in by the students.

The Disney videos were not movies based on children's literature read by primary-grade children. One was a comedy, and one was a cartoon. This indicated that the teacher did not use multimedia to support the literacy program.

The teacher's desk, indeed, held a prominent place in the classroom: It occupied the center of the front of the room. One could not help but conclude that its position placed the teacher in full control, a result quite consistent with other aspects of the room arrangement.

## SUMMARY

An examination of the physical culture of two first-grade classrooms to determine their learning environments led us to formulate the following conclusions: Using our blueprints, a thoughtful environment was found in Classroom A, while a thoughtless environment was found in Classroom B.

### Classroom A

From the materials we found in this classroom, their accessibility and the room arrangement, we inferred that the teacher used a transactional model of learning: The children were encouraged to construct knowledge together; this was apparent from the room arrangement showing small-group activity. It was also made explicit from the freedom of choice, encouraged by the children's accessibility to the materials, as well as the limited control by the teacher. Indeed the classroom was their work area!

There were several indications that language was used for a variety of purposes: the charts and signs made by the teacher and the children; the message board used to send personal notes to each other; the learning logs used to observe the development of the embryo within the duck egg; and students' journals to respond to stories. In this classroom, the use of language was purposeful, relevant to the work of the children, varied, and never decontextualized.

There was evidence that students engaged in demonstrations of how language works through the use of big books by the teacher. Another testimony of modeling good language was denoted by the abundant use of children's literature in the reading program.

Another aspect related to a thinking environment that we uncovered by our examination of the physical culture within this classroom was the evidence of the teacher's professional growth and renewal. Instead of the prescriptive teacher's guide, there were several professional books and two current journals on her desk. One journal was opened and given a prominent place in the center of her desk. This, indeed, indicated that the teacher's own learning did not stop when she left graduate school.

Finally, there were signs left in this classroom that indicated the children's work was valued. To cite one piece of evidence, we found a book written, published, and illustrated by a child displayed next to prominent authors of children's literature.

## Classroom B

The physical culture in Classroom B told a different story about its environment; here thinking was not encouraged. In this classroom, the organization of the furniture as well as the lack of learning centers made a bold statement about the official school world that the teacher tailored: *The arrangement of students' desks kept them isolated to discourage collaborative talk and to encourage independent workskills and competition.* The position of the teacher's desk added to the story; the teacher sought control over the learning. Indeed, this evidence points to the transmission model of instruction used in this classroom: The teacher dispensed the knowledge to the students.

The kinds of books and their accessibility signified that there was a heavy reliance on the basal reading program for literacy instruction. The children's writing was limited to filling in the blanks in workbooks and to copying, whereas composing text was not used as part of the writing program. Because composing text is a thinking process, the evidence confirmed that within this classroom thinking was not encouraged.

The teacher was freed up from thinking as well. All of the teaching decisions were made by the publishers. All she needed to do was to follow the lesson plans in the Teacher's Guide. This reader in effect has become a "technician" whose role in reading instruction is to apply expertly prepared commercial materials, which she perceives to be an effective program (Shannon, 1989).

## REFERENCES

Cambourne, B. (1988). *The whole story: Natural learning and the acquisition of literacy in the classroom.* New York: Ashton Scholastic.

Campbell, K. (1987). Desk tops tell all. *The New York Times Magazine 13,* pp. 66–67.

Czikszentmihalyi, M., & Rochberg-Halton, E. (1981). *The meanings of things: Domestic symbols and the self.* New York: Cambridge University Press.

Deetz, J. (1977). *In small things remembered.* Garden City, NY: Anchor.

Dyson, A. H. (1993). *Social worlds of children learning to write in an urban primary school.* New York: Teachers College Press.

Geertz, C. (1973). *The interpretation of cultures.* New York: Basic Books.

Edwards, I. E. S. (1976). *Treasures of Tutankhamen.* New York: Ballantine.

Langer, E. J. (1989). *Mindfulness.* New York: Addison-Wesley.

Langer, E. J. (1993). A mindful education. *Educational Psychologist, 28*(1), 43–50.

Lawton, S., & Scane, J. (1992). Inferring values from the physical culture of the CEO's office. In K. Leithwood and D. Musella (Eds.), *Understanding school system administration: Studies of the contemporary chief education officer* (pp. 175–208). Bristol, PA: Falmer Press.

McCracken, G. (1988). *Culture and consumption.* Bloomington: Indiana University Press.

Perkins, D. N. (1992). *Smart schools: From training memories to educating minds.* New York: The Free Press.

Shannon, P. (1989). *Broken promises.* New York: Bergin & Garvey.

Wells, G., & Chang-Wells, G. L. (1992). *Constructing knowledge together: Classrooms as centers of inquiry and literacy.* Portsmouth, NH: Heinemann.

# STRATEGIES FOR THINKING AND LEARNING

# Chapter 15

# Thinking Apprenticeships: Cognitive Learning Environments (TACLE)

Patricia Antonacci
*Fordham University*

James M. Colasacco
*Yonkers Public Schools*

There is a growing dissatisfaction with our nation's schools. Daily reminders from the media that schools have become places where teachers no longer teach and students no longer learn persist. Beleaguered educators insist that by holding fast to the instructional models that have become an American tradition, their crumbling institutions will be transformed. Strengthened by a commonsense philosophy (Mayher, 1990), educators are convinced that what worked for so many students for so long should work for today's students. However, these notions of demanding more of the old to improve the quality of education not only flies in the face of reality, but also resists the search for viable solutions to major dilemmas.

Indeed, our children are not learning. Our educational institutions are not the *Smart Schools* that Perkins (1992) described as places that develop habits of mind and dispositions of thought. Students are not reflecting on their own learning; neither are they becoming self-regulated learners. Furthermore, not all students are problem solvers, engaged in critical and creative thinking; nor are they graduating with the multiple literacies that are required in this information age. However, if educators persist at refurbishing the traditional instructional models as the solution to their troubled schools, they will further entrench their schools in the kinds of teaching and learning that appear to be the source of these problems. In fact, holding on to these very models of instruction is what has placed our nation's schools and their children deeper and deeper into the dark ages of learning.

Indeed, our schools are in need of a renaissance. Pervasive change is required by schools that wish to develop students into thinkers and problem solvers who are

**259**

self-regulated learners, equipped with multiple literacies. However, such change is not easy: A quick-fix or a prepackaged program promising to meet the demands of a *Smart School* will no doubt thwart any progress and bring us back to our starting position. What is demanded is an active response to the needs of today's students, for whom the traditional instructional models no longer work.

This chapter is about our response to create an effective instructional system for a group of urban elementary-school children. The design of our instructional system started by a simple written proposal to the NYNEX/CIBA "Principal's Grant" to procure a new science program. However, as we began to write the proposal, the problems of our school were brought into focus. It soon became apparent that merely winning another grant would not ensure the kind of learning and instruction that is necessary for today's students. Although the writing of the grant itself proved to be a significant event that caused us to change our stance toward the educational process in deep and profound ways, it was the process of "talking and thinking through" that made us come to value the most puissant concepts required for thoughtful learning. Even if we were not awarded the grant, we would proceed to implement the concepts of learning that became our new philosophy of education. We could not consider turning our backs and looking the other way. We knew that what guaranteed thoughtful learning environments was for the members of the learning community to embrace these beliefs.

What was so new and different about this kind of learning that we sought for our students? To construct an answer, we started with the following set of student outcomes necessary to create thoughtful students:

- Students would become *active learners.*
- Students would *develop language strategies required for collaborative problem solving.*
- Students would *think creatively* in problem solving.
- Students would develop *multiple literacies*, including more precise ways to use language for science and math.
- Students would develop *metacognitive strategies and self-regulatory behaviors.*
- Student would become *reflective learners*, possessing habits of mind which lead to self-regulated learning and dispositions for thought.
- Students would become *responsive to their community's problems.*

Abandoning all traditional instructional models, we sought to design a dynamic instructional system that we called Thinking Apprenticeships: Cognitive Learning Environments (TACLE). The system was developed to include the following components: apprenticeships, dialogue as education, authentic contexts, and a program of authentic assessment. Each of the components serves the system to work interactively and interdependently, with one component supporting the others by facilitating their operations. A brief description of each component follows.

Within the *apprenticeship model*, experts from the community, the scientific industry, as well as from the school, are utilized. The expert–novice relationship within the apprenticeship model is also maintained through the multiage grouping of the children within the instructional system. Children from the third, fourth, fifth, and sixth grades work together in small groups.

Another significant component of the instructional system is *dialogue for education*, which indeed has become the cornerstone of TACLE. Students' language is no longer viewed as inadequate; rather, collaborative talk has become the resource that they use in learning. The development of multiple literacies is accomplished through the use of a variety of language functions and different language contexts that include learning logs, storytelling, games, writing newsletters, interactive multimedia technology and so on. For each activity that the group may be working on, literacy responses are central to task completion.

In order to build *authentic contexts* as learning environments, real problem solving within the children's community became an integral part of students' learning science and mathematics, as well as social studies. Students go out into the community to identify, to analyze, and to solve environmental problems that surround their existence. Rotating from group to group, they view the problems and work toward solutions from different perspectives. For one problem, small groups will work with the biologist; others will work with the naturalist; another group will work with the literacy teacher. The technology expert works with a group who prepares the work that they receive for publication. In some cases and at some times, groups work together to complete their jobs.

For TACLE to be a dynamic instructional system, a program of *authentic assessment* was designed as an integral part of the system that is linked to each work activity. Its purpose is to inform the members of the community of learners, both the experts and the apprentices. Teacher observation and student portfolios, as well as school portfolios, provide the continuous feedback for reflection needed to ensure the dynamic nature of the instructional system that is essential to meet student outcomes.

A more complete description of TACLE follows. This next part of the chapter is organized around a theoretical discussion of each of the components of the instructional system with reference to how they have been implemented within the large urban elementary school.

## THINKING APPRENTICESHIPS: COGNITIVE LEARNING ENVIRONMENTS (TACLE)

TACLE was developed to respond to the traditional models of instruction that no longer work for today's students. The complex and dynamic instructional system includes at least the following four components: (a) apprenticeships, (b) dialogue as education, (c) authentic contexts, and (d) an authentic assessment program.

## Apprenticeships

### *What is an Apprenticeship?*

What comes to mind when we say the word *apprentice*? Probably it will make you think of a laborer on the journey to becoming skilled, or a person who is learning a trade or a profession under the watchful guidance of the expert. This was the way that most learning took place before the creation of schools. Apprenticeships existed in the home (and still do today) as well as on the job. In the home, apprenticeships occur when young children learn to speak, take care of themselves, cook, or perform other household chores. In the shops, people learned a craft or a trade alongside the craftsmen or the tradesmen.

Do you remember being an apprentice under the careful guidance of your parent? Maybe it was your mother who taught you how to set the table for dinner. First, she showed you several times, telling you what she was doing. Then she allowed you to help her; you worked alongside her and she coached and encouraged you through the chore that would someday be yours. This happened several times. Finally, you were allowed to perform on your own, but with your mother nearby. If you made a mistake and placed the forks on the right side of the plate instead of the left, your mother was there to correct you and tell you why the forks needed to be on the left side of the plate. When your mother no longer needed to be of assistance to you in setting the table for dinner, she disappeared and you took over.

Within this type of apprenticeship, learning is depended on by the novice who is engaged in a meaningful task and sees it demonstrated by an expert. Each part of the task is made clearly visible to the young apprentice. The expert coaches the apprentice through the task until assistance is no longer needed. However, when the apprentice needs assistance from the expert, the specialized help is offered. If part of the process needs to be demonstrated, the expert enters into the joint activity by modeling to the novice only the part that is necessary to be learned. When it is clear to both the expert and to the apprentice that the task can be executed independently by the apprentice, the expert fades.

Such apprenticeships occur in natural contexts for learning and include the important ingredients for thinking environments. Could such apprenticeships be used as models to transform the American classroom into authentic contexts such as Smart Schools as defined by Perkins (1992)? Cognitive apprenticeships were proposed as alternatives to traditional models of classroom instruction (Collins, Brown, & Holum, 1991) in which thinking is often invisible to students. Through cognitive apprenticeships the thinking required in learning is made visible to the students. Within the instructional design of TACLE, apprenticeships have been incorporated as one component. The nature of apprenticeships applied to formal schooling demonstrate how they serve to promote authentic contexts through which thoughtful teaching and learning can be achieved.

### Cognitive Apprenticeships

One important intention of apprenticeships is to make visible those aspects of thinking and learning that are often obscure to young learners when traditional models of instruction are used. The cognitive apprenticeship described here was designed by Collins et al. (1991) by identifying the elements in a traditional apprenticeship and applying them to school learning. Four important aspects of traditional apprenticeship that have been adapted for use in the cognitive apprenticeship model (Collins et al., 1991) are as follows:

*Modeling and Demonstrating.*   In traditional apprenticeships the expert demonstrated or modeled to the novice how to complete a task from start to finish, making "target processes visible, often by explicitly showing the apprentice what to do" (Collins et al., 1991, p. 8). While the expert worked through to task completion, the novice watched and learned. In the cognitive-apprenticeship model, the demonstration phase assumes a prominent role in learning. Defined as "the process of offering behavior for imitation" (Gallimore & Tharp, 1990, p. 178), modeling is a powerful means of learning that continues into the adult world, one that Cambourne (1988) suggested is a necessary condition for all learning.

Rogoff (1990) offered a clear explanation of how demonstration assists student instruction by applying Vygotsky's sociocultural theory of learning. She describes *demonstration* as a jointly undertaken cultural activity in which the teacher models the task, thereby providing guidance and explanation to the child. As a result, the student is able to appropriate and internalize the cultural ways of carrying out the activity.

*Scaffolding.*   In the traditional apprenticeship model, scaffolding is the support the expert gives to the novice. It is provided when the novice needs it, that is, at any given time while the task is being learned. The master craftsman may come in and demonstrate the entire process, or show the expert one small part of the process. In the classroom in which the cognitive apprenticeship model is employed, the teacher or some other student provides the support to the student who needs it at any point in the process. The expert tells the novice how to perform the task, demonstrates or models the process by showing the student how to do it, gives the student a hint or a sufficient explanation that will bring the novice to independence in performing the task.

It is clear that learning is a joint effort. The adult or more competent student provides assistance to the student who needs to be brought to a level of independent activity. It must be emphasized here that competence can be reached by the students in more effective ways when they are scaffolded at the point at which they need it. Thus the teacher or the expert must be responsive to the needs of the students; the teacher must be deliberate in appropriating the support at the time it is needed. Vygotsky has identified this area within a student's conceptual development as the *zone of proximal development*, which he defined as "the distance between the actual development level as determined by independent problem solving and the level of potential development as determined through problem solving under adult guidance or in collaboration with more capable peers" (Vygotsky, 1978, p. 86). Students are brought to development in culturally appropriate ways through collaboration with a teacher or more competent peers.

*Fading.*   When the support is no longer needed, it is slowly removed. Within the classroom, when a student becomes the expert, he no longer needs the assistance of the teacher, and the support is, therefore, removed.

*Coaching.*   The final element identified within the traditional model of apprenticeship and used in designing the cognitive model of apprenticeship is coaching. Throughout the entire apprenticeship experience, the novice has a coach. The coach supports, encourages, diagnoses problems, discusses solutions, and offers challenges.

The apprenticeship model could not exist without the important component of collaborative talk, because it is only through dialogue that the novice–expert can exist. In the demonstration of a craft, for example, the expert shows the learner how to construct each of the parts, but a critical part of this process is talk. The expert is responsive during the process, scaffolding the learner whenever it is necessary, with both learner and expert involved in asking and answering questions and commenting on what must be done. Without collaborative talk, learning would not occur. Both components, apprenticeships and dialogue, work interactively and interdependently, supporting the dynamic nature of TACLE. Therefore, a discussion follows on the foundation of dialogue with specific reference to its role in the construction of knowledge, the social aspects of language, and learning through collaborative talk.

## Dialogue as Education

### The Nature of Language

Parents are convinced that talking to their infants and toddlers is the primary tool for helping their children to learn to speak and to speak to learn. This same principle of learning is not valued by teachers who insist on silence in the classroom. However, no longer can the critical role of collaborative talk in the construction of knowledge be denied.

In traditional models of learning that are pervasive in America's classrooms, knowledge is transmitted. Our readers who attended school in United States will recall their teachers' dependency on textbooks to impart the facts. You will recollect what it took (and in most cases still takes) to be a good student: attentive listening in class to teacher explanations; reading prescribed texts with predetermined assignments; and solitary study for tests. This type of student behavior leads to retention of prescribed sets of ideas, information, and skills. Learning within this context is what Wells and Chang-Wells (1992) refer to as *cultural reproduction*, because students receive culturally valued knowledge that is transmitted to them by the experts standing beyond the walls of their classrooms.

Within the traditional models of instruction, learning is a private event. A contrasting approach is taken by the sociocultural theorists. Vygotsky (1986) viewed learning as a social activity, in which the interdependence of the student with society holds a prominent place within this event. He further explained that individual activity is a response to society; and that people within society and their activity define a culture: "every function of the child's cultural development appears twice: on the social level, and later, on the individual level; first, between people (interpsychological), and then inside the child (intrapsychological) . . . all the higher functions originate as actual relations between human beings" (1981, p. 30). Because in learning, in the development of their individual concepts, and in the construction of knowledge children work together with others, we are compelled to consider the social milieu of learning.

It is through language that learning becomes social, because language is social through and through (Bakhtin, 1981). Nystrand (1986) explained Bakhtin's stance that each and every utterance, is "the product of the reciprocal relationship between speaker and listener" (pp. 34–35). Language creates the bond that a child shares with the community of learners. Each word becomes a "shared territory" (Volosinov & Bakhtin, 1986) that the individual uses with others to construct meaning. How Bakhtin (1986) explained meaning with respect to language suggests important implications for the design of educational contexts: Language is never decontextualized; meaning does not exist outside of context. Bakhtin went far beyond the generally acceptable explanation that a word has many meanings depending on the way it is used in context; rather, he believed that the meaning of a word is related to its context and for each different context in which a word is used, another meaning is derived. Therefore, for Bakhtin, language meaning is radically contextual, shaped by social relations within a situation, but attached to the cultural and the historic communities. Finally, and most important, in considering talk to construct meaning, it is necessary to understand the dialogic nature of language as explained by Bakhtin. The language user is never alone in using language, because the utterance of "the word is a territory shared by both the addressor and the addressee" (Volosinov & Bakhtin, 1986, p. 86).

### Peer Collaboration

These concepts related to language use—how language is used for meaning and how knowledge is constructed through language—are critical in the design of any instructional system that provides the impetus to incorporate collaborative talk as the dominant social structure. The focus of our discussion therefore turns from the sociocultural foundations of learning through language to collaborative talk as the primary mode to construct knowledge.

Students work in small groups of three or four. They work on problems that they have identified as existing in their own communities. Through collaborative talk they internalize new ideas. How does this occur? Where do these new ideas come from? Certainly, they are not transmitted by the teacher; rather, new ideas are formed through social interaction over a point of interest. For example, one task might be to explore possible solutions to an environmental problem that exists in the students' community. An important part of their work is to brainstorm solutions to real problems that exist in their neighborhoods. They begin by asking questions. This strategy is demonstrated by the "expert scientist." As they talk, they ask useful questions which they write down, another strategy that is demonstrated by the "literacy expert."

At first, questions are tentative, but then they lead to new questions. The talk is truly collaborative, with members of the group bringing each other into the dialogue. The more capable students help to reframe questions for those who need help. An array of solutions is arrived at slowly and deliberately, some partial solutions and others well-thought-out. But always, there are questions to negotiate meaning, questions to clarify, both for the addressor and the addressee.

It is clear what the students are doing: They are negotiating shared meanings; their questions are being used to clarify, to extend and qualify their tentative hypotheses. Solutions to the problems are not as important as the processes the students use in trying to reach a viable solution-strategy. Within this social milieu, the students become members of a community of learners, constructing knowledge and building concepts from a Vygotskian perspective; first, interpsychologically, second, intrapsychologically. By this he meant that before a concept is developed within an individual, it is first constructed from interactions with others. Collaborative talk or joint dialogue is the vehicle that facilitates the construction of knowledge. Therefore, a student's concept development is mediated and assisted through joint social events (Bruner, 1987).

### Exploratory Talk for Learning

Barnes (1992) refers to the students' collaborative language as *exploratory talk*. The role of exploratory talk is crucial in learning; therefore, our discussion turns to the nature of this type of language for thinking.

In defining exploratory talk, Barnes (1992) described it as the opposite of final draft language. Exploratory talk is not talk to present ideas to the teacher or to a public audience; conversely, it is talk that is used to engage in understanding, to shape ideas and to express them for the purpose of testing out a new concept or idea. It is talk used for "thinking out loud"; it is talk that enables students to "monitor their own thought and, reshape it" (Barnes, 1992, p. 28). Exploratory talk is marked by "frequent hesitations, rephrasings, false starts, and changes of directions" (p. 28). So it is thinking out loud, what Vygotsky (1986) calls *inner speech*, or inner dialogue.

How is exploratory talk encouraged, and how is it sustained? There are indeed factors that support learning through talk just as there are conditions that inhibit students from using exploratory talk for learning. Barnes (1992) called the approach that fosters learning through talk an *open approach*. Students learning in the open approach ask questions of themselves as well as others, actively rather than passively; they encourage group members to make inquiries; they make tentative statements rather than complete, definitive ones; they accept the language of each member of the group, even when it appears to be diverse; they keep an open mind to new possibilities; and finally, they deal with disagreements and differences through verbal clarification. In short, in the open approach, talk among group members is collaborative; knowledge is constructed through the social relationship established within this community of learners.

What stands out as the most obvious factor that inhibits exploratory talk is the teacher. The dominant classroom structure within traditional instructional models assumes one of the following forms: whole-class instruction, in which the teacher talks to the entire class; or individually assigned tasks, in which students work alone while the teacher checks the assignment (Goodlad, 1984). This model of instruction discourages any form of exploratory talk. The expectation on the part of the teacher or any class member that all verbalizations must strictly adhere to the rules of language is another obstacle to students who try to engage in talk for learning. When the teacher asks all the questions, rather than encouraging the students to ask questions actively, talk for learning is again thwarted. Because learning is social in nature, the presence of the teacher in the group, even when there is small-group learning, may impede or stimulate talk for learning. This depends on the teacher's expectations for learning and the relationship the teacher has established with the members of the group.

## Authentic Contexts

### *Authentic Contexts Stimulate Exploratory Talk*

As a complex dynamic instructional system, TACLE was designed to offer opportunities to students to solve the real problems of their own community. Authentic contexts became the third component in creating effective learning environments. To legitimize the context for learning, experts from the community, who have a vested interest in solving the neighborhood's problems, work alongside the students. At times, the experts and novices work together in school; at other times they work in the community to identify and analyze the problems.

The traditional dominant social structure found in school—the teacher lecturing in front of the classroom—is gone. When you enter this context, you will not find a preformulated curriculum with specific textbooks. There are no assigned chapter readings, followed by questions with the "one right answer." The designated subject areas, such as science, mathematics, and language arts, with their specific time slots, have been eliminated. Students work on problems that cut across all curricular areas. Finally, the usual formal and informal classroom tests have no part in the authentic contexts for learning.

The students and the experts are, however, sincere in their quest for a solution to the community's problems. They work together, talking and reading about other problems around the world that may be comparable. They talk about possible strategies that they might consider in finding a solution. Their language is as real as the context in which they talk to explore their problems. Indeed, these are the real events that shape the authentic contexts upon which TACLE is designed.

### Authentic Contexts Lead to a State of Mindfulness

There is an exuberance within the community of learners; the students and teachers face their daily tasks with a renewed vigor. They are in the state of *mindfulness* (Langer, 1989, 1993).

Traditional models of education cause both teachers and students to be mindless in the fulfillment of their daily school functions. Langer (1989) described their daily context as placing them in "a premature cognitive commitment, a mindset."

To understand the mindless context into which traditional models of schooling often place teachers and students is to realize why so often they are committed to mindless behavior. For example, consider the elementary-school teacher who teaches her children to read from a basal reader. The teacher is locked into following the manual that guides her through each lesson. The same format is used daily with different stories. She follows the publisher's suggestions, rarely deviating lest she experience a sense of guilt. The students write in their workbooks, completing page after page of fill-in-the-blank exercises to reinforce their reading skills and place them at a level of automaticity. Both teacher and students repeat the same behaviors over and over with very little thought. Their goal is to "get through two readers" and to "cover" all of the skills. Thought does not have to play a part in their teaching and learning: The instruction consists of prepackaged daily lessons. The teacher need only deliver them accordingly, while the learning involves filling in the "one right answer" that can be found in the text of the basal reader if students fail to remember it.

Most learning in schools consists of repetition, practice, and involves tasks that are decontextualized. These ingredients are at the roots of mindless behavior (Langer, 1989). To create mindfulness Langer (1993) suggested "conditional instruction that respects variability and multiple frames for information" (p. 49). It is clear that authentic contexts which defy repetition and mindless practice will lead learners from their traditional categories of thinking to more creative and productive thought, placing them in the state of mindfulness.

### Multiple Literacies are Developed Within Authentic Contexts

School districts across the United States are busy writing curricula with the hope of preparing their students for the demands of the workplace. Much time and energy is spent writing standards and student outcomes for literacy, which indeed have become *the* priority. The results are long lists of goals and objectives related to simply learning how to read and write, outlined in detail, along with some understanding of the computer. Society is changing so rapidly and along with that change come different ways that knowledge is represented. Literacy, reading and writing, will always be given a prominent place within our schools, but we must begin to think of literacy in new ways so that each child can live in society. We need to go beyond the mechanics of learning to read and write. Children must enter the school and continue using society's tools to represent meaning.

This means that we need a broader view of literacy. Literacy involves much more: "Paulo Freire enjoins us not to dissociate 'reading the word' from 'reading the world' " (Papert, 1993, p. 10). In his current book, *The Children's Machine*, Papert is incisive in his description of how our nation's schools have introduced technology into their curricula: Most schools have isolated technology in the computer lab and have made computer literacy an add-on. This is an example of a narrow definition of literacy. Graves' (1983) ideas about literacy instruction offer a clarification without a prescription: The notion of critical literacy suggests that teachers must confirm the experiences that students bring to school; furthermore, children need to be legitimated and supported as people who matter and who can be a part of their own learning. Thus, as Paulo Freire has pointed out, schools cannot be mere places for instruction; schools can no longer transmit the dominant culture; they must be places of culture. It is at this point that the development of literacies begins.

### A Program of Authentic Assessment

Assessment is at the heart of TACLE. It is an ongoing process that began at its inception and will occur even after the students have been dismissed for their summer vacation. Assessment is what makes instruction relevant and useful to each student.

### Criteria for a Program of Authentic Assessment

In order to design an instructional system that would be dynamic as well, we recognized the need for ongoing confirmation and feedback of each component. Therefore, we worked to develop a viable program of authentic assessment for our instructional system. The blueprints of our assessment program were drawn up from the set of criteria listed as follows:

- A program of assessment should be consistent with our instructional philosophy.

- A program of assessment should be both formative as well as summative.
- A program of assessment should be built on shared decision making: Students, teachers, and administrators, as well as the community and parents, should be part of the assessment and evaluation program, because each provides input and receives feedback.
- A program of assessment should be feasible; any data-collection process should not interfere with learning and will be subject to revision.
- A program of assessment should lead to student and teacher empowerment, including revision of the instructional system to meet individual and group needs.
- A program of assessment should inform both students and teachers.
- A program of assessment should lead to reflective teaching and learning.
- Student portfolios of samples of performance along with anecdotal records will be kept.

### Processes Involved in Assessment

Since TACLE is designed on an authentic-learning context, a program of authentic assessment has to deliberately focus on what actually occurs during instruction and learning. Assessment needs to ask questions about the appropriateness of instruction and of student activities. *Teacher observation* is the most valuable tool that has become a major process of an authentic-assessment program.

Observation during instruction indeed has many advantages in assessing learning. For one, consider the paper-and-pencil tests to determine how individual students achieve. Using this procedure changes the context in which learning occurs; the product alone, without the student's learning processes, is measured; and finally, there are limitations in what actually can be measured with traditional paper-and-pencil tests.

TACLE is an instructional system that is built on the apprenticeship model in which social interaction plays a major role in learning. Observation, as a primary source for studying the student learning within the context, is extremely appropriate. Within a Vygotskian perspective, the usefulness of teacher observation in social interaction to determine the relevancy of instruction is prominent.

### Observation Should Inform Teaching and Learning

Vygotsky introduced the concept of the *zone of proximal development* for assessing the appropriateness of instruction. If we use the apprenticeship model as explained by Rogoff (1990), who has interpreted Vygotsky (1978), learning occurs within the novice–expert relationship over a cultural exercise that is mutually undertaken. The expert assists the novice through modeling, explanation, and guidance. Through teacher observation, the expert begins to understand the extent of the participation in the task by the novice, which may or may not lead to learning or the development of concepts. To enhance learning by the novice, the expert teacher must be aware of the learner's zone of proximal development with relation to the nature of the joint activity. Moll (1990) outlined three characteristics of the zone that will lead to a more definitive critique of teaching.

1. Establishing a level of difficulty. This level, assumed to be the proximal level, must be a bit challenging for the student, but not too difficult.
2. Providing assisted performance. The adult (or another competent student) provides guided practice to the child with a clear sense of the goal or outcome of the child's performance.
3. Evaluating independent performance. The most logical outcome of the zone of proximal development is the child performing independently (p. 7).

The student's zone is a band between what the learner can do independently and the upper limit at which the learner performs with the assistance of a more capable person. It guides our instruction, and it is based on the capacities of the student. We know our instruction is good "only when it proceeds ahead of development; (then it) awakens and rouses to life an entire set of functions which are in the stage of maturing, which lie in the zone of proximal development" (Vygotsky, 1956, p. 278, cited in Gallimore & Tharp, 1990, p. 200). Following the characteristics of the zone as a guide in observing instruction and learning, it becomes clear that observation is a powerful source of informing the teacher about the student's learning. It also makes apparent the need to link assessment and instruction.

### A Program of Authentic Assessment Leads to Reflective Learning

One of the major goals of TACLE was to develop thoughtful students who possess habits of mind for self-regulated learning. We felt that a surefire way of reaching our goal would be to empower students by giving them a visible and dynamic role in their own assessment. Realizing that thinking needed to be pervasive in the instructional aspects of the program, we also understood the consequences of teaching students to think about their own learning processes. Thus, we did not leave to chance the development of their *metacognitive strategies*.

The concept of metacognition has been around for almost 20 years, but it has rarely been in practice in our classrooms. Flavell (1977) explained it as the phenomenon of knowing about one's own cognitive processes. We do indeed want students to become aware of their own cognitive processes. We also want them to be able to manage their learning, and to be responsive to their learning environments by taking control of them. By having students become part of the assessment process, we sought ways to sharpen students' metacognitive strategies and develop their self-regulatory behaviors.

Palincsar and Brown (1989) described what it means to be self-regulated learners: Students "are able to use three main types of knowledge in a flexible manner: (1) knowledge of strategies for accomplishing learning tasks efficiently, (2) metacognitive knowledge, and (3) real-world knowledge" (p. 20). Indeed, the development of metacognitive strategies along with the habit and the disposition of learners to use these skills when warranted would create lifelong learners.

In order to develop metacognitive strategies and self-regulatory behaviors in students, teachers do not have to climb inside their students' heads. A simple method to ascertain such behaviors is to ask students questions about their own learning strategies and to get students to ask themselves questions about their own learning. Is this at all possible? Interviews with second- and sixth-grade students related to their understanding of the reading process were conducted by Myers and Paris (1978). Their findings suggest that there are wide discrepancies in the metacognitive strategies of children as a result of age and experience. Further, Garner (1987) found that when questions regarding metacognitive strategies are contextually defined, more information is yielded.

Based on the current research related to metacognition, we employed the students in TACLE as active agents in their own assessment, knowing that probing their own learning processes in authentic contexts would inform both students and teachers. For example, the explicit kind of questions that are posed by experts (teachers and other expert students), as well as the students, provide the necessary feedback for "knowing what to do when one gets stuck" and "understanding what needs to be known to get the task completed successfully." Such assessment is ongoing; it occurs on a daily basis when students are actively engaged in learning; such assessment is nonjudgmental, and occurs in a risk-free environment; such assessment empowers the students and the teachers to change when feedback indicates a necessity to do so. Without this component, our instructional system would not achieve its dynamic nature.


## SUMMARY

During the past decade, there have been resonant pleas for change within our nation's schools. The beginning of our response took the shape of a simple instructional model. As we proceeded, we became more aligned to our students' needs, and we knew that restructuring a complex learning environment was essential to make significant differences in students' learning. TACLE resulted in the construction of a dynamic instructional system. The inclusion of its four components leads to a thinking environment in which students develop more than simple, factual knowledge that eventually becomes static. TACLE is not a place where instruction is delivered; it is a thoughtful, learning environment.

Children target real problems within their community. They work alongside children of different ages and with experts analyzing the problems to find solutions. Students work in a context in which they experience actual work. They see many different kinds of demonstrations of a variety of work activities they engage in; clearly, the processes are made visible to the students. The children help each other and are helped by experts. They engage in *real talk*, talk for learning, talk for getting a job done. The children are not apprehensive about their grades, because they know how things are going. They are a real part of their assessment. They talk about "what they know" and about "what they need to know." In short, TACLE is on its way to becoming successful in producing thoughtful learners, thereby shaping significant changes within one school.

## REFERENCES

Bakhtin, M. M. (1981). *The dialogic imagination: Four essays by M. M. Bakhtin.* Austin: University of Texas Press.

Bakhtin, M. M. (1986). *Speech genres and other late essays.* Austin: University of Texas Press.

Barnes, D. (1992). *From communication to curriculum* (2nd ed.). Portsmouth, NH: Heinemann.

Bruner, J. (1987). *The child's construction of the world.* New York: Methuen.

Cambourne, B. (1988). *The whole story: Natural learning and the acquisition of literacy in the classroom.* New York: Ashton Scholastic.

Collins, A., Brown, J. S., & Holum, A. (1991, Winter). Cognitive apprenticeship: Making thinking visible. *American Educator*, pp. 6–46.

Flavell, J. H. (1977). *Cognitive development.* Englewood Cliffs, NJ: Prentice-Hall.

Gallimore, R., & Tharp, R. (1990). Teaching mind in society: Teaching, schooling, and literate discourse. In L. C. Moll (Ed.), *Vygotsky and education: Instructional implications and applications of sociohistorical psychology.* New York: Cambridge University Press.

Garner, R. (1987). *Metacognition and reading comprehension.* Norwood, NJ: Ablex.

Goodlad, J. I. (1984). *A place called school: Prospects for the future.* New York: McGraw-Hill.

Graves, D. (1983). Writing: Teachers and children at work. Portsmouth, NH: Heinemann.

Langer, E. J. (1989). *Mindfulness.* New York: Addison-Wesley.

Langer, E. J. (1993). A mindful education. *Educational Psychologist, 28*(1), 43–50.

Mayher, J. S. (1990). *Uncommon sense: Theoretical practice in language education.* Portsmouth, NH: Heinemann.

Moll, L. C. (Ed.). (1990). *Vygotsky and education: Instructional implications and applications of sociohistorical psychology.* New York: Cambridge University Press.

Myers, M., & Paris, S. G. (1978). Children's metacognitive knowledge about reading. *Journal of Educational Psychology, 70*, 680–690.

Nystrand, M. (1986). The structure of textual space. In M. Nystrand (Ed.), *What writers know* (pp. 75–86). New York: Academic Press.

Palincsar, A. S., & Brown, A. L. (1989). Instruction for self-regulated reading. In L. B. Resnick & L. E. Klopfer (Eds.), *Toward the thinking curriculum: Current cognitive research* (pp. 19–39). Alexandria, VA: Association of Supervision and Curriculum Development.

Papert, S. (1993). *The children's machine: Rethinking school in the age of the computer.* New York: Basic Books.

Perkins, D. (1992). *Smart schools: From training memories to educating minds.* New York: Free Press.

Rogoff, B. (1990). *Apprenticeship in thinking.* New York: Oxford University Press.

Volosinov, V. N., & Bakhtin, M. M. (1986). *Marxism and the philosophy of language*. Cambridge, MA: Harvard University Press.

Vygotsky, L. S. (1978). *Mind in society* (M. Cole, S. Scribner, V. J. Steiner, & E. Souberman, Eds.). Cambridge, MA: Harvard University Press.

Vygotsky, L. S. (1981). The genesis of higher mental functions. In J. Wertsch (Ed.), *The concept of activity in Soviet psychology*. Armonk, NY: Sharpe, Inc.

Vygotsky, L. S. (1986). Thought and language (translated & revised by A. Kozulin). Cambridge, MA: The MIT Press.

Wells, G., & Chang-Wells, G. L. (1992). Constructing knowledge together: Classrooms as centers of inquiry and literacy. Portsmouth, NH: Heinemann.

# Chapter 16

# A Case for Case-Based Instruction

Angelo V. Ciardiello
*Fordham University*
*Iona College*
*Jane Addams High School, Bronx, New York*

The educational reform movement of the 1980s and 1990s issued a call for changes in traditional teacher–student roles, learning strategies, and instructional materials. Generally, the reformers have criticized the teacher domination and student passivity that characterize many classroom lessons. Some have advocated techniques that incorporate critical-thinking procedures and process learning and view the teacher as a facilitator who actively engages students in their own instruction (Goodlad, 1984; Sizer, 1984, 1992).

Several approaches to instruction have been offered to enhance these changing roles and methodologies. Cooperative learning and reciprocal teaching are just two strategies (D. Johnson & R. Johnson, 1991; Palincsar & Klenk, 1992). There is another technique, which is not new but is receiving greater attention in schools today, that provides opportunities for greater teacher–student collaboration in the learning process. It is called *case-based instruction*. Learning through cases has been a successful technique for decades in professional business schools and law schools. The Harvard Business School utilizes the case-method approach in its curriculum and highlights four important factors that distinguish this process. First, it is *situational*. It is an approach that is steeped in the context of the real world. Second, it is a *narrative*. It is presented in story form with a series of episodes that contains a beginning, middle, and end. Third, it focuses on the objective of *active participation* rather than passive reflection. Fourth, it engages the student in *decision making* (Christensen & Hansen, 1987; McNair, 1954).

Recently, educators have advocated case-based instruction as an important training device in teacher education programs (Kowalski, Weaver, & Henson,

1990). It has also been recognized as an important vehicle in teaching specific disciplines such as mathematics and language arts (Barnett, 1991; Tiedt, 1992). Social studies educators have also stressed the importance of case studies in actively involving students in learning concepts (Martorella, 1991b; Newmann & Oliver, 1967). Indeed, the Bradley Commission on teaching history in the schools strongly recommends the case method and narrative teaching as the most effective way to teach the subject. The authors of the report claim that case studies provide a "context for data" and a "thick narrative" that stimulate understanding of factual and conceptual information (Gagnon, 1989, pp. 44, 290).

There is strong theoretical support in the literature for the relevance of case-method instruction in the social studies. Cornbleth (1985) argued that social studies is an "ill-structured domain" because it deals with issues that are not bounded or clearly delineated. Such an amorphous and unstructured discipline is not suited to teaching by algorithm. Case studies are types of knowledge representation most suited to content domains like the social studies that cannot be routinized. In ill-structured domains, important information tends to be uniquely contained in individual cases.

Cases provide the opportunity to reexamine a variety of thematic dimensions from different vantage points and in new situations. Spiro, Vispoel, Schmitz, Samarapungavan, and Berger (1987) advanced the theory of cognitive flexibility, which claims that knowledge of a domain is most effectively learned by "criss-crossing" it in many directions and by noting the interconnectedness between different aspects. The instructional metaphor of a "crisscrossed landscape" and the theory of cognitive flexibility are appropriate to the ill-structured domain of social studies. By its very nature, the field of social studies is an integrated one in that it represents "the social sciences simplified for pedagogical purposes" (Wesley, 1950, p. 34). One can crisscross the landscape of social studies by examining historical themes as they intersect and overlap economic and sociological themes. By using a case-study approach in social studies, one can analyze a situation from a number of thematic perspectives.

## CASE-METHOD INSTRUCTION
## AND THE CHANGING ROLE OF THE TEACHER

In order to effectively apply the case method in the classroom, the teacher must alter traditional methods of teaching, such as lecturing and recitation. Researchers recommend several teaching methods that are based on the cognitive-apprenticeship approach to education (Hmelo, 1993; Williams, 1992). These methods include *modeling, coaching*, and *scaffolding*. Through modeling, teachers as subject specialists demonstrate how to read and analyze a case. Through cognitive coaching, they observe and challenge students to analyze cases, and they provide immediate feedback. Concurrently, they assist students in handling the complex task of case analysis—an assignment that many students cannot do alone.

Case-method instruction incorporates other changes into the role of the teacher. Teachers can serve as curriculum makers. Indeed, they can be an integral part of the curriculum constructed and enacted in the classroom (Clandinin & Connelly, 1992). Wassermann (1992) successfully trained high school teachers to construct original case studies in 11th-grade social studies classes. These teacher-made cases, which utilized a narrative approach, served as the curriculum for the course.

Another new role for teachers is that of reflective practitioner. Reflective practitioners are professionals who observe and study their practice in order to discover the understandings already embedded in it (Schon, 1991). They must become role models of thinking in action. Instead of focusing on covering course content, they must concentrate on fostering habits of intelligent thinking (Newmann, 1988; Sizer, 1992). They must avoid lecturing to students, because the practice of teaching is too complex an activity to be left to teacher-talk alone. Several cognitive researchers agree that "wisdom cannot be told" (Bransford, Franks, Vye, & Sherwood, 1989; Erickson & MacKinnon, 1991; Gragg, 1940).

In addition, the process of metacognition plays a role in case-method instruction. Through this process, teachers develop an awareness of the tacit understandings revealed by the patterns of spontaneous activity that make up case-method instruction. By developing control strategies, they are then able to monitor their teaching skills.

## CASE-METHOD INSTRUCTION
## AND THE CHANGING ROLE OF STUDENTS

As the dominant role of the teacher diminishes in case-method instruction, the involvement of the student increases correspondingly. Indeed, both students and teachers become partners in the interpretation and analysis of issues embedded in cases. More and more, the students assume responsibility for their own learning as they acquire knowledge from reading and sharing ideas through group investigation. The instructional metaphor describing the change is "student as worker" rather than "student as passive absorber of information" (Sizer, 1992; Wassermann, 1992).

Case-study methods provide students with the reasoning skills and critical-thinking skills to make informed judgments. They develop the appropriate habits of thinking, such as learning how to gather sufficient data to support an argument and the ability to distinguish between relevant and irrelevant information. Students also learn how to develop conclusions based on concrete evidence.

A recent empirical investigation of the effects of case-method instruction in social studies revealed some interesting findings. Adam (1992) discovered in her qualitative research with 11th-grade students that they developed more tolerance to other students' viewpoints and expressed a greater sensitivity to the feelings of others in class discussions. Furthermore, she ascertained that they manifested a greater desire to continue the investigation of the issues outside the classroom and even discussed the cases with parents and friends. The students even expressed positive attitudes about social studies while involved in case-study analysis.

## CASE MATERIALS AND NEW TECHNOLOGIES

When the students involved in the Adam (1992) study were asked to identify the factor in case-study analysis that contributed most to their involvement, they referred to the nature of the case materials. They believed that the cases were relevant not only to historical circumstances, but also to their own personal lives. Cases are interesting to read because they immerse the reader into human experiences. They are complex situations extracted from real events that appear in the form of narratives (Wassermann, 1992). They focus intensively on limited situations rather than broad, panoramic events (Newmann & Oliver, 1970). These situations reflect major concepts or big ideas from the curriculum that are worthy of in-depth investigation. Furthermore, cases often include follow-up material such as graphic data, photographs, works of fiction, and so on, in order to broaden students' knowledge of the situation. Perhaps most important for the purpose of case analysis are the study questions that focus student thinking about the issues and provoke deeper examination of the data and materials (Wassermann, 1992). It is essential that the guide questions be constructed in an open-ended fashion in order to stimulate discussion and encourage the development of sound judgment. Getting the right answer is not the goal, but rather to encourage students to reason from data and to rationally defend their opinions of the case.

A relatively new instructional tool that presents case materials in an effective way is interactive video. This method provides students with an opportunity to get directly involved in historical events (Martorella, 1991a). One of the most interesting new forms of interactive video is hypertext—which are documents that can be distributed across both print and nonprint media. It is a nonlinear system of linked information (McKnight, Dillon, & Richardson, 1991).

Hypertext is a form of technology that is consistent with recent cognitive principles of case-based instruction. In particular, the theory of cognitive flexibility, which stresses the multiple and nonsequential dimensions of knowledge representation, lends support to a method of representing knowledge that is nonlinear. In fact, hypertext is case-based (Spiro, 1993). It can be manipulated to fit students' varying educational needs. This kind of technology provides an alternative means of knowledge representation that is not bounded by traditional forms of print media.

Bransford and Stein (1993) labeled these video-based anchors as *macrocontexts* because they situate instruction within the context of meaningful problems. The problem in the macrocontext is presented as a true story that makes the investigation less complex because the data is embedded in real-world settings. Macrocontexts solve the problem of what philosopher Alfred Whitehead (1929) called "inert knowledge," a type of learning which can only be accessed in limited situations. Too often traditional learning environments stress this kind of instruction that is not adaptable to varying contexts and hence has no transfer value. Macrocontexts provide students with the flexibility to access information from different sources to solve problems.

## CASE-BASED LEARNING STRATEGIES

Case-study analysis does not depend on any single instructional strategy. It can be taught in many different ways (Dunwiddie, 1967). However, recent literature supports two alternative techniques for training students in case-study analysis (Bittner, 1990; Wasserman, 1992). Bittner (1990) suggested a structured approach in which the teacher models the proper method for effectively analyzing a case. She recommends an instructional tool known as IRAC (Issues, Rules, Analysis, and Conclusion), which is used in legal-case methods of instruction. Through this procedure students are taught how to identify the major issues, apply the appropriate rules, analyze the case, and make an informed judgment about the results. It is a systematic approach to case analysis. The key element in this procedure is teachers' design of logical organization.

An alternative strategy is more student-centered and involves cooperative learning procedures. Wasserman (1992) advocated a three-step method entitled "play-debrief-replay." This procedure involves students in brainstorming sessions in which they respond to study questions that are part of each case. The author labels this free flow of ideas as the "play" segment of case analysis. The second stage involves the teacher assisting students in extracting the meanings of the case from their initial generated ideas. When the students have reviewed their supporting data as well as accepted new information, then they are ready to move to the last phase. At this point they proceed to support or refute the arguments of the case. The key elements in this technique is student involvement.

## CONCLUDING REMARKS

Case-based instruction incorporates many characteristics found in problem-centered learning, a technique that is used widely in medical-school training (Williams, 1992). Both of these teaching methods rely on cognitive apprenticeship and anchored instruction. Perhaps the most significant similarity is the fact that both types of instruction begin with a problem to be solved. Williams indicated that the first phase of problem solving occurs when students generate their own hypotheses necessary to solve the problem. This phase is also known as the *problem-finding phase.* Getzels (1979) informed us that it is the most creative segment of problem solving because it incorporates divergent thinking and discovery. This skill is particularly valuable in case-study analysis in which it is necessary to generate multiple student perspectives pertaining to the same event (Bransford, 1993). The skill is also important in the real world, where problems are approached from many different angles and generally have a number of potential solutions. Case-study instruction and problem-centered learning provide a context for students to identify and create their own problems in the process of clarifying goals. Learning through cases provides an authentic learning environment where real-world problems provide the basis for instruction. Cognitive researchers have discovered what classroom teachers know from experience— students have problems learning from decontextualized instruction. When learning begins with authentic problems embedded in cases, students are motivated to find the solutions.

## REFERENCES

Adam, M. E. (1992). *The response of eleventh graders to the use of the case method of instruction in social studies.* Unpublished master's thesis, Simon Fraser University, Burnaby, British Columbia.

Barnett, C. (1991). Building a case-based curriculum to enhance the pedagogical content knowledge of mathematics teachers. *Journal of Teacher Education, 42,* 263–272.

Bittner, M. (1990). The IRAC method of case study analysis: A legal model for the social studies. *The Social Studies, 81,* 227–230.

Bransford, J. D (1993, July). *Teaching problem solving.* Paper presented at the Fordham University Reading Institute, New York.

Bransford, J. D., Franks, J. J., Vye, N. J., & Sherwood, R. D. (1989). New approaches to instruction: Because wisdom can't be told. In S. Vosniadou & A. Ortony (Eds.), *Similarity and analogical reasoning* (pp. 470–479). New York: Cambridge University Press.

Bransford, J. D., & Stein, B. S. (1993). *The ideal problem solver: A guide for improving thinking, learning and creativity* (2nd ed.). New York: Freeman.

Christensen, C. R., & Hansen, A. J. (1987). *Teaching and the case method: Text, cases and readings.* Boston: Harvard Business School.

Clandinin, D. J., & Connelly, F. M. (1992). Teacher as curriculum maker. In P. Jackson (Ed.), *Handbook of Curriculum and Research* (pp. 363–393). New York: Macmillan.

Cornbleth, C. (1985). Critical thinking and cognitive processes. In W. B. Stanley (Ed.), *Review of research in social studies education: 1973–1983* (pp. 11–63). Washington, DC: National Council for the Social Studies and Boulder, CO: ERIC Clearinghouse for Social Studies/Social Science Education and Social Science Education Consortium.

Dunwiddie, W. (1967). Using case studies in social studies classes. *Social Education, 31,* 397–400.

Erickson, G. L., & MacKinnon, A. M. (1991). Seeing classrooms in new ways: On becoming a science teacher. In D. A. Schon (Ed.), *The reflective turn: Case studies in and on educational practice* (pp. 15–36). New York: Teachers College Press.

Gagnon, P. (Ed.). (1989). *Historical literacy: The case for history in American education.* New York: Macmillan.

Getzels, J. W. (1979). Problem-finding: A theoretical note. *Cognitive Science, 3,* 167–172.

Goodlad, J. (1984). *A place called school.* New York: McGraw-Hill.

Goodlad, J. (1990). *Teachers for our nation's schools.* San Francisco: Jossey-Bass.

Gragg, C. I. (1940). Because wisdom can't be told. In M. P. McNair (Ed.), *The case method at the Harvard Business School* (pp. 6–15). New York: McGraw-Hill.

Hmelo, C. E. (1993). *Learning in school and learning in life: An exploration of issues.* Unpublished manuscript, Vanderbilt University, Nashville, TN.

Johnson, D. W., & Johnson, R. (1991). *Learning together and alone: Cooperative, competitive, and individualistic learning* (3rd ed.). Englewood Cliffs, NJ: Prentice-Hall.

Kowalski, T. J., Weaver, R. A., & Henson, K. T. (1990). *Case studies on teaching.* New York: Longman.

Martorella, P. M. (1991a). Harnessing the new technologies to the new social studies curriculum. *Social Education, 55,* 55–57.

Martorella, P. H. (1991b). *Teaching social studies in middle and secondary schools.* New York: Macmillan.

McKnight, C., Dillon, A., & Richardson, J. (1991). *Hypertext in context.* New York: Cambridge University Press.

McNair, M. P. (Ed.). (1954). *The case method at the Harvard Business School.* New York: McGraw-Hill.

Newmann, F. M. (1988). Can depth replace coverage in the high school curriculum? *Phi Delta Kappan, 69,* 345–348.

Newmann, F. M., & Oliver, D. W. (1967). Case-study approaches in social studies, *Social Education, 31,* 108–113.

Newmann, F. M., & Oliver, D. W. (1970). *Clarifying public controversy: An approach to teaching social studies.* Boston: Little, Brown.

Palincsar, A. S., & Klenk, L. (1992). Examining and influencing contexts for intentional literacy learning. In C. Collins & J. N. Mangieri (Eds.), *Teaching thinking: An agenda for the 21st century* (pp. 297–316). Hillsdale, NJ: Lawrence Erlbaum Associates.

Schon, D. A. (Ed.). (1991). *The reflective turn: Case studies in and on educational practice.* New York: Teachers College Press.

Sizer, T. (1984). *Horace's compromise: The dilemma of the American high school.* Boston: Houghton Mifflin.

Sizer, T. (1992). *Horace's school: Redesigning the American high school.* Boston: Houghton Mifflin.

Spiro, R. J. (1993, July). *Hypertext: New ways of thinking about complex curriculum.* Paper presented at Fordham University Reading Institute, New York.

Spiro, R. J., Vispoel, W., Schmitz, J., Samarapungavan, A., & Berger, A. (1987). Knowledge acquisition for application: Cognitive flexibility and transfer in complex content domains. In B. C. Britton (Ed.), *Executive control processes* (pp. 177–197). Hillsdale, NJ: Lawrence Erlbaum Associates.

Tiedt, I. M. (1992). Responding to the call of stories: Learning from literary "case studies." *Phi Delta Kappan, 73,* 802–805.

Wesley, E. B. (1950). *Teaching social studies in high schools* (3rd ed.). Boston: Heath.

Wasserman, S. (1992). A case for social studies. *Phi Delta Kappan, 73,* 793–801.

Whitehead, A. N. (1929). *The aims of education.* New York: Macmillan.

Williams, S. M. (1992). Putting case-based instruction into context: Examples from legal and medical education. *Journal of the Learning Sciences, 2*(4), 367–427.

# Chapter 17

# Responding to Literary Texts

Richard T. Vacca
*Kent State University*

Evangeline V. Newton
*John Carroll University*

For much of this century, reading instruction in American elementary schools has been guided by a belief that children will learn to read well through mastery of linguistic artifact. The teaching of "reading skills" has become the *raison d'être* of instruction in classrooms where reading is believed to be a text-driven event. The study of literary texts has been similarly conceptualized, with student attention focused on mastery of "a special vocabulary for describing the properties of poems and the establishment of standard methods of explication" (Tompkins, 1980, p. 223).

Although skills-based reading instruction and text-based literary interpretation evolved from different curricular preoccupations, practitioners of each viewed comprehension as the process of extracting indigenous meaning from a printed text. Not surprisingly, they generated philosophically compatible instructional paradigms that embraced certain assumptions about the roles of text, teacher, and reader in classroom interaction: The text was to be regarded as the locus of meaning. The teacher's role was to impart information about the properties of text through classroom activities focused on its structure, language, and conventions. The reader's task was judicious application of that information. The ultimate instructional goal, *comprehension*, was demonstrated by readers through their command of factual information in the text. Comprehension of a literary text was called *interpretation, explication*, or *exegesis*. It was demonstrated by identifying the "truth" or "deep" meaning in a literary text.

In recent years, however, extensive research in several fields—literacy acquisition, cognitive psychology, psycholinguistics, literary criticism, and the sociology of classroom interaction—has offered new insights into how readers construct meaning with texts. This chapter examines one facet of those insights with enormous implications for language-arts classrooms: the interaction of readers with literary text. What does contemporary research tell us about readers' instinctive responses to the literature they read? How does response research alter traditional conceptualizations of readers and literary text? How can a reader's spontaneous interaction be nurtured and enriched in a contemporary classroom? What is meant by a "response-based" literature curriculum? How does it alter the traditional teacher–reader–text relationship in American literature classrooms?

## DEFINING *RESPONSE*

As early as 1938, Rosenblatt (1983) wrote in *Literature as Exploration* that English teachers had fundamentally misunderstood the activity of reading literature. There was no such thing, she claimed, as a "generic" reader or a "generic" literary text. Rather, each reader brought to the reading act distinctive personality traits, worldviews, and preoccupations of the moment that influenced his or her understanding of that text. Furthermore, through the act of reading literature the reader could become aware of "potentialities for thought and feeling within himself." Rosenblatt's (1983) seminal work offered our first definition of *response* by arguing that *thought* and *feeling* were legitimate components of literary interpretation. Furthermore, a text's meaning was dependent on the unique natures of both reader and text.

Her innovative ideas, however, were not widely endorsed, probably because New Criticism was quickly rooting in American universities. Based loosely on the poet T. S. Eliot's (1959) declaration that the writer's task was to represent emotion in his work by constructing an "objective correlative" of his own experience, the New Critics emphasized the primacy of text in meaning making. They warned against contamination of literary analysis through reader bias, popularizing the notion of text-as-objective-artifact. Their curricular agenda subordinated the reader's uniqueness, emphasizing instead the study of genre and literary technique to help readers interpret text "correctly." The reader's task became to ferret out the truth inherent in poems, not to probe his or her own thoughts, feelings, or unique responses to the text. The New Critics' influence on literature instruction in American classrooms cannot be underestimated. In fact, a recent study of junior high schools revealed that even today most instructional time in literature classrooms is spent on teaching comprehension through literary terms and concepts (Zancanella, 1988).

The worksheet in Fig. 17.1, from a seventh-grade literature class, demonstrates a New Critical approach. Note how this assignment assumes that the text harbors an objective meaning. Focus on words and images will expose that meaning. The first question, for example, solicits the writer's point; the second asks how

*Understanding Symbols, Imagery*

Read the poem carefully. This poem relies heavily on symbols and images to achieve its desired effect.

1. Make a general statement on the effect of the poem. How does the poet feel about 4:00 A.M.?

_____

_____

2. Now let's analyze how he achieves this effect. First, consider the images. Most of them are visual ones. List *five* images (word or phrase) which reflect the mood of the poem:

_____

_____

3. Symbols are also used (sometimes within the images) to suggest other things to us that we can relate to. Comment on the significance and appropriateness of the following symbols (in context with his subject—4 A.M.).

a. "swaying vessel of emptiness" _____

_____

_____

b. "dead planets" _____

_____

_____

c. "cellblock sealed in ice" _____

_____

_____

d. "blank screen" _____

_____

_____

e. "pool of ashes" _____

_____

_____

f. "the very dirge" _____

_____

_____

4. The last two stanzas (or couplets, in this case) contain a shift in the images and symbols. Comment on the following:

a. "bandages of light" _____

_____

_____

b. "a life buoy in bruised waters" _____

_____

5. What are your thoughts on the last line? Does it seem appropriate there? Odd? Why?

_____

_____

FIG. 17.1 Example of worksheet for Edward Hirsch's "4 A.M." based on New Critical precepts.

the writer achieves this effect through "five images—word or phrase—which reflect the mood of the poem." In addition, the worksheet asks students to explain symbols which have been identified as "keywords or phrases." When Olivia, an eighth grader, was asked to write an essay on symbolism in Dunbar's "Sympathy," she also assumed a New Critical stance:

> In the poem "Sympathy," the poet, Paul Lawrence Dunbar, feels sympathy towards the caged bird because his parents had been physically "caged" and because he and his entire race were and still are facing a psychological cage that exists in the minds of all racist people. He uses the metaphor of a caged bird to express the oppression of the people of his race and of all minority races. He compares the life and struggle of a caged bird to the life and struggle of an African-American. He also uses word imagery to further his point. . . . His mastery of words and phrases causes the reader to feel "sympathy" for the caged bird and listen more closely to its song.

From an academic perspective, Olivia does what is expected of her, and she does it well. But conspicuously absent from the process of literary analysis is Olivia's own voice, beliefs, or disposition. She volunteers no personal opinions. In fact, there is no evidence that she liked—or disliked—the poem.

These two assignments, while formatted differently, are both rooted in text-centered comprehension paradigms: students are asked to extrapolate meaning by analyzing linguistic elements in the text.

## Psycholinguistic Contributions to Response Theory

For most of this century, reading was regarded as a word recognition process. It was believed that readers required only a generic knowledge of sound–symbol relationships to construct meaning. Consequently, reading instruction in American schools has been conceived as a kind of "technology" in which "skills are arranged sequentially and hierarchically and exercises are multiplied and duplicated to teach the skills" (Goodman, 1987a, p. 368).

But in the 1960s new developments in psycholinguistics and cognitive psychology generated a different view of reading, one focused on "the interaction of readers' knowledge and expectations with the constraints in connected discourse" (Cooper, 1985, p. xii). In 1969, Goodman conducted an extensive study of oral-reading errors, which he called *miscues*. He concluded that errors were not random or the consequence of ignorance about symbol–sound relationships. In fact, an examination of the nature of specific reading errors provides insight into how the reading process functions in a particular reader at a particular time.

Consequently, the reading process is "less a matter of extracting sound from print than of bringing meaning to print" through a reader's continuous and deliberate employment of semantic (meaning), syntactic (grammar), and graphophonemic (print) cues in a text (Smith, 1988, p. 2). Furthermore, efficient reading of a text depends largely on how well its structure and content fit the readers' prior knowledge and linguistic schema. The better the fit, the fewer cues a reader will need to construct meaning. Goodman (1987b) attributed the major difference between the psycholinguistic and earlier conceptualizations of the reading process to "how much active control the reader exerts, how important reader characteristics are, how much text characteristics control the process, and whether meaning is in the writer, the text, or the reader" (p. 827).

Further support for a psycholinguistic view of reader as director of the meaning-making process comes from a growing body of research in early literacy. Halliday (1975), for example, discovered that oral language development is a "saga in learning to mean." Studies by Harste, Burke, and Woodward (1982, 1984) indicated that language is learned through interpretation. Language learners, then, are architects who construct meaning from linguistic and environmental cues. In addition, oral and written language develop in a parallel, not sequential, manner as children attempt to make sense of their world.

Bloome (1985) noted that learning to read also means learning "culturally-bound ways of thinking" (p. 138). Most children learn to read in the social context of a classroom where they are also taught "culturally appropriate ways of interacting," which influence how they construct meaning (p. 138). This perspective has profound implications for reading instruction, which must now concern itself not only with what knowledge students need to become proficient readers, but also with the influence of classroom dynamics on how that knowledge is acquired and transmitted.

The psycholinguistic model has caused many teachers of literature to question New Critical assumptions about the relationship between a reader and a text.

### Early Response Research

As the psycholinguists were offering new perspectives on the reader–text relationship, research on the teaching of literature began to suggest that teachers should expand their instructional approaches. In 1964, Squire examined 52 written responses of 9th- and 10th-grade students to four short stories. He suggested that teachers stop limiting themselves to postreading discussions. Instead, he recommended that students explore conflicting interpretations by reviewing the different reading processes that had produced them. Two years later, Wilson (1966) conducted a similar study of 54 college freshman in two English classes. He identified seven categories of student response to three novels, and concluded that self-involvement was an early and necessary step in the interpretive process.

In another seminal work, Purves and Rippere (1968) examined the kinds of statements students and critics made after reading a literary work. They determined that readers approach a literary text on four nonhierarchical levels: engagement–involvement, perception, interpretation, and evaluation. Purves and Rippere advised teachers to demonstrate the interpretive consequence of each approach and recommended that the process of "examining one's engagement" begin "early in the child's schooling" (p. 61).

Largely as a result of proliferating research in literacy acquisition and literary instruction, *reader response* began to develop as a school of literary criticism in universities. Unlike their New Critical rivals, reader-response theorists conferred primal importance on the reader–text relationship in the process of literary interpretation (Jefferson & Robey, 1986). With its epistemological roots in hermeneutics and phenomenology, reader-response theory held that meaning evolves from the interaction of diverse influences, including that of reader, writer, and text within a historical and linguistic context.

So, as reading theorists and researchers in early literacy directed attention to the learner's role in language acquisition, literary theorists revived and developed new perspectives on Rosenblatt's (1983) seminal work. *Response* quickly became a shorthand term for new ways of defining the relationship between a reader and a text.


## RESPONSE THEORY: A FRAMEWORK

In a later work, *The Reader, the Text, the Poem*, Rosenblatt (1978) developed what she refers to as a "transactional" view of the reader–text relationship. When readers approach a text, Rosenblatt believes, they adopt one of two stances, *efferent* or *aesthetic*. These stances will vary according to the readers' purpose and the text's nature. Because the goal of an efferent reading is information retrieval, a reader's stance will be objective. But the goal of an aesthetic reading is to focus on "what happens during the actual reading event" (p. 27). This, she claims, is the special province of literary text because readers savor the experience of reading literature. Consequently, "the poem—the literary work—is evoked during the transaction between reader and text" (p. 27). And because the experience has differed from reader to reader, the poem that is evoked may differ markedly as well.

Although response theorists represent a variety of epistemological orientations, they share a perception of readers as actively engaged in the process of constructing meaning from text. Iser (1980), for example, believes readers fill in information gaps when reading texts (e.g., missing description or chronology). According to his approach, called *phenomenological*, as readers interact with a text, they supply necessary details from their own imaginations. Thus they construct their own unique meanings. When students were asked to read the following poem by Hayden, they invented a history of the relationship between the father and son:

Those Winter Sundays

Sundays too my father got up early
and put his clothes on in the blueblack cold,
then with cracked hands that ached

from labor in the weekday weather made
banked fires blaze. No one ever thanked him.

I'd wake and hear the cold splintering, breaking.
When the rooms were warm, he'd call,
and slowly I would rise and dress,
fearing the chronic angers of that house,

Speaking indifferently to him,
who had driven out the cold
and polished my good shoes as well.
What did I know, what did I know
of love's austere and lonely offices?

—*Robert Hayden* (1991, p. 821)

For example, note how three of the students, Ray, Linda, and Jane, responded:

The kid took every little thing his father did for him for granted. (Ray)

The son feels that *his* son probably feels the same way about him. This is because both men, as fathers have a difficult job during the week and probably don't enjoy it. (Linda)

Love warmed the house for *everyone* to sleep in late while he did chores. (Jane)

In each case, the text offers no concrete support for the student's assertion. Each student has dipped into the text itself for interpretive material, but constructed meaning by using his or her own feelings to weave an appropriate fiction. Iser (1980) asserted that a literary text must be understood as an opportunity for readers to use their imaginations to work things out for themselves.

Mailloux (1990) found most response theories to be based on psychological, intersubjective, or social archetypes of the reading experience, with each weighting the reader–text relationship somewhat differently. Bleich (1975, 1978) and Holland (1975, 1985) asserted the total authority of a reader. Bleich (1975) focused chiefly on the idiosyncratic nature of literary interpretation. A critic of conventional language-arts pedagogies that ask students to separate their thoughts from their feelings, Bleich (1975) introduced the term *subjective criticism* to suggest that literary response "begins in complete subjectivity and is then transformed into judgments that appear to be objective" (p. 49).

In her response to Jackson's "The Lottery," Sarah, a high school senior, demonstrates Bleich's notion that response begins in "complete subjectivity":

I did not like "The Lottery" because the story seemed senseless. The people seemed senseless. I do not understand why a town would annually kill a citizen just for the hell of it. I don't see how this can be compared to anything in real life. Even the Holocaust isn't the same. They weren't killing their own family by luck of the draw. . . . Growing up in a rural town myself, I see all the things at home in this story. This is probably another reason why I disliked it so much. It shows how narrow-minded people in the country can be. If something is a tradition, no matter how stupid or dangerous it may be, it will remain a tradition. God forbid if anyone should try to change anything in these small towns. It scares me to think that if one of these "traditions" was to stone someone in the community every year, they would still do it. These attitudes are what made me want to leave so desperately and never go back, but even so, I still have ties to my home.

Note how candidly Sarah works through her initial reaction to this text, and how—perhaps inadvertently—she emerges with a seemingly "objective" interpretation.

Similarly, Holland (1985) emphasized the psychological makeup of an individual reader. He believes readers "DEFT" a text, "re-creating our identities through our own characteristic patterns of *d*efense, *e*xpectation, *f*antasy, and *t*ransformation" (p. 14). For Holland (1985), literary analysis is self-examination. Petrosky (1977) drew on the work of Anna Freud, Piaget, and Erikson to demonstrate that a reader's response to literature depends largely on his or her cognitive and ego operations in current and prior developmental stages. Petrosky believes that adolescents, like adults, respond to literature based on their prior experience and knowledge. But unlike adults, adolescents are sometimes "clumsy and confused by symbols and meanings" (p. 37). He believes our language-arts pedagogies should respect this.

Fish (1980) focused attention on the character of literary experience, attacking the New Criticism's canon of *textual objectivity*, which he called a "dangerous illusion . . . of self-sufficiency and completeness" (p. 83). Because the text is mercurial, Fish argued, the reader should regard language as an experience. In lieu of the traditional "What does this text mean?", Fish suggested asking students, "What does this text do?"

Although reader-response theorists obviously represent a variety of epistemological orientations, they share a perception of readers as actively engaged in the process of constructing meaning with text. This perception is relatively new to the academy and ushers in a host of pedagogical possibilities.

## TOWARD A RESPONSE-BASED CURRICULUM

For most teachers, the major challenge in a response curriculum lies in understanding the altered roles of reader and text. Because all interpretation evolves from a reader's aesthetic interaction with text, instruction must focus on eliciting and then nurturing these interactions.

First, the teacher must create an environment in which students feel free enough to respond openly. Open responses are not final responses. They are, however, crucial to further exploration in which students clarify and extend their initial thoughts and feelings. Second, teachers must demonstrate that meaning is constructed socially as well as in the self. These two features of a response curriculum may require teachers to reconceptualize their own instructional roles by encouraging students to develop independent interpretations and then share them with classmates. Traditionally, teachers have sought to "expound the wisdom and truth of our texts . . . in the service of a secular scripture" (Scholes, 1985, p. 12). But if meaning construction begins in the "self" and evolves within a classroom community, multiple understandings of the same text are possible, even desirable.

Furthermore, these principles should be well modeled for children from their earliest encounters with print. Hickman (1984) saw the teacher as a director of classroom experiences, who "arranges available time, provides materials, controls the physical setting of the classroom, and presents certain expectations about what is to happen" (p. 282).

In an oral-reading activity with very young children, for example, teachers can assist the response process through a "My Own Feelings Chart" (see Table 17.1). Before reading, teachers identify significant moments or sentences in a story they plan to read aloud. These are printed on a large chart and displayed in front of the classroom. As teachers finish reading each sentence listed, they

TABLE 17.1
"My Own Feelings" Chart on *Koala Lou* by Mem Fox

| STORY MOMENTS . . . | HOW DO I FEEL NOW? |
|---|---|
| "But it was her mother who loved her most of all." | happy<br>glad<br>like hugging |
| "Soon her mother was so busy she didn't have time to tell Koala Lou that she loved her." | sad |
| SHE would enter the Olympics! | excited<br>happy<br>fun |
| "At last the day of the Bush Olympics arrived." | excited<br>scared<br>happy |
| "Koala Lou came second." | sad<br>angry<br>mad<br>tired |
| "And she hugged her for a very long time." | happy<br>glad |

ask students to describe their feelings at that moment about what they have just heard. Teachers then record students' descriptive phrases beside each event.

Postreading discussion begins with an examination of how students' responses differed or evolved during the reading event. R. Yopp and H. Yopp (1992) described a similar "Feelings Chart" in which students are asked to speculate about how each of the characters in a story is responding to specific plot events. Both activities sensitize young children to the importance of feelings during a reading event. They also demonstrate that a range of emotions is possible and that individual responses sometimes vary profoundly from reader to reader.

Middle- and upper-grade teachers should continue to offer students similar opportunities to share honest reactions to a variety of literary texts without penalizing them for overlooking predetermined "truths" in those texts. Bleich (1975) used feeling or affect to help older students chronicle their responses as a catalyst for classroom discussion. His affective-associative heuristic has been widely adopted in secondary and university classrooms. After students have read a text, they are asked to write in response to the question, "How does this poem make you feel?" Next they are asked to review their first response and then consider, "What in your own life might have influenced how you responded to the poem?"

Note the following responses from two students, Jeanette and Caroline, who had just read Updike's "A & P":

Jeanette:
    . . . I feel I have a connection with Sammy. He is struggling to explore and be free from the monotonous chores of work. Yet he is still and probably will be forever stuck in that social class in that small town. (affective)
    The reason I relate to this is because I have moved around my whole life. I have grown up in four different states and have already experienced two different colleges. I feel sorry for those people who stay in their same town or the same state their whole life. I experienced this while in school in Indiana. I discovered that many of those people whom I had met, have never been outside of Indiana. . . . One weekend my friends and I borrowed a car & drove to Columbus, Ohio. It was no big deal for me, as I have made plenty of trips there, but they had never seen a big city before. They had never been outside of Washington, Ind. where they graduated from a class of 25. (associative)

Caroline:
    I didn't like the short story "A & P" by John Updike. I think it was because of the fact that it was a male watching females, and the fact that I am a female. I didn't care for the long descriptive details. The author did describe everything very clearly. I felt as though I was right there in the store. I could see the boy at the cash register staring with his mouth open and the three girls flaunting themselves around the store. . . . Maybe if it was written about men being watched I would feel differently about it. (affective)
    The way I associated with "A & P" was through the experience of working in a grocery store. When I worked as a cashier I can remember how my coworkers

and I would people watch. I can also relate to standing up for something and supporting it, even though I knew the results would not be in my favor. (associative)

These two students were influenced by very different elements in the story, despite any similarities they might share as teenage and female readers. With their polar responses as a discussion catalyst, their teacher can help them understand that the same text may produce conflicting emotions and multiple understandings because each reader's comprehension is influenced by prior knowledge, experience, and literary schema. Furthermore, when such untutored responses are explored through whole-class or small-group discussion, the classroom becomes a community of learners whose collective experience often results in additional and more penetrating insights.

Most teachers in American schools structure their lessons around three main activities: reading, writing, and talking. All three activities play a central role in a response curriculum because discussion and composition strategies are used to assist meaning construction before, during, and after reading events. Although individual response strategies naturally vary according to reading purposes and curricular goals, they share a fundamental principle: Readers construct meaning actively, by drawing on their cumulative prior knowledge (i.e., worldview, beliefs, experiences, feelings, literary schema). In addition, those meanings are enriched and often reconstructed when shared with others through writing and/or discussion.

## Discussion Strategies

As they plan lessons, teachers should consider how prereading discussion can facilitate response by helping students activate pertinent background knowledge. Students' own prior experiences and learning can then be used to introduce content, dilemmas, or themes that will be raised in the text.

When teaching Sophocles' *Antigone*, for example, a teacher might ask students to recall a personal occasion when they had challenged authority (Newton, 1990). Recollections might include a statement of the issue, sample arguments on both sides, and its resolution. Students might also be asked to recall any consequences of their choice. Shared either in small groups or with the whole class, these memories can be used to prepare students for Antigone's authority conflict.

Anticipation Guides are another effective way to introduce content issues, to activate students' background knowledge, and to invite them to draw on personal opinions when reading literary text. Table 17.2 shows an Anticipation Guide for Sophocles' *Oedipus Rex*, in which readers are asked to reflect on their own feelings about three issues raised in the play.

Although prereading strategies sometimes limit student response by identifying central themes in advance, they do not require students to embrace a specific perspective on those themes. Instead, they focus and scaffold the reading expe-

TABLE 17.2

Anticipation Guide for Sophocles' *Oedipus Rex*

Directions: Put a check under "Agree" for each of the following statements that you believe to be true. Check "Disagree" for those you believe to be false. Be ready to discuss/explain your reasoning.

| Agree | Disagree | |
|-------|----------|---|
| _____ | _____ | A human being should seek the truth even when he/she knows the consequences will be disastrous for those he loves. |
| _____ | _____ | No one can escape his/her fate because it has been preordained. |
| _____ | _____ | A person must accept whatever happens to him/her as the will of God, and never question or challenge that will. |
| _____ | _____ | If one commits a foolish act in his/her youth, he/she is forever responsible for it. |

rience so that students may respond to and comprehend a difficult text more efficiently. Moreover, as the Anticipation Guide in Table 17.2 demonstrates, such strategies can also invite debate of conflicting perspectives.

Teachers using response-centered strategies for discussion during and after reading must help students understand the meaning-construction process so that their classrooms become a cooperative—not competitive—community of readers. Wollman-Bonilla (1993) advised teachers to follow six strategies as they facilitate literature discussions:

1. Discourage competition among participants.
2. Participate as students' equals in group activities.
3. Model exploratory, collaborative talk.
4. Remember that group meanings are constructed collectively.
5. Clearly state learning goals and expectations for student participation.
6. Invite students to create their own discussion guidelines.

In many elementary and secondary classrooms, student-generated guidelines are displayed. They can be helpful prompts when students are uncertain about how to extend a discussion.

Literature Circles are a special kind of student-generated talk. They offer meaningful opportunities for readers to become critical thinkers while engaged in ongoing dialogue about their reading. As members of Literature Circles, students are given choices about which books they wish to read. Those who select the same text gather together to share responses, raise questions, and debate interpretations.

Discussions begin as group members share their written or oral reactions to the text they have read. These personal statements then direct subsequent conversation. Sometimes students use them to brainstorm or build a web of potential discussion topics. In any case, ensuing discussion is generated from these ideas. The classroom possibilities for this small-group strategy are endless. Noden and Vacca (1994), for example, suggested that some circles be formed as "literature teams," in which group members share different books on the same subject, or different books by the same author. However structured, all meetings should be concluded by establishing a focus for the next gathering (Short & Klassen, 1993).

### Writing Strategies

Writing activities nurture response in several ways. "Free response" is one strategy that uses writing during the actual reading event (Santa, Dailey, & Nelson, 1985). Before reading, students are asked questions designed to activate pertinent background knowledge. They are then directed to read until they reach an italicized or underlined sentence or phrase the teacher has determined in advance as a temporary stopping place. At this point, students are instructed to "write down their reactions in the margin" (p. 347). Later, they can review the story and use their impromptu responses as a stimulus for class discussion or for longer written reflections and essays.

Perhaps the most adaptable vehicle for eliciting response is the journal. Journals can be used both during and after reading. They help readers record response, construct meaning, or work through the challenges of a difficult text. They may be read privately or shared with teachers and peers. Naturally, the format of a response journal will depend largely on its instructional purpose.

Even very young readers should be invited to write responses to the literature they read. Fig. 17.2, for example, shows the first page of Eli's third-grade Reading Response Log. Whenever Eli read a book independently, he entered its title, the date, and a few brief comments. Each page of the Log contains a separate response for every book Eli had listed. Some responses were followed by drawings of a story event or a character. Note his responses to two different texts, Rylant's *Green Time* and Lobel's *Small Pig*:

*Green Time*:
I liked it. In the beginning, Henry and Mudge went on a picnic. There was a bee on Henry's pear. When Henry picked it up he got stung. He was yelling Ow! Ow! After awhile the pain went away and Henry was fine.

*Small Pig*:
I didn't like it. It was about a pig that liked to sit in the mud and sink. One day the farmer's wife was cleaning the house. Then she cleaned the farm and sucked up the mud in the vacuum. So he went to the city and sat in wet concrete and it dried. The farmer had to get him out.

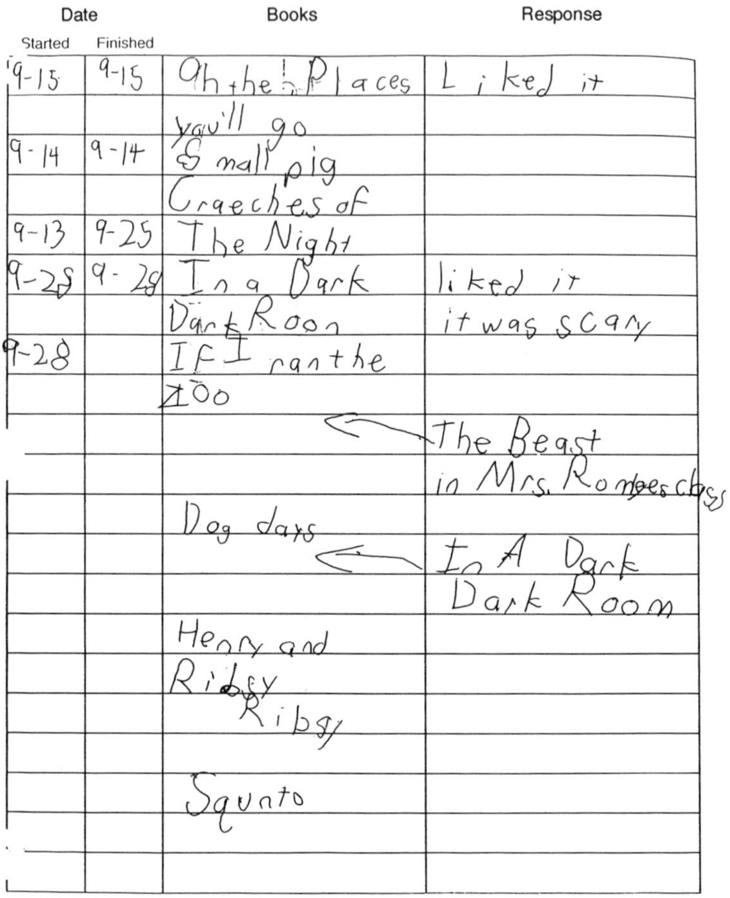

| Date | | Books | Response |
|---|---|---|---|
| Started | Finished | | |
| 9-15 | 9-15 | Oh the! Places you'll go | Liked it |
| 9-14 | 9-14 | Small pig | |
| 9-13 | 9-25 | Craeches of The Night | |
| 9-28 | 9-28 | In a Dark Dark Roon | liked it  it was scary |
| 9-28 | | IF I ran the ZOo | |
| | | | ⟸ The Beast in Mrs. Rombes chss |
| | | Dog days | |
| | | | ⟸ In A Dark Dark Room |
| | | Henry and Ribsy Ribsy | |
| | | Squnto | |

FIG. 17.2.   Eli's third-grade Reading Response Log.

In both entries, Eli's "response" was a cursory expression of like or dislike followed by a plot summary. Such responses are typical and developmentally appropriate for young readers, particularly since much of their classroom time is spent learning elements of story grammar. When readers are offered many opportunities to write about how they are affected by what they read, these early retellings are gradually supplanted by more sophisticated responses.

Hancock (1993) cited studies suggesting that if students are encouraged to write continually "while in the process of reading a text," they will gradually expand the scope of their responses (p. 466). In her own study of middle-school students, Hancock identified three standard response modes: (a) personal meaning making; (b) character and plot involvement; and (c) literary criticism. She believes teachers should use journal writing as an opportunity to assess students' response patterns and write back comments to help them expand the scope of their responses.

As part of a ninth-grade Reading Workshop, Olivia was required to write a daily response about what she was reading. Her teacher commented after each entry. Following are Olivia's initial and final entries for Dickens' *A Tale of Two Cities*, and her teacher's replies:

First entry:
    I don't really like a *Tale of Two Cities* from what I have read. I don't really like the way Dickens writes—I think he uses too many words and the point is often lost in them. I do, however, like the way he develops the characters. I think he does a good job of inserting subtle details about the character's personalities in the plot. Another thing I like is the symbolism Dickens uses. I can't usually pick it out (with a few exceptions like the dream about the man buried alive), but I think that's because I usually don't understand what is going on due to all the words he uses. I think if I knew the plot *before* I read it, I would have a much easier time understanding the book.

Teacher's reply:
    Good point—But I'm really torn about exposing too much too soon. Dickens' use of foreshadowing makes the act of discovery so much fun (well, challenging at least).

Notice how in this first entry, Olivia briefly raises all three response modes. She cites her difficulty constructing meaning, makes generic references to character development, and becomes a literary critic of Dickens' style. Her teacher's comments acknowledge Olivia's dissonance, but move her beyond abstraction by calling attention to Dickens' deliberate use of foreshadowing. Hancock (1993) advises teachers to make comments that are "suggestive," but not "demanding." By her final entry, Olivia's responses are more focused and in-depth. Her teacher's remarks bring closure to this reading experience:

Final Entry:
    In Book the Third, the whole novel seems to come together. Up until this point, a lot of the characters and events either swirled together and it seemed like they were the same or seemed to have nothing to do with each other. I still have a few questions. Who is the Marquis' wife talking about when she refers to the sister of the dead girl? I like Carton the best of all the characters—I think he was brave and seemed to have the most spine. I don't like Lucie all that much—I think she's sort of mealy-mouthed. I think it's admirable how she cared for her father and how she cared for everyone around her, but she was too weak a character for my liking. I Like Charles Darnay and Jarvis Lorry equally—I think they're both strong characters. Overall, I liked *A Tale of Two Cities*, but I thought in a lot of places, particularly in the beginning, it was very hard to understand.

Teacher's Reply:
    Good, Olivia. This is pretty typical of Dickens' books (the complexity). His plots are all involved, and they're fun to "discover."

Some response journals are conceived as dialogues. Sometimes called "partner" or "buddy" journals, they are meant to be shared with friends who read entries and write back. The Double-Entry Journal allows readers to "dialogue" with authors (R. Yopp & H. Yopp, 1992). As they are reading, students identify meaningful passages and write them on the left side of a notebook sheet. On the right side, they record their responses to each passage, indicating why it caught their attention. Passages are selected because they have affected the reader in some way. Writing about how they were affected offers students an intimate view of their own comprehension processes.

Hancock (1993) offered teachers the following guidelines to share with students as they write in literature-response journals:

1. Feel free to write your innermost feelings, opinions, thoughts, likes, and dislikes.
2. Take the time to write down anything that you are thinking while you read.
3. Don't worry about the accuracy of spelling and mechanics in the journal.
4. Record the page number on which you were reading when you wrote your response.
5. One side only of your spiral notebook paper, please.
6. Relate the book to your own experiences and share similar moments from your life or from books you have read in the past.
7. Ask questions while reading to help you make sense of the characters and the unraveling plot.
8. Make predictions about what you think will happen as the plot unfolds.
9. Talk to the characters as you begin to know them.
10. Praise or criticize the book, the author, or the literary style.
11. There is no limit to the types of responses you may write. (p. 472)

### Metacognitive Strategies

Because meaning construction is facilitated by fluent reading, some instructional activities should also focus attention on the metacognitive dimensions of the reading process. Baker and Brown (1984) described metacognition in reading as three-dimensional knowledge: of text, of task, and of self. Students' knowledge of text involves an awareness of how different kinds of texts are structured. Task knowledge depends on understanding the requirements of specific assignments. Self-knowledge stems from a student's insight into his or her own meaning-making behaviors as a reader.

Before a reading event, metacognitive awareness may be developed through simple questions which focus student attention on the reading process. Students may be asked, for example, what options they will have when encountering an unfamiliar word. They may anticipate idiosyncratic textual structure by recalling other books they have read by the same author.

After a reading experience, students should be asked to reflect on their own comprehension process. The value of metacognitive writing in a response curriculum is that it helps students become aware of how they, themselves, construct meaning. When they track their reading behaviors, students come to understand impediments to fluent reading and can review strategies that helped them work through a difficult reading task.

Note how two young women, Katina and Camille, reconstruct their reading of *The Odyssey*:

> Katina:
> At the beginning, I thought it was very boring, very dull. I just couldn't get into it. I brought it home one weekend and just did not even touch it. Then my mother said I should go and buy the *Cliff Notes*. I did, I read them, they were no help. I realized I now was forced to read the story. And I admit, it started off dull but throughout the story it kept my interest and my attention and after awhile the chapters no longer seemed to drag on, but they flew by.

> Camille:
> While reading Books IX–XII of *The Odyssey*, I was either very confused or totally understood what was going on. Sometimes it took me at least three books to understand the first one. . . . The one book I didn't like was the Book of the Dead. I felt there were too many people and names to follow. I was frustrated reading it because I wasn't sure where the characters were coming from.

When Katina writes of using *Cliff Notes*, she articulates a strategy to help her build interest in the text. If Camille is aware that "too many people and names" interfered with her aesthetic interaction in Book X, she will also understand something of her personal response to the events in that chapter.

Probst (1988) asserted the value of group participation for developing students' own "sense of uniqueness" as they observe differences between themselves and their peers. Metacognitive writing after a whole- or small-group discussion offers students an opportunity to revisit their initial responses and to understand how those responses ripen and mature in a collaborative setting.

Following are two meta-analyses in which students were asked to recall a small-group discussion and then account for some difference between their interpretation and that of other group members. When recalling discussion of Frost's "Never Again Would Birds' Song Be the Same," Kate writes that her lack of biblical schema limited her understanding of the poem.

> I am kind of taking a stab in the dark at this poem. I think that my interpretation differs in that even though I tried to give it a religious meaning, my knowledge of religion greatly falls short of everyone else. I did not grow up with religion and I am embarrassed to admit that I don't know the story about Adam and Eve. I always thought it was another fairy tale.

Newton (1991) shares the meta-analysis of another young woman following a group discussion of Faulkner's "A Rose for Emily":

> The biggest difference I saw . . . was that there was alot of symbolism that I had totally looked over. . . . I did not realize the significance of Emily putting the watch on the chain as a symbol of her not being able to deal with time passing. When I read it, it confused me so I re-read it, still not understanding its reasoning. I just couldn't understand what the big deal was about the men hearing the ticking of the clock hidden beneath her clothing. I feel that I overlooked this because I am a very literal reader and all around person. I expect to be told the truth, flat out! Not in a round about way, where the person implies what he or she is trying to say.

These comments suggest that group members helped this reader recognize symbolism she had missed when she read independently. Her observation that she is a "very literal" reader may be the result of comparison with the meaning-making behaviors she observed in her peers. In any case, it is an important insight that may help her comprehend more efficiently in future reading events.

## CONCLUDING REMARKS

For most of this century, literary instruction in American schools was a text-driven event. Students were taught how to extrapolate the meaning of a text through application of a formalized set of linguistic skills. But research in cognitive psychology, linguistics, literacy acquisition, reading instruction, and literary theory has resulted in a reconceptualization of the role of reader, text, and context in the comprehension process.

Responding to literature is now believed to be a reader-driven event. As readers engage with text, they construct meanings that are influenced by their own knowledge, values, and prior literary and life experience. Readers are also influenced by the contexts or purposes for which they are reading. Furthermore, when readers share their perceptions of a text within a classroom community, their own responses are often extended and enriched.

Instruction from a response-based perspective must, therefore, focus on eliciting and nurturing readers' first interactions with text. It must also focus on sharing both the process and result of those first interactions with peers. Classroom discussion, writing tasks, and metacognitive activities can play a central role in facilitating meaning construction before, during, and after reading events.

## REFERENCES

Baker, L., & Brown, A. L. (1984). Metacognitive skills and reading. In P. D. Pearson (Ed.), *Handbook of reading research* (Vol. 2, pp. 353–394). New York: Longman.

Bleich, D. (1975). *Readings and feelings: An introduction to subjective criticism.* Urbana, IL: National Council of Teachers of English.

Bleich, D. (1978). *Subjective criticism.* Baltimore, MD: Johns Hopkins University Press.

Bloome, D. (1985). Reading as a social process. *Language Arts, 62*(2), 134–142.

Cooper, C. R. (1985). Introduction. In C. R. Cooper (Ed.), *Researching response to literature and the teaching of literature: Points of departure* (pp. ix–xix). Norwood, NJ: Ablex.

Eliot, T. S. (1959). The problem of *Hamlet.* In G. B. Harrison (Ed.), *Major British writers II* (pp. 845–847). New York: Harcourt Brace.

Fish, S. (1980). Literature in the reader: Affective stylistics. In J. Tompkins (Ed.), *Reader-response criticism: From formalism to poststructuralism* (pp. 70–100). Baltimore, MD: Johns Hopkins University Press.

Fox, M. (1988). *Koala Lou.* San Diego: Harcourt Brace.

Goodman, K. S. (1969). Analysis of oral reading miscues: Applied psycholinguistics. *Reading Research Quarterly, 5,* 9–30.

Goodman, K. S. (1987a). Acquiring literacy is natural: Who skilled Cock Robin? *Theory into Practice, 26,* 368–373.

Goodman, K. S. (1987b). Transactional psycholinguistic model. In H. Singer & R. B. Ruddell (Eds.), *Theoretical models and processes of reading* (3rd ed., pp. 813–839). Newark, DE: International Reading Association.

Halliday, M. A. K. (1975). *Learning how to mean.* London: Edward Arnold.

Hancock, M. R. (1993). Exploring and extending personal response through literature journals. *The Reading Teacher, 46*(6), 466–474.

Harste, J. C., Burke, C. L., & Woodward, V. A. (1982). Children's language and world: Initial encounters with print. In J. Langer & M. T. Smith-Burke (Eds.), *Reader meets author: Bridging the gap* (pp. 105–131). Newark, DE: International Reading Association.

Harste, J. C., Woodward, V. A., & Burke, C. L. (1984). Examining our assumptions: A transactional view of literacy and learning. *Research in the Teaching of English, 18*(1), 84–107.

Hayden, R. (1962). Those winter Sundays. In X. J. Kennedy (Ed.), *Literature: An introduction to fiction, poetry, and drama* (5th ed., p. 821). New York: HarperCollins.

Hickman, J. (1984). Research currents: Researching children's response to literature. *Language Arts, 61*(3), 278–284.

Holland, N. (1975). *Five readers reading.* New Haven, CT: Yale University Press.

Holland, N. (1985). Reading readers reading. In C. Cooper (Ed.), *Researching response to literature and the teaching of literature: Points of departure* (pp. 3–21). Norwood, NJ: Ablex.

Iser, W. (1980). The reading process: A phenomenological approach. In J. Tompkins (Ed.), *Reader-response criticism: From formalism to poststructuralism* (pp. 50–69). Baltimore, MD: Johns Hopkins University Press.

Jefferson, A., & Robey, D. (1986). *Modern literary theory: A comparative introduction.* Totowa, NJ: Barnes & Noble.

Mailloux, S. (1990). The turns of reader-response criticism. In C. Moran & E. F. Penfield (Eds.), *Conversations: Contemporary critical theory and the teaching of literature* (pp. 38–54). Urbana, IL: National Council of Teachers of English.

Newton, E. V. (1990). *Antigone* and Kent State: Teaching ancient as modern tragedy. *Teaching English in the Two-Year College, 17*(4), 267–272.

Newton, E. V. (1991). Developing metacognitive awareness: The response journal in college composition. *Journal of Reading, 34*(6), 476–478.

Noden, H., & Vacca, R. T. (1994). *Whole language in middle and secondary classrooms.* New York: HarperCollins.

Petrosky, A. (1977). Genetic epistemology and psychoanalytic ego psychology: Clinical support for the study of response to literature. *Research in the Teaching of English, 11*(1), 28–38.

Petrosky, A. (1982). From story to essay: Reading and writing. *College Composition and Communication, 33,* 19–36.

Probst, R. E. (1988). *Response and analysis: Teaching literature in junior and senior high school.* Portsmouth, NH: Boynton/Cook.

Purves, A. C., & Rippere, A. (1968). *Elements of writing about a literary work: A study of response to literature* (Research Report No. 9). Urbana, IL: National Council of Teachers of English.

Rosenblatt, L. (1978). *The reader, the text, the poem: The transactional theory of the literary work.* Carbondale: Southern Illinois University Press.

Rosenblatt, L. (1983). *Literature as Exploration* (4th ed.). New York: Modern Language Association of America.

Santa, C. M., Dailey, S. C., & Nelson, M. (1985). Free response and opinion proof: A reading and writing strategy for middle grade and secondary teachers. *Journal of Reading, 28,* 346–352.

Scholes, R. (1985). *Textual power: Literacy theory and the teaching of English.* New Haven, CT: Yale University Press.

Short, K. G., & Klassen, C. (1993). Literature circles: Hearing children's voices. In B. E. Cullinan (Ed.), *Children's voices: Talk in the classroom* (pp. 66–85). Newark, DE: International Reading Association.

Smith, F. (1988). *Understanding reading: A psycholinguistic analysis of reading and learning to read* (4th ed.). Hillsdale, NJ: Lawrence Erlbaum Associates.

Squire, J. R. (1964). *The responses of adolescents while reading four short stories.* Champaign, IL: National Council of Teachers of English.

Tompkins, J. (1980). *Reader-response criticism: From formalism to poststructuralism.* Baltimore, MD: Johns Hopkins University Press.

Wilson, J. R. (1966). *Responses of college freshmen to three novels* (Research Report No. 7). Champaign, IL: National Council of Teachers of English.

Wollman-Bonilla, J. E. (1993). "It's really special because you get to think": Talking about literature. In B. E. Cullinan (Ed.), *Children's voices: Talk in the classroom* (pp. 47–65). Newark, DE: International Reading Association.

Yopp, R. H., & Yopp, H. K. (1992). *Literature-based reading activities.* Boston, MA: Allyn & Bacon.

Zancanella, D. A. (1988). Relationships between five teachers' personal approaches to literature and their teaching of literature. *Dissertation Abstracts International, 49,* 3293-A.

# Author Index

# Subject Index